THE SENATE
AND
THE LEAGUE OF NATIONS

The Delegates may also meet at such other times and upon such other occasions as they shall from time to time deem best and determine.

ARTICLE IX.

In the event of a dispute arising between one of the Contracting Powers and a Power not a party to this Covenant, the Contracting Power involved hereby binds itself to endeavour to obtain the submission of the dispute to judicial decision or to arbitration. If the other Power will not agree to submit the dispute to judicial decision or to arbitration, the Contracting Power shall bring the matter to the attention of the ~~Body of Delegates~~ *Executive Council.* The Delegates shall in such a case, in the name of the League of Nations, invite the Power not a party to this Covenant to become *ad hoc* a party and to submit its case to judicial decision or to arbitration, and if that Power consents it is hereby agreed that the provisions hereinbefore contained and applicable to the submission of disputes to arbitration or discussion shall be in all respects applicable to the dispute both in favour of and against such Power as if it were a party to this Covenant.

Executive Council In case the Power not a party to this Covenant shall not accept the invitation of the ~~Delegates~~ to become *ad hoc* a party, it shall be the duty of the Executive Council immediately to institute an inquiry into the circumstances and merits of the dispute involved and to recommend such joint action by the Contracting Powers as may seem best and most effectual in the circumstances disclosed.

ARTICLE X.

If hostilities should be begun or any hostile action taken against the Contracting Power by the Power not a party to this Covenant before a decision of the dispute by arbitrators or before investigation, report and recommendation by the Executive Council in regard to the dispute, or contrary to such recommendation, the Contracting Powers ~~shall~~ *engage* thereupon cease all commerce and communication with that Power and ~~shall~~ *to* also unite in blockading and closing the frontiers ~~of~~ that Power to all commerce or intercourse with any part of the world, ~~employing~~ *and to combine* jointly any force that may be necessary to accomplish that object. The Contracting Powers ~~shall~~ *undertake to* also unite in coming to the assistance of the Contracting Power against which hostile action has been taken, ~~combining~~ their armed forces in its behalf.

ARTICLE XI

In case of a dispute between states not parties to this Covenant, any Contracting Power may bring the matter to the attention of the Delegates *or the Executive Council,* who shall thereupon tender the good offices of the League of Nations with a view to the peaceable settlement of the dispute.

If one of the states, a party to the dispute, shall offer and agree to submit its interests and cause of action wholly to the control and decision of the League of Nations, that state shall *ad hoc* be deemed a Contracting Power.

6

FACSIMILE PAGE OF WILSON'S DRAFT OF THE LEAGUE OF NATIONS COVENANT

THE SENATE
AND
THE LEAGUE OF NATIONS

BY

HENRY CABOT LODGE

CHARLES SCRIBNER'S SONS
NEW YORK   LONDON
1925

CONTENTS

THE SENATE
AND
THE LEAGUE OF NATIONS

THE SENATE
AND
THE LEAGUE OF NATIONS

CHAPTER I

BEGINNING OF THE WILSON ADMINISTRATION AND THE QUESTION OF PANAMA CANAL TOLLS

My purpose in writing the ensuing pages is to give an account of the opposition and consequent debate which arose in the Senate of the United States when that body was asked by President Wilson to give their advice and consent to the Treaty of Versailles containing the Covenant of the League of Nations. Whatever the future may have in store for us, the importance of the Senate debate and of their rejection of the Treaty in 1919 and 1920 cannot, I think, be questioned. It so happened that having been unanimously selected as Republican minority leader after the death of Senator Gallinger in the summer of 1918, I was again unanimously chosen by my colleagues leader of the Republicans in the Senate after March 4, 1919, and at the same time I became Chairman of the Committee on Foreign Relations of which I had been a member for twenty-three years. These positions brought with them grave responsibilities and also, I think, gave me opportunities for acquiring knowledge and information as to the phases and conditions of this momentous transaction which perhaps in some respects were not so fully possessed by anyone else. I shall tell the story, of course, from my own standpoint; and in order that those who read this account may understand what was done, and the situation in the Senate, it is necessary for me to explain my own relations with Mr. Wilson before and after he entered the White House, to consider carefully what he said and did, and, at the same time, in order to complete the picture, to endeavor to describe the conditions in the Senate and the attitude both of those who opposed and of those who supported the President.

President Wilson was inaugurated on the 4th of March, 1913. He had been elected by a minority of the popular vote because the Republican party was divided at the election. Mr. Taft and Colonel Roosevelt polled together 7,604,463 votes, Mr. Taft receiving 3,484,956 and Colonel Roosevelt 4,119,507. Mr. Wilson received 6,293,019 and therefore was, as I have just said, a minority President, polling 1,311,444 votes less than the combined Roosevelt and Taft vote. The result had been foreseen long before the votes were cast, and the Republicans, torn by their own dissensions, had but little of the bitterness of party feeling toward their political opponents which usually arises after a close and doubtful election. The success of Mr. Wilson was wholly owing to Republican divisions.

A few days after his inauguration I called upon Mr. Wilson simply to pay my respects. It was my intention and, I think, that of Republicans in Washington generally, to make no attempt to oppose the new President merely for the sake of opposition. I said to Mr. Wilson when I saw him: "You do not, of course, remember me, Mr. President, but I had the pleasure of sitting next to you at the alumni dinner at a Harvard Commencement." He replied very pleasantly: "Senator, it is not necessary to recall our meeting at Cambridge, because a man never forgets the first editor who accepts one of his articles. You were the first editor who accepted an article written by me." I had for the moment entirely forgotten that I had first known him in that connection. I had been

for a time one of the editors of the *International Review*
and I had accepted an article from Mr. Wilson, who was
then, I may say, unknown to the public. His recalling
to me this incident in such a pleasant way led me to
look at some of my letter files, and I found there, rather
to my surprise, a letter from Mr. Wilson in regard to an
article on "Cabinet Government in the United States"
which I published in August, 1879. Mr. Wilson's letter
to me was written from Wilmington, North Carolina.

After his administration had begun, the question arose
of repealing the act by which Congress had authorized a
discrimination in the matter of tolls in favor of American
vessels passing through the Panama Canal, and I supported the position of the President. I was present at
a meeting which he held at the White House, consisting,
I think, of the committees of the two Houses on Foreign
Relations and Foreign Affairs respectively, where a very
animated discussion took place and Senator O'Gorman,
Senator William Alden Smith of Michigan, and perhaps
one or two others opposed the President's proposition
to repeal the law imposing the tolls discrimination. The
President made an argument in favor of his position
and showed, as I remember, a strong feeling in regard
to it. He then made the statement, now well known,
that the action which he asked from Congress was necessary to enable him to carry on his foreign policy. This
position he defined in his message to Congress of March
5, 1914. These were his words:

"I ask this of you in support of the foreign policy of
the administration. I shall not know how to deal with
other matters of even greater delicacy and nearer consequence if you do not grant it to me in ungrudging
measure."

What his precise purpose was or in what way this action
aided his conduct of our foreign relations has not yet been

disclosed. Mr. Walter Hines Page, who had much to
say about this question of Panama tolls in his correspondence, was puzzled as to the motive, but finally said
he thought afterwards that what the President meant
was that it would help him to preserve the peace of the
world which, some months after this Panama tolls debate, was shattered by the war with Germany. I confess
that this explanation did not seem to me to explain
anything because no one foresaw the great war at the
time of the Panama Message, and the fact that we had
taken the action in regard to the tolls desired by
the President seemed, from all that is known of that
period, to have had no weight either with the Allies or
with Germany. I do not know to this day what he meant
by its being necessary to repeal the tolls discrimination
in order to enable him to conduct the foreign relations
of the country, and I have never found anybody who was
better informed on this point than I. This assertion by
Mr. Wilson at the time, however, undoubtedly had great
weight, especially with members of his own party.

Subsequently, on the 9th of April, 1914, I spoke in the
Senate at some length on the question of the tolls. Mr.
Wilson called me up on the telephone very soon after-
ward and thanked me for my speech and for all that I
had said in support of his position. He also wrote to
me cordially regarding my reply to Senator Bristow in
the Panama tolls debate, made in the Senate on February
18th. I then said:

"Mr. President, I do not believe that the President of
the United States is the least embarrassed, as the Senator
from Kansas (Mr. Bristow) suggests, and I should not
undertake to interfere in such a debate as we have been
listening to here today were it not that the Senator
seemed to take a view of the President's attitude in regard to the Panama tolls which I do not share. I listened
to all the Senator from Kansas said, and he left me with

the impression that, in his opinion, the influence of corporations, both foreign and domestic, had been very strong in determining the attitude of the President with reference to the repeal of what is known as the exemption clause in the Panama Canal act. Whoever else may have changed his mind, I do not think that the President has changed *his* mind on that question at all. My own impression is that he has held his present view for a long time. Of this I am certain: The President did some of us who are on the Committee on Foreign Relations the honor of consulting with us about this matter, and I am sure that in dealing with it he is guided entirely by what he thinks is for the honor and credit of the United States in our relations with foreign nations. I think he has no other object in view. I think he feels, unless I greatly misunderstand him, as some of the rest of us have felt, that the position we held not very many years ago in the way of prestige and standing among the nations of the world has been lost or greatly impaired. I think he feels that the time has come to retrace some of the steps that have been taken subsequently in late years. I think he has the conviction that in one way or another—and I am laying no blame now at anybody's door—the United States has fallen into an unfortunate and unhappy position, where she has incurred the active dislike of many nations and the distrust of many more, instead of the friendship and respect which she once possessed. The President does not like, in my judgment, to see the United States in the attitude of an outlaw among the nations. He feels that we should have all the prestige, all the influence which is our due and which we have ever had among the nations of the earth. He believes, I think, that prestige and influence are not to be obtained by disregarding the international obligations or by reversing policies long held by the United States simply to gratify some passing whim or some passion of the moment. I believe also that the President regards the foreign relations of the country as above the party.

"I do not hold a position in this Chamber which calls upon me or entitles me to be the President's defender, but I cannot sit in silence, as a member of the opposition and of the minority, and hear what I consider an injustice done to the President of the United States, in whose hands rests the conduct of all our foreign relations, without making a protest against it simply in my capacity as an American citizen. I have always held very strongly the opinion that in the matter of foreign relations it is our duty always to stand by the President of the United States just so far as it is possible to do so without violating one's own convictions. I have always tried to follow that course in my public life, and therefore I shall not now consent to censure him because he has taken a certain view of our international duties in regard to toll exemption—a view which I think he has probably always held—or charge that he is doing something inconsistent and improper as a party leader which, I confess, seems to me absurd.

"I am myself a pretty rigid Republican and party man. Yet I have known things which in some way crept into Republican platforms that I would not have voted for if they had been brought up here as the basis of legislation, because my conscience and my sense of duty would have forbidden it. Cases constantly arise where party conventions in their resolutions travel out of the line of their duty, which is simply to set forth general principles and not undertake to regulate the details of legislation. It is entirely within the province of the President, if he chooses, to say that in an act in which he can have no participation—for he does not sign a constitutional amendment—he does not feel justified in injecting a new article into the party creed. I see no inconsistency between his taking that position and saying at the same time that there is another paragraph in that platform to which in duty and in conscience he cannot agree. If there were inconsistency, I do not see that that in the least affects the merits of the tolls question upon which the President has taken recently and publicly such a decided stand.

"I differ as widely as possible from the President of the United States on general political principles, but on the question of foreign relations, speaking, as I have already said, merely as an American citizen, I wanted to make my protest against an injustice being done, as I think has been done this morning, to the purposes and motives of the President of the United States. When he is dealing with foreign relations, in some respects of a most perilous and difficult character, if he says, on his high responsibility, to the Congress of the United States that a certain step in foreign relations is necessary to ·the good name and possibly to the security of the United States, perhaps from a situation where serious loss or serious injury might be incurred—if he says all this on his high responsibility, I think it becomes the duty of all men, who look upon foreign relations as I do, not to try to block his path but to give him such aid and assistance in our humble way as we are conscientiously able to give."

"Mr. Clark of Wyoming. Mr. President, will the Senator from Massachusetts permit me to ask him a question before he takes his seat?

"Mr. Lodge. Certainly.

"Mr. Clark of Wyoming. The Senator's last statement was a little broader than I care to accept. Am I correct in my understanding of the Senator's notion that the Senator would aid the President of the United States in carrying out a policy which the President thought was the best policy, or a necessary policy, but which the Senator from Massachusetts, from his own investigation, thought was not a good policy and was a dangerous policy if carried out?

"MR. LODGE. I certainly should not support the President in any policy which I believed to be wrong or which went against my conscience; but where I have no policy to substitute, and he is engaged in a difficult situation, I am ready at least not to throw obstacles in his way, and so far as I honestly and conscientiously can, I am going to give my support.

"MR. CLARK of Wyoming. I agree with the Senator's last statement, but further than that I decline to go.

"MR. LODGE. I did not mean to suggest that I would support any man whom I believed to be wrong, unpatriotic, or doing something which I thought an injury to the country; but I say that on a question of foreign relations, where my desire is to support the Executive, if I do not feel that what he is trying to do is wrong, I will go just as far as I conscientiously can in giving him my support, whether he is of my party or of some other party.

"I was a member of the Senate when a President of the United States of the Democratic Party made a declaration in regard to Venezuela which was thought by many persons to bring us to the verge of war with England. I did not happen to agree with the view that it involved us in any danger of war, and I thought the President was entirely right in the attitude he took. I thought so then, and I think so now. He was widely and bitterly criticized at the time by many men who belonged to my own party; but I was unable to see my way, for party advantage, to oppose the President when I believed he was doing not only what he honestly thought was best but something to which I could give conscientious support.

"I am anxious to go as far as I can in supporting any President when he is dealing with a difficult and complicated foreign situation, because the great responsibility

of initiating and shaping our foreign policy must rest
with the Executive and cannot rest anywhere else."

I print here Mr. Wilson's note in regard to this speech
in reply to Senator Bristow, as follows:

"The White House,
          Washington   February 19, 1914.

My dear Senator:

May I not express my sincere appreciation of your
generous action yesterday in replying as you did to the
criticisms of Senator Bristow?   I feel honoured by your
confidence and your general comprehension of my
motives.

Sincerely yours,

WOODROW WILSON."

I mention these little incidents merely to show that
my relations with President Wilson when he first came
to the White House and for many months afterwards
were entirely friendly and without any hostile prejudice
on my part.   There was indeed no reason why they
should have been otherwise.

Upon the questions which arose in connection with
the tariff, and later regarding the bill for the establishment of the Federal Reserve Bank system, I took as to
the former the Republican position, which I had always
held, in favor of the protective tariff policy.   At the
time of the Bank Bill I was at home, having passed
through a very serious operation, and was unable to be
present during the debate or when the vote was taken;
but I wrote a letter, which was printed in the Record,
explaining that I could not vote for the bill because I
felt that under it there was a latitude given for the issue
of bank currency which it seemed to me might threaten
the stability of our whole financial system by undue is-

suance of paper money.* I may say that the bill, which
was largely amended in the Senate, has, in practical

* My letter, addressed to my colleague, Senator Weeks, was as follows:

(Copy)

New York, December 17, 1913.

My dear Senator Weeks:

I am, as you know, unable to be in Washington before the holidays.
I cannot, therefore, be present and give my vote in person upon the
final passage of the currency bill. This I greatly regret; so much,
indeed, that I am unwilling to have the bill acted upon in the Senate
without making public record of the reasons which would govern my
vote, were I able to give it, upon the passage of the bill.

The many details of this most important law I have had no opportunity to master as they should be mastered by anyone who
presumes to discuss them. Fortunately for me, however, there is no
one who has a more thorough knowledge, not only of every feature
of this particular bill but also of the far-reaching and difficult questions
which must be involved in any bill of this character, than you. This
mastery of the subject you have demonstrated in debate, and therefore
with the most absolute confidence I authorized you to pair me upon
all amendments as you yourself voted, without any statement or
explanation on my part.

When, however, the Senate comes to a final vote upon the bill as
a whole, there are certain general principles involved upon which I
have very strong convictions. By these convictions my vote, could I
be present and give it in person, would be decided.

I quite agree that there are provisions covering the details of the
system proposed which would effect marked improvements in the
system, or lack of system, of our banking laws as they now exist.
This could hardly be otherwise, as many of these details are taken
from the report of the Monetary Commission. But these improvements, which are not only most desirable, but which are very necessary,
are not sufficient, in my opinion, to command my vote for the bill if
they are linked with general principles which are both perilous and
unsound.

Let me briefly state the objections which seem to me so grave as
to make the adoption of the beneficial provisions of the bill impossible
without a sacrifice of the fundamental principles upon which, as I
believe, all sound and enduring banking laws must rest.

Throughout my public life I have supported all measures designed
to take the Government out of the banking business. I voted for the
withdrawal of the Treasury notes and hoped that I should live to see
the legal tenders also withdrawn—the Government confined to coining
gold, silver, and copper, and wholly free from responsibility for note
issues. I believe very strongly that banking should be done and bank
notes issued by banks rigidly supervised by the Government, but that
the Government itself should have no part in either function. This
bill puts the Government into the banking business as never before in
our history, and makes, as I understand it, all notes Government
notes when they should be bank notes.

This bill as it stands seems to me to open the way to a vast
inflation of the currency. There is no necessity of dwelling upon this
point after the remarkable and most powerful argument of the senior
Senator from New York [Mr. Root]. I can be content here to follow

operation, worked much better than I expected, but I think that the dangers pointed out in my letter still exist and, under pressure of war, were made apparent.

the example of the English candidate for Parliament who thought it enough 'to say ditto to Mr. Burke.' I will merely add that I do not like to think that any law can be passed which will make it possible to submerge the gold standard in a flood of irredeemable paper currency.

The guaranty of bank deposits seems to me a direct encouragement to bad and reckless banking. I cannot but think that it may have results like those which followed Jackson's deposit of the surplus in the State banks.

The powers vested in the Federal board seem to me highly dangerous, especially where there is political control of the board. I should be sorry to hold stock in a bank subject to such domination.

I will not attempt to enumerate any other objections. Still less shall I undertake to argue upon those which I have mentioned, for that would be impossible in a letter.

I merely desire, as I have already said, to make public record of the reasons which lead me to ask you to pair me against the passage of this bill. I had hoped to support this bill, but I could not vote for it as it stands, because it seems to me to contain features and to rest upon principles in the highest degree menacing to our prosperity, to stability in business, and to the general welfare of the people of the United States.

I am, as always

Very sincerely yours,
(Signed)   H. C. LODGE

CHAPTER II

MEXICO

MEANTIME the controversy with Mexico, which Mr. Wilson had inherited from the previous administration, became acute. It is not necessary here to trace in detail the events connected with that period. It is sufficient to say that President Wilson declined to recognize General Huerta because Huerta had not, in his opinion, been constitutionally elected. This policy disregarded, of course, the accepted international practice of not interfering with the internal affairs of another nation, and if generally applied in South America would have had disastrous results. I was not, however, disposed at that time to urge the recognition of Huerta, whose methods did not differ essentially from those employed by the men who had taken possession at different times of the Mexican government; but there was a fair question as to the wisdom of recognizing him as President at that moment. Out of this situation grew the affair at Tampico, which finally resolved itself into a demand on our part that our flag be saluted, everything else that we had demanded being, as I remember, practically conceded. Mr. Wilson, however, decided that we must insist on the salute to the flag, with which I sympathized, and this being refused he sent an expedition to Vera Cruz designed to take possession of the city. He had been grossly misinformed as to the situation by his agents in Mexico, and he had a fixed idea that the people would welcome us at Vera Cruz and that we should take possession of the city without opposition. I made some memoranda at the time as to consultations with the

President in regard to invoking the support of Congress; these I quote verbatim as they have the value always possessed by contemporary evidence:

"Friday, April 17, 1914.

"This morning at 9 o'clock to the White House (not office) at request of the President. Present, Shively [Senator Shively of Indiana, acting in the absence of Senator Stone—Chairman of the Foreign Relations Committee] and I, Flood and Cooper of House. He told us crisis was approaching over Tampico incident and he might be obliged to use Navy and Army. Said he wished to know whether we thought that he should call on Congress for authority. I said that he had the power undoubtedly to act or take possession of a port for protection of American lives and property without action by Congress. Had often been done when Congress not in session (Boxer rebellion) and therefore could be done even if Congress in session; but as Congress was in session I thought it would be better to ask Congress for authorizing resolution. Others agreed. The President said that was his view. He talked a little of possibilities; mentioned, as he did in January, committee going to city."

"Monday, April 20th.

"Called to White House (executive office) from Capitol at 2 o'clock P.M. Shively, H. C. L., Flood and Cooper of House. President was to deliver his message at 3. He said he wished to read his message and take our opinion upon it. As it was already in print for the press it could not be changed. But he read it. It seemed to me weak and insufficient, although of course well expressed. He then produced the resolution which he wished passed. It was the same as that which afterwards passed the House and authorized hostilities against Huerta by name.

This seemed to me most unsatisfactory, in reality a declaration of war against an individual. I said that I thought we ought to speak of protection to the lives and property of American citizens as the true and international ground. Pres. said that would widen too much and lead to war. I thought it war in any event. He said that he wanted immediate action because he wished to intercept a cargo of arms for Huerta due that evening at Vera Cruz on German ship. I suggested that he could not stop the ship without a war blockade. He said that his plan was to take Vera Cruz and seize the cargo after it was landed. I pointed out that he would then be cutting off arms from Huerta and letting them go to Villa, which would be in the nature of an alliance. He said this was due to circumstances and could not be helped. He then gave to each of us a copy of the resolution which he wished to have passed.

"At 3 P.M. he read his message to the Houses.

"The House at once took up the resolution and while they were at work our committee on For. Relations met. Objection to the President's resolution naming Huerta was unanimous. Then everyone tried his hand at resolutions. Finally there was general and informal agreement to a resolution drafted by me with a preamble setting forth broad international grounds drawn by Root. When we reassembled after the recess I perceived at once that the Democrats had seen the President. Swanson offered as a substitute for the House resolution my resolution exactly as drawn, except for the insertion of the word "certain" before the word "affronts," and had omitted the preamble. It was something to get rid of Huerta's name in the resolution but without the preamble we were left to go to war in silence as to the real and only truly justifying international grounds. The committee reported my resolution as thus amended and we made our fight in the Senate.

"I there offered my resolution with the Root preamble as a substitute, but it was beaten by a straight party vote. That resolution was as follows:

"Resolved, etc. That the state of unrestricted violence and anarchy which exists in Mexico, the numerous unchecked and unpunished murders of American citizens and the spoliation of their property in that country, the impossibility of securing protection or redress by diplomatic methods in the absence of lawful or effective authority, the inability of Mexico to discharge its international obligations, the unprovoked insults and indignities inflicted upon the flag and the uniform of the United States by the armed bands in occupation of large parts of the Mexican territory have become intolerable;

"That the self-respect and dignity of the United States and the duty to protect its citizens and its international rights require that such a course be followed in Mexico by our Government as to compel respect and observance of its rights.

"That to this end the President is justified in the employment of the armed forces of the United States to enforce his demand for unequivocal amends for affronts and indignities committed against the United States; that the United States disclaims any hostility to the Mexican people or any purpose to make war upon them."

As I set down this official record it seems almost incredible that the President of the United States should have seriously proposed to have the Congress and the government of which he was the head substantially declare and practically make war against an individual, a single man whom he wished to name in the resolution. At the moment I did not grasp its full significance or realize the light which it threw upon Mr. Wilson himself. I, however, saw even then what I afterwards came clearly to perceive, that the reason for the extraordinary proposition to make General Huerta the subject of the resolution authorizing the President to seize a Mexican city was that the salute to the flag, which was never given, was a mere excuse. General Huerta had declined to obey Mr. Wilson, he had made himself a stumbling block in Mr. Wilson's path and he had interfered with Mr. Wilson's plans, which was an unforgivable offense. The purpose of the seizure of Vera Cruz was to punish the recalcitrant Mexican, and Mr. Wilson wished to tell the truth and make the United States punish the offender, the man who had dared to thwart him personally. His egotism, so little comprehended then, was so vast that he did not hesitate to say to the world that Huerta's resistance to him must be punished. He succeeded in ultimately overthrowing Huerta, but the Senate declined to allow the United States to declare war upon an individual and thus prevented the President from advertising his own purpose and making a public display of the penalty which he intended to exact from a man who had dared to refuse compliance with his wishes.

In the course of the debate I said:*

. . . "Let us be under no misapprehension as to where this resolution, either in the form passed by the House or in that reported by the Committee on Foreign Relations, leads. It leads to armed intervention. The first step that will be taken under it will be the seizure of Vera Cruz. Does anyone suppose for one moment that we can seize Vera Cruz without some show of resistance on the part of those who now hold it? It is inconceivable. The day we take Vera Cruz we have intervened; you cannot narrow that fact; we have intervened, and if we are to stand by the President, as everyone intends so to stand, in seeking atonement for the insult to the flag, we say that intervention should rest on grounds so broad that the civilized world cannot contest the righteousness of the act.

* Congressional Record—Senate. April 21, 1914, p. 6967.

"We are engaged at this moment, Mr. President, not only in dealing with the gravest responsibility that can come before the American Congress, but we are engaged, as not often happens, in a great historic transaction. The grounds of our action here today will lie before the world and will come to the tribunal of history.

"If we are to intervene for any cause or at any point in Mexican territory, I want it to be done on broad, sufficient grounds. I want to strip the transaction of any personal character whatever. I want to lift it up from the level of personal hostility and place it on the broad ground of great national action, taken in the interest and for the protection of American lives in a foreign country, and for the purpose of restoring peace and order, if we can, to the unhappy people just across our border. I want to place it on a ground where we shall all be content to have it rest. I want to place it upon a ground where the nations of the earth, in whose presence we are acting today, shall admit the justice and the high motives of our action. I want to place it upon a ground upon which we shall not fear to appeal to the judgment seat of history."

That speech shows that what I now write is not wisdom after the event.

As a result of this expedition sent forth by Mr. Wilson against General Huerta, 19 Americans were killed and 71 wounded. The Mexican losses were 126 killed and 195 wounded. This was war, and personally I felt that it was the duty of every American to stand by the administration when the country was actually involved in what was an act of war against a foreign power. The first or second day after the landing at Vera Cruz (April 21st or April 22nd) I went to the White House in the morning, I think with Senator Stone, chairman of the Committee on Foreign Relations, and, I believe, Senator Shively.

There may have been members of the House Committee on Foreign Affairs also present but this I do not recall at the moment. We found Mr. Wilson in a state of great agitation and very much disturbed. He had never meant to have war. Owing to his misinformation he was taken completely by surprise by the fighting at Vera Cruz and he was thoroughly alarmed. His one idea seemed to be that there must be no further warlike operations and he was then looking for an escape through the intervention of the Argentine Republic, Brazil and Chile, which was known afterwards as the A-B-C mediation, and which he hoped they would offer. While we were discussing the situation Mr. Bryan, then Secretary of State, appeared, I suppose to report progress on this effort, and he seemed even more disturbed and more anxious than Mr. Wilson because the fighting at Vera Cruz was peculiarly unpalatable to him in view of his extreme zeal in desiring to maintain peace everywhere at any price. What struck me most in the conversation was the President's evident alarm and his lack of determination as to his policy. He evidently had not thought the question out or in any way determined beforehand what he would do in certain very probable contingencies. Of course he ought never to have sent the fleet and the Marines to Vera Cruz unless he had been prepared not only for the peaceful surrender of the city but also for the resistance which might and, as a matter of fact, actually did take place. It must have been clear to everybody that armed resistance was likely to occur; but it was only too obvious that the President had made no preparation in his own mind for this most probable event. All he seemed desirous of doing, the fighting having occurred, was to get out of the trouble in any way possible without continuing the war which he had himself begun.

I quote again from memoranda made at the time:

"April 25, 1914.

"Word came from the White House this afternoon that the President wished to see me at 6 o'clock (executive office). Present, Stone, Shively, H. C. L., Flood and Cooper. President informed us that Brazil, Argentine and Chile had offered mediation and good offices. He had accepted and read us his reply. We all approved acceptance. That fact, in itself a good thing, shows our readiness for a peaceful solution but also, which is infinitely more important, improves our relations with three most important South Amer. States and unites them with us. I asked President if mediation was to be confined to Tampico incident. He said 'Certainly not,' that his note meant settlement by general pacification of Mexico. I said that I so understood it but that I wished to make perfectly sure. We then talked of continuing preparations which the note provided for. President said that they would go on but he thought it would have a bad effect to call out militia and volunteers immediately after note. I said that it should not be done at once but urged strongly that if we were to intervene we ought to put at least 200,000 men into Mexico as rapidly as possible. That we ought to use overwhelming force and stifle resistance at once. This was quickest and most humane. Nothing so bad as a 'little war.'

"I then brought up the Canal; urged the importance of sending a strong body of troops and heavy coast artillery, for permanent defense at both ends, a cruiser or destroyer for the Gatun Lake and, if it were possible, to pass a dreadnought through the canal to the Pacific, which would not only protect entrance to canal but soothe Japan. So we parted.

"Acceptance of the South American mediation very valuable. To have refused would have been a terrible blunder. Whether they can succeed in getting a basis for pacification of Mexico we cannot tell. It seems most improbable.

"But the effort can do no harm unless the President, who has been thoroughly frightened by Vera Cruz, accepts some humiliating terms in order to escape. He assured us that offer of mediation was wholly voluntary, without any suggestion from us of any kind. I heard from Spring-Rice * in evening at embassy that Jusserand † had hinted to Brazil, Argentine and Chile to move."

It is not necessary for me here to trace the subsequent transactions in regard to Huerta. He finally died in an American prison, having been driven from power in Mexico as Mr. Wilson desired. In this sense Mr. Wilson's war to remove Huerta was successful, but the political and physical destruction of one man, who had been chosen by familiar if illicit methods to be President of another and friendly country, was not a very glorious feat. I shall not attempt to follow the course of our tangled relations with Mexico and the general anarchy which ensued, for the A-B-C mediation had no practical results. Suffice it to say that two years later the President sent into Mexico an expedition headed by General Pershing, with an army of 10,000 men, to repress and capture Villa, who for a time had apparently been selected as a friend and ally of our administration. In that connection I took part in another consultation with the President, of which I made a memorandum the same evening. It was just after the affair at Carrizal, where a troop of our cavalry had been ambushed, some of our men killed and seventeen carried off as prisoners. The memorandum is as follows:

"June 25, 1916.

"Sent for to White House. Evening at 8 o'clock. Senator Stone, Flood (Chairman House Com. Foreign

* Then British Ambassador.
† Then French Ambassador.

Affairs) and I, present. The President told us of Arredondo's insolent note, and of his own note to Carranza demanding C's intentions. Both then had gone to press.*

"He said he was collecting evidence as to just what happened at Carrizal. What was he to do next? If Carranza refused to give up the prisoners he thought he should order Pershing to march on Chihuahua where the prisoners were and take it but he did not want war. Stone suggested that to fight an action and capture a city belonging to a country with which legally we were

* The notes referred to are as follows:

"I am directed by my Government to inform Your Excellency, with reference to the Carrizal incident, that the Chief Executive, through the Mexican War Department, gave orders to General Jacinto B. Trevino not to permit American forces from General Pershing's column to advance farther south, nor to move either east or west from the points where they are located, and to oppose new incursions of American soldiers into Mexican territory. These orders were brought by General Trevino to the attention of General Pershing, who acknowledged the receipt of the communication relative thereto. On the 22nd instant, as Your Excellency knows, an American force moved eastward quite far from its base, notwithstanding the above orders, and was engaged by Mexican troops at Carrizal, State of Chihuahua. As a result of the encounter several men on both sides were killed and wounded and 17 American soldiers were made prisoners."

You are hereby instructed to hand to the Minister of Foreign Relations of the de facto Government the following:

"The government of the United States can put no other construction upon the communication handed to the Secretary of State of the United States on the 24th of June by Mr. Arredondo, under instruction of your Government, than that it is intended as a formal avowal of deliberately hostile action against the forces of the United States now in Mexico, and of the purpose to attack them without provocation whenever they move from their present position in pursuance of the objects for which they were sent there, notwithstanding the fact that those objects not only involve no unfriendly intention towards the Government and people of Mexico, but are on the contrary, intended only to assist that Government in protecting itself and the territory and people of the United States against irresponsible and insurgent bands of rebel marauders.

"I am instructed, therefore, by my Government to demand the immediate release of the prisoners taken in the encounter at Carrizal, together with any property of the United States taken with them, and to inform you that the Government of the United States expects an early statement from your Government as to the course of action it wishes the Government of the United States to understand it has determined upon, and that it also expects that this statement be made through the usual diplomatic channels, and not through subordinate military commanders."

at peace closely resembled war. The President then said we must shut out arms from Mexico and to do that a blockade would be necessary but he did not wish to declare war. I said that unless war was formally declared no blockade could be established, for a general blockade was purely a belligerent right. He said he would ask the lawyers at the State Dept. It seems incredible that he should not have known, for it is the A B C of international law. He then said that we might say to other nations that we should regard it as an unfriendly act to permit the export of arms to Mexico. I said that course seemed to me likely to lead to many serious complications as we were at that moment exporting arms and munitions of war to Europe. He said Yes, he feared so, that he was just thinking aloud. He did not know how many men Pershing had with him; said he left all that to the War Dept. He did not know how far Pershing was from Chihuahua, the place he proposed to capture. It seemed to me odd that the Commander-in-chief should not have enough curiosity to know these facts. He wanted evidently to do just enough to allay public feeling and avoid war. He was willing to commit one or two acts of war but not declare war. He was torn between fear of losing votes and fear of war. He was in a nervous condition, as when I saw him after Vera Cruz, although not so collapsed as he was then."

This memorandum in regard to my conversation with the President after the affair at Carrizal is the last memorandum I made in regard to Mexico. It is shown by the date to have occurred nearly two years after the beginning of the Great War in Europe and it seemed to me better to conclude the Mexican question, so far as I had any personal conversations with the President in regard to it, before beginning on the history of the Great War so far as that war concerned the United States.

At this point, however, I think it is well that I should

explain why I have given a brief account of my action on the Panama Canal tolls and of my personal relations with Mr. Wilson at the beginning of his Administration, in order to show the personally friendly character of those relations. I do this because in this connection I wish to take occasion now to say once for all that I never had the slightest personal hostility to Mr. Wilson. During the protracted contest of the League, it was constantly said by the newspapers which were supporting Mr. Wilson and the League that I was actuated in my attitude by a personal hostility to the President. Nothing could be more absolutely untrue. I never had any personal hostility to Mr. Wilson, as I have just said, and there was no possible reason why I should have any personal hostility. In all the speeches and debates of that time I never attacked him personally or otherwise than courteously and always on public questions. He had never crossed my path in any way and never had inflicted any personal injury upon me; in fact, it was impossible for him to do so. My opposition to Mr. Wilson in connection with the war and the League rested entirely on public grounds, which I shall explain fully before I complete this brief account of the events of that time so far as they concern me. The questions involved in the war and the League were altogether too serious to be decided on any ground of personal feeling or to be caused by any personal hostility, even had such hostility existed. In the war with Germany and the events growing out of the war, the very highest interests of the people of the United States were deeply concerned and also, as I shall later explain, as it seemed to me, the character and the methods of our Government under the Constitution were involved and perhaps imperiled. In dealing with issues of such moment, I do not believe that there was a single man among Mr. Wilson's opponents in the Senate who was moved to take the position which he took by

any personal feeling whatever. Those who opposed Mr.
Wilson and the League, not only the Senators who voted
for the League with the reservations which bore my
name but those who would not vote for it in any form
or under any consideration, were determined by the deepest convictions of duty and were not influenced by any
other consideration than that of the public weal and the
safety of the United States.

CHAPTER III

BEGINNING OF THE WORLD WAR

I HAPPENED to be abroad during the summer of 1914 and was in England when the war began. The crowding events of those days as they came upon us in London, so near to the scene of action and involving as they did the safety of the British Empire, made an impression upon all who watched the developments of the days as they passed, which no one, I think, could ever forget. My sympathies were from the very first strongly with the Allies. I believed then, as I have continued to believe ever since, that nothing less was at stake on the result of the conflict than the freedom and civilization of the Western world. While I was in London during the first six weeks of the war, I gave a statement to the correspondent of the New York *Sun* which was printed in that newspaper in New York on August 23, 1914, and which is as follows:

"I will not comment on the war except to say that no other such calamity has ever befallen humanity or civilization. The mind recoils even from an attempt to picture the sacrifice of life and the misery and suffering which those who began this war have brought on mankind.

"My interest is in regard to my own country and her attitude in this great conflict of nations. Fortunately the United States is outside the widespread circle of the war The United States is at peace with all nations and I trust will remain so. From such a convulsion as this we have already suffered severely financially and by the

25

loss of some of our best markets and commerce, and are bound to suffer still more. This cannot be helped.

"What we should remember above all is that we have a national duty to perform. That duty is the observance of strict neutrality as between the belligerents, with all of whom we are at peace. But strict neutrality is not enough. It must be an honest neutrality, as honest as it is rigid. Neutrality, while preserving its name, can often be so managed as to benefit one belligerent and injure another. This is no time for neutrality of this kind on the part of the United States. Our neutrality now, as I have said, must not only be strict but rigidly honest and fair. Honor and interest alike demand it.

"President Wilson's Administration, in its eagerness to maintain neutrality, has made one new departure from practices which have hitherto been unbroken. Heretofore Governments have not undertaken to interfere with private persons or institutions who desired to lend money to belligerents. If we had been unable to borrow money or obtain supplies from abroad while we were cut off from all supplies from the South during the Civil War the boundaries of the country of which Mr. Wilson is President might possibly be far different today. But the Administration in its earnestness to maintain strict neutrality during the present war has thought fit to make this new departure by preventing, as far as it can, private individuals from lending money to belligerents. This makes it difficult to understand what theory of neutrality it favors. If the despatches are correct in regard to the purchase by the United States Government of certain German ships now lying useless in New York harbor, the Administration regards as impairing strict neutrality permission to private persons to lend a hundred million dollars to France to be spent in the purchase of supplies in the United States, while at the same time it appears to think it is consonant with honest neutrality to give

$25,000,000 of the public money outright to Germany for ships which Germany cannot use.

"This proposed purchase of German ships by the American Government to be run as Government vessels is calculated to hamper and check exports from the United States. We are suffering severely from the injury to our trade and commerce by the loss of our best markets, consequent on the war, but there are certain articles that Europe must have even now and these exports should be encouraged in every possible way. Half a dozen ships owned by the Government can carry only an insignificant fraction of the exports we desire to make, but they will check all private enterprise and prevent Americans from purchasing ships as they would otherwise do in large numbers, because they will fear Government competition. We need every possible outlet for our exports at this moment and Government ships will simply check some of the most important channels and give us one ship where we might have ten.

"Far more grave, however, than the interference with trade will be the international complications which these Government owned ships (purchased from Germany) are certain to produce. Are they to be regarded and treated as merchantmen, or are they public vessels of the United States on the same footing as our ships of war? It seems impossible that they should be treated as merchantmen under the rules of international law. If one of them should be stopped when classed as a merchantman it would be at the worst only a diplomatic incident for which reparation could easily be made; but if a ship of the United States engaged in commerce and yet retaining the character of a public vessel should be stopped for any reason, that would be an act of war. If one of the German cruisers which are now said to be roaming over the Atlantic should hold up one of those Government owned vessels because she believed this vessel was carrying contraband of war, the arrest would constitute an act of war against the United States. If England or France believed that one of these Government owned vessels was carrying supplies, say oil, to Germany by way of Holland, and should stop that ship as they would a merchantman and turn her back, it would be an act of war. In neither of these supposed cases, if the vessel were a simple merchantman, would the act of Germany, England or France be an act of war.

"In purchasing these vessels we should begin with a breach of strict neutrality by giving $25,000,000 to Germany. We should hamper and check the outward flow of our exports, which are of immense importance at this time. Worst of all, we should have half a dozen vessels afloat which might at any moment involve us in war with any or all the belligerents. It is an experiment so dangerous that I earnestly hope that it will not be attempted. I repeat that our duty, honor and interest alike demand at the present moment that our neutrality should be as honest as it is strict."

I made this statement because the attitude of the Administration as to the purchase of the German ships which had sought asylum in New York harbor (they were not interned and were free to go at any moment), coupled with the apparent hostility to exports to the allies and to loans, constituted not only in essence a breach of neutrality, but were in reality a help to Germany. After events seemed to show that Mr. Wilson was not a German sympathizer or indeed in sympathy with any of the belligerents; but that this attitude as to exports and the purchase of German ships was part of the scheme afterwards developed to put the United States in a position where the President could come forward and play the great rôle of peace-maker for the entire world. It was a personal ambition which was the key to this as to other actions, as large as it was hopeless and futile, but chargeable with all sorts of dangerous possibilities.

Being most anxious not to embarrass the British Government in any way, I spoke to my friend, Lord Harcourt, then Secretary for the Colonies, about it, and he was very anxious that I should make such a statement as I proposed to make just at that critical time. I felt at the moment a keen regret that the United States had not made a protest as to the invasion of Belgium and the breach of her neutrality. The invasion of Belgium by Germany, of course, came very suddenly, but there was fair reason to expect it and there was an opportunity for the United States to make a protest and with it a record upon which the American people could always look back with pride and satisfaction. How much that protest would have availed, no one can say. I never felt at all certain that it would have had any effect, although there were many people in the United States and elsewhere who believed that it might have gone far toward stopping the war at the outset. This I doubt very much. I think that all the correspondence which has been since published showing the attitude of Germany and of the Emperor makes it very clear that Germany meant to bring on the war at that moment, and if this view is correct a protest by the United States might have given her pause, but I do not believe it would have prevented her action.

The President, when the war came, issued a proclamation of neutrality, which was in accordance with the settled policy of our Government in the past, beginning with Washington's famous declaration of neutrality as between Great Britain and France in 1793. I felt that this was the correct policy at that moment and so stated again, I think, in public when I returned to the United States. When the President, however, went further and made his statement on August 19, 1914, that, "The

United States must be neutral in fact as well as in name during these days that are to try men's souls. We must be impartial in thought as well as in action, must put a curb upon our sentiments as well as upon every transaction that might be construed as a preference of one party to the struggle before another," I could no longer sympathize with such an idea of neutrality as this. The neutrality which he urged upon us to be maintained even "in thought" could only have been achieved in the presence of such a war as was then convulsing Europe by a vast and organized hypocrisy. Proper neutrality, and the only one possible, was one maintained honestly and officially by the Government in all its acts in accordance with the principles of International Law. The President's demand was, to my thinking, a perfectly unsound as well as utterly impractical position to take.

We had a rather vivid example of the President's conception of neutrality in the subsequent attempt made in January, 1915, to buy the German ships which had taken asylum and were laid up at the wharves in New York harbor and to which I have already referred. A bill was brought forward to establish a Shipping Board and a corporation, which was done at a later period, to own and manage in behalf of the Government a fleet of merchant vessels. Under the bill as it stood it was impossible to purchase the German ships, which would have meant an expenditure of about 35 million dollars. Even in that time of great expenditures 35 millions would have been very valuable to the German Government and it would also have relieved them of their anxiety about the ships. To this the Republicans and some Democrats in the Senate were very much opposed. I offered an amendment providing that under the shipping bill no vessels belonging to any belligerent should be purchased. This amendment was rejected by the Committee on Commerce, the Democrats controlling the committee. Subsequently I offered the amendment in the Senate. We made up our minds that this bill should not pass, and the only way surely to prevent it was by a parliamentary obstruction, usually called a "filibuster." We entered upon this policy of resistance early in January, kept it up until the 4th of March and succeeded in preventing action on the bill.

It seemed right to me then, and has always seemed right to me since, that with this great war in progress party lines should be abandoned in the Congress, and to that belief I adhered throughout, not only during the neutral years but after we entered the war ourselves. The Republican Party after the war began, in both the Senate and the House, not only put no obstacle whatever in the way of legislation desired by the Administration for the conduct of the war but aided that legislation in every possible way. It would require a volume to follow the events of the war in detail from the outset and show the course pursued in the Senate in regard to it. I shall only touch on the salient points, my purpose being to make clear the attitude of Mr. Wilson and why I, at least, became more and more dissatisfied with his policy and ceased to have any confidence in his conduct of our relations during the trying and eventful years which followed the beginning of the war in 1914.

CHAPTER IV

THE LUSITANIA

THE *Lusitania* was torpedoed by a German submarine on the 7th of May, 1915, and many American citizens, non-combatants, women and children, were savagely and cruelly drowned. The country was horrified, and at that moment the popular feeling was such that if the President, after demanding immediate reparation and apology to be promptly given, had boldly declared that the time had come when the rights and safety of American citizens were so endangered that it was our duty to go to war, he would have had behind him the enthusiastic support of the whole American people. He would have had it with more enthusiasm and fervor at that moment, I firmly believe, than he did when we finally went to war in 1917, because in the interval he had paltered with the issues raised by Germany through her attacks upon our shipping and her violation of our rights, and had so confused the whole question that the mind of the people generally was not so clear upon our duty and the necessity of action as it was immediately after the sinking of the *Lusitania*. He made a speech in Philadelphia on May 10, 1915, three days after the destruction of the ship, in which he used the phrase, "There is such a thing as a man being too proud to fight. There is such a thing as a nation being so right that it does not need to convince others by force that it is right." Mr. Wilson was given to making phrases and they were not always fortunate. This was probably the most unfortunate phrase that he ever coined. He discovered at once by the expression of feeling all over the country that, although he was usually very shrewd in gauging popular feeling, he had made, by his "too proud to fight," a rather ghastly mistake. It was not the moment for fine words or false idealism. That phrase of "too proud to fight" and his subsequent correspondence in regard to the *Lusitania* incident, which evaded the issue and clouded it with words, destroyed my confidence in him because he had shown himself destitute of the strength, patriotism, courage and unselfishness which were so sorely needed at that precise moment in any man who was called upon to stand at the head of the American nation. The phrase "too proud to fight," uttered at such a moment, shocked me, as it did many others, and I never again recovered confidence in Mr. Wilson's ability to deal with the most perilous situation which had ever confronted the United States in its relations with the other nations of the earth.

In 1916 a controversy arose due to a speech I made at Brockton, and I give a brief account of it here because it completes what I have to say about the destruction of the *Lusitania*.

The summer of 1916 was of course occupied with the Presidential election. The Republican Party made an admirable nomination, taking as their candidate Mr. Justice Hughes, then on the Supreme Court bench. Mr. Wilson made his contest on the cry: "He kept us out of war," and on that noble principle he succeeded in carrying the country, although the vote was very close. During that campaign, a question came up in regard to the *Lusitania* and the correspondence which followed it. I had received information from a trustworthy source—in fact, from two entirely separate witnesses—that weak as Mr. Wilson's notes in regard to the *Lusitania* were, he had intended to go further and was considering an additional note or cablegram which would have removed all danger of our going to war with Germany,—there really was none at that moment,—but which would have put us in a lamentable position. The strong opposition of Mr. Garrison, then Secretary of War, and others as I afterwards learned stopped the sending of this note. I think it important, in my own interest, to give an account of that controversy. I fully expected that after the campaign I should be assailed for having made the attack, and I therefore prepared a very careful statement of the whole question so as to be ready for the assault, but the attack never came. It then seemed to me evident that the subject was one which the President did not care to pursue. I now give the statement which I had prepared at the time, and which is entirely contemporary:

On October 25th, 1916, I received the following letter from Honorable Grafton D. Cushing, who had been Speaker of the Massachusetts House of Representatives and Lieutenant Governor of the Commonwealth, who has been a friend of mine for many years and in whom I have absolute confidence:

"October 24, 1916.

"Dear Senator Lodge:—

Dr. Charles H. Bailey of Tufts Medical School came in to see me today to give me the substance of conversations which he had with Breckinridge, the Assistant Secretary of War, on a trip across the continent. The facts may be perfectly well known to you but I have asked Dr. Bailey to put them in typewritten form and I am sending them on to you in case there is any use to be made of them.

Dr. Bailey is evidently a perfectly reliable man and if you care to question him further he will be very glad to call on you.
Yours very truly,
GRAFTON D. CUSHING."

Dr. Bailey's letter which he enclosed was a clear and explicit account of a conversation which he had with Mr. Breckinridge, former Assistant Secretary of War under the present [Wilson] administration. The letter interested me very much because it showed that the note of May 13th, commonly known as the "strict accountability" note, was never intended seriously; that at the time it was sent it did not mean what it purported to mean on its face. The note of June 9th and subsequent events had conclusively shown that the note of May 13th meant nothing. The only new point in Dr. Bailey's report of Mr. Breckinridge's conversation was that the "strict accountability" note of May 13th meant nothing and was intended to mean nothing at the moment when it was written and sent. I added nothing else to what all the world already knew.

In a speech at Brockton on October 26th I alluded to the statement by Dr. Bailey, without mentioning names, merely to illustrate the character of the Administration's management of our foreign relations in connection with the destruction of American lives on the *Lusitania*. What I said attracted some attention in the press and I felt that it was necessary for me to give my authority for my statements. I communicated with Dr. Bailey, who told me that I was entirely at liberty to use his letter and who confirmed all that was said in the letter, in the strongest way. I made the following speech at Somerville on October 28th:

"As a concrete instance both of the indifference of this Administration to the rights of Americans to be protected in their lives when lawfully beyond the borders of the United States, and of the paltering way in which this question has been dealt with, I need only cite some recent events.

"On the 7th of May, 1915, the *Lusitania* was destroyed by a submarine and the lives of more than 100 American citizens, lawfully on board, were sacrificed. On May 10th, the President, speaking at Philadelphia, made the famous remark about the nation being "too proud to fight." This statement was not well received by the country and the Administration made haste to disclaim it. On the 13th of May the President wrote a note to Germany, in which occurred the following passage: 'This Government has already taken occasion to inform the Imperial German Government that it cannot admit the adoption of such measures or such a warning of danger to operate as in any degree an abbreviation of the rights of American shipmasters or of American citizens bound on lawful errands as passengers on merchant ships of belligerent nationality; and that it must hold the Imperial German Government to a *strict accountability* for any infringement of those rights, intentional or incidental.' The concluding paragraph of the note was as follows: 'The Imperial German Government will not expect the Government of the United States to omit any word or any act necessary to the performance of its sacred duty of maintaining the rights of the United States and its citizens and of safeguarding their free exercise and enjoyment.'

"The note thus framed was agreed to by the cabinet and in this form it was sent. On the 8th of June Mr. Bryan resigned from the cabinet and on the 9th of June the second note to Germany concerning the operation of submarines was sent. The second note sounded a retreat from the very strong language used in the first note.

"In the meantime it became publicly known that the Austrian Ambassador had sent word to Berlin that the first note really meant nothing but was intended merely to satisfy public opinion, and that he had this information from the Secretary of State, Mr. Bryan. It is not necessary to discuss the propriety of Mr. Bryan's action in making such a statement to the representative of a foreign power; but that it was true has been shown in the process of time by the fact that Germany was not held to a 'strict accountability' and that no disavowal, no apology for the destruction of American lives on the

Lusitania and no offer of reparation has ever been made. These facts, all within public knowledge, prove what I have already said of the indifference of this Administration to the protection of Americans in the first of rights— the right of life—when lawfully beyond our borders, and the rapid shifting of policy in order to meet the varying currents of public opinion in the United States and to avoid doing anything. This case is complete as it stands.

"There was, however, one feature which does not affect or modify the essential point, but about which there was much speculation at the time, and that was why Mr. Bryan allowed his name to be appended to a very strong note, couched in the most extreme language possible to diplomacy, and yet resigned so that he need not affix his signature to the very mild note of June 9th, a note which even a man of very strong pacifist tendencies could not have objected to.

"It was currently reported at the time that the reason for this apparently inexplicable action on Mr. Bryan's part was the fact that the first note as finally sent was not the note to which he had appended his signature.

"Within a few days there has come into my possession direct information upon this subject, contained in the following letter which was addressed to Hon. Grafton D. Cushing, who forwarded it to me. The writer, Dr. Charles H. Bailey, professor in the Tufts Medical School, is a gentleman of high standing and undoubted veracity, and his letter is as follows:

'Boston, Mass., Oct. 24, 1916.
'The Hon. Grafton Cushing,
  'Massachusetts Chairman of the Hughes
  'National College League,
    '719 Barristers Hall, Boston, Mass.
'Dear Sir:
  'As you requested, I am submitting to you herewith in writing a report of a conversation between ex-Assistant

Secretary of War Breckinridge and myself. Leaving San Francisco on July 15, 1916, I rode from that city as far as Omaha, Neb., with Mr. Breckinridge. During the trip I asked Mr. Breckinridge if he would be willing to answer certain questions with regard to the conduct of our national affairs during his connection with the present administration. Receiving an affirmative reply, I asked him among other things as to the truth of the published report that following the so-called strict accountability note Secretary Bryan had informed Ambassador Dumba that the central powers need not take the note too seriously as it was written for political effect and home consumption only. He said that in all essential details I had stated the matter correctly, which led him of his own accord to tell me the following: This is not, of course, a verbatim report, but simply a brief outline of the story as told me by Mr. Breckinridge.

'He stated that following the completion of the "omit no word or no act" note, to the satisfaction of the cabinet, Mr. Wilson without the knowledge of any member of the cabinet except Secretary Bryan, himself wrote a postscript which he sent with the note to the State Department for codification. Mr. Breckinridge stated that both Mr. Garrison and he had seen this postscript and he told me what he claimed were its exact words, which, however, I cannot repeat exactly, but the substance was that the Imperial German Government was not to put too serious an interpretation on the words "omit no word or act." On the contrary he would be inclined, provided the German government did not see fit to yield to the demands of the United States, to use his efforts toward submitting the whole matter to an impartial international tribunal, the decision to be made only after the war. Both note and postscript were submitted to and signed by Secretary Bryan.

'This, according to Mr. Breckinridge, was too good for Mr. Bryan to keep to himself, with the result that it reached Secretary Garrison's ears, who immediately, with two or three (I do not remember which) other members of the Cabinet, called on Mr. Wilson and demanded that he withdraw the postscript under the threat that otherwise they would resign and make the matter public. Mr.

Wilson immediately yielded and Secretary Garrison and the others left.

'Immediately after this President Wilson summoned Secretary Bryan to the White House and when the latter left President Wilson had the assurance of his resignation; whether at Mr. Wilson's request, because Secretary Bryan had been responsible for the matter reaching Secretary Garrison's ears, or whether presented by Secretary Bryan because there had been a previous understanding between Wilson and Bryan that the latter would sign the note proper only with the understanding that such a nullifying postscript should be sent and the President was now unable to fulfil the agreement, Mr. Breckinridge was unable to state.

'I asked Mr. Breckinridge if he would be willing to bring such knowledge as he possessed to the active support of Mr. Hughes. He said that he was still at heart a Democrat, but that neither he nor any other patriotic American could support Wilson. Whether, however, he would be willing to actively support Hughes, he said that he could not say at that early date.

'With best wishes for the success of your campaign, I am,

'Sincerely yours,
'CHAS. HERVEY BAILEY.
'Tufts Medical School, Boston, Mass.'

"This adds nothing to the main facts which, as I have said, are wholly within the public knowledge. It simply throws an additional light on the shifty character of this administration in its foreign policies. It is also of interest in one way, for it shows apparently that Mr. Bryan's reason for resigning was the highly creditable one of objecting to having his signature go out appended to a document differing in an essential point from the one which he had signed.

"It brings out very vividly the point I have been trying to make. It shows the signal failure of this administration to protect American citizens. It shows the writing of one note to meet a rush of public sentiment, the writing of another to gratify one racial group, and of another to gratify another racial group—trying, in the maddened search for votes, to get them by doing the worst of all things in American politics, trying to draw race lines among Americans who ought to have only one allegiance and tradition—the allegiance and tradition of the American Republic."

At the conclusion of my speech Professor Bailey said to the press: "I was present when Senator Lodge made the statement tonight and there is nothing more which I can add, as he quoted directly from my letter to Mr. Cushing. I can only say that Senator Lodge's statement is absolutely correct."

The publication of Dr. Bailey's letter attracted much attention and brought a statement from Mr. Breckinridge in which he denounced Dr. Bailey for repeating the conversation which he had held with an actual stranger on the train, but he neither denied the fact of the conversation nor the essential point in the report of his conversation. It seemed to me necessary, however, in view of the comments in the press and Mr. Breckinridge's statement, to take the matter up again, and at Fitchburg, on Monday, October 30th, I spoke as follows, and gave a letter which I had received from Mr. Jeffries, a gentleman in Boston whose family were well known to me and who had been for some six weeks with Mr. Breckinridge during the previous summer.

"As additional evidence of the truth of what I said at Somerville on Saturday evening about the preparation of a postscript to the *Lusitania* note I give the following letter which has come to me from Mr. J. T. L. Jeffries of Boston:

'Dear Senator Lodge:
'I have noted in Boston papers your remarks connecting President Wilson with a postscript to one of the so-called *Lusitania* notes. According to the papers you

state that the effect of this postscript was to vitiate the
force of the note, or purposely to inform the Imperial
Government that the vigor displayed in earlier parts of
the note was designed for Anglo-American consumption
solely. According to the press accounts this postscript
was added rather surreptitiously and under star-chamber
proceedings, and was withdrawn only because the few
manly members of the cabinet happened to discover its
existence by luck and naturally threatened to turn the
government upside down.

'I assure you, sir, I deeply regret being drawn into
this affair; but I cannot sit idly by and see you called a
liar when I know your statements are true.

'My friend Major Breckinridge several times made to
me remarks similar to those reported by Professor Bailey.
I cannot swear to every minute detail, for my memory is
only human; but the general substance of your statement
is correct to my personal knowledge.

'As I have telegraphed to Major Breckinridge to tell
him of my proposed action, and as his remarks were not
secret, and as Professor Bailey has already involved the
Major, I feel obliged to state that I know your statement
is true. With regard to Major Breckinridge, he is one of
the finest examples of the American gentleman, and his
distinguished family has been famous for its chivalry in
the South for years. His statement also is unquestion-
ably true beyond any possibility of doubt.

'Believe me, dear Senator Lodge,
'Yours truly,
'JOHN TEMPLE LLOYD JEFFRIES.'

"The writer of this letter, Mr. John Jeffries, is a
member of a very well known family in Boston, a gentleman of honor and now known to me personally. The
evidence that Mr. Breckinridge made the statement at-
tributed to him about the postscript I therefore think
cannot be successfully controverted, and if Mr. Breckinridge made the statement it can be absolutely believed.

"Mr. Breckinridge has published one or two telegrams
in which he refers to Dr. Bailey and myself in a very

angry manner, which is not important, but he characterizes his own conversation, which Dr. Bailey reported, as 'backstairs gossip.' He does himself a great injustice by this because he was a member of the Wilson administration and a most excellent Assistant Secretary of War. He denies that there was any threat of resignation by Mr. Garrison and others but he entirely fails to deny the essential point, which was that the postscript was written and that he and Mr. Garrison saw it. Mr. Garrison said yesterday in Washington: 'I am not being interviewed on any subject. I have no statement of any kind to make.'

"So that he also refuses to deny the existence of the postscript, which he certainly would have done if it had been a mere fabrication by Dr. Bailey. Dr. Bailey is a gentleman of the highest character, standing and veracity. I have no doubt that he stated the conversation in substance with absolute truth."

Mr. Jeffries' letter is self-explanatory but he further emphasized it by the statement which he gave to the press the next day and which is as follows:

"I was travelling in California this last summer and for six weeks was more or less in the company of Breckinridge at San Francisco. Breckinridge not only told me the story of the *Lusitania* note postscript several times but I heard him tell it to others. In my opinion he repeated it to a great many people.

"I assume full, absolute and undivided responsibility for every particle of the statement made by me to Senator Lodge. That statement was made by me alone, without the aid, countenance, advice or encouragement of any of my friends, or of any of my relatives, or of any person whatsoever.

"I have never understood that the information I and others received was given as 'gossip' or as 'backstairs gossip.' In all the time that I have known of the *Lusi-*

tania diplomata I have never given to any one a hint of my knowledge or opinion. So far as I am concerned the subject would not have been mentioned this side of doomsday. I have not mentioned the subject until Major Breckinridge was already involved heels over head and until the matter was publicly blazoned in the press. Nor did I mention the subject until after telegraphing Major Breckinridge of my proposed statement, a telegram to which he has not replied. Even then I should not have mentioned the matter had not Democratic leaders deliberately tried to create the impression that Senator Lodge lied. For me to permit a candidate to go before the electorate accused of charges which I know to be false, as in the case of Senator Lodge, would have been to intentionally deceive and mislead the people. Such action would vitiate the fundamental principles of republican government and would be morally equivalent to treason."

On the night of my Fitchburg speech, October 30th, the President issued a statement which is as follows:

"In reply to your telegram let me say that the statement made by Senator Lodge is untrue. No postscript or amendment of the *Lusitania* note was ever written or contemplated by me except such changes that I myself inserted, which strengthened and emphasized the protest. It was suggested after the note was ready for translation that an intimation be conveyed to the German Government that a proposal for arbitration would be acceptable, and one member of the cabinet spoke to me about it, but it was never discussed in cabinet meeting and no threat of any resignation was ever made, for the very good reason that I rejected the suggestion after giving it such consideration as I thought every proposal deserved which touched so grave a matter.

"It was inconsistent with the purpose of the note. The public is in possession of everything that was said to the German Government.

"WOODROW WILSON"

To that I replied at North Adams, on Ocotber 31st, as follows:

"The President of the United States has denied that there was any postscript to the *Lusitania* note and we are all bound, of course, to accept the President's denial just as he makes it. I need hardly say that I would not willingly bring an unfounded charge against any one high or low and if misled in doing so I would be quick to retract it. The President makes one' mistake. The statement which he characterizes as untrue, that there was such a postscript was not mine, but was made by Mr. Breckinridge, a former Assistant Secretary of War, according to the evidence of two independent witnesses, both gentlemen of high character, responsibility and veracity, and Mr. Breckinridge was in a position to know, if, as he is reported to have said, he had seen the postscript.

"Bearing in mind the public and hitherto uncontroverted fact that Mr. Bryan had informed the Austro-Hungarian ambassador that the 'strict accountability' note of May 15th meant nothing, which fact was at once cabled by the Ambassador to Berlin, it seemed to me that Mr. Breckinridge's statement as testified to by independent witnesses ought properly to be laid before the public.

"The President, it will also be observed, says that the clause proposing arbitration 'was suggested' and that after consideration he rejected it. This suggestion rejected by the President covered the exact proposition said by Mr. Breckinridge to have been embodied in the postscript, and may have been what Mr. Breckinridge had in mind when talking to Dr. Bailey and Mr. Jeffries about the postscript which was rejected without having been referred to the cabinet, and it may also have been the reason for Mr. Bryan's statement to the Austro-Hungarian ambassador that the 'note meant nothing.'

"I would also call your attention to a statement by

Mr. Charles Warren, a Republican presidential elector of New Jersey, who states that he was told by a member of President Wilson's official family that the proposition to arbitrate the loss of life on the *Lusitania* was to be embodied in a note to Ambassador Gerard and was not to be a postscript to the 'strict accountability' note. He states further what Mr. Tumulty did to prevent such action, and Mr. Tumulty, when Mr. Warren's statement was brought to his attention, said that he apprised the President that there was a proposition for arbitration from a member of the Cabinet. I mention this only because the President and Mr. Tumulty both agree that there was a proposition for arbitrating the loss of American lives on the *Lusitania* to accompany the 'strict accountability' note, which was suggested by some one, considered by the President and by him rejected.

"As I have previously pointed out, the suggestion for a proposition of arbitration to accompany the 'strict accountability' note, whether as a postscript or as a separate note, by cable, or post, or in any form, and the methods of its suggestion, consideration and rejection are only of interest as throwing light on the manner in which our foreign relations have been dealt with by this Administration. This question of the arbitration proposition does not in the least alter the essential fact that the 'strict accountability' note meant nothing, as Mr. Bryan declared to the Austro-Hungarian Ambassador, and as events since that time have painfully demonstrated. The utter emptiness of the note of May 15th with its threat of 'strict accountability' and 'omit no word or act' has been strikingly shown once more within forty-eight hours, if press reports are to be believed, by the destruction of lives of Americans rightfully on board the steamship *Marina*, which was blown up by a submarine."

Before I come to an examination of the President's statement and my reply it ought to be said that the New

York *Herald* stated that they knew of this proposed addition to the *Lusitania* note at the time, but that the information had been given to them in confidence and they could not use it. There also appeared two statements from Mr. Charles Warren, a Republican presidential elector in New Jersey, which I referred to in my North Adams speech and which I now give in full, as follows:

"The real facts concerning Mr. Bryan's resignation," said Mr. Warren, "came to me directly from an unimpeachable source—from a member of President Wilson's official family. It wasn't really a postscript to the *Lusitania* note that was to be sent to Berlin but an additional note in which Ambassador Gerard was instructed to convey to the German government the information that the note had been written solely for American consumption. Secretary Bryan signed the first note on condition that the second should be sent.

"The second note was actually written and got as far as the telegraph office before it was recalled. It was the President's secretary, Mr. Tumulty, who prevented its being forwarded to Ambassador Gerard. He realized the political danger to his chief of such a message and went to Lindley M. Garrison, the Secretary of War. Mr. Tumulty urged Mr. Garrison to exert his influence with the President to prevent the sending of the message and Mr. Garrison said that he had no influence but directed the secretary to Postmaster General Burleson. The Postmaster General went to the President, but Mr. Wilson did not agree. He urged that the American people did not want war, were opposed to getting into war, and that the course laid down in his instructions to Ambassador Gerard was in accordance with the feelings of the country. This argument satisfied Postmaster General Burleson, who withdrew his objection.

"Mr. Tumulty then sought Mr. Lansing, who at that

time was a counselor of the State department. Lansing and Tumulty went back to the President and succeeded in convincing him of the importance of withdrawing the supplemental instruction to Ambassador Gerard. It was when Mr. Bryan was informed definitely that this instruction to Mr. Gerard had been withheld that he resigned as Secretary of State."

In his second statement Mr. Warren said:

"My source of information cannot be impeached. The story of this remarkable incident was told to me without any pledge of confidence. It is correct and can be substantiated if necessary. I felt at liberty to give out the information after Senator Lodge made his statement. There were two notes, the *Lusitania* note and an additional note, which was known only to President Wilson and Secretary of State Bryan, setting forth that the contents of the first note was for home consumption only and was not to be taken seriously. In some way Mr. Tumulty, the President's secretary, became apprised of the facts and realized at once how grave the effects would be if the facts became known. He went to a cabinet officer and told him it would be the political death of Mr. Wilson. The cabinet officer thoroughly agreed with Mr. Tumulty, who asked the cabinet member to go with him to see the President. The cabinet officer, however, suggested that Mr. Tumulty get Mr. Burleson to accompany him, saying that the Postmaster General would have more influence with the President. Mr. Tumulty saw Mr. Burleson and the latter accompanied him to the President.

"In the meantime Mr. Tumulty had recalled the second note, which was then at the cable office. This was the note declaring that the *Lusitania* note was only for home consumption.

"Mr. Burleson tried to persuade the President. Mr. Wilson said that the people didn't want war. He declared that if the note was not sent it would lead to difficulties between the two countries. The President persuaded Mr. Burleson that it was the right thing to do.

"Then Mr. Tumulty went to Mr. Lansing, who was at that time Counselor to the State Department. As soon as Mr. Lansing was told of the facts he realized that it would be a most serious mistake to send that second note. Mr. Lansing got a number of influential men together and they went with him to Mr. Wilson. They argued with the President and finally persuaded him not to send the note.

"It was then that Mr. Bryan resigned as Secretary of State. Mr. Bryan's signature to the so-called *Lusitania* note was conditional upon the sending of the additional note. There was a wordy war over it, and when the President directed that the second note be withdrawn and not sent, Mr. Bryan got out of the Cabinet."

It must be borne in mind in considering this question that the essence of Mr. Breckinridge's reported conversation was that at the time of the "strict accountability" note and after it had been agreed to in the Cabinet there was a proposition to send in some form an additional note informing the German government that the "strict accountability" note meant nothing serious and that we would be ready to accept a proposal of arbitration from the German government, the question to be arbitrated after the close of the war. The proposition of arbitration to accompany the "strict accountability" note is the essential point in the statement.

The President at the conclusion of his statement says that "the public is in possession of everything that was said to the German government." That sentence alleges a fact which no one had ever questioned. It was admitted on all sides that the proposition for arbitration was not sent. The President also says in his statement, "No postscript or amendment to the *Lusitania* note was ever written or contemplated by me." That is a denial of the fact that there was a postscript or addition to the note. It is not a denial that there was a proposition of arbitration, to accompany the note in some form, considered at the time the note was sent.

In my reply I said;

"The President of the United States has denied that there was any postscript to the *Lusitania* note and we are all bound, of course, to accept the President's denial just as he makes it." I have far too much respect for the great office of President of the United States to bandy words with the holder of that office or to engage in charges or countercharges, but I was very careful to say that I accepted the denial "just as he makes it," and the denial the President made was that there was a postscript or addition.

The President then goes on to say:

"It was suggested after the note was ready for transmission that an intimation be conveyed to the German government that a proposal for arbitration would be acceptable and one member of the cabinet spoke to me about it, but it was never discussed in cabinet meeting and no threat of resignation was ever made for the very good reason that I rejected the suggestion after giving it such consideration as I thought every proposal deserved which touched so grave a matter."

Now let me contrast that with Mr. Breckinridge's statement. Mr. Breckinridge said that the President, after the *Lusitania* note had been agreed upon in the Cabinet, prepared a proposal for arbitration and did not submit it to the Cabinet but showed it to Mr. Bryan. The President says, "It was suggested . . . that an intimation be conveyed to the German government that a proposal for arbitration would be acceptable." He does not say who suggested it, but he admits Mr. Breckinridge's statement that there was such a scheme proposed. He agrees with

Mr. Breckinridge that it was not submitted to the Cabinet, and he agrees with Mr. Breckinridge that it was shown to one member of the Cabinet (Mr. Bryan). He agrees with Mr. Breckinridge that he considered it, and he agrees with Mr. Breckinridge that he rejected it. He denies that there was any threat of resignation; but he does not deny that there was protest against it by some member of the Cabinet.

It will thus be seen that on the vital point of a proposal of arbitration to accompany the *Lusitania* note the President admits the whole substance of Mr. Breckinridge's conversation.

The two other persons who are entirely familiar with all the facts are Mr. Bryan and Mr. Breckinridge. Mr. Bryan says: "I take it for granted that the President will deal with the matter as he deems wise, if indeed any attention need be paid to it after Mr. Breckinridge's denial." In other words, Mr. Bryan denies nothing and rested on Mr. Breckinridge's denial; and Mr. Breckinridge had not denied the vital point in his reported conversation.

Mr. Garrison, who also knew the facts, stated as follows:

"I am not being interviewed on any subject. I have no statement of any kind to make."

It will thus be seen that none of the persons who knew just what happened ever denied the essential point in Mr. Breckinridge's reported conversation, and that the President himself admitted it. It is for this reason that I said at North Adams that "I would not willingly bring an unfounded charge against anyone high or low and if misled in doing so I would be quick to retract it." It will be observed that I did not retract it. I did not retract it then, and I never have retracted it. On the contrary, I believe that the statements of Dr. Bailey and of Mr. Jeffries which I brought to public attention were in substance and in essence absolutely correct. Whether the addition was in the form of a postscript, of an amendment, or an unofficial note to the German government, or a note to Mr. Gerard, is wholly unimportant. It makes no difference whether the proposition was to go by mail, or by cable, or by wireless. The point is that at the very time the *Lusitania* note was drafted, agreed upon and sent, it was seriously contemplated sending, in some form, an intimation to the German government that the note was not seriously meant and that a proposal of arbitration would be accepted.

This clearly shows that at the very moment of its despatch the note did not mean or intend serious action, which subsequent events abundantly proved to be the case.

*   *   *   *   *

Since writing the preceding account of the controversy which I had with President Wilson with reference to the *Lusitania* note, there has appeared in the press a series of articles, later published in book form, by Mr. David Lawrence, the well known Washington correspondent. The book, published by Doran & Company, is entitled "The True Story of Woodrow Wilson." Mr. Lawrence was in a position during the war to know Mr. Wilson well and to hear his views on many subjects. His study of Mr. Wilson's qualities and character is from a most friendly point of view and his book as a whole is eulogistic. Mr. Lawrence, however, has not undertaken, on certain incidents in Mr. Wilson's career, either to suppress the truth or to suggest what is false. On the contrary, he has endeavored, I think, to give a truthful account of some incidents which have not been properly represented, and as his statement in regard to my controversy with Mr. Wilson in the campaign of 1916 absolutely confirms my position and is based on some sources of information which were not at my disposal but which were accessible to Mr. Lawrence, I reprint it here as a very complete justification, if any were needed, of what I said at the time in regard to it.

In Chapter 9 of his book, beginning on page 144, Mr. Lawrence says:

"Perhaps the most dramatic episode of that entire pre-war period in America, if not indeed in Mr. Wilson's first administration, occurred when the first note was sent to Germany denouncing the destruction of the *Lusitania* in May 1915 with more than 100 American lives aboard. The Secretary of State, Mr. Bryan, had not given up hope that moral force could and would prevail. President Wilson read the note to the Cabinet. It was strong in tone stating that 'the Imperial German Government will not expect the Government of the United States to omit any word or act' in obtaining a satisfaction of its demands. The Cabinet approved, but in a conference between Mr. Bryan and the President, afterwards, there was renewed discussion of the effect of the note. Mr. Bryan thought the note might provoke war and could not bring himself to believe that he should sign a note which would cause war as he had committed himself to the pacifist position. Mr. Bryan reasoned with the President that the American people did not want war, that it was not in keeping with Christian doctrines for America to threaten war, and that almost all the world was engaged in conflict anyway and some nation should keep its head and remain aloof, especially a nation like America composed of many races and able to understand the racial complexities of the European conflict.

"Secretary Bryan had been negotiating treaties with thirty nations whereby disputes would be submitted to a commission of inquiry during the sessions of which the disputants agreed for at least nine months not to engage in hostilities. All the important nations of the world with the exception of Germany, Japan, Mexico and Turkey, had either accepted the principle of such treaties or had ratified pacts of that kind with the United States.

"The Secretary of State pleaded with the President to give Germany another chance to accept the principle of an investigation treaty. Mr. Bryan was convinced that the Germans did not want war with America and that they would look upon the suggestion as a diplomatic loophole—a way out of an embarrassing situation. For, even if they had intended to send instructions to torpedo the *Lusitania*, he could not bring himself to believe that they would repeat such an act when once the effect on American opinion was known in Berlin.

"President Wilson yielded to Mr. Bryan's persuasive arguments and permitted him to draft an instruction to Ambassador Gerard to be sent simultaneously with the *Lusitania* note advising the German Government of the willingness of the United States to submit the questions at issue to a commission of investigation on the principle of the Bryan treaties.

"This instruction to Ambassador Gerard which has been variously called a 'postscript' or a 'supplementary note' was never sent from Washington. It was under the circumstances as exciting as it was significant. It would have made a world-wide sensation at the time but the swift passage of events since those dramatic days has, to some extent, robbed the incident of its true importance in the history of the neutrality period. The supplementary instruction to Ambassador Gerard reached the State Department from the White House and was about to be put into code and cabled to Berlin. No one knew about it except the President and the Secretary of State. Robert Lansing was Counsellor of the State Department, and it was natural that he should learn of the supplementary instruction as it reached the telegraph office. He could not understand it and immediately communicated with Private Secretary Tumulty in an effort to learn its significance. Mr. Tumulty communicated with his close friend, the Secretary of War, Mr. Garrison, who said he knew nothing about the supplementary instruction as it had not been discussed in the Cabinet meeting. Mr. Lansing made it clear that the supplementary instruction was a recession, in his judgment, from the strong words contained in the note itself. Word was passed to other members of the Cabinet and soon Mr. Wilson was besieged with requests to reconsider. Meanwhile the note itself was held up at the State Department until the matter could be canvassed further. Private Secretary Tumulty made an eloquent speech to his chief pointing out the danger of such a step, that possible misunderstandings might grow from it, that Germany might get the impression the United States could not fight for her rights and that it was essential Germany be told she must respect American rights without equivocation.

"There were no direct threats of resignation made to Mr. Wilson by members of his Cabinet but the President saw fire in the eyes of his advisers. He finally ordered the supplementary instruction suppressed and the note went forth to Berlin with the strong words undiluted by any suggestion of weakness.

"Later on, in the campaign of 1916, the secret leaked out in garbled fashion and was never clearly explained. Senator Lodge of Massachusetts made a speech in Boston, reading from a letter sent him by Professor Charles H. Bailey of the Tufts Medical School, in which Mr. Bailey repeated a conversation he had had with Henry C. Breckinridge who was Assistant Secretary of War under Secretary Garrison at the time of the so-called 'postscript' episode. The Massachusetts Senator was endeavoring to prove that Mr. Wilson's strong words were tempered with hints that they were not meant seriously and that Germany was destroying American rights because she knew or believed the United States would not, under the Wilson administration, defend those rights. President Wilson issued from his headquarters at Long Branch, New Jersey, a statement in reply to an inquiring telegram from Walter Lippman, then one of the editors of the *New Republic,* Mr. Wilson said:

'In reply to your telegram, let me say that the statement made by Senator Lodge is untrue. No postscript or amendment of the *Lusitania* note was ever written or contemplated by me, except such changes that I myself inserted which strengthened and emphasized the protest. It was suggested, after the note was ready for transmission, that an intimation be conveyed to the German Government that a proposal for arbitration would be acceptable, and one member of the Cabinet spoke to me about it, but it was never discussed in Cabinet meeting and no threat of any resignation was ever made, for the very good reason that I rejected the suggestion after giving it such consideration as I thought every proposal deserved which touched so grave a matter. It was inconsistent with the purpose of the note. The public is in possession of everything that was said to the German Government.'

"The foregoing statement is one of the most remarkable pieces of adroit fencing which came from Mr. Wilson's pen. He had a theory that a diplomatic denial was absolutely essential in many cases because the end justified the means. In this case every line of Mr. Wilson's statement is true—literally taken.

"In the first place, Mr. Wilson was right in saying that there was no postscript to the *Lusitania* note itself nor was there any amendment of the note. Mr. Wilson was right when he said that he never wrote or contemplated writing any postscript or amendment. Mr. Bryan composed the supplementary instruction for Ambassador Gerard and it was not a part of the original note but a separate communication. Mr. Wilson also revealed that 'it was suggested after the note was ready for transmission that an intimation be conveyed to the German Government that a proposal for arbitration will be acceptable.' He uses the word 'intimation' to cover the instruction which was to be sent to Ambassador Gerard. It was true that only one member of the Cabinet spoke to Mr. Wilson about it—that was Mr. Bryan. When the President stated that the suggestion was 'inconsistent with the purpose of the note' he revealed the conclusion he finally reached, which was contrary to his first decision. To his mind, the postscript, amendment or supplementary instruction did not exist officially because it was never sent to Germany, and he spoke the real truth when he said 'the public is in possession of everything that was said to the German Government.'

"Senator Lodge, did, however, have in his possession during that campaign the elements of one of the biggest secrets of the administration, and if he had worded his accusation in a slightly different fashion it would have been impossible to deny the existence of a supplementary instruction. On the other hand, since the instruction was not sent to the German Government Mr. Wilson regarded the affair as of no importance externally. It was of vital importance internally however because it was the basic cause a month later of the resignation of Mr. Bryan as Secretary of State."

As I have already said in the foregoing pages, Mr. Wilson's reply when I made the charge was very ingenious. It was in reality based on a single word which I had used and which enabled him to make an apparently complete denial. His denial was possible only by making it turn on that one word. The word was "postscript," as pointed out by Mr. Lawrence in his book. That was the word given to me in the account which I had from two sources in reference to the additional communication which had been drafted and which President Wilson was thinking of sending to soften the "strict accountability" note. "Postscript" was not the correct word. I ought to have said and did say in substance at the time that it was an additional communication. Whether it was to be sent by cable, or wireless, or mail, did not matter; the fact was that it was an additional communication. Mr. Wilson avoided this by adhering to the word "postscript" and saying that there was no *postscript*, which he could deny, "postscript" being the technical word. This Mr. Lawrence has brought out very clearly in his statement which I have quoted above and it is of value, as I have said, because he got the truth from sources not open to me but which, knowing them as I do, are beyond contradiction.

Experience with Mr. Wilson's denials was not confined to me or to what I said. There were other instances. I shall cite but two additional cases and in the language of Mr. Robert Edwards Annin, who, in his admirable book "Woodrow Wilson, a Character Study," published by Dodd Mead & Company in 1924, on pages 325 *et seq.* says:

"In February [1920] Mr. Lansing was publicly dismissed in a way which caused the President's best friends to look askance, and evoked remonstrance even from members of the Cabinet. Almost simultaneously another unfortunate incident became public. It appeared that one of Mr. Lansing's last official acts had been the drafting of a note to the Allies regarding the territorial settlements on the eastern shores of the Adriatic. No sooner was Mr. Lansing dismissed than it was asserted in Paris dispatches, that the note contained a threat from President Wilson that, unless such settlements should meet his approval he would withdraw the Versailles treaty from the Senate. This was at first received with incredulity. How the President could logically withdraw the treaty after his passionate asseverations that its failure would endanger civilization and break the heart of the world was incomprehensible. A disclaimer by the White House was issued through the Associated Press on February 17th. It read:

'Emphatic denial that President Wilson had threatened to withdraw the treaty of Versailles and the American-French treaty from the Senate—was made today at the White House. Officials characterized as an "absolute falsehood" the statement of Pertinax in the "Echo de Paris," that *the postscript of Mr. Wilson's memorandum from which the note was drawn up contained such a threat.*'

"A careful reading of this statement will show that it really denied nothing about the note, *as sent*. It referred only to the President's memorandum from which Mr. Lansing drew up the note, and, impliedly, placed the blame for any threat upon the late Secretary of State.

"But such a position was promptly recognized as untenable since the 'erroneous White House announcement' was, within an hour, recalled and retracted; and virtual admission made that the Paris despatches had told the truth.

"This was confirmed a day or two later by the publication of the offending 'postscript' which stated that, in the given contingency, 'the President would take into serious consideration the withdrawal of the United States from the treaty of Versailles and from the treaty between the United States and France.'

"The President's friends had a hard time with this whole matter. The Associated Press somewhat blandly stated that the discredited denial 'obviously did not come from the President himself' but refrained from stating why this was 'obvious.' Nor is that clear even yet. What is very obvious is the improbability that such a statement would have been issued from the White House without Presidential authority; and that the President would have overlooked such a blazing indiscretion in a subordinate. Finally the apparent explicity and actual ambiguity of the statement are strongly suggestive of other incidents in Mr. Wilson's career.

"This unfortunate matter was no doubt a fresh blow to Mr. Wilson's influence and prestige. To explain his petulant threat to wreck a treaty upon which he had passionately asserted hung the future of civilization, was more than difficult—it was impossible."

Senator Seldon P. Spencer, of Missouri, also had some experience with Mr. Wilson of a similar kind, although in his case as in mine the denial was not retracted as it had been in the instance just given above. Again I shall quote from Mr. Annin who, on pages 351 *et seq.* of his "Woodrow Wilson," says:

"Few of our Presidents have more often been attacked in the matter of veracity than President Wilson. In so far as his lapses occurred in the course of political business, the public—present and future—will probably judge them as lightly as those of his predecessors and successors. The political 'passing the lie'—which is as much a part of the game as 'pointing with pride' or 'viewing with alarm'—will probably not be of much more interest.

"Having relaxed our morals to this point we may as well go a step further. Even as to such incidents as would not seem to fall strictly within the political, as distinct from the personal, category, the degree, or even the fact of condemnation may be determined largely by the point of view. In other words the matter of conscious or unconscious motive may be allowed for.

"The conviction that motive or purpose must determine the moral quality of action may thus glide easily into the theory that the end justifies the means. Hence the honest opportunist may wake up to find himself a practical casuist wielding the weapons of the sophist. If then there exist the power of self-deception almost any course of action may seem justifiable if it but contribute to the desired result.

"Senator S. P. Spencer (Mo.) campaigning for his own reelection had asserted (in attacking Article X of the covenant) that at the eighth plenary session of the Peace Conference, President Wilson had declared that the peace of the world depended upon armed strength; and led the delegates present,—and particularly the Roumanian delegates—'to believe that if at any time in the future their territorial boundary lines as established by the treaty of peace should become endangered, an American Army and American Navy would be sent to preserve the integrity of their territory.' *

"This provoked a telegram from the President's Secretary, Mr. Tumulty, which said:

'The excerpt from the speech of Senator Spencer has been called directly to the President's attention, and he authorized me to say that Senator Spencer's statement is absolutely and unqualifiedly false.'

"Upon Mr. Spencer's questioning Mr. Tumulty's authority to speak for the President in this matter, the latter sent Spencer this dispatch:

'I have just been shown your statement that my secretary's denial of the previous statement by you that I had promised military aid to Roumanians and Serbs, was issued by him without my knowledge and sanction; and that you did not believe that I had made any such denial or that the matter had ever been called to my

* This whole matter is set forth in Senator Spencer's speech in the Senate of May 9, 1921.

attention by Mr. Tumulty, and that I requested him to issue the denial to which you refer. I reiterate the denial. The statement you made was false.'

"Upon Mr. Spencer's appeal for the minutes of the eighth plenary session, no direct reply was made to him; but a statement was issued from the White House on Oct. 7th, 1920, stating,

'The President has no stenographic report of the eighth plenary session, at which the promise is alleged to have been made; and—so far as the President knows —*there is no such record in the country.*'

"In March, 1921, the Harding administration succeeded, and on April 15th, upon Senator Spencer's request, Secretary Hughes handed him the desired record. It is of interest to note that the record essentially confirmed Senator Spencer's assertions.

"More surprising, and disconcerting to Mr. Wilson's friends, was Secretary Hughes' statement (in a letter which accompanied the document) that of 'Protocol No. 8' (the record in question) five hundred copies had been received by the State Department in July, 1919; and three hundred more in February, 1920.

"The pertinent extract from protocol No. 8 was this:

'*The President of the United States speaking in English:*
'. . . and back of that lies this fundamentally important fact that, when the recisions are made the Allied and Associated powers guarantee to maintain them. . . . And yet there underlies all of these transactions the expectation on the part—for example—of Roumania, and of Czechoslovakia and of Serbia that, if any covenants of this settlement are not observed, the United States will send her armies and her navies to see that they are observed.'

"When President Wilson denied not only the fact as to what he himself had said, but that any copies of the record were to his knowledge, in the country, it is immaterial whether, in this last respect, he told the truth or not. The suppression of the fact that he apparently had made no attempt to inform himself would fix the quality of the statement. The motive was to deceive. Mr. Wilson's critics quite naturally made much of the incident, and his admirers were silent and troubled."

As I have already said, my intention in presenting all the facts in the controversy which I had with the President during the campaign of 1916 was in preparation for an attack which I expected on the subject in the Senate. That attack, as I have also said, never came; but there was one rather amusing incident which I had always supposed was due to the argument which I made in regard to the President's attitude about the sinking of the *Lusitania*. It so happened that on January 13, 1917, the One Hundredth Anniversary of the Church of St. John in Washington was celebrated. Some time before, the rector of the Church, Dr. Roland Cotton Smith, an old friend of mine, asked me if I would make an address on the occasion of this celebration,—something I was very glad to do for him; and also the subject appealed to me for there were many memories connected with the old church. He told me that the President was to be there and make a brief address and also Secretary Lansing, who was one of his parishioners. Shortly before the date fixed for the commemoration services, Dr. Smith came to see me and said that the President had informed him that if I was to speak he could not speak or be present. I said at once to Dr. Smith that, of course, I would withdraw, that nothing would be more unpleasant to me than to think that I had interfered in any way with the ceremonies connected with the commemoration. Dr. Smith declined to permit me to do this and the result was that the President did not come, nor did Mr. Lansing speak, although he was present, nor did Mr. Lane, who also attended that Church. The celebration passed off very well, but I could not but be amused at the President's attitude. He seemed to be wholly unconscious of the fact that men in public life, in high office, charged with the conduct of public business, cannot allow mere personal feeling to interfere with the public business, and that it was quite possible for men occupying such positions, who were not personally on good terms, to transact the public business without involving any personal question. So far as I was concerned, I had no personal feeling whatever. The President and I had had a political controversy during a campaign and I had not gone beyond the limits of fair debate, nor said anything about him personally with which he could find fault, and therefore I had no objection to meeting him at any time in any way. But President Wilson was very sensitive to criticism from anyone, especially from members of his own party who ventured to disagree with him, and in a less degree with any expression of disapprobation from members of the party opposed to him. I had had a slight experience of this once before in speaking on May 27, 1916, at a meeting of the friends of the League to Enforce Peace called here by a committee headed by ex-President Taft and President Lowell of Harvard. They asked me to speak and I very gladly consented to do so, and then I said that I had heard that the President was to be there and was to speak last. I said I had occasion to speak many times with different Presidents and be present when they spoke, and that the President always at any gathering spoke first. The right of way was his and it was only proper that it should be so. As I recall, President Lowell, with whom I talked about it, agreed with me, but he came to me afterwards and said that the President declined to speak first, insisting that he should speak last and that I should speak before he did. Whether he thought that if I spoke last I might take occasion to criticise him, which of course I never should have done under any circumstances—it would have been in the

worst possible taste—I cannot say; but I could at the
time think of no other reason than that he feared something of that sort being done. Although it never would
have been done by anybody speaking after the President
under like conditions, he evidently had an uneasy feeling that something of the kind might happen. It occurred to me afterwards that the fact probably was
that Mr. Wilson did not fancy face-to-face debate with
anybody; that it was not me especially to whom he objected, but he did not like to be followed by any other
speaker. His attitude was the schoolmaster's attitude;
that is, the attitude of some schoolmasters. He addressed
his class and there could be no reply, no criticism on what
he said from the advantageous position of teacher and in-
structor. I have no desire to do him the slightest injustice, but these two incidents made me think that he had
no liking for what is called commonly in political cam-
paigns a "Joint Debate." But be that as it may, the
little incident of his refusal to speak at St. John's Church
passed by like so many other things and was forgotten,
except perhaps by those few in charge of the ceremonies
and familiar with the details.

CHAPTER V

QUESTIONS OF NEUTRALITY

WHEN Congress came together in December, 1915, we were met at once by the questions growing out of our neutrality. Great Britain quite rightly was enforcing her blockade against the German ports, and this blockade was one of the two or three absolutely vital elements of success in the struggle against Germany. Very naturally, however, the arrest or seizure of neutral ships by English cruisers raised many legal questions and caused much feeling among those whose ships were stopped and especially among those whose trade was illicit. There was a movement on foot to attack Great Britain in the Senate on the ground of violations of international law,—an enterprise which was made difficult by the fact that Great Britain was in the main following very closely the course pursued by the Government of the United States during the Civil War and the decisions made by our Supreme Court in regard to cases arising out of the efforts of English blockade runners to reach the Southern States with supplies and then bring out cotton. The practical danger at the moment was that the Administration might be persuaded to put an embargo on American vessels which were carrying munitions of war and arms in large amounts to the Allies and especially to Great Britain. Supplies of this character from the United States were vital to the Allies, and nothing would have given their cause a harder blow than to have the United States stop these exports of arms and munitions. In that connection, I made one or two memoranda of conversations which I had with Mr. Lansing, the Secretary of State, and Mr. Wilson, which show the course of events here at that time and also my own attitude in regard to the policy of the embargo. My first conversation of which I made any note occurred on the 12th of January, 1916, and is as follows:

"January 12, 1916.

"On reaching home found urgent request from Lansing to see me. Telephoned I would come over to his house. Found him there. He talked about the *Persia;* difficulty of getting evidence and especially as to nationality of submarine. I agreed that he could not go on without some evidence and suggested that the submarine would probably turn out to be Bulgarian!

"Then talked to him about unwisdom and danger of having committee investigation of pending negotiations.

"Also urged that Administration get their friends to line up against embargo. He said they would.

"He then came back to the *Persia.* Asked what they should do if submarine proved to be either German or Austrian. I said, 'break off relations.' That troubled him, but it was obvious that this was the point of seeing me, to find out if I would sustain them in severance of relations."

"January 14, 1916.

"Further talk with Lansing as to embargo and investigation by Foreign Relations Committee of pending negotiation as demanded in Hoke Smith's resolution, to which I offered amendments. Smith's object of course to make trouble with England. Urged Lansing again to have President speak to his people about embargo."

By way of explanation, I ought to say that the case of the *Persia* was that of a steamship which had been blown up in the Mediterranean (the lives of American citizens and American property being involved) and in

which an American Consul lost his life. I do not mean
to dwell on the case of the *Persia*, but the conversation that I had with Mr. Lansing indicates the attitude
of the Administration at that moment. The movement
in the Senate against Great Britain and the attack upon
her conduct of the blockade were to be led and managed
by my friend, Senator Hoke Smith of Georgia, who I
was told had been preparing very elaborately during the
summer for this work. As a basis for his discussion, he
had introduced the following resolution:

"Whereas the executive department, through the Secretary of State, has protested the legality of the orders
of Great Britain virtually blockading the neutral
ports of northern Europe; and
"Whereas the responsibility for the preservation of the
commercial rights of citizens of the United States
rests upon the Congress as well as upon the executive
department, THEREFORE be it
"RESOLVED: That the Committee on Foreign Relations
be requested to investigate the subject and to suggest to the Senate the action, if any, they may deem
advisable."

He then, on December 10, 1915, made an elaborate
speech in regard to it, which I think was to be the fore-
runner of a still further and even more extended discussion. I made a brief reply, as follows:

"Mr. President, I have no intention at this moment of
discussing any of the many points raised by the Senator
from Georgia in his very elaborate and able argument,
but I desire to offer an amendment to his resolution extending the scope of the inquiry and investigation if it
is to be ordered by the Senate and made by the Committee on Foreign Relations.

"I think, Mr. President, that neutral rights possessed
by us should be insisted upon and investigated in every
place where it can be proved that they have been violated,

but I think also that we are equally bound to fulfill our neutral duties rigidly and strictly, although I have observed in some quarters that our sense of our rights is a little more vivid than our sense of our duty.

"I wish to extend the scope of the resolution by my amendment, because if we are to take up this question of the violation of our rights, I want to put it not on the lowest ground alone, but on the highest ground as well. I think it is of great importance that we should vindicate our rights as a neutral in trade if those rights have been violated, but I think it is far more important that we should extend protection and assure security to American citizens wherever they rightfully are, for I do not believe that any government can long retain the respect of its own people if it does not give them the protection to which they are entitled.

"I think Americans should be protected in their lives and in their liberty everywhere. I do not think they ought to be murdered in detail and obscurely in Mexico or openly and wholesale on the high seas.

"Although I am as anxious as anyone can be to care for our rights in trade if they are violated, to me American lives are more important than American dollars. The body of an innocent child floating dead on the water, the victim of the destruction of an unarmed vessel, is to me a more poignant and a more tragic spectacle than an unsold bale of cotton.

"If this investigation is to go on, and especially if Congress is to take action, I want it to take in all the violations of our rights that may have occurred. The most important is the violation which has affected American lives or the security of an American citizen—man, woman or child—and the next most important are those pointed out by the President of the United States in his message the other day, when he referred to the destruction of property accompanied by destruction of life, in the United States, and stated that conspiracies in alien interests are going on within our own borders.

"I think if we are to investigate and inquire with a view to action such deeds as these should not be omitted. I am not willing to get into a passion over an infringement of our trade and then allow American citizens to lose their lives and pass it by in frigid silence.

"I do not wish to see this country when it looks into the book of time close the pages on which are written the outrages that have been committed against American citizens in Mexico and on the high seas and be blind to what is written there and fix its whole attention on the pages where is reckoned up the profit and loss account in dollars. I think the United States stands for something higher in the world than mere trade and mere dollars. I do not want to see our citizens wronged in their property, but I think we should also stand, and above all, for morality and humanity in the dealings of nations with each other.

"These are the reasons, Mr. President, why I desire to have the scope of this inquiry enlarged. I shall be very glad if the Senator will allow the resolution to go over so that my amendment may be printed and that the Senate before it votes may have an opportunity to read it.

"MR. SMITH of Georgia. Mr. President——

"The PRESIDENT pro tempore. The Secretary will state the amendment.

"MR. LODGE. I should like to have it read so that the Senate may see it in print.

"The SECRETARY. It is proposed to add to the resolution:

RESOLVED FURTHER, That the Committee on Foreign Relations be also requested to investigate and report upon the law and the facts involved in the attacks upon or the destruction by belligerents of the following vessels:

The GULFLIGHT, FALABA, LUSITANIA, ARABIC, ANCONA, HES-
PERIAN, and PETROLITE.   And also to investigate and
report upon the law and the facts involved in the incidents referred to by the President of the United States in
his annual message, when he said, referring to certain
persons: 'They have formed plots to destroy property;
they have entered into conspiracies against the neutrality
of the Government; they have sought to pry into every
confidential transaction of the Government in order to
serve interests alien to our own.' "

What I said before offering the amendments to the
Smith resolution and have just quoted, although very
brief, for I did not undertake to argue the question at
any length, seemed to be well received throughout the
country. At all events, the discussion on the violations
of neutrality by the British began to fade out after December 10, 1915. Soon after that time, I had an interview with the President of which I made a memorandum,
and which I think is worth quoting in full:

"January 20, 1916.
"Took to the White House an invitation to the President to speak in Boston before Real Estate Exchange.
Tumulty and Forster asked me to give it to President
personally, which I did. As I turned to go, he said,
greatly to my surprise, that he wished to thank me for
having advised with Mr. Lansing. I said I was very glad
if I could be of service on any international question. I
then talked with him about embargo and investigation
by committees of Congress on pending negotiations in
same vein as I had with Lansing. He said he fully agreed
with me on both points and that 'there must be no embargo in any form.' I hope he will stand to this. So
far as the Allies are concerned this is the one practical
and vital point."

Just at this time there arose another question involving neutral rights which in its gravity overshadowed all

others. This was the question of armed merchantmen.
In the entire range of international law there is hardly a
subject which has been during centuries so fully discussed diplomatically and in the courts, both in careful
opinions and in well weighed decisions, as this; nor is
there one in which the principles have been more completely settled or more widely agreed to than the international rules as to the status of armed merchantmen of
neutral states or of belligerents in time of war. Broadly
speaking, it has been universally agreed both in law
and practise that a belligerent or a neutral merchantman
has the right to go armed without losing its neutral character in the one case or its noncombatant character in
the other, provided only that the armament is purely defensive and used only for defense; the character and use
of the armament being of course questions of fact in
each case. It was equally well settled that neutral passengers and neutral goods could be carried on such armed
merchantmen and retain their neutral character. Such
had been the policy of the United States, and its principles had been upheld in a series of decisions by our
Supreme Court in which the leading cases had behind
them the great authority of John Marshall. The retention of the neutral character of armed merchantmen
carried with it all the privileges and protection of neutral
ships in time of war, such as warning from any enemy
vessel and security for the lives of the crews and passengers upon a neutral or belligerent merchantman before attack or in case of destruction by an enemy vessel
of war whether public or letter-of-marque. At the beginning of the war with Germany the United States
sent a circular letter dated September 19, 1914, to the
representatives of foreign powers, signed by Mr. Lansing,
then Acting Secretary of State, setting forth the position of the United States as to armed merchantmen of
belligerent nationality—a position in accordance with the

rules and principles of international law, long established, and accepted as I have briefly stated them. The attitude of the government of the United States in this note was absolutely correct. On the 7th of November, 1914, Mr. Lansing, in a note to Mr. Gerard, our Ambassador in Berlin, dissented from the German view and restated the position taken by the United States in the note of September 19th of the same year.

In the President's note of May 13th, 1915, signed by Mr. Bryan, just after the sinking of the *Lusitania,* occurs this passage:

"American citizens act within their indisputable rights in taking their ships and in traveling wherever their legitimate business calls them upon the high seas and exercise those rights in what should be the well-justified confidence that their lives will not be endangered by acts done in clear violation of universally acknowledged international obligations, and certainly in the confidence that their own Government will sustain them in the exercise of their rights."

Thus far the position was not only correct but perfectly sound and in full accord with the established rules and principles of the law of nations. It had, however, become only too clear that an adhesion to these rules and principles interfered very seriously with the operation of submarines as commerce destroyers, by the requirements for warning to the merchantman and for the removal, protection and security of the crews and passengers on such merchantman when made the subject of submarine attacks without warning and with wholesale destruction of all on board.

It was, therefore, with a shock of amazement and even alarm that the people of the United States in January, 1916, read in the newspapers a note from Mr. Lansing to our Ambassadors and Ministers proposing, to put it briefly, that for the benefit of submarine warfare practically all the privileges and protection given by International Law to belligerent merchantmen should be swept away. There was no doubt, despite its somewhat irregular mode of appearance, as to the authenticity of the note. As a matter of course none of the allied powers would have accepted it, but it was a change in the unbroken custom and policy of the United States which was in the last degree discreditable. I said in the Senate, speaking of this note:

"It is a hesitating and faltering argument in behalf of clearing away all the laws which have been established by the general assent of civilized nations and by the dictates of humanity in favor of the protection of the lives of neutrals who may have taken passage on a belligerent merchantman."

Moreover, this note not only involved our abandonment of all the principles of international law, but was also a gross violation of our neutrality and made us an efficient ally of Germany in a very important point. It seems to be connected naturally with the conversations, or negotiations, or understandings, which were attempted with Germany the following Autumn and which I shall discuss at another point.

The question of armed merchantmen did not, however, end here.

CHAPTER VI

THE COMING OF WORLD WAR POLICIES

Meantime in the general field of international relations the paltering with the *Lusitania* case went on. Other ships were torpedoed. More fruitless notes were exchanged. In March, 1916, came the destruction of the *Sussex*. Americans were on board and three were injured. More notes. In one *Sussex* note, Germany was notified "that unless the Imperial Government declares and effects abandonment of the present method of submarine warfare against passenger and freight carrying vessels the Government of the United States can have no choice but to sever diplomatic relations with the German Empire altogether." Brave words. More notes. More conversations. The resumption of submarine warfare in an extreme form was threatened. Nothing effective was done. The Presidential campaign was on and the noble cry of "He kept us out of war" was echoing through the country. Just as our Ambassador to Berlin arrived in his native land, German submarines sank six vessels in the neighborhood of Nantucket, which, of course, was not allowed to interfere with the inspiring acclaim that "He kept us out of war." Soon after his arrival, Mr. Gerard, who had come to America principally through the urging of Von Jagow, saw Mr. Wilson at Shadow Lawn near Long Branch. After the election, Mr. Gerard saw Mr. Wilson on several occasions. Exactly what was said in those conferences is not known and probably never will be, but Mr. Gerard's statement that before he left "he was impressed with the idea that Mr. Wilson desired above all things both to keep and to make peace" remains and is sufficient. Despite the obstacles Mr. Gerard says, "Nevertheless, I think that the inclination of the President was to go very far towards the forcing of peace." Fortified by his reelection on the great declaration that "He kept us out of war," which gave keen pleasure to the Germans and helped still further to mislead them, it is evident that informal negotiations and conversations were carried on as the year 1916 was drawing to its close and that Mr. Wilson had good reason to believe that the opportunity was at hand when he, and he alone, could come forth and figure as the maker of peace, a rôle which he desired and for which he was well fitted by his indifference as to the terms of the peace, provided he made it. He had never felt, judging by what he had said in the past, that the issues of the war concerned the United States, which he had begun to confuse with his own personality. In December, the Chancellor, Bethmann-Hollweg, announced to the Reichstag that "In a deep moral and religious sense of duty towards this nation and beyond it to humanity, the Emperor now considers that the moment has come for official action towards peace." This, of course, appealed strongly to the President, especially by its allusion to the "deep moral and religious sense" which was then affecting the Kaiser, and he sent to Mr. Gerard and our other representatives with the Central Powers a "peace note," dated December 18, 1916. Similar notes were sent to the Allied Powers and to the neutral countries. The note was coolly received by the Allies, and the British argumentative answer was far from favorable, except as to the generalities about the loveliness of peace, which Mr. Wilson stated so well. The Central Powers were more cordial, for the whole peace movement originated with them as they were anxious to win and eager to bring the war to an end at a time when they could get off with valuable spoils already temporarily in their hands. The President intimated, with some modestly deprecatory phrases, that he was ready to play the part of mediator and peace-maker.

When Mr. Gerard returned to Berlin, everything on the surface appeared to be most cheerful, and at a dinner to Mr. Gerard given by the American Association of Commerce and Trade friendly words were freely exchanged. The dinner was on January 6th, 1917, and on January 22d the President, addressing the Senate, referred to his notes of December 18th and to the replies of the Entente Powers. In that speech the President set forth his plan for a "League for Peace" in general outline. Peace, once made, was to be preserved by an organized "major force" which was to crush any recalcitrant who would not accept the peace. Mr. Wilson also declared for an autonomous Poland, and outlined his plan for the "freedom of the seas," which were always free in time of peace, and the plan applied therefore to making the seas free equally in time of war. An "autonomous Poland" did not warm the German heart, and the President's plan for freedom of the seas did not excite fervent gratitude in England, which at the moment was preserving her own life by her navy and a blockade. It was in this speech that Mr. Wilson declared in favor of a "Peace without victory," which appealed to no one and was of the same unfortunate quality as its predecessor, "Too Proud to Fight," which still glares out rather luridly, even in the cold, gray light of history. But Mr. Wilson's proposition and his unhappy phrase were not appreciated at the time, for they all and much else, went down to temporary oblivion in the crash which was at hand. Some of the statements of the President were not liked in Germany, but nevertheless his plan for making peace, at a moment when no peace of any value could be made, seemed to be prospering, and Mr. Gerard had felt warranted in telling the German Government not only of the President's earnest desire for peace but "that the President was ready to go very far in the way of coercing any nation which refused a reasonable peace." This statement, it is worth repeating, was made to the German Government. The skies looked for the moment very fair for the President's project, but dark clouds were already beginning to gather on the horizon. Through our Naval attaché came reports not to be doubted that ruthless submarine warfare was being resumed. It had been resumed in fact long before the final public step was taken. The extreme party, the followers of Tirpitz, had gained the upper hand over the Chancellor, and on the 31st of January the resumption of unrestricted submarine warfare and the creation of the war zones about Great Britain and Belgium were formally announced.

So far as Germany was concerned, it was a colossal mistake. With all her military skill and high administrative efficiency, Germany had blundered steadily and persistently in regard to other nations. She had blundered grossly as to Belgium and as to England in holding to the belief that neither would fight. The mental heaviness of Germany showed itself in her utter inability to form any reasonable opinion as to other people and other nations. Her stupidity in this direction was almost beyond belief. In regard to the United States, Germany had a settled conviction that the American people neither could nor would fight. She believed that half a million Americans of German descent would rise in arms if war with Germany was attempted; that the German-Americans would never permit us to enter the war; that we could not pass a conscription law if we did enter the war or transport troops to Europe. Such dull witted ignorance seems hard even to imagine, but the facts and the evidence are beyond contradiction. It may be said that in the case of the United States, at the time of Mr. Wilson's peace movement in 1916, Germany had some reason for believing her opinion about then making peace to be correct. The Germans had seen the efforts of our Government to break the British blockade; they had watched the correspondence growing out of the destruction of the *Lusitania* and repeated invasions and complete disregard of our rights and the apparent contentment of our Government with the awkward devices and clumsy notes of the German Government to secure evasion and delay. They must have read Mr. Lansing's remarkable revision of international law in regard to armed merchantmen as set forth in his note of January 10th, 1916. Finally, as Mr. Gerard says, they interpreted very naturally Mr. Wilson's victory at the polls on the declaration that he "kept us out of war" as a mandate from the American people to avoid war at all hazards. Yet all these things were but palliations, hardly even excuses, for their really marvelous stupidity as to the American people. Moreover, they entirely overlooked one vital element in the problem of 1916-1917, and that was Mr. Wilson himself. They evidently failed to consider the fact that Mr. Wilson was himself committed to the peace movement of that period. It was, indeed, his movement. Mr. Wilson may have been touched by the Kaiser's solemn reference to "moral and religious duty," but he could not have been really misled by the pompous sham of the Kaiser's declaration of policy. He must have had grounds more relative than this for his belief that Germany was ready to join in his attempt to make peace at that precise moment. Mr. Wilson was an able man and an astute one as well. In the conversations and secret, if informal, negotiations of that autumn and winter he must have received assurances and promises from the German Government which convinced him that the German Government would stand by him in his plans for peace. Now, in an instant, he discovered on January 31st that he had been played with and deceived. His projects, which were his own, and in the success of which he would have played a leading and shining rôle, were dashed to pieces, and he was made to appear in a somewhat ridiculous light. He was naturally very angry. The Germans had blundered again by not knowing their man or understanding him. They had crossed Mr. Wilson's path and upset his plans. What the sinking of the *Lusitania* and the invasion of American rights at sea could not do, they did by their ultimatum of January 31st. On February 3d, Count Bernstorff was dismissed and Mr. Gerard recalled, and the breaking off of diplomatic relations with Germany was announced to the Congress. The German Government put a finishing and characteristic touch to this performance by offering Mr. Gerard a treaty to sign and holding him a semi-prisoner—a wanton insult. The stupidity of the German Government in all this affair is such that ordinary language fails to describe it. We can only repeat what Dr. Johnson said of Thomas Sheridan, "Sherry is dull, naturally dull; but it must have taken him a great deal of pains to become what we now see him. Such an excess of Stupidity, Sir, is not in nature."

At last, after long delay, on April 2d, 1917, the President spoke and spoke most effectively and finely, and on the 6th of April we declared war. It is not necessary for me to follow the course or the details of that vast struggle. At the very outset, before the declaration of war, I did my utmost, both in committee and on the floor of the Senate, to carry through the resolution desired by the Administration for the arming of merchantmen, and this course I followed throughout the war in common with my party associates. In my speech supporting the declaration of war I was the first to urge the sending of American troops—no matter how few—to France. I did this not only because I fervently believed that it would be of immense moral value but because I feared that Mr. Wilson who had depicted a "peace without victory" might desire to have a war without fighting. I need not have been troubled on this point. Once the war was declared, Mr. Wilson was swept along by the irresistible tide of events and by the uncontrollable power of public opinion, for the American people did not go to war to lose but to win.

Soon after we went to war I was called several times to the White House, and I think it well to insert here some memoranda which I made in my diary in regard to certain very interesting consultations with the President during that spring and summer:

"May 18, 1917.

"With Gallinger and Knox at White House. President has at last discovered that without the Republicans he would not and could not get his legislation. Two days ago he gathered a number of members of both Houses and both parties, of whom I was one, to talk over the shipping legislation and listen to Denman, one of the President's pet obscurities suddenly drawn to light, who discoursed to us. Denman's ignorance of his subject almost equals his vanity, which perhaps is too severe a comparison for the former. Tonight the President had us three Republicans alone for the same general purpose of appearing to consult us. We were there nearly two hours. He was most polite and talked well, as he always does so far as expression goes. We discussed revenue, food control and censorship chiefly. The two latter were his objects, but we chatted cheerfully and of course made no promises. We told him perfectly pleasantly some truths which he ought to have heard from those who surround him, but with few exceptions they are too small or too subservient and are afraid to tell him the truth or what they really think. They are wise in their generation, for the President said of some one not long ago; 'I do not like Mr So-and-so. He disagrees with me.'

"I watched and studied his face tonight as I have often done before—a curious mixture of acuteness, intelligence and extreme underlying timidity—a shifty, furtive, sinister expression can always be detected by a good observer.

"I wonder if the future historian will find him out? He has only to read and compare the President's messages and papers and follow his mistaken policy in order to discover him.

"His war message, to which he was driven by events, was a fine one, but he has not changed his spots. I wonder if some historian of the future will see the aforesaid spots. They are all there. The man is just what he has been all along, thinking of the country only in terms of Wilson, never of the country's interest alone."

"August 17, 1917. Friday.

"This afternoon at the White House. Martin, Swanson, J. S. Williams, Pomerene, Lodge, Brandegee, Knox. Meeting arranged with the President by Martin. 'All Americans,' as J. S. W. remarked. President came in, greeted us very pleasantly and after a few words upon indifferent matters said, 'You have come to talk about these peace plans. I have only received the official text of the Pope's letter this afternoon.' Evidently it was on his mind and he was adrift as he was the evening I saw him after Carrizal. He went on: 'The great difficulty is that there is no one with whom to negotiate. You cannot negotiate with a Government like that of Germany, which frankly says that no treaty, no agreement, is binding and which so acts. This is what we ought to say, and yet if we do, the reply is that we are undertaking to say what the Government of the Germans shall be, and one of the principles for which we are fighting is that every people has the right to settle its own form of government. There again the Pope does not touch the objects for which we are fighting.' Williams said that 'the Bishop of Rome had no more concern or power in the business than the Archbishop of Canterbury; that he was not a Government; that for a thousand years he had been closely allied with the House of Hapsburg; that this note came from Vienna and was devised by Berlin.' The President said that was all true, and then, with a smile, 'but I could hardly address him as the Bishop of Rome.' Williams replied that he did not intend that, but that with every diplomatic politeness he should be told that it was none of his business. Knox said the answer should be, 'that there could be no peace, no real peace, until we and our Allies were able to dictate it.' Everybody agreed to the proposition, but the President was of opinion that this could not be said at this time. Then Knox said, 'Mr. President, what you said at the beginning is the proper answer. Tell the Pope with the utmost politeness that his note does not approach in the most remote way any of the objects for which the United States went to war —that it cannot be discussed by us, and stop there.' This seemed to strike the President very favorably—in fact he seemed greatly relieved, and I am curious to see if he follows that sound and simple line in his reply.

"Martin, I think it was, said that he supposed the President would not determine on his answer without consulting with our Allies and the President said, 'Certainly not.' Knox then asked a most vital question: 'Have we any agreement or understanding with our Allies?' The President answered, 'None whatever. I told Mr. Balfour to whom alone I spoke about it that I thought it best and wisest that there should be no understandings, formal or informal; but of course he knew that we should never go back on them, and that binds us in honor.' In other words there were no 'understand-

ings,' except one 'that binds us in honor,' of the most
sweeping kind. We were all extremely glad to hear this,
but it was an odd way of putting it.

"Every one present had something to say. All talked
well. I waited as it happened until all had spoken and
then I said, 'Mr. President, we have a practical question
before us in the Senate. We have resolutions of German
origin, all proceeding on the same line, all proposing
negotiations on the basis of the *status quo ante bellum.*
If we should accept a peace leaving everything as it was
in July, 1914, you who advised war and everyone of us
who voted for the declaration of war would be guilty of
the blackest of crimes. We could never be justified.'
As I said this the President nodded approvingly at each
sentence and said, 'yes, yes.' I continued, 'In my
opinion we ought to say that this is no time to consider
or discuss peace, and never any peace that rests on the
status quo ante bellum. In fact you might say that to
the Pope too in proper form, and then in the Senate
we ought to lay all the peace resolutions on the table
and kill them.' The President said, 'I fully agree. I
hope you will care for the resolutions in the Senate in
exactly that way.' I brought the same point around again
later and he made the same reply. This was the object
I had in view. I wanted him to declare in the presence
of others that he meant to go through with the war to a
complete victory. He so declared and such I believe is
his intention now. Whether he will steadily adhere to it
no man can tell; but he is at least committed. He is a
man of words not of action, but in this interview he
gave way to phrases less than I ever saw on the other
occasions when I have met him. He went off once, something about 'heart-breaking sorrow,' but otherwise
talked simply and well. He had been adrift and troubled
about the Pope's note. I think in that we helped him

with our various suggestions and stiffened him.* He appeared better than at the other times when I have seen him."

"August 23, 1917.

"Dined at the White House to meet Japanese Commission. I was amused by the invitation, reflecting how short a time ago the President refused to appear at the St. John's Church Centennial because I was to speak. My sin was that I had told the truth about the *Lusitania* note. The dinner was the usual dull affair, although I had an interesting but very limited conversation with Gen. Sugano, next to whom I sat at dinner. I say the conversation was limited because his English was hardly superior to my Japanese, and he spoke no French."

Then came the days, terrible days, when the war moved on and the Army and Navy and the whole American people went to work to do their part in winning the war. They had to struggle against the awful obstacles created by our lack of preparation, by the utter refusal of the Wilson Administration, benumbed by the President's desire to make peace, to make ready for the inevitable conflict drawing ever nearer and looming more darkly as the months sped by. By the really terrible energy of the American people, by the toil of the Army and Navy, by sacrifices of money and of men made necessary by unpreparedness, we managed in some way to do in one year the work of ten. When the New Year of 1918 arrived our ships and our men were ready, our soldiers had begun to appear in the camps and trenches of France and the stream of men and supplies and ships was running with ever increasing volume—a stream which in the next eight months would have assumed the dimensions of a torrent—a swelling tide going on faster and faster to flood.

* The reply to the Pope sent immediately after this consultation was much better in tone than his previous notes.

At the very opening of the fateful year of 1918, Mr. Wilson addressed the Congress on January 8th. The address, to which I have already alluded, is short, and I print it here in full because it is in so many ways so significant and reveals so completely Mr. Wilson's steady adherence to his policy of bringing about a peace which should be due to him and in which he should play the part of the mediator and maker of world peace by him arranged:

"Gentlemen of the Congress:

"Once more, as repeatedly before, the spokesmen of the Central Empires have indicated their desire to discuss the objects of the war and the possible bases of a general peace. Parleys have been in progress at Brest-Litovsk between Russian representatives and representatives of the Central Powers to which the attention of all the belligerents has been invited for the purpose of ascertaining whether it may be possible to extend these parleys into a general conference with regard to terms of peace and settlement. The Russian representatives presented not only a perfectly definite statement of the principles upon which they would be willing to conclude peace but also an equally definite programme of the concrete application of these principles. The representatives of the Central Powers, on their part, presented an outline of settlement which, if much less definite, seemed susceptible of liberal interpretation until their specific programme of practical terms was added. That programme proposed no concessions at all either to the sovreignty of Russia or to the preferences of the populations with whose fortunes it dealt, but meant, in a word, that the Central Empires were to keep every foot of territory their armed forces had occupied,—every province, every city, every point of vantage,—as a permanent addition to their territories and their power. It is a reasonable conjecture that the general principles of settlement which they at first suggested originated with the more liberal statesmen of Germany and Austria, the men who have begun to feel the force of their own peoples' thought and purpose, while the concrete terms of actual settlement came from the military leaders who have no thought but to keep what they have got. The negotiations have been broken off. The Russian representatives were sincere and in earnest. They cannot entertain such proposals of conquest and domination.

"The whole incident is full of significance. It is also full of perplexity. With whom are the Russian representatives dealing? For whom are the representatives of the Central Empires speaking? Are they speaking for the majorities of their respective parliaments or for the minority parties, that military and imperialistic minority which has so far dominated their whole policy and controlled the affairs of Turkey and of the Balkan states which have felt obliged to become their associates in this war? The Russian representatives have insisted, very justly, very wisely, and in the true spirit of modern democracy, that the conferences they have been holding with the Teutonic and Turkish statesmen should be held within open, not closed doors, and all the world has been audience, as was desired. To whom have we been listening, then? To those who speak the spirit and intention of the Resolutions of the German Reichstag of the ninth of July last, the spirit and intention of the liberal leaders and parties of Germany, or to those who resist and defy that spirit and intention and insist upon conquest and subjugation? Or are we listening, in fact, to both, unreconciled and in open and hopeless contradiction? These are very serious and pregnant questions. Upon the answer to them depends the peace of the world.

"But, whatever the results of the parleys at Brest-Litovsk, whatever the confusions of counsel and of purpose in the utterances of the spokesmen of the Central Empire, they have again attempted to acquaint the world with their objects in the war and have again challenged their adversaries to say what their objects are and what sort of settlement they would deem just and satisfactory. There is no good reason why that challenge should not be responded to, and responded to with the utmost candor. We did not wait for it. Not once, but again and again, we have laid our whole thought and purpose before the world, not in general terms only, but each time with sufficient definition to make it clear what sort of definitive terms of settlement must necessarily spring out of them. Within the last week Mr. Lloyd George has spoken with admirable candor and in admirable spirit for the people and Government of Great Britain. There is no confusion of counsel among the adversaries of the Central ·Powers, no uncertainty of principle, no vagueness of detail. The only secrecy of counsel, the only lack of fearless frankness, the only failure to make definite statement of the objects of the war, lies with Germany and her Allies. The issues of life and death hang upon these definitions. No statesman who has the least conception of his responsibility ought for a moment to permit himself to continue this tragical and appalling outpouring of blood and treasure unless he is sure beyond a peradventure that the objects of the vital sacrifice are part and parcel of the very life of Society and that the people for whom he speaks think them right and imperative as he does.

"There is, moreover, a voice calling for these definitions of principle and of purpose which is, it seems to me, more thrilling and more compelling than any of the many moving voices with which the troubled air of the world is filled. It is the voice of the Russian people. They are prostrate and all but helpless, it would seem, before the grim power of Germany, which has hitherto known

no relenting and no pity. Their power, apparently, is
shattered. And yet their soul is not subservient. They
will not yield either in principle or in action. Their conception of what is right, of what it is humane and honorable for them to accept, has been stated with a frankness,
a largeness of view, a generosity of spirit, and a universal
human sympathy which must challenge the admiration
of every friend of mankind; and they have refused to
compound their ideals or desert others that they themselves may be safe. They call to us to say what it is
that we desire, in what, if in anything, our purpose and
our spirit differ from theirs; and I believe that the people
of the United States would wish me to respond, with
utter simplicity and frankness. Whether their present
leaders believe it or not, it is our heartfelt desire and
hope that some way may be opened whereby we may be
privileged to assist the people of Russia to attain their
utmost hope of liberty and ordered peace.

"It will be our wish and purpose that the processes of
peace, when they are begun, shall be absolutely open and
that they shall involve and permit henceforth no secret
understandings of any kind. The day of conquest and
aggrandizement is gone by; so is also the day of secret
covenants entered into in the interest of particular governments and likely at some unlooked for moment to
upset the peace of the world. It is this happy fact, now
clear to the view of every public man whose thoughts do
not still linger in an age that is dead and gone, which
makes it possible for every nation whose purposes are
consistent with justice and the peace of the world to
avow now or at any other time the objects it has in view.

"We entered this war because violations of right had
occurred which touched us to the quick and made the life
of our own people impossible unless they were corrected
and the world secured once for all against their recur-
rence. What we demand in this war, therefore, is nothing

peculiar to ourselves. It is that the world be made fit and safe to live in; and particularly that it be made safe for every peace-loving nation which, like our own, wishes to live its own life, determine its own institutions, be assured of justice and fair dealing by the other peoples of the world as against force and selfish aggression. All the peoples of the world are in effect partners in this interest, and for our own part we see very clearly that unless justice be done to others it will not be done to us. The programme of the world's peace, therefore, is our programme; and that programme, the only possible programme, as we see it, is this:

"I. Open covenants of peace, openly arrived at, after which there shall be no private international understandings of any kind but diplomacy shall proceed always frankly and in the public view.

"II. Absolute freedom of navigation upon the seas, outside territorial waters, alike in peace and in war, except as the seas may be closed in whole or in part by international action for the enforcement of international covenants.

"III. The removal, so far as possible, of all economic barriers and the establishment of an equality of trade conditions among all the nations consenting to the peace and associating themselves for its maintenance.

"IV. Adequate guarantees given and taken that national armaments will be reduced to the lowest point consistent with domestic safety.

"V. A free, open-minded, and absolutely impartial adjustment of all colonial claims, based upon a strict observance of the principle that in determining all such questions of sovereignty the interests of the populations concerned must have equal weight with the equitable claims of the government whose title is to be determined.

"VI. The evacuation of all Russian territory and such a settlement of all questions affecting Russia as will secure the best and freest coöperation of the other nations of the world in obtaining for her an unhampered and unembarrassed opportunity for the independent determination of her own political development and national policy and assure her of a sincere welcome into the society of free nations under institutions of her own choosing; and, more than a welcome, assistance also of every kind that she may need and may herself desire. The treatment accorded Russia by her sister nations in the months to come will be the acid test of their good will, of their comprehension of her needs as distinguished from their own interests, and of their intelligent and unselfish sympathy.

"VII. Belgium, the whole world will agree, must be evacuated and restored, without any attempt to limit the sovereignty which she enjoys in common with all other free nations. No other single act will serve as this will serve to restore confidence among the nations in the laws which they have themselves set and determined for the government of their relations with one another. Without this healing act the whole structure and validity of international law is forever impaired.

"VIII. All French territory should be freed and the invaded portions restored, and the wrong done to France by Prussia in 1871 in the matter of Alsace-Lorraine, which has unsettled the peace of the world for nearly fifty years, should be righted, in order that peace may once more be made secure in the interest of all.

"IX. A readjustment of the frontiers of Italy should be effected along clearly recognizable lines of nationality.

"X. The peoples of Austria-Hungary, whose place among the nations we wish to see safeguarded and assured, should be accorded the freest opportunity of autonomous development.

"XI. Rumania, Serbia, and Montenegro should be evacuated; occupied territories restored; Serbia accorded free and secure access to the sea; and the relations of the several Balkan states to one another determined by friendly counsel along historically established lines of allegiance and nationality; and international guarantees to the political and economic independence and territorial integrity of the several Balkan states should be entered into.

"XII. The Turkish portions of the present Ottoman Empire should be assured a secure sovereignty, but the other nationalities which are now under Turkish rule should be assured an undoubted security of life and an absolutely unmolested opportunity of autonomous development, and the Dardanelles should be permanently opened as a free passage to the ships and commerce of all nations under international guarantees.

"XIII. An independent Polish state should be erected which should include the territories inhabited by indisputably Polish populations, which should be assured a free and secure access to the sea, and whose political and economic independence and territorial integrity should be guaranteed by international covenant.

"XIV. A general association of nations must be formed under specific covenants for the purpose of affording mutual guarantees of political independence and territorial integrity to great and small states alike.

"In regard to these essential rectifications of wrong and assertions of right we feel ourselves to be intimate partners of all the governments and peoples associated together against the Imperialists. We cannot be separated in interest or divided in purpose. We stand together until the end.

"For such arrangements and covenants we are willing to fight and to continue to fight until they are achieved; but only because we wish the right to prevail and desire a just and stable peace such as can be secured only by removing the chief provocations to war, which this programme does remove. We have no jealousy of German greatness, and there is nothing in this programme that impairs it. We grudge her no achievement or distinction of learning or of pacific enterprise such as have made her record very bright and very enviable. We do not wish to injure her or to block in any way her legitimate influence or power. We do not wish to fight her either with arms or with hostile arrangements of trade if she is willing to associate herself with us and the other peace-loving nations of the world in covenants of justice and law and fair dealing. We wish her only to accept a place of equality among the peoples of the world,—the new world in which we now live,—instead of a place of mastery.

"Neither do we presume to suggest to her any alteration or modification of her institutions. But it is necessary, we must frankly say, and necessary as a preliminary to any intelligent dealings with her on our part, that we should know whom her spokesmen speak for when they speak to us, whether for the Reichstag majority or for the military party and the men whose creed is imperial domination.

"We have spoken now, surely, in terms too concrete to admit of any further doubt or question. An evident principle runs through the whole programme I have outlined. It is the principle of justice to all peoples and nationalities, and their right to live on equal terms of liberty and safety with one another, whether they be strong or weak. Unless this principle be made its foundation no part of the structure of international justice can stand. The people of the United States could act upon no other principle; and to the vindication of this principle they are ready to devote their lives, their honor, and everything that they possess. The moral climax of this the culminating and final war for human liberty has come, and they are ready to put their own strength, their own highest purpose, their own integrity and devotion to the test."

The importance of this brief address by the President on January 8, 1918, is at once apparent. It will be observed that the President takes as his text the parleys in progress at the moment at Brest-Litovsk, which he seems to regard as a very significant and valuable incident, and his view as to what it portends is a very rosy one. He praises the Russians and their attitude. That he was somewhat misled in this respect is obvious, because within the next two months these parleys culminated in treaties between Germany, Northern and Southern Russia and Ukraine. The treaties then made were forced by the Germans and they were disgraceful arrangements, especially to the Germans, who took advantage of their situation, and not creditable to the Russians, who, broken as they were at the moment, yielded with an almost painful weakness to the German dictation. Proceeding from that point, the address deals with the German attitude at that moment and makes a very proper demand that the Germans should define their principles, which were subsequently defined (if they can be called principles) by the treaties ultimately made at Brest-Litovsk or bearing that name. The President then states what were known as the fourteen points, which at a later day were to play a very important part when Germany was beaten and the peace of Versailles was in process of construction. It may be as well at this juncture, in order to make the situation clear, to say just a word in regard to the fourteen points. The first one related to "open covenants" of peace which were to be "openly arrived at." Under our system of government, it is needless to say that no secret treaties are possible, because they all have to go before the Senate of the United States. It is also recognized by everybody that no negotiations can be carried on between countries if everything that is said informally among the negotiators is to be printed the next morning in the newspapers. Any such course as that would practically put a stop to all negotiations. The practical result in this instance was, it is safe to say, that no great treaty was ever made with greater secrecy in the making than the treaty which issued from the decisions of the representatives of five, four, and, in the end, three Powers, and on which the provisions of the Versailles Treaty were based. The second proposition in regard to the freedom of the seas disappeared from consideration before the Powers met at Versailles to make the Treaty with Germany. Nothing was ever done about it. As a matter of fact, it was impracticable from the beginning, there being no trouble whatever about the freedom of the seas outside territorial waters in time of peace, and in time of war Great Britain could hardly be expected to concede the freedom of the seas when her very existence, and, indeed, very largely the existence of the Allies, depended upon the power of blockade.

The third proposition was in essence for universal free trade. That was never, I think, seriously considered by anyone.

The fourth related to a reduction of armaments. Nothing was done about that in the Treaty of Versailles, except the disarmament of Germany, which was made as complete as possible. The League has since then done nothing about it, except pass very excellent resolutions * to inform the world as Mr. Snodgrass informed the mob in *Pickwick*, when he took off his coat, "that he was going to begin." But a long step was taken in this direction and some real reductions made in naval armaments by the Conference on the Limitation of Armaments held at Washington in the winter of 1921-1922.

* Another and verbally a more vigorous scheme for disarmament is now (October 1924) before the League at Geneva.

The fifth point related to the adjustment of colonial claims, which seem to have been settled by the victorious Allied Powers taking all the colonial possessions of Germany everywhere.

Point six related to the evacuation of Russian territory, and that of course was not dealt with at all according to the methods set forth by Mr. Wilson, but was more or less temporarily and violently disposed of in the process of events which could not have been foreseen at that time and certainly were not foreseen at all by the makers of the Versailles Treaty.

Then follow seven, eight, nine, ten, eleven, twelve and thirteen, all relating to the boundaries of Europe and the claims of the different European countries which had been engaged in the war. It is not necessary to go into the details. The propositions made by Mr. Wilson, although stated rather vaguely in some cases, were such as met general approbation but were carried out in their own way by the representatives of the Powers.

The fourteenth, and last point, was for a general association of nations, which took form in the Versailles Treaty as the covenant of the League of Nations.

The four points made by President Wilson subsequently on the 4th of July, 1918, in a speech at Mt. Vernon, were of a more general character and did not add in any way to the definite points made in the fourteen set forth on January 8, 1918.

Important as these fourteen points were, for they played a very considerable part in subsequent negotiations, they were less significant than the fact that Mr. Wilson just then should renew his plans for his own mediation and for making peace himself at that particular moment. There was nothing in the situation in January, 1918, to warrant an attempt to bring about a peace at that time. We were very far from being on the eve of victory. The great German drive of the spring of 1918, which forced the Allies back as far as Amiens and which was perhaps the most critical moment in the whole war, was yet to come. The American troops were beginning to arrive in large numbers, but the great body was still to be sent. The turn of the tide, which began in the summer of 1918, was still far distant and not to be felt before the victorious advance of the Allies, with the fresh troops from America pouring in in great numbers, could even start. It was a moment most unfavorable to us and the Allies in which to begin a talk of peace. It was a moment favorable to Germany and adverse to the Allies, for Germany was just then crushing Russia and, as I have said, the American troops were not yet arriving in the large numbers which were necessary. This renewed attempt to make peace on the part of the President simply showed how that idea of peace under his direction still dominated his whole policy, and that there was no moment, however inauspicious, which in any way could cool his eagerness to get a peace of some sort at any time without regard to the vast, deep-reaching issue for which all the terrible sufferings of the war had been endured.

CHAPTER VII

THE COMING OF PEACE

ON November 11, 1918, the war came to an end by Germany's acceptance of the armistice, the terms of which were dictated by the Allies and the United States. I felt very strongly that it was essential at once to make peace with Germany and bring all fighting to an end. It seemed to me a grave mistake to undertake at that time to form a League which would be certain to occupy a great deal of time, cause long delays and exercise an influence on the peace of the world, so fervently desired, which would probably be in the highest degree prejudicial. Therefore, within six weeks after the armistice, on the 21st of December, 1918, I made a speech in the Senate discussing the terms of peace to be made by Germany and concluded with the following statement:

"We have now at this moment a league of nations. They have been engaged in compelling Germany to make peace and in restoring peace to the world. It has taken four years of the bloodiest war ever known to get that peace. By this existing and most efficient league the peace once signed must be carried out and made effective. Therefore, it is well to reflect that entering upon a new and larger league of nations involves somewhat heavy responsibilities and dangers which must be carefully examined and deliberately considered before they are incurred. The attempt to form now a league of nations— and I mean an effective league, with power to enforce its decrees—no other is worth discussing—can tend at this moment only to embarrass the peace which we ought to make at once with Germany. The American people desire as prompt action on peace with Germany as is consistent with safety. The attempt to attach the provisions for an effective league of nations to the treaty of peace now making with Germany would be to launch the nations who have been fighting Germany on a sea of boundless discussion, the very thing Germany most desires. It would cause wide differences of opinion and bring long delays. If the attempt was successful and a league of nations, with the powers about which I have ventured to inquire vested in it, were to come here before the Senate, it might endanger the peace treaty and force amendments. It certainly would lead to very long delays. Is not the first duty of all the countries united against Germany to make a peace with Germany? Is that not the way to bring peace to the world now? Ought we not to avoid, so far as possible, all delays? Ought we not, speaking only for ourselves, to have a treaty here before the Senate which will not involve interminable discussions about the provisions of a league? Is it not our first duty and our highest duty to bring peace to the world at this moment and not encumber it by trying to provide against wars which never may be fought and against difficulties which lie far ahead in a dim and unknown future? I have merely glanced at these outlying questions, my purpose being simply to show that they ought none of them to be pressed at this time; that the making of peace with Germany and the settlement of the questions inseparably connected with it is enough and more than enough for the present without embarrassing it with questions which involve the settlement of the unknown, without the attempt to deal with all possible questions that ever may arise between nations. To enter on these disputed fields which are not necessary to the making of the peace with Germany seems to me perilous and more likely at this moment to lead to trouble and to a failure of the German peace and its associated questions than to anything else."

What I feared was even then coming to pass. Mr. Wilson had made up his mind to go to Paris and make the treaty himself. IIis going seemed to me a most serious mistake, but I never saw any reason for publicly criticizing the President at that moment for doing it. Nevertheless, I was convinced that in the interest of the peace of the world it was a grievous error. Mr. Wilson then occupied the greatest and most powerful position which any man in public life had occupied in modern times. The United States, although it came into the war late,—and I was one of those who thought we ought to have gone in immediately after the sinking of the *Lusitania*, which would probably have saved the world a year and a half or two years of war, innumerable lives and countless treasure,—the United States, nevertheless, when it went in had by marvellous exertions on the part of the American people and of the officers of the Army and Navy sent over an army to the number of two millions and had two million more men ready to go; we had poured out money in loans to the Allied Nations, and we turned the wavering scale. I do not say that we won the war, which was said more or less loudly by every nation engaged. The war had gone on for four years and if it had not been for the fighting of England and France, of Belgium and Italy, and the enormous sacrifices made by those Powers, there would have been no scale to turn in 1918. Yet it is none the less true that we came at a vital moment and rendered a decisive service. Mr. Wilson with all the glory of this great achievement, won by the people of the United States and by her Army and Navy, about him, could have had a dominant authority in determining peace. If he, remaining in the White House, had only said to Europe: "The United States asks no territory and seeks no conquests"; if he had said, as he later did say, that we sought no reparation: and then, what he never said at any time, that the boundaries to be fixed in Europe were nothing to us, that we wanted a peace which would put it beyond Germany's power for many years to attempt again to destroy the peace of the world and the freedom and civilization of mankind and that all we asked of the Allies was to make such a peace as that with Germany and make it at once and have it agreed to as rapidly as possible; if he had taken this position he would have rendered an unrivalled service to humanity. If he had only done these things he would have had the world at his feet. If he had followed the advice of Mr. Lansing, which, as Mr. Lansing's book shows, was offered to him, and had let the League wait, we should have had peace in the world, a general peace before the existing Congress came to an end in March. He could have done this best by staying here and sending men to represent him, but what Mr. Wilson was thinking of, as was made perfectly obvious subsequently, was himself and the League. He wished to have a League of Nations, of which it was generally expected, I suppose by himself as well as by others, that he would be the head. Therefore he went to Paris. Therefore all the negotiations for peace were hampered and delayed and soon after the New Year began the general propositions to be embodied in the League were known to the press and public of the country.

Mr. Wilson returned from Paris on the 24th of February, landing at Boston, where he spoke on that evening at Mechanic's Hall and challenged his opponents to test the sentiment of the nation on the League. The committees of the House and Senate were invited to dine with him on the evening of the 26th and I give the following brief account of that dinner which I made at the time:

February 26, 1919.

"Dinner to the Committee on Foreign Affairs of the House and the Foreign Relations Committee of the Senate at the White House. It was a large and very pleasant dinner. After dinner we went into the East Room. The President answered questions for two hours about the draft of the constitution of the League of Nations, and told us nothing. He did not seem to know it very thoroughly and was not able to answer questions. For example, he did not know that it was not stated by whom mandatories were to be appointed until I pointed it out to him. He was civil and showed no temper. We went away as wise as we came. I may add as a matter of very vivid recollection that while I asked him one or two questions the principal questioning was done by Senator Knox and more particularly by Senator Brandegee, and the President's performance under Brandegee's very keen and able cross-examination was anything but good."

The most interesting statement made by the President after the dinner was as to the authorship of the original draft of the League on which the covenant as adopted was based. The President said that there were, as he recalled, four drafts—British, Italian, French and American—and that the British draft was the one used as the basis for the League covenant in the Treaty. To those who had had an opportunity to compare the covenant of the League as brought back by Mr. Wilson at that time with the proposal for the League published in a pamphlet by General Smuts, this announcement of the fact that the British draft was the one on which the League was based, was no surprise. In this connection it may be well to say here that when the President received the Committee on Foreign Relations at the White House on

August 19th, the following conversation took place in regard to the original draft of the covenant:

The CHAIRMAN. "You were kind enough to send us the draft of the American plan. When we were here in February, if I understood you rightly—I may be incorrect but I understood you to say that there were other drafts or plans submitted by Great Britain, by France, and by Italy. Would it be possible for us to see those other tentative plans?"

The PRESIDENT. "I would have sent them to the committee with pleasure, Senator, if I had found that I had them. I took it for granted that I had them, but the papers that remain in my hands remain there in a haphazard way. I can tell you the character of the other drafts. The British draft was the only one, as I remember, that was in the form of a definite constitution of a league. The French and Italian drafts were in the form of a series of propositions laying down general rules and assuming that the commission, or whatever body made the final formulation, would build upon those principles if they were adopted. They were principles quite consistent with the final action. I remember saying to the committee when I was here in March—I have forgotten the expression I used—something to the effect that the British draft had constituted the basis. I thought afterwards that that was misleading, and I am very glad to tell the committee just what I meant.

"Some months before the conference assembled, a plan for the league of nations had been drawn up by a British committee, at the head of which was Mr. Phillimore—I believe the Mr. Phillimore who was known as an authority on international law. A copy of that document was sent to me, and I built upon that a redraft. I will not now say whether I thought it was better or not an improvement; but I built on that a draft which was quite different, inasmuch as it put definiteness where there had been what seemed indefiniteness in the Phillimore suggestion. Then, between that time and the time of the formation of the commission on the league of nations, I had the advantage of seeing a paper by Gen. Smuts, of South Africa, who seemed to me to have done some very clear thinking, particularly with regard to what was to be done with the pieces of the dismembered empires. After I got to Paris, therefore, I rewrote the document to which I have alluded, and you may have noticed that it consists of a series of articles, and then supplementary agreements. It was in the supplementary agreements that I embodied the additional ideas that had come to me not only from Gen. Smuts's paper but from other discussions. That is the full story of how the plan which I sent to the committee was built up."

The CHAIRMAN. "Of course, it is obvious that the Gen. Smuts plan has been used. That appears on the face of the document."

The PRESIDENT. "Yes."

The CHAIRMAN. "Then there was a previous draft in addition to the one you have sent to us? You spoke of a redraft. The original draft was not submitted to the committee?"

The PRESIDENT. "No; that was privately, my own."

The CHAIRMAN. "Was it before our commission?"

The PRESIDENT. "No; it was not before our commission."

The CHAIRMAN. "The one that was sent to us was a redraft of that?"

The PRESIDENT. "Yes. I was reading some of the discussion before the committee, and some one, I think Senator Borah, if I remember correctly, quoted an early version of article 10."

Senator BORAH. "That was Senator Johnson."

Senator JOHNSON of California. "I took it from the *Independent.*"

The PRESIDENT. "I do not know how it was obtained but that was part of the draft which preceded the draft which I sent to you."

Senator JOHNSON of California. "It was first published by Mr. Hamilton Holt in the *Independent;* it was again subsequently published in the *New Republic,* and from one of those publications I read it when examining, I think, the Secretary of State."

THE PRESIDENT. "I read it with the greatest interest, because I had forgotten it, to tell the truth, but I recognized it as soon as I read it."

Senator JOHNSON of California. "It was the original plan?"

The PRESIDENT. "It was the original form of article 10; yes."

The CHAIRMAN. "I was about to ask in regard to article 10, as the essence of it appears in article 2 of the draft which you sent, whether that was in the British plan— the Smuts plan—or the other plans?"

"Of course if there are no drafts of these other plans, we can not get them."

The PRESIDENT. "I am very sorry, Senator. I thought I had them, but I have not."

When Mr. Bullitt, who had been connected with the Peace Conference at Paris, testified before the Foreign Relations Committee, he presented a draft of the League covenant showing Mr. Wilson's changes and corrections in his own hand, and I print that here in this same connection: *

"(Seal: Woodrow Wilson)

COVENANT.

PREAMBLE.

"In order to secure **international** peace **and security** and ~~orderly government~~ by the prescription of open, just,

* Mr. Wilson's additions are printed in bold-face.

and honorable relations between nations, by the firm establishment of the understandings of international law as the actual rule of conduct among governments, and by the maintenance of justice and a scrupulous respect for all treaty obligations in the dealings of organized peoples with one another, and in order to promote international cooperation, the Powers signatory to this covenant and agreement jointly and severally adopt this constitution of the League of Nations.

ARTICLE I.

"The action of the Signatory Powers under the terms of this ~~agreement~~ covenant shall be affected through the instrumentality of a Body of Delegates which shall consist of the ambassadors and ministers of the contracting Powers accredited to H. and the Minister of Foreign Affairs of H. The meetings of the Body of Delegates shall be held at the seat of government of H. and the Minister for Foreign Affairs of H. shall be the presiding officer of the Body.

"Whenever the Delegates deem it necessary or advisable, they may meet temporarily at the seat of government of B. or of S., in which case the Ambassador or Minister to H. of the country in which the meeting is held shall be the presiding officer pro tempore.

"It shall be the privilege of any of the contracting Powers to assist its representative in the Body of Delegates by any method of conference, counsel, or advice that may seem best to it, and also to substitute upon occasion a special representative for its regular diplomatic representative accredited to H.

ARTICLE II.

"The Body of Delegates shall regulate their own procedure and shall have power to appoint such committees as they may deem necessary to inquire into and report upon any matters that lie within the field of their action.

"It shall be the right of the Body of Delegates, upon the initiative of any member, to discuss, either publicly or privately as it may deem best, any matter lying within the jurisdiction of the League of Nations as defined in

this Covenant, or any matter likely to affect the peace of
the world; but all actions of the Body of Delegates taken
in the exercise of the functions and powers granted to
them under the Covenant shall be ~~first~~ formulated and
agreed upon by an Executive Council, which shall act
either by reference or upon its own initiative and which
shall consist of the representatives of the Great Powers
together with representatives drawn in annual rotation
from two panels, one of which shall be made up of the
representatives of the States ranking next after the Great
Powers and the other of the representatives of the minor
States (a classification which the Body of Delegates shall
itself establish and may from time to time alter), such
a number being drawn from these panels as will be but
one less than the representatives of the Great Powers;
and three or more negative votes in the Council shall
operate as a veto upon any action or resolution proposed.

"All resolutions passed or actions taken by ~~the Body
of Delegates upon the recommendation of~~ the Executive
Council, except those adopted in execution of any direct
powers herein granted to the Body of Delegates themselves, shall have the effect of recommendations to the
several governments of the League.

"The Executive Council shall appoint a permanent
Secretariat and staff and may appoint joint committees,
chosen from the Body of Delegates or consisting of specially qualified persons outside of that Body, for the study
and systematic consideration of the international questions with which the Council may have to deal, or of questions likely to lead to international complications or disputes. It shall also take the necessary steps to establish
and maintain proper liaison both with the foreign offices
of the signatory powers and with any governments or
agencies which may be acting as mandatories of the
League of Nations in any part of the world.

ARTICLE III.

"The Contracting Powers unite in guaranteeing to
each other political independence and territorial integrity as against external aggression, but it is understood
between them that such territorial readjustments, if any,

as may in the future become necessary by reason of changes in present racial conditions and aspirations or present social and political relationships, pursuant to the principle of self-determination, and also such territorial readjustments as may in the judgment of three-fourths of the Delegates be demanded by the welfare and manifest interest of the peoples concerned, may be effected if agreeable to those peoples and to the State from which the territory is separated or to which it is added; and that territorial changes may in equity involve material compensation. The Contracting Powers accept without reservation the principle that the peace of the world is superior in importance to every question of political jurisdiction or boundary.

ARTICLE IV.

"The Contracting Powers recognize the principle that the establishment and maintenance of peace will require the reduction of national armaments to the lowest point consistent with domestic safety and the enforcement by common action of international obligations; and the ~~Delegates are~~ Executive Council is directed to formulate at once plans by which such a reduction may be brought about. The plan so formulated shall be binding when, and only when, unanimously approved by the Governments signatory to this Covenant.

"As the basis for such a reduction of armaments, all the Powers subscribing to the Treaty of Peace of which this Covenant constitutes a part hereby agree to abolish conscription and all other forms of compulsory military service, and also agree that their future forces of defence and of international action shall consist of militia or volunteers, whose numbers and methods of training shall be fixed, after expert inquiry, by the agreements with regard to the reduction of armaments referred to in the last preceding paragraph.

"The ~~Body of Delegates~~ Executive Council shall also determine for the consideration and action of the several governments what direct military equipment and armament is fair and reasonable in proportion to the scale of forces laid down in the programme of disarmament; and these limits, when adopted, shall not be exceeded without the permission of the Body of Delegates.

"The Contracting Powers further agree that munitions and implements of war shall not be manufactured by private enterprise or for private profit, and that there shall be full and frank publicity as to all national armaments and military or naval programmes.

ARTICLE V.

"The Contracting Powers jointly and severally agree that, should disputes or difficulties arise between or among them which cannot be satisfactorily settled or adjusted by the ordinary processes of diplomacy, they will in no case resort to armed force without previously submitting the questions and matters involved either to arbitration or to inquiry by the Executive Council of the Body of Delegates or until there has been an award by the arbitrators or a decision by the Executive Council; and that they will not even then resort to armed force as against a member of the League of Nations who complies with the award of the arbitrators or the decision of the Executive Council.

"The Powers signatory to this Covenant undertake and agree that whenever any dispute or difficulty shall arise between or among them with regard to any question of the law of nations, with regard to the interpretation of a treaty, as to any fact which would, if established, constitute a breach of international obligation, or as to any alleged damage and the nature and measure of the reparation to be made therefor, if such dispute or difficulty cannot be satisfactorily settled by the ordinary processes of negotiation, to submit the whole subject matter to arbitration and to carry out in full good faith any award or decision that may be rendered.

"In case of arbitration, the matter or matters at issue shall be referred to three arbitrators, one of the three to be selected by each of the parties to the dispute from outside their own nationals, when there are but two such parties, and the third by the two thus selected. When there are more than two parties to the dispute, one arbitrator shall be named by each of the several parties and the arbitrators thus named shall add to their number others of their own choice, the number thus added to be limited to the number which will suffice to give a deciding voice to the arbitrators thus added in case of a tie vote among the arbitrators chosen by the contending parties. In case the arbitrators chosen by the contending parties cannot agree upon an additional arbitrator or arbitrators, the additional arbitrator or arbitrators shall be chosen by the ~~Body of Delegates~~ **Executive Council.**

"On the appeal of a party to the dispute the decision of the arbitrators may be set aside by a vote of three-fourths of the Delegates, in case the decision of the arbitrators was unanimous, or by a vote of two-thirds of the Delegates in case the decision of the arbitrators was not unanimous, but unless thus set aside shall be finally binding and conclusive.

"When any decision of arbitrators shall have been thus set aside, the dispute shall again be submitted to arbitrators chosen as heretofore provided, none of whom shall, however, have previously acted as arbitrators in the dispute in question, and the decision of the arbitrators rendered in this second arbitration shall be finally binding and conclusive without right of appeal.

"If for any reason it should prove impracticable to refer any matter in dispute to arbitration, the parties to the dispute shall apply to the Executive Council to take the matter under consideration for such mediatory action or recommendation as it may deem wise in the circumstances.

"The Council shall immediately accept the reference and give notice to the ~~other party or~~ parties, and shall make the necessary arrangements for a full hearing, investigation, and consideration. It shall ascertain and as soon as possible make public all the facts involved in the dispute and shall make such recommendations as it may deem wise and practicable based on the merits of the controversy and calculated to secure a just and lasting settlement. Other members of the League shall place at the disposal of the Executive Council any and all information that may be in their possession which in any way bears upon the facts or merits of the controversy, and the Executive Council shall do everything in its power by way of mediation or conciliation to bring about a peaceful settlement. The decisions of the Executive Council shall be addressed to the disputants, and shall not have the force of a binding verdict. Should the Executive Council fail to arrive at any conclusion, it shall be the privilege of the members of the Executive Council to publish their several conclusions or recommendations, and such publication shall not be regarded as an unfriendly act by either or any of the disputants.

"Every award by arbitrators and every decision by the Executive Council upon a matter in dispute between States must be rendered within twelve months after formal reference.

ARTICLE VI.

"Should any contracting Power break or disregard its covenants under Article V, it shall thereby ipso facto become at war with be deemed to have committed an act of war against all the members of the League, which shall immediately subject it to a complete economic and financial boycott, including the severance of all trade or financial relations, the prohibition of all intercourse between their subjects and the subjects of the covenant-breaking State, and the prevention, so far as possible, of all financial, commercial, or personal intercourse between the subjects of the covenant-breaking State and the subjects of any other State, whether a member of the League of Nations or not.

"It shall be the privilege and duty of the Executive Council of the Body of Delegates in such a case to recommend what effective military or naval force the members of the League of Nations shall severally contribute, and to advise, if it should think best, that the smaller members of the League be excused from making any contribution to the armed forces to be used against the covenant-breaking State.

"The covenant-breaking State shall, after the restoration of peace, be subject to perpetual disarmament and to the regulations with regard to a peace establishment provided for new States under the terms Supplementary Article IV.

ARTICLE VII.

"If any power shall declare war or begin hostilities or take any hostile step short of war against another Power before submitting the dispute involved to arbitrators or consideration by the Executive Council as herein provided, or shall declare war or begin hostilities, or take any hostile step short of war, in regard to any dispute which has been decided adversely to it by arbitrators chosen and empowered as herein provided, the Contracting Powers hereby bind themselves engage not only to cease all commerce and intercourse with that Power but also to unite in blockading and closing the frontiers of that Power to commerce or intercourse with any part of the world and to use any force that may be necessary to accomplish that object.

ARTICLE VIII.

"Any war or threat of war, whether immediately affecting any of the Contracting Powers or not, is hereby declared a matter of concern to the League of Nations and to all the Powers signatory hereto, and those Powers hereby reserve the right to take any action that may be deemed wise and effectual to safeguard the peace of nations.

"It is hereby also declared and agreed to be the friendly right of each of the nations signatory or adherent to this Covenant to draw the attention of the Body of Delegates or of the Executive Council to any circumstances anywhere which threaten to disturb international peace or the good understanding between nations upon which peace depends.

"The Delegates and the Executive Council shall meet in the interest of peace whenever war is rumored or threatened, and also whenever the Delegate of any Power shall inform the Delegates that a meeting and conference in the interest of peace is advisable.

"The Delegates may also meet at such other times and upon such other occasions as they shall from time to time deem best and determine.

ARTICLE IX.

"In the event of a dispute arising between one of the Contracting Powers and a Power not a party to this Covenant, the Contracting Power involved hereby binds itself to endeavor to obtain the submission of the dispute to judicial decision or to arbitration. If the other Power will not agree to submit the dispute to judicial decision or to arbitration, the Contracting Power shall bring the matter to the attention of the ~~Body of Delegates~~ **Executive Council.** The Delegates shall in such a case, in the name of the League of Nations, invite the Power not a party to this Covenant to become ad hoc a party and to submit its case to judicial decision or to arbitration, and if that Power consents it is hereby agreed that the provisions hereinbefore contained and applicable to the submission of disputes to arbitration or discussion shall be in all respects applicable to the dispute both in favor of and against such Power as if it were a party to this Covenant.

"In case the Power not a party to this Covenant shall not accept the invitation of the ~~Delegates~~ **Executive Council** to become ad hoc a party, it shall be the duty of the Executive Council immediately to institute an inquiry into the circumstances and merits of the dispute involved and to recommend such joint action by the Contracting Powers as may seem best and most effectual in the circumstances disclosed.

ARTICLE X.

"If hostilities should be begun or any hostile action taken against the Contracting Power by the Power not a party to this Covenant before a decision of the dispute by arbitrators or before investigation, report and recommendation by the Executive Council in regard to the dispute, or contrary to such recommendation, the Contracting Powers shall **engage** thereupon to cease all commerce and communication with that Power and ~~shall~~ also **to** unite in blockading and closing the frontiers of that Power to all commerce or intercourse with any part of the world, **and to** employ~~ing~~ jointly any force that may be necessary to accomplish that object.   The Contracting Powers ~~shall~~ also **undertake to** unite in coming to the assistance of the Contracting Power against which hostile action has been taken, ~~combining~~ **and to combine** their armed forces in its behalf.

ARTICLE XI.

"In case of a dispute between states not parties to this Covenant, any Contracting Power may bring the matter to the attention of the Delegates **or the Executive Council,** who shall thereupon tender the good offices of the League of Nations with a view to the peaceable settlement of the dispute.

"If one of the states, a party to the dispute, shall offer and agree to submit its interests and cause of action wholly to the control and decision of the League of Nations, that state shall ad hoc be deemed a Contracting Power. If no one of the states, parties to the dispute, shall so offer and agree, the Delegates shall, through the Executive Council, of their own motion take such action and make such recommendation to their governments as will prevent hostilities and result in the settlement of the dispute.

ARTICLE XII.

"Any Power not a party to this Covenant, whose government is based upon the principle of popular self-government, may apply to the Body of Delegates for leave to become a party. If the Delegates shall regard the granting thereof as likely to promote the peace, order, and security of the World, they ~~may~~ **shall** act favourably on the application, and their favourable action shall operate to constitute the Power so applying in all respects a full signatory party to this Covenant. This action shall require the affirmative vote of two-thirds of the Delegates.

ARTICLE XIII.

"The Contracting Powers severally ~~agree~~ that the Present Covenant and Convention is accepted as abrogating all treaty obligations inter se which are inconsistent with the terms hereof, and solemnly engage that they will not enter into any engagements inconsistent with the terms hereof.

"In case any of the Powers signatory hereto or subsequently admitted to the League of Nations shall, before becoming a party to this Covenant, have undertaken any treaty obligations which are inconsistent with the terms of this Covenant, it shall be the duty of such Power to take immediate steps to procure its release from such obligations.

SUPPLEMENTARY AGREEMENTS.

I.

"In respect of the peoples and territories which formerly belonged to Austria-Hungary, and to Turkey, and in respect of the Colonies formerly under the dominion of the German Empire, the League of Nations shall be regarded as the residuary trustee ~~with sovereign right of ultimate disposal of continued~~ with the right of oversight or administration in accordance with certain fundamental principles hereinafter set forth, and this reversion and control shall exclude all rights or privileges of annexation on the part of any Power.

"These principles are, that there shall in no case be any annexation of any of these territories by any State either within the League or outside of it, and that in the future government of these peoples and territories the rule of self-determination or the consent of the governed to their form of government, shall be fairly and reasonably applied, and all policies of administration or economic development be based primarily upon the well considered interests of the people themselves.

II.

"Any authority, control, or administration which may be necessary in respect of these peoples or territories other than their own self-determined and self-organized autonomy shall be the exclusive function of and shall be vested in the League of Nations and exercised or undertaken by or on behalf of it.

"It shall be lawful for the League of Nations to delegate authority, control, or administration of any such people or territory to some single State or organized agency which it may designate and appoint as its agent or mandatory; but whenever or wherever possible or feasible the agent or mandatory so appointed shall be nominated or approved by the autonomous people or territory.

III.

"The degree of authority, control, or administration to be exercised by the mandatory State or agency shall in each case be explicitly defined by the ~~League~~ Executive Council in a special Act or Charter which shall reserve to the League complete power of supervision ~~and of intimate control~~, and which shall also reserve to the people of any such territory or governmental unit the right to appeal to the League for the redress or correction of any breach of the mandate by the mandatory State or agency or for the substitution of some other State or agency, as mandatory.

"The mandatory State or agency shall in all cases be bound and required to maintain the policy of the open door, or equal opportunity for all the signatories to this Covenant, in respect of the use and development of the economic resources of such people or territory.

"The mandatory State or agency shall in no case form or maintain any military or naval force, **native or other,** in excess of definite standards laid down by the League itself for the purpose of internal police.

"Any expense the mandatory State or agency may be put to in the exercise of its functions under the mandate, so far as they cannot be borne by the resources of the people or territory under its charge upon a fair basis of assessment and charge, shall be borne by the several signatory Powers, their several contributions being assessed and determined by the Executive Council in proportion to their several national budgets, unless the mandatory State or agency is willing to bear the excess costs; and in all cases the expenditures of the mandatory Power or agency in the exercise of the mandate shall be subject to the audit and authorization of the League.

"The object of all such tutelary oversight and administration on the part of the League of Nations shall be to build up in as short a time as possible out of the people or territory under its guardianship a political unit which can take charge of its own affairs, determine its own connections, and choose its own policies. The League may at any time release such a people or territory from tutelage and consent to its being set up as an independent unit. It shall also be the right and privilege of any such people or territory to petition the League to take such action, and upon such petition being made it shall be the duty of the League to take the petition under full and friendly consideration with a view to determining the best interests of the people or territory in question in view of all the circumstances of their situation and development.

IV.

"No new State ~~arising or created from the old Empire of Austria-Hungary, or Turkey~~ shall be recognized by the League or admitted into its membership except on condition that its military and naval forces and armaments shall conform to the standard prescribed by the League in respect of it from time to time.

"~~As successor to the Empire,~~ The League of Nations is empowered, directly and without right of delegation, to watch over the relations inter se of all new independent States arising or created, ~~out of the Empire,~~ and shall assume and fulfill the duty of conciliating and composing differences between them with a view to the maintenance of settled order and the general peace.

V.

"The Powers signatory or adherent to this Covenant agree that they will themselves seek to establish and maintain fair hours and humane conditions of labour for all those within their several jurisdictions who are engaged in manual labour and that they will exert their influence in favour of the adoption and maintenance of a similar policy and like safeguards wherever their industrial and commercial relations extend.

VI.

"The League of Nations shall require all new States to bind themselves as a condition precedent to their recognition as independent or autonomous States, and the Executive Council shall exact of all States seeking admission to the League of Nations the promise, to accord to all racial or national minorities within their several jurisdictions exactly the same treatment and security, both in law and in fact, that is accorded the racial or national majority of their people.

VII.

"Recognizing religious persecution and intolerance as fertile sources of war, the Powers signatory hereto agree, and the League of Nations shall exact from all new States and all States seeking admission to it the promise, that they will make no law prohibiting or interfering with the free exercise of religion, and that they will in no way discriminate, either in law or in fact, against those who practice any particular creed, religion, or belief whose practices are not inconsistent with public order or public morals.

VIII.

"The rights of belligerents on the high seas outside territorial waters having been defined by international convention, it is hereby agreed and declared as a fundamental covenant that no Power or combination of Powers shall have a right to overstep in any particular the clear meaning of the definitions thus established; but that it shall be the right of the League of Nations from time to time and on special occasion to close the seas in whole or in part against a particular Power or particular Powers for the purpose of enforcing the international covenants here entered into.

IX.

"It is hereby covenanted and agreed by the Powers signatory hereto that no treaty entered into by them, either singly or jointly, shall be regarded as valid, binding, or operative until it shall have been published and made known to all the other signatories.

X.

"It is further covenanted and agreed by the signatory Powers that in their fiscal and economic regulations and policy no discrimination shall be made between one nation and another among those with which they have commercial and financial dealings."

It was, then, after the dinner at the White House on February 26, 1919, that Senator Knox and I, apprehending the coming of the League, each made a speech just as Congress was closing. Senator Knox's speech delivered on the 1st of March was one of great ability, as all his speeches were, and ought to have commanded, as it did, the attention of this country and of Europe; but it ought also to have commanded the attention of the President if he had been capable of taking advice. On the 28th of February, I spoke in the Senate, taking similar ground. The speech will be found in Appendix I.

My effort and that of Senator Knox at that time was to try, by showing the objections to the League proposed, to make it apparent that the thing to do was to make peace and deal with the League later when we could take our time in doing so, and thereby to demonstrate that the League should not be yoked with the treaty of peace and thus create the risk of dragging them both down together.

My speech, as I have said, was delivered on the 28th of February, 1919. Upon the 4th of March, the following Tuesday, the then existing session of Congress would come to an end. On the morning of Sunday, March 2nd, Senator Brandegee came to my house soon after breakfast and told me that it seemed to him of the last importance that at that juncture some declaration should be made, securing for it if possible the signatures of more than one-third of the Senate, to the effect that a League of Nations such as it was understood was to be proposed, and the outlines of which had been given through the press, could not be passed. I was very much struck by the proposition, and he had no difficulty in convincing me of its essential and even vital importance. We discussed it for some time and then went to see Senator Knox and asked him to draft the declaration, which he did, and we went over his draft with him later in the day. I then took the draft on Monday morning and went first to see Senator Cummins, who was one of the oldest and most distinguished Senators on our side, and asked him to consider it and told him that I hoped he would be ready to sign it. He went over it with care, suggested two amendments, as I remember, to which no one could object and which I regarded as improvements, and then those of us who had been interested in getting it up signed it and proceeded to circulate it on our side of the chamber. We did not think it desirable to ask any Democrats to sign. We knew there were Democratic Senators opposed to the League, but we did not wish to involve or embarrass them, and we also were able to exercise a greater freedom in taking this position than was possible for them. Just before midnight on the 3rd of March I arose in the Senate and read the declaration and the signatures, which made certain the printing of the declaration in the Record. Its consideration was clearly out of order in the condition of the existing business; one objection was certain to put it over and that objection was made by Senator Swanson of Virginia. Our purpose, however, had been served. The declaration went out to the world and before the next morning we had by the arrival of Senator Elkins of West Virginia and a telegram from Senator Fall of New Mexico two additional signatures, making in all thirty-nine signers. One-third of the Senate was of course 32, so that it was perfectly clear that a proposal for a League of Nations which did not have reservations meeting the objections expressed in the declaration could not pass the Senate; that is the Senate would not advise and consent to it. The declaration with the signatures read as follows:

"Whereas under the Constitution it is a function of the Senate to advise and consent to, or dissent from, the ratification of any treaty of the United States, and no such treaty can become operative without the consent of the Senate expressed by the affirmative vote of two-thirds of the Senators present; and

"Whereas owing to the victory of the arms of the United States and of the nations with whom it is associated, a peace conference was convened and is now in session at Paris for the purpose of settling the terms of peace; and

"Whereas a committee of the conference has proposed a constitution for a league of nations and the proposal is now before the peace conference for its consideration: Now, therefore, be it

"*Resolved by the Senate of the United States in the discharge of its constitutional duty of advice in regard to treaties,* That it is the sense of the Senate that while it is their sincere desire that the nations of the world should unite to promote peace and general disarmament, the constitution of the league of nations in the form now proposed to the peace conference should not be accepted by the United States; and be it

"*Resolved further,* That it is the sense of the Senate that the negotiations on the part of the United States should immediately be directed to the utmost expedition of the urgent business of negotiating peace terms with Germany satisfactory to the United States and the nations with whom the United States is associated in the war against the German Government, and that the proposal for a league of nations to insure the permanent peace of the world should be then taken up for careful and serious consideration.

"The undersigned Senators of the United States, Members and Members elect of the Sixty-sixth Congress, hereby declare that, if they had had the opportunity, they would have voted for the foregoing resolution:

Henry Cabot Lodge.
Philander C. Knox.
Lawrence Y. Sherman.
Harry S. New.
George H. Moses.
J. W. Wadsworth, Jr.
Bert M. Fernald.
Albert B. Cummins.
F. E. Warren.
James E. Watson.
Thomas Sterling.
J. S. Frelinghuysen.
W. G. Harding.
Frederick Hale.
William E. Borah.
*Walter E. Edge.
Reed Smoot.
Asle J. Gronna.

William M. Calder.
Henry W. Keyes.
Boies Penrose.
Carroll S. Page.
George P. McLean.
Joseph Irwin France.
Medill McCormick.
Charles Curtis.
*Lawrence C. Phipps.
Seldon P. Spencer.
Hiram Johnson.
Charles E. Townsend.
William P. Dillingham.
I. L. Lenroot.
Miles Poindexter.
Howard Sutherland.
*Truman H. Newberry.
*L. Heisler Ball

Added the next morning.
Davis Elkins of West Virginia
Albert B. Fall of New Mexico."

I call attention to this declaration and the manner in which it was made and then published not only to the people of the United States but to the people of Europe, because it has an especial significance which must not be

* Senators Elect.

overlooked. The United States and the Senate were much criticized in Europe, and the President and the Allied Powers kept urging directly or by implication the proposition that we were bound to accept the Versailles Treaty because President Wilson had negotiated and signed it. On the part of the President, this was an attempt to overthrow the powers of the Senate and thus indirectly to violate and set aside the provisions of the Constitution. On the part of the Allied Powers, it was the business of their official representatives to know what our constitutional provisions were and that no treaty would bind the United States unless accepted and approved by the Senate, whether with or without amendments or reservations. The public men of England and France, especially those of England, knew this fact; in any event, it was their business to know it, whether they actually knew it or not.

There are certain facts of which courts of law take judicial cognizance, and all nations engaged in negotiations with the United States were bound to take judicial cognizance of the Constitution of the United States so far as it affected the treaty-making power, and therefore were bound to know that the treaties made by the President could not become law and binding unless two-thirds of the Senate gave advice and consent to them after they had been submitted to the Senate by the President. If they did not know this fact, then it was their own fault alone if they thought that the United States was bound in any way by the President's action in making and signing a treaty. Moreover, the Senate, by its declaration of March 4th, gave formal notice that more than one-third of that body would not accept the covenant of the League of Nations as it appeared in the first draft. The attempt, therefore, made in Europe, to suggest that the Senate was bound by the President's action, was childish and worse than childish; it was dishonest.

In addition to these provisions of the Constitution of

the United States, it was also a matter of public notoriety that at the November election just preceding the Armistice the President's party had been badly defeated at the polls, the Republican party having carried, by a net gain in popular majority of 1,200,000 votes, both the House and Senate. The President at the end of a great war just closing in victory had made a personal appeal to the American people to give him a Democratic Congress, and the voters had rejected his request and placed his opponents in power in both the House and Senate. Under the ministerial system of Europe this would have meant an immediate change in the government. Under the Constitution of the United States the Chief Executive could not be displaced in the middle of his term; but the American people had done all that was possible to take power away from Mr. Wilson. In view of existing conditions, with victory in the field actually hovering over our country, such a defeat for an administration was unheard of. Yet Europe apparently took no notice of the startling result of the American elections but persisted in believing that Mr. Wilson was still all-powerful and that the Senate, if it resisted him, would soon be overruled, and if it were not, successful resistance would be an act of bad faith. It is not easy fitly to characterize such an attitude of mind which was as disingenuous as it was absurd, and for the prime ministers and statesmen, who knew perfectly well about the provisions of the Constitution of the United States and the meaning of the election results, to make any such pretense, as they did, in order to shelter their own shortcomings, of belief in the President's power, was as indefensible as it was stupid. There is reason to believe that Great Britain and Europe have for the time being at least acquired a better understanding of the powers of the United States Senate than they pretended to enjoy in the winter and spring of 1918 and 1919.

President Wilson himself, however confident he may have been of securing the assent of the Senate, knew very well what the Constitution of the United States provided and what had happened at the November election. This is shown by a brief correspondence by cable, which has never been made public before and which I now give. It tells its own story.

Shortly after the adjournment of Congress, when I had returned to Boston for a few days, I received through the State Department, the following cablegram, dated March 9, 1919, from Mr. Henry White, who was one of the delegates of the United States to the Conference at Paris:

"I should be grateful if you would cable, in cipher through the Department of State, to me the exact phraseology of amendments modifying the League of Nations covenant which Senate considers important. It is our desire to meet the Senate's views as closely as it is possible to obtain acquiescence therein of other nations anxious for recognition of their own special interests, which immediately they will insist upon in the covenant if we in addition demand exemptions in favor of ours. Two days ago, I wrote you fully, but feel use of cable desirable time being so important. Please send full report of your and Knox speeches by next courier."

It was Mr. White's understanding, and in fact he wrote to me, that his despatch to me was personal and that he had not consulted the President in regard to it, and of course I had absolute confidence in his entire good faith. By an arrangement, however, with the French Government, President Wilson and his agents had complete control and a pretty thorough censorship of all despatches sent out from Paris as well as those from the United States admitted to Paris, and this despatch to me could not have gone out if it had not had the approval of those charged with the censorship. They certainly never would have allowed such a despatch addressed to me to go through if it had not been approved by the President without Mr. White's knowledge. Moreover, the despatch was sent in Department cipher to the State Department and, therefore, was known to some of the officers of the State Department at Washington. It is as certain as anything can be that Mr. White's despatch could not possibly have reached me unless it had the approval of the President and the Department of State. I considered this request very carefully and saw at once that if I should suggest amendments or reservations it would put me in a very false position, for the new Congress had not assembled, the new Foreign Relations Committee had not been organized, and I should not only appear as speaking for them and for the Republicans of the Senate, which I had no right to do, but I should also be committing myself individually to propositions upon which I might wish in the future to make modifications or perhaps very vital changes. I consulted Senator Brandegee, Senator Knox, who was in Florida, by telephone, and also Mr. Root, who was in New York. They all agreed with me as to the nature of the reply and Mr. Root sent me some valuable suggestions as to the wording of my answer, which I was only too glad to adopt as I did not feel that I could improve upon them. I now quote the letter which I received from Mr. Root:

"March 13, 1919.

"Dear Lodge:

"Chandler Anderson has been in with a copy of Harry White's cable to you. Brandegee sent it to him with a request that he should consult me about the answer. I enclose a suggestion for an answer which we have worked out with considerable discussion.

"It seemed to both of us that the fundamental consideration in replying to this despatch must be that your relations as a Senator to the proposed League of Nations Convention are and must necessarily continue to be direct relations with the President of the United States, and that you should not enter into any discussion as to the terms of the proposed treaty with a subordinate of the President for several reasons:—

"First, that you would be committing yourself as an independent agent of Government, while the President would not be at all committed by what his subordinate may choose to say. It is a wise rule not to enter into a discussion with an unauthorized agent where you will be bound and the other principal will not.

"A second reason is that any views which the Senate may have, to be effective must reach the President's mind by an entirely different avenue of approach from that of information communicated by a subordinate. They should be presented not as an appeal to his judgment, but with the compelling force of expression by a co-equal power to which his judgment must yield, or his action must fail.

"It seemed to us also that White unwittingly was inviting action on your part which would result in the Senate's assenting to public repudiation and flouting by the President, accompanied by private consultation,—a position which of course you cannot agree to. I hardly think that White appreciates the attitude which the President has assumed towards the Senate. If he did appreciate the fact, I think he would not have sent this cablegram; but, of course, you cannot explain it to him in your cable answer.

"We also agreed that quite apart from these considerations it was a very extraordinary proceeding for the President to refrain from asking the advice of the Senate while it was in session, and then as soon as the Senate had separated to allow a subordinate to seek to commit one member of the Senate as to what the whole Senate would agree to; and that in view of the official relations of White and yourself to the subject matter you are not at liberty to make any expression whatever to him as to what the Senate will or will not do, or will or will not agree to, until the Senate has been consulted, and has acted and authorized the statement. It may be that Harry White has sent this despatch without any consultation with the President but the effect is the same.

"If the President wants to know what the Senate will be satisfied with, there is only one means of ascertaining, and that is the natural and customary way,—to convene the Senate in extraordinary session. That is the proper official course. If I were not sure that Harry White does not appreciate the real force and effect of his cablegram to you, I should resent the attempt to carry on the business in this kind of backdoor way.

"The President appears to be in continual wireless communication both with Washington and with Paris, and it is a fair presumption that he knew of this despatch. I think White would hardly have sent it without communicating with the President. If that be the case, a comparison between the despatch and the President's public utterances in this country would be very interesting. At all events, the net is spread in plain sight of the bird, and you are the bird.

"The Union League Club here will pass a resolution tonight providing for a petition to the President to convene an extraordinary session of the Senate. I think that is the course he ought to follow, and that the country will be inclined to think so.

"With these views, the answer we suggest is as follows:

"'Your cable March ninth. The President expressed 'no willingness to receive any communication from the 'Senate while that body was in session. If he now wishes 'to have amendments drafted which the Senate will con-'sent to, the natural and necessary course is to convene the

'Senate in the customary way. Manifestly, I cannot now 'speak for the Senate or consult its members, nor can they 'consult with each other, nor can the President consult 'them while they are at their homes in forty-eight States.'

"You will perceive that this assumes that White wishes the information for the President's benefit, which is the proper attitude for him to occupy so long as he is a member of the Commission. It avoids either entering into a discussion of the subject, or refusing to discuss it.

"I wish you great success in your discussion with Lowell. I assume that he occupies substantially the same attitude that Taft does. I think it a great mistake for Taft while he knows perfectly well that the so-called constitution [of the League of Nations] is in serious need of amendment to take a course tending to help Wilson to put it through without amendment.

"I have been studying the paper and trying to dispossess my mind of the prejudice against it created by the way in which it has been presented,—a way exceedingly offensive to me. The more I study it, the more satisfied I am that it has some very useful provisions, some very bad ones, some glaring deficiencies, and that if it is not very materially amended not merely in form but in substance, the world will before very long wake up to realize that a great opportunity has been wasted in the doing of a futile thing.

"Faithfully yours,
"ELIHU ROOT.

"Honorable H. Cabot Lodge,
    "56 Beacon Street,
        "Boston, Mass."

To the debate between President Lowell of Harvard College and myself to which Senator Root refers in his letter I shall allude later (pp. 129 *et seq.*). It is not necessary for me now to say anything further in regard to the debate except that when it was over it seemed that President Lowell apparently agreed with most of my criticisms and favored changes on the points to which I especially called attention. The sole value of the debate from my standpoint was that being widely published it helped to bring the questions raised by the covenant of the League of Nations sharply to the attention of the country, which was what I desired to do beyond anything else.

After hearing from Senator Knox and Senator Brandegee and after receiving this letter from Mr. Root, I sent the following cablegram, which, as I have said, embodies what was my own opinion and that of Senators Knox and Brandegee and of Mr. Root in whose language I think no improvement could be made:

"Have considered your cable March 9th. The President expressed no willingness to receive any communication from the Senate while that body was in session. If he now wishes to have amendments drafted which the Senate will consent to, the natural and necessary course is to convene the Senate in the customary way. Manifestly I cannot now speak for the Senate or consult its members nor can they consult with each other nor can the President consult them while they are at their homes in forty-eight States."

This cable message closed this incident and we received no more requests for statements as to what amendments or reservations the Senate desired or would accept. The effort to obtain this information officially failed, but the attempt to secure it is none the less instructive.

CHAPTER VIII

THE QUESTION OF CONSISTENCY

BEFORE tracing the story of the contest in the Senate over the Treaty of Versailles and more particularly the Covenant of the League of Nations, I think it is well, in order to avoid later digressions or interruptions, that I should make a brief statement in regard to the charge of inconsistency which was constantly brought forward against me during the debate. I wish to dispose of that matter, as I have already disposed of the entirely false charge that I was in any degree influenced by a personal hostility to Mr. Wilson which, as a matter of fact, never existed. To this end it is necessary for me briefly to state the course and development of my own opinions in regard to the vital question of a League of Nations.

At the opening of a public debate with President Lowell of Harvard on the 19th of March, 1919, in Boston, I said:

"I have also been charged with inconsistency. In the autumn of 1914, Theodore Roosevelt made a speech in which he brought forward the idea of a League of Nations for the prevention of future wars. In the following June, of 1915, speaking at Union College in New York on Commencement, I took up the same idea and discussed the establishment of a League of Nations backed by force."

I spoke of it only in general terms. The following are the essential parts of that address taken from my volume of War Addresses published in 1917:

"In differences between nations which go beyond the limited range of arbitrable questions peace can only be maintained by putting behind it the force of united nations determined to uphold it and to prevent war. No one is more conscious than I of the enormous difficulties which beset such a solution or such a scheme, but I am certain that it is in this direction alone that we can find hope for the maintenance of the world's peace and the avoidance of needless wars. Even if we could establish such a union of nations there might be some wars which could not be avoided, but there are certainly many which might be prevented.

"It might be easily said that this idea, which is not a new one, is impracticable; but it is better than the idea that war can be stopped by language, by speech-making, by vain agreements, which no one would carry out when the stress came, by denunciations of war and laudations of peace, in which all men agree, for these methods are not only impracticable but impossible and barren of all hope of real result. It may seem Utopian at this moment to suggest a union of civilized nations in order to put a controlling force behind the maintenance of peace and international order; but it is through the aspiration for perfection, through the search for Utopias, that the real advances have been made. At all events, it is along this path that we must travel if we are to attain in any measure to the end we all desire of peace upon earth. It is at least a great, a humane purpose to which, in these days of death and suffering, of misery, and sorrow among so large a portion of mankind, we might well dedicate ourselves. We must begin the work with the clear understanding that our efforts will fail if they are tainted with the thought of personal or political profit or with any idea of self-interest or self-glorification. We may not now succeed, but I believe that in the slow process of the years others who come after us will reach the goal. The effort and the sacrifice which we make will not be in vain when the end in sight is noble, when we are striving to help mankind and lift the heaviest of burdens from suffering humanity."

I spoke again in favor of the plan for a League in the following winter at a meeting in Washington of the League to Enforce Peace. I then said:

"The limit of voluntary arbitration has, I think, been reached. It has done much. It has taken out of the range of arms a large mass of questions which once were causes, frequently of war, constantly of reprisals, and by the general consent of civilized mankind has put them before a tribunal and had them there decided.

"If we have reached the limit of voluntary arbitration, what is the next step? I think the next step is that which this League proposes and that is to put force behind international peace, an international league or agreement, or tribunal, for peace. We may not solve it in that way, but if we cannot solve it in that way it can be solved in no other.

"You cannot keep order in your cities unless you put force behind the will of the community and behind the peace of the citizens. The peace of your states is maintained by force. It rests upon the militia and the constabulary of the states. The peace of the United States can only be secured and maintained by an ample, thorough, national defense.

"We have not that defense now.

"I trust that we are entered on the path which will lead us to the upbuilding of our national defense, both in the army and in the navy. I hope this not only to make our own peace secure, but because we as a nation will find it very difficult to induce others to put force behind peace if we have not force to put behind our own peace.

"I know, and no one, I think, can know better than one who has served long in the Senate, which is charged with an important share of the ratification and confirmation of all treaties—no one can, I think, feel more deeply than I do the difficulties which confront us in the work which this League has undertaken.

"But the difficulties cannot be overcome unless we try to overcome them. I believe much can be done.

"Probably it will be impossible to stop all wars, but it certainly will be possible to stop some wars and to diminish their number.

"The way in which this problem must be worked out must be left to this League and to those who are giving this great question the study which it deserves. I know the obstacles. I know how quickly we shall be met with the statement that this is a dangerous question which you are putting into your agreement, that no nation can submit to the judgment of other nations, and we must be careful at the beginning not to attempt too much. I know the difficulties that arise when we speak of anything which seems to involve an alliance.

"But I do not believe that when Washington warned us against permanent alliances he meant for one moment that we should not join with the other civilized nations of the world if a method could be found to diminish war and encourage peace.

"It was a year ago that in delivering the Chancellor's address at Union College, I made an argument on this theory, that if we were to promote international peace at the close of the present terrible war, if we were to restore international law as it must be restored, we must find some way in which the united forces of the nations could be put behind the cause of peace and law.

"I said then that my hearers might think that I was picturing a Utopia, but it is in the search for Utopias that great discoveries have been made. 'Not failure, but low aim, is crime.'

"This League certainly has the highest of all aims for the benefit of humanity, and because the pathway is sown with difficulties is no reason that we should turn from it. It is the vision of a perhaps impossible perfection which has led humanity across the centuries. If our aspirations are for that which is great and beautiful and good and beneficent to humanity, even when we do not achieve our end, even if the results are little, we can at least remember Arnold's lines:

> 'Charge once more, then, and be dumb!
> Let the victors, when they come,
> When the forts of folly fall,
> Find your body by the wall!' "

The speech which I have quoted above was printed from a shorthand report and I never saw it until it appeared. There were one or two verbal mistakes in it which I have corrected.

Continuing the extract from my debate with President Lowell, I quote the following:

"But the more I reflected upon it and the more I studied it the more difficult the problem appeared to me. It became very clear to me that in trying to do too much we might lose all; that there were many obstacles and many dangers in the way; and that it would require the greatest skill and self-restraint on the part of the nations to make any league that would really promote and strengthen and make more secure the peace of the world.

"In January, 1917, the President of the United States brought forward a plan for a League for Peace in an address to the Senate, and I discussed it at some length, showing the dangers of the proposition and the perils which it would bring, not only to peace but to the United States." *

The message of the President, despite its importance, and the speech which I made in reply, were both lost sight of in the feverish days that followed, which were filled with the events that were rapidly carrying the country into war. This reply to the President I could not have presented in the Symphony Hall debate, but I refer to it here. What I then said in January, 1917, in discussing the President's plan of a League for Peace shows completely the change which I have already indicated and which came in my opinions and my views as to the possibility and desirability of a League of Nations, backed by force, during the year which had elapsed since I spoke with the President at the Washington meeting of the League to Enforce Peace. It also shows conclusively that nearly two years before the League of Nations became a question for action by the Senate, my attitude in regard to it had changed from what it had been in July, 1915, and that I had made the fact of the change known

* I print this address by the President in full in Appendix II, and I also give in Appendix III in full, the speech I made on February 28, 1917, in reply to the President's address.

as publicly as I could in my speech in the Senate in reply to the message of the President.

I return once more to the quotation from my debate with President Lowell, and what I am about to quote is the portion of the speech which I am particularly desirous of preserving because it contains a statement regarding my consultations with Colonel Roosevelt in regard to this momentous subject. That part of my speech is as follows:

"During all this time, I may say, I was in consultation or I was talking with Theodore Roosevelt in regard to it. His position and mine did not then differ.

"On December 21 I made a speech in the Senate in which I discussed the 14 points and some of the momentous questions raised by the proposition for a League of Nations.

"Colonel Roosevelt wrote an article in the Kansas City *Star* upon that speech, approving it and commending it. I read a single paragraph from it:

'Our need is not as great as that of the vast scattered British Empire, for our domains are pretty much in a ring fence. We ought not to undertake the task of policing Europe, Asia and Northern Africa; neither ought we to permit any interference with the Monroe doctrine, or any attempt by Europe or Asia to police America. Mexico is our Balkan Peninsula. Some day we will have to deal with it. All the coasts and islands which in any way approach the Panama Canal must be dealt with by this nation, and by this nation in accordance with the Monroe doctrine.'

"On January 3 of the present year—the Friday before his death—he dictated another editorial which appeared in the Kansas City *Star* after his death. I wish time would permit me to read it all, but I will read only one paragraph:

'. . . Let each nation reserve to itself and for its own decision, and let it clearly set forth, questions which are nonjusticiable. . . . Finally, make it perfectly clear that we do not intend to take a position of an international Meddlesome Mattie. The American people do not wish to go into an overseas war unless for a very great cause, and where the issue is absolutely plain. Therefore, we do not wish to undertake the responsibility of sending our gallant young men to die in obscure fights in the Balkans or in Central Europe, or in a war we do not approve of. Moreover, the American people do not intend to give up the Monroe doctrine. Let civilized Europe and Asia introduce some kind of police system in the weak and disorderly countries at their thresholds. But let the United States treat Mexico as our Balkan Peninsula and refuse to allow European or Asiatic powers to interfere on this continent in any way that implies permanent or semi-permanent possession. Every one of our Allies will with delight grant this request if President Wilson chooses to make it, and it will be a great misfortune if it is not made.'

"Two weeks before his death I was with Theodore Roosevelt for some hours, seeing him for two mornings in succession. The draft of the covenant of the League of Nations now before the country was not then before us, but we discussed fully the League of Nations in all its bearings. We were in entire agreement.

"The position that I have taken, and now take, had his full approval. The line I have followed in the Senate and elsewhere was the one he wished to have followed. I do not say this to transfer any responsibility from my shoulders to his. All I do and all I say is on my own responsibility alone. But it is a help and a strength to me to feel that I have behind me the approval, the support of the great American, the great patriot, the great man whose death has been such a grievous loss, not only to the United States, but to the entire world in this hour."

This seems to be the point where I ought properly to insert a brief statement which I made on the floor of the Senate on the question of my inconsistency. I had grown rather weary of the continual repetition by my opponents who, lacking arguments on the merits of their

own proposition, thought it was important to show that
I had been inconsistent in my views, and it seemed to
me desirable to answer this reiteration of my speech at
Union College in 1915 once for all. I need hardly repeat
what everyone knows, that personal inconsistency on a
political question has no bearing on the merits of the
question, or that without changes of opinion, without
the ability of men to learn and to take up new views,
the world would stagnate because every advance in any
realm of thought or activity necessarily involves some inconsistency with the past. Inconsistency as a reproach
has no force whatever unless it is so constant and so frequent as to indicate that the man responsible for the inconsistencies has no stability and is ready to shift his
opinions at any moment to serve some immediate or personal end. So much by way of preface. On the 16th of
September, 1919, I made a speech in the Senate, of
which I give the following extract:

"The mere fact that a man happens to have changed
his mind, if he has changed it, does not bear on the merits
of any question; and even if a man happens to be a
convert, some good work has been done by converts from
the days of St. Paul to the present time.

"Mr. President, the President of the United States has
now seen fit to refer to the speech that I made in 1915,
and as he has done that, I think perhaps it is worth while
for me to say a little about it.

"On May 6, 1914, at the unveiling of the Barry monu-
ment in Washington, President Wilson said:

'There are just as vital things stirring now that concern the existence of the nation as were stirring then,
and every man who worthily stands in the presence
should examine himself and see whether he has the full
conception of what it means that America should live
her own life. Washington saw it when he wrote his
Farewell address. It was not merely because of passing and transient circumstances that Washington said
that we must keep from entangling alliances.'

"I pause a moment to say that Washington did not say that we should keep clear from 'entangling alliances' in the Farewell Address. He said that we should keep clear of *permanent alliances,* and that temporary alliances would be sufficient to meet an emergency—as they were in the war just closed.

"I merely mention this because the phrase 'entangling alliances,' which is so familiar to the country, was the utterance of Thomas Jefferson in his first inaugural. He warned us against 'entangling alliances.' He too, like Washington, I know is considered antiquated by many people. I merely recall it for the benefit of Jeffersonian Democrats, if any still survive.

"In Washington, on January 6, 1916, addressing the Pan American Congress, President Wilson said:

'The Monroe Doctrine was proclaimed by the United States on her own authority. It always has been maintained and always will be maintained upon her own responsibility.'

"I think I am not to blame for wishing it to be maintained now.

"That is what I said then, but I think perhaps if we are investigating inconsistencies I will go a little further to-day. In a speech at Shadow Lawn September 30, 1916, the President said:

'The certain prospect of the success of the Republican party is that we shall be drawn in one form or another into the embroilments of the European war.'

"I now quote from the interview at the White House on August 19, 1919:

Senator McCumber. 'Would our moral conviction of the unrighteousness of the German war have brought us into this war if Germany had not committed any acts against us without the league of nations, as we had no league of nations at that time?

The President. 'I hope it would eventually, Senator, as things developed.

Senator McCumber. 'Do you think that if Germany had committed no act of war or no act of injustice against our citizens that we would have gotten into this war?

The PRESIDENT. 'I do think so.

Senator McCUMBER. 'You think we would have gotten in anyway?

The PRESIDENT. 'I do.'

"On the 19th of August, 1914, the President said:

'The United States must be neutral in fact as well as in name during these days that are to try men's souls. We must be impartial in thought as well as in action, must put a curb upon our sentiments as well as upon every transaction that might be construed as a preference of one party to the struggle before another.'

"When we entered the war, on the 6th of April, 1917, evidently the President had seen reason to change his mind—very fortunately, as I think, and greatly to his credit. But if we are looking for inconsistencies they can be found even in the greatest men.

'The Great War—

"He said again in an address before the League to Enforce Peace, at Washington, May 27, 1916—

'The Great War, that broke so suddenly upon the world two years ago, and which has swept within its flame so great a part of the civilized world, has affected us very profoundly, and we are not only at liberty, it is, perhaps, our duty, to speak very frankly of it and of the great interests of civilization which it affects. 'With its causes and its objects we are not concerned. The obscure fountains from which its stupendous flood has burst forth we are not interested to search for or explore.'

"On the 19th of August, 1919, he stated to the committee, as I have just read, that we should have gone into the war anyway even if Germany had not committed acts which required us to go into the war. Again, I think, I may have pointed out certain inconsistencies.

"He then said in his speech at Des Moines on February 1, 1916:

'There are actually men in America who are preaching war, who are preaching the duty of the United States to do what it never would before, seek entanglements in the controversies which have arisen on the other side of the water—abandon its habitual and traditional policy and deliberately engage in the conflict which is now engulfing the rest of the world. I do not know what the standard of citizenship of these gentlemen may be. I only know that I for one cannot subscribe to those standards.'

"And yet today he is urging upon us a treaty which involves our entanglement in every European broil that comes up.

"He said, at Kansas City, on February 2, 1916:

'It would tear the heartstrings of America to be at war with any of the great nations of the world. We can show our friendship for the world and our devotion to the principles of humanity better and more effectively by keeping out of this struggle than by getting into it.'

"Subsequently we got into it. Now we are preparing to get into some more, as I think.

'We have been neutral—
"He said in the speech accepting renomination—
'We have been neutral not only because it was the fixed and traditional policy of the United States to stand aloof from the politics of Europe * * * but because it was manifestly our duty to prevent if it were possible, the extension of the fires of hate and desolation kindled by that terrible conflict.'

"That was on the 2d of September, 1916, and the following April we were at war. He said in Chicago on the 31st of January, 1916:

'I believe that we can serve the nations at war better by remaining at peace and holding off from this contest than we could possibly serve them in any other way. Your interest, your sympathy, your affection may be engaged on one side or the other, but it is your duty to stand off and not let this Nation be drawn into the war.'

"That was on the 31st of January, 1916, and in April, 1917, a little over a year later, we were at war, justly, rightly, and I commended his doing it; I do not criticize him because he was inconsistent, but he was inconsistent a year later.

"In the first *Lusitania* note of May 10, 1915, he said:

'Long acquainted as this Government has been with the character of the Imperial German Government and with the high principles of equity by which they have in the past been actuated and guided, the Government of the United States cannot believe that the commanders of the vessels which committed these acts of lawlessness did so except under a misapprehension of the orders issued by the Imperial German naval authorities.'

"He then said on May 10, 1915:

'The example of America must be a special example. The example of America must be the example of peace, not merely because it will not fight, but of peace because peace is the healing and the elevating influence of the world and strife is not. There is such a thing as a man being too proud to fight.'

"On October 14, 1915, he said:

'America stands apart in its ideals; it ought not to allow itself to be drawn, as far as its heart is concerned, into anybody's quarrel.'

"We went to war in April, 1917, and now we are making a treaty which involves us, by its terms, in literally everybody's quarrels for an indefinite future.

"On the 24th of October, 1918, he said:

'If you have approved of my leadership and wish me to continue to be your unembarrassed spokesman at home and abroad, I earnestly beg that you will ex-

press yourself unmistakably to that effect by returning a Democratic majority in both the Senate and the
House of Representatives.'

"I do not charge him with any inconsistency there.
That was simply a misapprehension and a misfortune—
a misfortune for him in making the appeal.

"On May 17, 1916, he said:

'Since the rest of the world is mad, why should we
not refuse to have anything to do with the rest of the
world in the ordinary channels of action?'

"Today we are supposed to have the ordinary channels
of action. Peace has come. He thought the rest of the
world was mad, but now he does not seem to be in favor
of having nothing to do with the rest of the world in
the ordinary channels of action. We are told that all
the hope of humanity is there.

"On December 8, 1914, he said:

'More than this, proposed at this time, permit me to
say, would mean merely that we had lost our self-pos-
session; that we had been thrown off our balance by
a war with which we have nothing to do, whose causes
cannot touch us.'

"I do not say whether he was right or wrong. This is
not the time to debate merits or demerits. I merely want
to point out that when we come to inconsistencies, they
can be found in many places.

"On July 23, 1915, he said:

'The Government of the United States and the Imperial German Government are contending for the
same great object; have long stood together in urging
the very principles upon which the Government of the
United States now so solemnly insists. They both are
contending for the freedom of the seas.'

"At that time we were contending for the same principle for which Germany was contending, and the principle for which she was contending at sea was the sub-

marine and the mine and interference with every form of neutral commerce. I have found nothing that contradicts that statement; it has never apparently been changed; but the freedom of the seas has gone with much else in the Paris treaty—well gone, I think, for it was a German freedom of the seas for which the President was then standing.

"On February 3, 1916, the President said:

'We believe that we can show our friendship for the world and our devotion for the purposes of humanity better by keeping out of this trouble than by getting into it.'

"On January 25, 1919, he said:

'This was a war not only to redeem France from an enemy but to redeem the world from an enemy.'

"In 1916 he thought to show our devotion to the world we ought at all hazards to keep out of the war then raging, but in 1919 he thought we were wise and that it was right that we should go in to redeem France and to defeat Germany. I think his second opinion was correct, and I am glad he changed his first opinion.

"On February 3, 1916, he said:

'I have no indictment against any form of government.'

"And on June 14, 1917, he said:

'They [the German Empire] impudently denied us the use of the high seas and repeatedly exercised the threat that they would send to their death any of our people who ventured to approach the coasts of Europe * * * This flag under which we serve would have been dishonored had we withheld our hand.'

"I think that is a very good imitation of an indictment against a certain form of government. I sympathized with the indictment but not with the refusal to indict.

On December 20, 1916, the President said:

'I take the liberty of calling attention to the fact that the objects of the statesmen of the belligerents on both sides are virtually the same as stated to their own people and to the world.'

"On April 1, 1917, speaking of the German war, he said:

'It is a war against all nations * * * The challenge is to all mankind.'

"On the next day he said:

'The world must be made safe for democracy. Its peace must be planted upon the tested foundations of political liberty.'

"Again an inconsistency. I think the second decision was right, and it would have been unfortunate if the President had not changed his mind. On April 2, 1917, the President also said:

'We do not wish to fight her [Germany] either with arms or hostile arrangements of trade, if she is willing to associate herself with us and other peace-loving nations of the world in the covenants of justice and fair dealing. We wish her only to accept a place of equality among the peoples of the world—the new world in which we live—instead of a place of mastery.'

"On December 4, 1917, he said:

'This intolerable thing of which the masters of Germany have shown us the ugly face, this menace of combined intrigue and force, which we now see clearly as the German power * * *.'

"Mr. President, I have merely introduced a few quotations. I could go on at great length piling up contradictions as to other matters, but I do not think the fact that the President has changed his mind in regard to the war in Europe, in regard to entangling alliances, and in regard to our mixing in the broils of Europe has any relation whatever to the merits of the case. I never should have thought of citing these instances if the President had not become distressed by inconsistencies.

"Mr. President, in conclusion I wish to read just a few words from the close of the speech to which I have re-

ferred, and which was delivered by me in the Senate
on Thursday, February 1, 1917:

'As an example of what I mean, let me call your attention to the resolution offered by the Senator from
Idaho. It meets with my full approval at the present
time, for I now see in this tortured and distracted
world nothing but peril in abandoning our long and
well-established policies, which have behind them not
only the authority of Washington and Jefferson and
Adams and Monroe, but a long acceptance by the
American people. Let it not be forgotten that if we
pass that resolution we close the door for the time being, so far as the Senate is concerned, upon a proposition that we should join a league for peace backed by
the organized major force of mankind.'

"That was the President's proposition.

'This resolution commits us without reserve to the
policy, in regard to foreign nations, of Washington,
Monroe, and Jefferson, whose statements are as clear
as the unclouded sun at noonday, and are not collec-
tions of double-meaning words under which men can
hide and say they mean anything or nothing. Let
there be no mistake about what we are doing in this
direction. I would not have our action misunderstood
there any more than I would wish to see a mistake
made if resolutions were adopted in a sense to which
I was opposed. There is no lurking place for a league
for peace "supported by the organized major force of
mankind" in the sentences of George Washington and
Thomas Jefferson set forth in the preamble to which
the resolution of the Senator from Idaho declares our
allegiance.

'This war will end; the passions of mankind will die
down; individual ambitions will vanish with the
evanescent beings who cherish them; but the Republic
and the American people will remain. Let us beware
how we take any steps which may precipitate this
country and the people who are to come after us, and
whose inheritance it is, into dangers which no man
can foresee. We cannot secure our own safety nor

build up the lasting peace of the world upon peace at any price. The peace of the world, to be enduring, must be based on righteousness at any cost.'

"That was the prediction which I made and the position which I ventured to take in February, 1917, before we entered the war. From that position at least I have never swerved. One of the reasons why I object to the provisions of this treaty is that it endangers the sovereignty and the independence of the United States. I think now, as I always have thought and believed, that the United States is the best hope of mankind and will remain so as long as we do not destroy it by mingling in every broil and quarrel that may desolate the earth."

CHAPTER IX

THE LEAGUE OF NATIONS

In the Congress which had gone out of existence on the 4th of March, 1919, some of the essential appropriation bills had failed and it was therefore absolutely necessary to have an extraordinary session of the Congress in order to pass the requisite supply bills before the beginning of the new fiscal year on the 1st of the following July. After some delay the President called the session to meet on May 19, 1919. I returned from Boston toward the end of April. The morning after I arrived Senator Borah came to my house to see me and talk over the course to be pursued in regard to the League of Nations and the Versailles treaty generally. He was the first member of the Senate I saw after my arrival, and I had then talked with no other Senator in regard to the situation. I said to him that in my opinion the first step must be the organization of the Senate, for we had only two majority, but that we were entitled to the control of the Senate and the appointment of committees and that it was very necessary that this matter should be successfully disposed of. With this of course he entirely agreed. I then said to him that I desired his opinion upon the situation as it appeared to me, and that the following conditions, as I saw them, existed. The great mass of the people, the man in the street, to use a common expression, the farmers, the shopkeepers, the men in small business, clerks and the like, in short the people generally, did not understand the treaty at all, had had no opportunity even to read the provisions of the League except in the draft which Mr. Wil-

146

son had brought back when he returned in February, and that knowing nothing about any of the details of the treaty their natural feeling was, "Now the war is over and let us have peace as quickly as possible." The second condition was that, what I may call the vocal classes of the community, most of the clergymen, the preachers of sermons, a large element in the teaching force of the universities, a large proportion of the newspaper editors, and finally the men and women who were in the habit of writing and speaking for publication, although by no means thoroughly informed, were friendly to the League as it stood and were advocating it. With these conditions existing, I said to Senator Borah, it seemed perfectly obvious to me that any attempt to defeat the treaty of Versailles with the League by a straight vote in the Senate, if taken immediately, would be hopeless, even if it were desirable. I said that of course I knew his attitude, that it had been familiar to me for some time and that personally I could not accept the League as it stood under any circumstances, but that I thought the interests and safety of the United States might be so protected by amendments or reservations that a large majority of the Republicans could vote for it. I told him that in any event there was only one thing to do and that was to proceed in the discussion of the treaty by way of amendment and reservation. He told me that he agreed entirely with my description of the situation, that he did not believe the treaty could possibly be beaten at that time by a direct vote, that he was against the treaty in any form whatever, whether with reservations or amendments or not, but that thinking I was right in my judgment of the conditions and the situation generally he would support any amendments or reservations which I and those who agreed with me should offer, although, of course, so far as he was personally concerned, after having voted for the reservations or amendments in the belief that they would make the treaty better and the League safer, on the final vote he would vote against the acceptance of the treaty by the Senate.

I mention this conversation with Senator Borah because I knew him to be not only a man of distinguished ability as a lawyer and as a student of our foreign affairs, but also a debater of the first rank, who had the question very deeply at heart and, I knew, would discuss every phase of it with great power and effect. To find him in agreement with me on the general situation, therefore, confirmed me in the opinions which I had formed as to the proper way of dealing with the treaty when it came before us. This conversation, which was followed by many others with other Senators, gave to the course which I had suggested the assurance of the support of all those Senators who would not under any circumstances vote for the treaty but were willing to acquiesce in perfecting amendments or reservations, and also the support of those who constituted the greater part of the Republican majority in the Senate and were anxious to adopt the treaty if it could be done with safety to the United States.

The treaty, however, was not then before us, and the first problem to be solved was that of organization. When the Republican conference met, I was unanimously chosen chairman of the conference, which under our present practice is equivalent to the floor leadership of the Senate. On the death, in 1918, of Senator Gallinger, who was then the Republican leader, I was chosen unanimously to succeed him as leader of the Minority; therefore, when I was again chosen leader in May, 1919, it was by reelection to the position which I already held. Senator Wadsworth was made Secretary and Senator Curtis, whip and later Vice-chairman, also by unanimous vote.

Then came the choice of a President *pro tempore* and

the election of chairmen of committees after they had
been decided upon by the Committee on Committees
which was to be appointed by the Chairman of the Conference. In regard to the President *pro tempore* and two
or three of the principal chairmanships there was much
controversy, and it took some time to settle the differences. It is not worth while to go over, now, the difficulties and the intricacies of a contest within the Party
for the important positions. There is only one point on
which I wish to say a word here in order to make the
situation clear. We had, as I have already said, only
two majority. A contest had been filed against Senator
Newberry of Michigan, and that contest ultimately developed into a conflict of great bitterness on the floor
of the Senate and in the attack made by the Democrats
upon Senator Newberry, which seemed to me nothing
more than a gross case of persecution and of endless misrepresentations, into which it is not necessary to enter
here. One of these misrepresentations, however, and a
very serious one, which was kept up for several years,
was that we owed our control of the Senate to the vote
of Senator Newberry. This was wholly untrue. In the
first place, Senator Newberry had been elected on the
face of the returns and had received his certificate from
the Governor of Michigan. The practice of both Houses
was well settled, that the Member or the Senator duly
identified who presented a certificate, correct in form and
complying with the law, was to be sworn in as having
the *prima facie* title to his seat whether there was a contest pending against him or not. Under the practice of
the Senate it was impossible to deprive Senator Newberry of his seat and right to vote, because his certificate
was in due form, properly drawn, and signed by the Governor of the State. No attempt indeed was made to prevent his being sworn in. In the second place, there is
another fact to be remembered, which will dispose of an-

other absolute misrepresentation, constantly made, that if Mr. Newberry had not been sworn in we could not have organized the Senate. If the Senate had refused, which they could not have done, to accept the certificate of the Governor of Michigan, and declined to have Mr. Newberry sworn in, we should have been left with 48 Republican Senators and 47 Democratic Senators, giving us a majority of one, which was practically no worse than a majority of two, because with a majority of two, if one Republican Senator had refused to support the Republican organization, that would have tied the vote on organization and the Vice President being a Democrat, would have voted to give the organization to the Democratic Party. A majority of one could have done no less, because if one Republican Senator in that event had refused to sustain the organization we should have been left in a minority by one and the only difference would have been that it would not have been necessary then to use the vote of the Vice President. Moreover, it must not be forgotten that even if the Senate had refused to allow Senator Newberry to take his seat, and no attempt, as I have said, was made to do that—he was sworn in without objection—the seat would have been vacant. Whoever was elected in Michigan it was not Mr. Ford, the Democratic candidate, because he was in the minority in any event and a candidate who has received only a minority vote cannot possibly be sworn in, even if his opponent is unseated, unless fraud is shown or mistakes in the returns which would prove that he really had a majority and was not a minority candidate. Therefore the swearing in of Senator Newberry had no effect whatever upon the power of the Republicans to secure the organization of the Senate, because every Republican, as the result showed, voted for the organization agreed to in the conference. The Republican Conference chose Senator Cummins for president *pro tem-*

pore and nominated their candidates for the Senate offices of Secretary and Sergeant-at-arms, and they were all elected by a solid Republican vote. Later the committees were made up and the committee lists of both parties were agreed upon by the representatives of each party and presented by me, and those were also accepted by the Senate.

This control of the organization of the Senate was, of course, extremely important as an essential step to enable us to conduct the business of the Senate, which we were entitled to do because we had a majority. All that concerns us here, however, is the formation of the Committee on Foreign Relations which, in view of the fact that the treaty of Versailles would come before that Committee for action in a very short time, made the membership of that committee, always of the first rank, of unusual consequence. I shall say nothing, therefore, about the other committees, but the Committee on Foreign Relations was made up as follows:

Republicans: *Lodge of Massachusetts (Chairman)
              *McCumber of North Dakota
              *Borah of Idaho
              *Brandegee of Connecticut
              *Fall of New Mexico
              *Knox of Pennsylvania
              Harding of Ohio
              New of Indiana
              Johnson of California
              Moses of New Hampshire
Democrats: *Hitchcock of Nebraska
              *Williams of Mississippi
              *Swanson of Virginia
              *Pomerene of Ohio
              *Pittman of Nevada
              Smith of Arizona
              Shields of Tennessee

* Those marked with an asterisk were old members. The others were put on in the new Congress.

It will be seen at once that this was a strong committee and such as the existing conditions demanded.

The Treaty of Versailles was signed on June 28, 1919, and at the same time another treaty was signed between France, Great Britain and the United States carrying a guarantee of protection to France if both Great Britain and the United States accepted it and ratified the treaty of Versailles. President Wilson returned at once to the United States after the signature of the treaty and arrived on July 9th. He appeared before the Senate on the 10th of July, made an address and presented the treaty of Versailles.

At this point it seems desirable to state the facts as to the fate of the treaty of guarantee made by Great Britain, the United States and France. In order that the case may be understood I give the text of that treaty, as follows:

"ASSISTANCE TO FRANCE IN THE EVENT OF UNPROVOKED AGGRESSION BY GERMANY

"AGREEMENT BETWEEN THE UNITED STATES AND FRANCE, SIGNED AT VERSAILLES JUNE 28, 1919.

"Whereas the United States of America and the French Republic are equally animated by the desire to maintain the Peace of the World so happily restored by the Treaty of Peace signed at Versailles the 28th day of June, 1919, putting an end to the war begun by the aggression of the German Empire and ended by the defeat of that Power; and,

"Whereas the United States of America and the French Republic are fully persuaded that an unprovoked movement of aggression by Germany against France would not only violate both the letter and the spirit of the

Treaty of Versailles to which the United States of America and the French Republic are parties, thus exposing France anew to the intolerable burdens of an unprovoked war, but that such aggression on the part of Germany would be and is so regarded by the Treaty of Versailles as a hostile act against all the Powers signatory to that Treaty and as calculated to disturb the Peace of the world by involving inevitably and directly the State of Europe and indirectly, as experience has amply and unfortunately demonstrated, the world at large; and,

"Whereas the United States of America and the French Republic fear that the stipulations relating to the left bank of the Rhine contained in said Treaty of Versailles may not at first provide adequate security and protection to France on the one hand and the United States of America as one of the signatories of the Treaty of Versailles on the other;

"Therefore, the United States of America and the French Republic having decided to conclude a treaty to effect these necessary purposes, Woodrow Wilson, President of the United States of America, and Robert Lansing, Secretary of State of the United States, specially authorized thereto by the President of the United States, and Georges Clemenceau, President of the Council, Minister of War, and Stéphen Pichon, Minister of Foreign Affairs, specially authorized thereto by Raymond Poincaré, President of the French Republic, have agreed upon the following articles:

ARTICLE I.

"In case the following stipulations relating to the Left Bank of the Rhine contained in the Treaty of Peace with Germany signed at Versailles the 28th day of June, 1919, by the United States of America, the French Republic and the British Empire among other Powers:

'ARTICLE 42. Germany is forbidden to maintain or construct any fortifications either on the left bank of the Rhine or on the right bank to the west of a line drawn 50 kilometres to the East of the Rhine.

'ARTICLE 43. In the area defined above the maintenance and assembly of armed forces, either permanently or temporarily, and military manœuvres of any kind, as well as the upkeep of all permanent works for mobilization are in the same way forbidden.

'ARTICLE 44. In case Germany violates in any manner whatever the provisions of Articles 42 and 43, she shall be regarded as committing a hostile act against the Powers signatory of the present Treaty and as calculated to disturb the peace of the world.'

may not at first provide adequate security and protection to France, the United States of America shall be bound to come immediately to her assistance in the event of any unprovoked movement of aggression against her being made by Germany.

ARTICLE II.

"The present Treaty, in similar terms with the Treaty of even date for the same purpose concluded between Great Britain and the French Republic, a copy of which Treaty is annexed hereto, will come into force when the latter is ratified.

ARTICLE III.

"The present Treaty must be submitted to the Council of the League of Nations, and must be recognized by the Council, acting if need be by a majority, as an engagement which is consistent with the Covenant of the League. It will continue in force until on the application of one of the Parties to it the Council, acting if need be by a majority, agrees that the League itself affords sufficient protection.

ARTICLE IV.

"The present Treaty will be submitted to the Senate of the United States at the same time as the Treaty of Versailles is submitted to the Senate for its advice and consent to ratification. * It will be submitted before ratification to the French Chamber of Deputies for approval. The ratifications thereof will be exchanged on the deposit of ratifications of the Treaty of Versailles at Paris or as soon thereafter as shall be possible.

"In faith whereof the respective Plenipotentiaries to wit: On the part of the United States of America, Woodrow Wilson, President, and Robert Lansing, Secretary of State, of the United States; and on the part of the French Republic, Georges Clemenceau, President of the Council of Ministers, Minister of War, and Stéphen Pichon, Minister of Foreign Affairs, have signed the above articles both in the English and French languages, and they have hereunto affixed their seals.

"Done in duplicate at the City of Versailles, on the twenty-eighth day of June, in the year of our Lord one thousand nine hundred and nineteen, and the one hundred and forty-third of the Independence of the United States of America.

(SEAL)	WOODROW WILSON.
(SEAL)	ROBERT LANSING.
(SEAL)	G. CLEMENCEAU.
(SEAL)	S. PICHON.

It will be observed that by Article IV of this treaty the President was bound explicitly to present it when he presented the treaty of Versailles. Nothing could be plainer than the language there used and there is no escape from it. It constituted a pledge of action which he, the maker and the signer of the treaty providing for

* The italics are mine.

assistance to France in the event of unprovoked aggression by Germany, could alone fulfill. He failed to do it. He did not present it as he had agreed to do at the time when he presented the treaty of Versailles, and this created much adverse comment which finally found expression on the floor of the Senate. Thereupon the President sent in on July 29th, 19 days after the presentation of the treaty of Versailles, the treaty which gave the guarantee of Great Britain and the United States for the protection of France. This treaty was meant to satisfy France for the refusal of the representatives of the great Powers to give to France, under the treaty of Versailles, the Rhine boundary. The treaty was duly referred to the Committee on Foreign Relations. It was never taken up and never reported out. It would have been quite useless to do so, even if the Committee had favored it, for I do not think there was the slightest chance that the Senate would ever have voted to accept it. There was no desire on the part of Senators of either Party at that stage to bind the United States irrevocably with agreements to go to war again under certain prescribed conditions.

Before describing the work of the Committee upon the treaty of Versailles and the covenant of the League of Nations, there are certain points which I think should be covered in regard to the President's action during the time when the treaty was in Committee and being there discussed. President Wilson was informed by leaders of his own Party, when he returned in July, that it would not be possible to pass the treaty through the Senate without some reservations and he was advised that it would be well for him to see me and one or two others of the leaders on the Republican side and find out whether some agreement could not be reached as to reservations which would secure the passage of the treaty. This, as I was told by members of his own Party who talked with him, he absolutely declined to do. He was determined then and always, as he had publicly announced at Boston, that the treaty must be passed just as it stood; in short, he intended to have the treaty agreed to exactly as he brought it home, without any change whatever. He could not fail to see, however, that in order to secure the passage of the treaty in the Senate, he must have Republican votes, because a two-thirds vote was necessary and his party was in a minority and not completely united. He therefore undertook to secure Republican votes by sending for Republican Senators individually and trying to persuade them to vote for the treaty as it stood. It was publicly stated that he had sent for the following Senators:

McCumber of North Dakota
Colt of Rhode Island
Nelson of Minnesota
Kenyon of Iowa
Kellogg of Minnesota
Capper of Kansas
McNary of Oregon
Page of Vermont
Sterling of South Dakota
McLean of Connecticut
Newberry of Michigan
Dillingham of Vermont
Fernald of Maine
Harding of Ohio
Lenroot of Wisconsin

I cannot say of my own knowledge that there were not others asked but those fifteen certainly were invited to the White House and there may have been a few more. In a general way it may be said that he received but one reply from the Republican Senators and that was that the treaty could not possibly pass without some reservations. The Senators who saw him in this way differed somewhat in their attitude as to what reservations were necessary, but the general statement to him was that it was hopeless to try to pass the treaty as it stood. I talked with some of the Senators who saw him and among them, as I remember very distinctly were: Senators Kenyon, Kellogg, Fernald, Dillingham, McCumber and Colt. I may have talked with others whom I do not now recall. As I have already said, these Senators differed in their views as to reservations, varying from Senator McCumber, who was ready to vote for the treaty in any event, no matter what reservations were put on, to those like Senator Fernald who would not vote for the treaty on any terms; but they all alike told the President that the treaty could not possibly go through without some reservations. These Senators also told me that the President manifested a great deal of feeling, said, what was quite true, that it was not a Party question and insisted that it was their duty to vote for the treaty just as he had presented it to the Senate.

The next and only remaining occasion when the President came in direct contact with Republican Senators was on August 19, 1919. The Committee on Foreign Relations had found great difficulty in getting any information as to the making of the treaty, the subjects discussed in Paris and the intent of the various provisions of the League of Nations agreed to by the signatories. They therefore instructed me to ask the President whether he would receive the committee. He replied in the affirmative, appointed the day and invited the committee to lunch with him after the conversation had been held. On that day all the members of the committee were present except Senator Shields. The conversation lasted for nearly three hours. Everything that was said was taken in shorthand and subsequently printed and is given as Appendix IV to this statement.

The President was very thoroughly questioned but was not able to give us much information such as we desired on some points, while on others relating to minutes of private conferences of the representatives of the great Powers he declined to furnish us with the reports, as appears in the shorthand notes of our conversation already referred to. He took the questioning, which was rather sharp at times, in good part, although at the end of the session when we went in to luncheon he seemed very much fatigued. It will not be necessary for me to say more here as to this meeting because all that transpired at the White House is given in the full report printed in the Appendix which I have just mentioned.

Having failed in securing any Republican votes on the terms and conditions which he desired, President Wilson then made up his mind to appeal to the country, and on September 3, 1919, he started on his journey across the Continent and began a series of speeches at Indianapolis, going from there westward and intending to return from the Coast by the southern route, in this way covering the Republican States of the North, the West and the Southwest. It became very obvious as the President proceeded that he was not meeting with the reception which he expected or awakening the enthusiasm for the League which he anticipated. As a whole the meetings and the events of the trip were disappointing. It was also apparent as the journey proceeded that the President was suffering from the strain, and was becoming not only weary but very nervous and excitable. He made his last speech at Pueblo, and then he broke down and came directly back to Washington where he had, as all know, a very serious illness, keenly regretted by everyone, of which it is not necessary for me to speak here.

Let me return, then, to the story of the treaty itself after it passed into the control of the Senate on the 10th of July.

The treaty of Versailles was printed as quickly as possible. It filled, with the English text alone, 264 quarto pages.

The Committee on Foreign Relations lost no time in taking up the heavy work which lay before it. To print such a document, which was really a volume, as I have just said, took time, but we succeeded in getting the text of the treaty before the Committee on July 14th. It is also to be remembered that the Committee gave public hearings which began on July 31st and necessarily added to the labors of the Committee and consumed many days. It was not possible to avoid those hearings. The treaty touched every country in Europe and also the Far East. American citizens—no others, under the Senate rules, were allowed to appear before the Committee—who came directly or by descent from these many countries affected by the treaty provisions and had an interest in the land of their birth or origin, desired to be heard on particular clauses affecting the various countries involved in the boundary settlements and on other points. Others were anxious to secure the influence of the United States in behalf of the requests of the countries from which they came to appear in Paris before the Conference. It is not necessary now to review these hearings because they are all printed in the proceedings of the Committee and are of value chiefly as showing the wide range of subjects which were forced upon the attention of the Committee and in regard to which they could not avoid giving a hearing to those American citizens who desired to discuss certain phases of the treaty of Versailles. I mention this in order to make complete my statements as to the work in which the Committee on Foreign Relations was engaged and to give some idea of its large extent, unavoidable owing to the character of the sweeping and elaborate provisions of the Versailles treaty. The Committee, apart from the hearings, devoted all its time to dealing with the treaty itself.

Amendments were first proposed to the text of the treaty. These amendments were as follows:

1st, an amendment to Article 3 of the League, defining the organization and vote of the Assembly, where it was proposed to add the following proviso:

"Provided, That when any member of the League has or possesses self-governing dominions or colonies or parts of empire, which are also members of the League, the United States shall have votes in the assembly or council of the League numerically equal to the aggregate vote of such member of the League and its self-governing dominions and colonies and parts of empire in the council or assembly of the League."

2d, an amendment to Article 15 of the League, defining the powers and duties of the Council, where the following was proposed:

"Whenever the case referred to the Assembly involves a dispute between one member of the League and another member whose self-governing dominions or colonies or parts of empire are also represented in the Assembly, neither the disputant members nor any of their said dominions, colonies or parts of empire shall have a vote upon any phase of the question."

Forty amendments were submitted proposing to strike out, in the phrase "Principal Allied and Associated Powers" wherever it appeared in articles of the treaty establishing commissions or defining their powers or duties, the words "and Associated," thus relieving the United States from having representatives on the commissions established by the League, with one exception. This exception was with regard to the Reparations Commission, fully defined in clause 2 of Annex II of the treaty, where it was proposed to add the following amendment:

"The Delegate of the United States shall have no vote in the proceedings of the Commission except concerning a matter wherein such Delegate is specifically instructed by his Government to take part in proceedings of the Commission and to cast and record the vote of the United States thereupon; but shall always have such right when Annex 3 to the reparation clauses or any section thereof is under consideration."

Six other amendments were submitted, designed, by substituting the word "China" for the word "Japan" in Articles 156, 157 and 158 of the treaty, to restore to China the rights renounced by Germany in the Province of Shantung.

These amendments which I have enumerated were, after much discussion, all adopted by the Foreign Relations Committee. They were supported by all the Republican members of the committee with the single exception of Senator McCumber, who, with the solid Democratic membership, voted against them in every case.

After the amendments were disposed of, the Committee then took up the reservations, and these reservations constituted the crucial point in the work of the Committee because there was a group of Senators who took the position that, although favoring certain reservations, they would support no amendments, not even an amendment embodying a proposition which they intended to vote for in the form of a reservation. Their objection was that amendments, if adopted, would require acceptance by all the Powers which were signatories of the treaty, that the representatives of the signatory Powers at the Versailles Conference had already scattered and that much time would be lost if amendments were submitted to them, which would be, as they said, necessary. Personally I never could see the force of this objection because just as much time would have been consumed by the consideration of reservations by each of the

Powers as by the consideration of amendments. Nevertheless, this view was held and therefore it was clear before the treaty was reported back from the Committee that amendments, in all probability, could not be adopted because the Democrats, with few exceptions, were certain to vote against them all, and that proved to be the case when the treaty came before the Senate. Therefore, as I say, the reservations involved the crucial points. In dealing with them and showing, as I intend to do, just what was adopted in the way of reservations, I think for greater clearness and a better understanding of the situation it is necessary to explain the conditions with which I was confronted.

We had in all forty-nine Republican Senators. There were fifteen Republican Senators who were ready to vote for reservations but would not vote for the treaty under any circumstances, whether reservations were adopted or not. They were known as the "irreconcilables." That left thirty-four Republican Senators who were ready to vote for the treaty with reservations, but there was a difference among the thirty-four as to the character of the reservations desired. There were eight or ten Republican Senators who were known as "mild reservationists," but they differed among themselves as to the degree of mildness which they were ready to accept. This situation introduced an element of difficulty and uncertainty in the problem with which I had to deal because I was Chairman of the Foreign Relations Committee as well as leader of the Republican majority. The fifteen irreconcilables could be counted upon to support all reservations; the stronger the reservations were the better they liked them. There were about eighteen Republican Senators who, like myself, were determined to have effective reservations; and then, lastly, there were eight or ten, some of whom were ready to accept the mildest kind of reservations and others who agreed generally with those who might be called the "middle group." It was essential of course from my point of view to secure, if possible, the vote of every Republican Senator for the reservations, and I need not say that under the conditions which I have tried to explain this required some compromises in language and form and a great deal of effort and discussion among ourselves. If I could secure a united Republican vote for reservations, there were three Democratic irreconcilables who could be depended upon to vote for all reservations and one more who generally voted with them. This was sufficient to make the reservations safe if we could secure, as I have said, a united Republican vote. There was another object which I had very much at heart, and that was that if we were successful in putting on reservations we should create a situation where, if the acceptance of the treaty was defeated, the Democratic party, and especially Mr. Wilson's friends, should be responsible for its defeat, and not the opponents of the treaty who were trying to pass it in a form safe for the United States.

With this explanation by way of preface, I will now take up the reservations and show briefly the result of many conferences and much private discussion in framing those reported from the Committee on Foreign Relations which were afterwards adopted by the Senate.

I can most briefly explain the work of the Committee by printing the first report of the treaty made by the Committee by a majority vote on September 10, 1919.

The Committee report explains the difficulties which the Committee had in securing the information which it very properly required. The report also carried with it the amendments which I have already discussed and four proposed reservations, accompanied with the statement that the Committee reserved the right to offer other reservations if they should so determine. The reservations accompanying the report were later modified and ten additional reservations were reported. The Committee report of September 10th discusses the question of the equality of voting, one of the most salient points in the contest over the League of Nations, because that was offered at the time in the form of an amendment. The same may be said of the Shantung question, which was also covered by amendments. None of these, therefore, appeared in the reservations as reported on September 10th, but they took their place among the reservations reported later.

The reservations covered by the report which I wrote as Chairman, and which had the approval of the majority of the Committee, provided for the right of unconditional withdrawal from the League, limited Article 10, reserved to the United States the right to say what questions were within its domestic jurisdiction and, fourth and last, declared that the United States would decline to submit for arbitration any question relating to the Monroe Doctrine. All these points are sufficiently explained in the report, which now follows:

"The treaty of peace with Germany was laid before the Senate by the President on July 10, 1919. Three days were consumed in printing the treaty, which was in two languages and filled 537 quarto pages. The treaty therefore was not in the possession of the Committee for action until July 14, 1919. The report upon the treaty was ordered by the Committee on September 4. Deducting Sundays and a holiday, the treaty has been before the Committee on Foreign Relations for 45 days. The Committee met on 37 of those working days, sitting whenever possible both in the morning and afternoon. The eight working days upon which the Committee did not sit were lost owing to unavoidable delays in securing the presence of witnesses summoned by the Committee. In view of the fact that six months were consumed by the peace conference in making the treaty, in addition to a month of work by the various delegations before the assembling of the conference, the period of six weeks consumed by the Committee in considering it does not seem excessive.

"These facts are mentioned because there has been more or less clamor about delay in the Committee. This demand for speed in the consideration of the most important subject which ever came before the Senate of the United States, involving as it does fundamental changes in the character of our Government and the future of our country for an unlimited period, was largely the work of the administration and its newspaper organs and was so far wholly artificial. Artificial also was the demand for haste disseminated by certain great banking firms which had a direct pecuniary interest in securing an early opportunity to reap the harvest which they expected from the adjustment of the financial obligations of the countries which had been engaged in the war. The third element in the agitation for haste was furnished by the unthinking outcry of many excellent people who desired early action and who, for the most part, had never read the treaty or never got beyond the words 'league of nations,' which they believed to mean the establishment of eternal peace. To yield helplessly to this clamor was impossible for those to whom was entrusted the performance of a solemn public duty.

"The responsibility of the Senate in regard to this treaty is equal to that of the Executive, who, although aided by a force of thirteen hundred assistants, expert and otherwise, consumed six months in making it, and the Senate and its Committee on Foreign Relations cannot dispose of this momentous document with the light-hearted indifference desired by those who were pressing for hasty and thoughtless action upon it. The Committee was also hampered by the impossibility of securing the full information to which they were entitled from those who had conducted the negotiations. The Committee were compelled to get such imperfect information as they secured from press reports, by summoning before them some of the accessible experts who had helped to frame the complicated financial clauses, and certain outside witnesses. As an illustration in a small way of the difficulties in securing information, it may be stated that no provision had been made to supply the Senate with the maps accompanying the treaty, and it was necessary to send to Paris to procure them. The only documents of the many asked for by the Committee which were furnished by the Executive were the American plan for the league of nations submitted to the commission on the league covenant, and the composite draft made by experts of that commission.

"The treaties with Poland and with France as well as the Rhine protocol, all integral parts of the treaty with Germany, were obtained by the Senate, prior to their transmission by the President, from the documents laid before the House of Commons and the Chamber of Deputies early in July by the Prime Ministers of England and France. The records of the peace conference and of the conferences of the representatives of the five great powers were asked for by the Committee and refused by the Executive. The Committee had before them the Secretary of State, who was one of the American delegates and a signer of the treaty, and they also had the privilege of a meeting with the President at the White House which they had themselves requested. The testimony of the Secretary of State and the conversation of the Committee with the President, published in the record of the Committee hearings, have been laid before the country by the press and it is not necessary to say anything further in regard to them because the people themselves know how much information in regard to the treaty was received by the Committee upon those two occasions.

"The character of the clamor for speedy action is well illustrated by the fact that it was directed solely against the Senate of the United States and its Commitee on Foreign Relations. The treaty provides that it shall go into force when ratified by Germany and by three of the principal allied and associated powers, which are the United States, France, Great Britain, Italy and Japan. Great Britain very naturally ratified at once, but no one of the other four has yet acted. Persons afflicted with inquiring minds have wondered not a little that the distressed mourners over delays in the Senate have not also aimed their criticism at the like shortcomings on the part of France, Italy, and Japan, an act of even-handed justice in faultfinding which they have hitherto failed to perform.

"Perhaps it is well also to note and to consider for a moment one of the reasons given for the demand for hasty action, which was to the effect that it was necessary to have prompt ratification in order to renew our trade with Germany, for even the most ardent advocate of unconsidered action was unable to urge that the channels of trade to the allied countries were not open. The emptiness of this particular plea for haste, now rather faded, is shown by the fact that we have been trading with Germany ever since the armistice. Between that event and the end of July we have exported to Germany goods valued at $11,270,624. In the month of June we exported more to Germany than we did to Spain. In July, by orders of the War Trade Board, the provisions of the trading-with-the-enemy act were set aside by the authorization of licenses to trade, and exports to Germany for the month of July amounted to $2,436,742, while those to Austria and Hungary were $1,016,518.

"It is an interesting fact that the exports in June to

Germany, before the relaxation of the trading-with-the-enemy act, were much larger than after that relaxation, brought about by allowing licenses, was ordered, an indication of the undoubted truth that our trade with foreign countries is not affected by the treaty, but is governed by the necessarily reduced purchasing power of all countries in Europe engaged in the war. As a matter of fact, therefore, we are trading with Germany, and it is a mere delusion to say that we cannot trade with Germany until the ratification of the treaty, because in order to do so, we require a new treaty of amity and commerce and the reestablishment of our consular system in that country. The United States, following the usual custom, was represented in Germany by Spain both in the consular and in the diplomatic service, after the outbreak of the war, and we can transact all the business we may desire through the good offices of Spanish consuls until a new consular treaty with Germany has been made.

"Before leaving this subject it may not be amiss to remark that Mr. Lloyd-George has recently made two important speeches expressing grave apprehensions as to the social and political unrest and the economic troubles now prevalent in England. He seems to have failed to point out, however, that the ratification of the covenant of the league of nations by Great Britain had relieved the situation which he had described. He was apparently equally remiss in omitting to suggest that prompt action by the Senate of the United States in adopting the covenant of the league of nations would immediately lower the price of beef.

"In reporting the treaty to the Senate for action the Committee propose certain amendments to the text of the treaty and certain reservations to be attached to the resolution of ratification and made a part of that resolution when it is offered.

"In regard to the amendments generally it should be

stated at the outset that nothing is more groundless than the sedulously cultivated and constantly expressed fear that textual amendments would require a summoning of the peace conference, and thereby cause great delay. There will be no necessity of summoning the peace conference, because it is in session now in Paris, with delegates fully representing all the signatory nations, as it has been for six months, and it seems likely to be in session for six months more. Textual amendments, if made by the Senate, can be considered in Paris at once, and the conference would be at least as usefully employed in that consideration as they now are in dividing and sharing southeastern Europe and Asia Minor, in handing the Greeks of Thrace over to our enemy, Bulgaria, and in trying to force upon the United States the control of Armenia, Anatolia, and Constantinople through the medium of a large American Army. Still more unimportant is the bugbear which has been put forward of the enormous difficulties which will be incurred in securing the adhesion of Germany. No great amount of time need be consumed in bringing German representatives to Paris. The journey is within the power of a moderate amount of human endurance, and it is also to be remembered that Germany is not a member of the league and need not be consulted in regard to the terms of the covenant. When Germany enters the league she will take it as she finds it.

AMENDMENTS

"The first amendment offered by the Committee relates to the league. It is proposed so to amend the text as to secure to the United States a vote in the assembly of the league equal to that of any other power. Great Britain now has under the name of the British Empire one vote in the council of the league. She has four additional votes in the assembly of the league for her self-governing dominions and colonies, which are most properly members of the league and signatories to the treaty. She also has the vote of India, which is neither a self-governing dominion nor a colony but merely a part of the Empire and which apparently was simply put in as a signatory and member of the league by the peace conference because Great Britain desired it. Great Britain also will control the votes of the Kingdom of Hedjaz and of Persia. With these last two of course we have nothing to do. But if Great Britain has six votes in the league assembly no reason has occurred to the Committee and no argument had been made to show why the United States should not have an equal number. If other countries like the present arrangement, that is not our affair; but the Committee failed to see why the United States should have but one vote in the assembly of the league when the British Empire has six.

"Amendments 39 to 44, inclusive, transfer to China the German lease and rights, if they exist, in the Chinese Province of Shantung, which are given by the treaty to Japan. The majority of the Committee were not willing to have their votes recorded at any stage in the proceedings in favor of the consummation of what they consider a great wrong. They can not assent to taking the property of a faithful ally and handing it over to another ally in fulfillment of a bargain made by other powers in a secret treaty. It is a record which they are not willing to present to their fellow citizens or leave behind them for the contemplation of their children.

"Amendment No. 2 is simply to provide that where a member of the league has self-governing dominions and colonies which are also members of the league, the exclusion of the disputants under the league rules shall cover the aggregate vote of the member of the league and its self-governing dominions and parts of empire combined if any one of them is involved in the controversy.

"The remaining amendments, with a single exception, may be treated as one, for the purpose of all alike is to relieve the United States from having representatives on the commissions established by the league which deal with questions in which the United States has and can have no interest and in which the United States has evidently been inserted by design. The exception is amendment No. 45, which provides that the United States shall have a member of the reparation commission but that such commissioner of the United States can not, except in the case of shipping where the interests of the United States are directly involved, deal with or vote upon any other questions before that commission except under instructions from the Government of the United States.

RESERVATIONS

"The Committee proposes four reservations to be made a part of the resolution of ratification when it is offered. The Committee reserves, of course, the right to offer other reservations if they shall so determine. The four reservations now presented are as follows:

'1. The United States reserves to itself the unconditional right to withdraw from the league of nations upon the notice provided in article 1 of said treaty of peace with Germany.'

"The provision in the league covenant for withdrawal declares that any member may withdraw provided it has fulfilled all its international obligations and all its obligations under the covenant. There has been much dispute as to who would decide if the question of the fulfillment of obligations was raised, and it is very generally thought that this question would be settled by the council of the league of nations. The best that can be said about it is that the question of decision is clouded with doubt. On such a point as this there must be no doubt. The United States, which has never broken an international obligation, can not permit all its existing treaties to be reviewed and its conduct and honor questioned by other nations. The same may be said in regard to the fulfillment of the obligations to the league. It must be made perfectly clear that the United States alone is to determine as to the fulfillment of its obligations, and its right of withdrawal must therefore be unconditional as provided in the reservation.

'2. The United States declines to assume, under the provisions of article 10, or under any other article, any obligation to preserve the territorial integrity or political independence of any other country or to interfere in controversies between other nations, members of the league or not, or to employ the military or naval forces of the United States in such controversies, or to adopt economic measures, for the protection of any other country, whether a member of the league or not, against external aggression or for the purpose of coercing any other country, or for the purpose of intervention in the internal conflicts or other controversies which may arise in any other country, and no mandate shall be accepted by the United States under article 22, Part I, of the treaty of peace with Germany except by action of the Congress of the United States.'

"This reservation is intended to meet the most vital objection to the league covenant as it stands. Under no circumstances must there be any legal or moral obligation upon the United States to enter into war or to send its Army and Navy abroad or without the unfettered action of Congress to impose economic boycotts on other countries. Under the Constitution of the United States the Congress alone has the power to declare war, and all bills to raise revenue or affecting the revenue in any way must originate in the House of Representatives, be passed by the Senate, and receive the signature of the President. These constitutional rights of Congress must not be impaired by any agreements such as are presented in this treaty, nor can any opportunity of charging the United States with bad faith be permitted. No American soldiers or sailors must be sent to fight in other lands at the bidding of a league of nations. American lives must not be sacrificed except by the will and command of the American people acting through their constitutional representatives in Congress.

"This reservation also covers the subject of mandates. According to the provisions of the covenant of the league the acceptance of a mandate by any member is voluntary, but as to who shall have authority to refuse or to accept a mandate for any country the covenant of the league is silent. The decision as to accepting a mandate must rest exclusively within the control of the Congress of the United States as the reservation provides and must not be delegated, even by inference, to any personal agent or to any delegate or commissioner.

'3. The United States reserves to itself exclusively the right to decide what questions are within its domestic jurisdiction, and declares that all domestic and political questions relating to its affairs, including immigration, coastwise traffic, the tariff, commerce, and all other domestic questions, are solely within the jurisdiction of the United States and are not under this treaty submitted in any way either to arbitration or to the consideration of the council or of the assembly of the league of nations, or to the decision or recommendation of any other power.'

"This reservation speaks for itself. It is not necessary to follow out here all tortuous windings, which to those who have followed them through the labyrinth disclose the fact that the league under certain conditions will have power to pass upon and decide questions of immigration and tariff, as well as the others mentioned in the reservation. It is believed by the committee that this reservation relieves the United States from any dangers or any obligations in this direction.

"The fourth and last reservation is as follows:

'4. The United States declines to submit for arbitration or inquiry by the assembly or the council of the league of nations provided for in said treaty of peace any questions which in the judgment of the United States depend upon or relate to its long-established policy, commonly known as the Monroe doctrine; said doctrine is to be interpreted by the United States alone, and is hereby declared to be wholly outside the jurisdiction of said league of nations and entirely unaffected by any provision contained in the said treaty of peace with Germany.'

"The purpose of this reservation is clear. It is intended to preserve the Monroe doctrine from any interference or interpretation by foreign powers. As the Monroe doctrine has protected the United States, so, it is believed by the Committee, will this reservation protect the Monroe doctrine from the destruction with which it is threatened by article 21 in the covenant of the league and leave it, where it has always been, within the sole and complete control of the United States.

"This covenant of the league of nations is an alliance and not a league, as is amply shown by the provisions of the treaty with Germany which vests all essential power in five great nations. Those same nations, the principal allied and associated powers, also dominate the league through the council.

"The Committee believe that the league as it stands will breed wars instead of securing peace. They also believe that the covenant of the league demands sacrifices of American independence and sovereignty which would in no way promote the world's peace but which are fraught with the gravest dangers to the future safety and well being of the United States. The amendments and reservations alike are governed by a single purpose and that is to guard American rights and American sovereignty, the invasion of which would stimulate breaches of faith, encourage conflicts, and generate wars. The United States can serve the cause of peace best, as she has served it in the past, and do more to secure liberty and civilization throughout the world by proceeding along the paths she has always followed and by not permitting herself to be fettered by the dictates of other nations or immersed and entangled in all the broils and conflicts of Europe.

"We have heard it frequently said that the United States 'must' do this and do that in regard to this league of nations and the terms of the German peace. There is no 'must' about it. 'Must' is not a word to be used by foreign nations or domestic officials to the American people or their representatives. Equally unfitting is the attempt to frighten the unthinking by suggesting that if the Senate adopts amendments or reservations the United States may be excluded from the league. That is the one thing that certainly will not happen. The other nations know well that there is no threat of retaliation possible with the United States because we have asked nothing for ourselves and have received nothing. We seek no guarantees, no territory, no commercial benefits or advantages. The other nations will take us on our own terms, for without us their league is a wreck and all their gains from a victorious peace are imperiled. We exact nothing selfish for ourselves, but we insist that we shall be the judges, and the only judges, as to the preservation of our rights, our sovereignty, our safety, and our independence.

"At this moment the United States is free from any entanglements or obligations which legally or in the name of honor would compel her to do anything contrary to the dictates of conscience or to the freedom and the interests of the American people. This is the hour when we can say precisely what we will do and exactly what we will not do, and no man can ever question our good faith if we speak now. When we are once caught in the meshes of a treaty of alliance or a league of nations composed of 26 other powers our freedom of action is gone. To preserve American independence and American sovereignty and thereby best serve the welfare of mankind the Committee propose these amendments and reservations."

CHAPTER X

THE LEAGUE IN THE SENATE—THE VOTES AND THE DEBATE

THE President, as I have already said, started on his tour through the country on the 3d of September. On September 10th the report of the Foreign Relations Committee was presented to the Senate, together with the amendments to the treaty agreed to by the Committee, and four reservations. For the reasons I have already given, the amendments were rejected in the Senate, as a sufficient number of Republicans believed that amendments would delay the adoption of the treaty by the other signatories. It is only necessary to give here the votes on the amendments offered by Senator Moses and Senator Johnson of California, on one of the amendments offered by Senator Fall (because the other Fall amendments were practically identical), and on the amendments which I offered in regard to Shantung. The debate, which went on steadily from day to day, although the amendments were first before the Senate, covered both amendments and reservations and the entire general question of the treaty and the covenant of the League of Nations. I think I can say, what I believe was generally admitted, that the debate which ensued was one of the most remarkable, if not the most remarkable, which had ever occurred in the Senate of the United States. Very great ability was shown in the discussion, and I think I can assert now without partiality that those who opposed the treaty and those who favored reservations and would not vote for the treaty without them, were far the stronger side. Of course this opinion has nothing whatever to do with the merits of the question. I am referring now only to the merits of the debate as a debate. The weight of ability and knowledge rested decidedly with those who were opponents of the treaty, whether "irreconcilables" or reservationists. The support given to the treaty and to Mr. Wilson's position was, in the field of debate, as a whole ineffective and weak. The proof of what I say is shown by the steady advance of opposition to the League of Nations as presented by Mr. Wilson, among the mass of the American people. That opposition became stronger day by day as, owing to the debate, the average American came to understand the questions to be decided and especially the leading issues involved in Article X, the equality of voting, the Monroe Doctrine and Shantung. The votes on the amendments to which I have referred were as follows:

The amendment of Senator Johnson of California, providing for equality of voting in the council and the assembly of the League, was defeated on October 27th by a vote of 38 to 40. Eight Republican Senators voted against the amendment and three Democratic Senators voted or were paired in favor of it.

The amendment of Senator Moses was voted upon on October 27th and was defeated by a vote of 32 to 49. That amendment also dealt with the question of equality of voting. Ten Republican Senators voted or were paired against the amendment and three Democratic Senators supported it.

The committee amendments, six in number, which proposed to restore to China the rights renounced by Germany in favor of Japan, were all defeated on October 16th by a vote of 35 to 55. Three Democratic Senators voted for the amendments and 15 Republicans voted or were paired against them.

The series of amendments proposed by Senator Fall and reported by the committee were voted upon on

October 2d. Their purpose was, as has been said, to relieve the United States from representation on the various commissions established by the League. A record vote was taken on three of these amendments and they were defeated by large majorities, the first by 30 to 58, one Democratic Senator supporting it and 16 Republican Senators voting against it. The other two amendments were also defeated by practically a similar vote and at the suggestion of Senator Fall the remaining amendments of the series were acted upon by a *viva voce* vote and were all defeated.

Then on the 6th of November I reported from the Committee the resolution of ratification, which contained some very important clauses not usual in resolutions of ratification, and fourteen reservations which included the four that were recommended in the report of September 10th.

I shall now review those reservations one by one and show the votes, because the votes are very important for a just understanding of the position of the Senate as opposed to that of the President.

The first action taken was in connection with an amendment to the text of the resolution of ratification. That amendment was to insert the following:

"1. The reservations adopted are hereby made a part and condition of this resolution of ratification, which ratification is not to take effect or bind the United States until the said reservations and understandings adopted by the Senate have been accepted by an exchange of notes as a part and a condition of this resolution of ratification by at least three of the four principal Allied and Associated Powers, to wit, Great Britain, France, Italy, and Japan."

To this proposal many amendments were offered, but they were all voted down by varying votes, the highest being 63 against to 25 in favor, the lowest being 46 against to 42 in favor. After the rejection of all the amendments offered to this provision it was adopted on November 7th as reported by the committee, the vote being 48 to 40, one Republican, Senator McCumber, voting against the committee recommendation and four Democrats voting or being paired in favor of it.

The first reservation voted upon was that dealing with the question of withdrawal from the League.

The last clause of Article 1 of the covenant of the League of Nations provided that "Any member of the League may, after two years' notice of its intention so to do, withdraw from the League, provided that all its international obligations and all its obligations under this covenant have been fulfilled at the time of its withdrawal."

The committee report, already given, makes the following statement:

"The provision in the league covenant for withdrawal declares that any member may withdraw provided it has fulfilled all its international obligations and all its obligations under the covenant. There has been much dispute as to who would decide if the question of the fulfillment of obligations was raised, and it is very generally thought that this question would be settled by the council of the league of nations. The best that can be said about it is that the question of decision is clouded with doubt. On such a point as this there must be no doubt. The United States, which has never broken an international obligation, can not permit all its existing treaties to be reviewed and its conduct and honor questioned by other nations. The same may be said in regard to the fulfillment of the obligations to the league. It must be made perfectly clear that the United States alone is to determine as to the fulfillment of its obligations, and its right of withdrawal must therefore be unconditional as provided in the reservation."

This gives the reason for the reservation reported to the Senate, which was as follows:

"2. The United States so understands and construes Article 1 that in case of notice of withdrawal from the league of nations, as provided in said article, the United States shall be the sole judge as to whether all its international obligations and all its obligations under the said covenant have been fulfilled, and notice of withdrawal by the United States may be given by a concurrent resolution of the Congress of the United States."

Several amendments to the reservation were voted down and then on the adoption of the amendment as reported by the Committee the vote was 50 yeas and 35 nays. Five Democrats were paired or voted for the reservation and all the Republicans voted in favor of it.

The next reservation dealt with the famous article 10, which was the provision of the League of Nations upon which the controversy centered more than upon any other. This article as it stands in the treaty, in the League covenant, is as follows:

"The Members of the League undertake to respect and preserve as against external aggression the territorial integrity and existing political independence of all Members of the League. In case of any such aggression or in case of any threat or danger of such aggression the Council shall advise upon the means by which this obligation shall be fulfilled."

It would require a volume to give even an abstract of the discussion which arose over Article 10 and the reservation made to it by the Senate. The statement in the Committee report alluded to this reservation as follows:

"This reservation is intended to meet the most vital objection to the league covenant as it stands. Under no circumstances must there be any legal or moral obligation upon the United States to enter into war or to send its Army and Navy abroad or without the unfettered action of Congress to impose economic boycotts on other

countries. Under the Constitution of the United States
the Congress alone has the power to declare war, and all
bills to raise revenue or affecting the revenue in any way
must originate in the House of Representatives, be passed
by the Senate, and receive the signature of the President.
These constitutional rights of Congress must not be impaired by any agreements such as are presented in this
treaty, nor can any opportunity of charging the United
States with bad faith be permitted. No American
soldiers or sailors must be sent to fight in other lands at
the bidding of a league of nations. American lives must
not be sacrificed except by the will and command of the
American people acting through their constitutional representatives in Congress."

In a general way this statement in the report sums up
the objections to Article 10 as presented by Mr. Wilson,
and from the beginning there was no doubt that a majority of the Senate would not accept Article 10 as it
stood; but there was a long and protracted discussion
outside the Senate among individual Senators in order
to secure a reservation which would command the vote
of all those opposed to the Article. I personally went
over this reservation to Article 10 again and again with
groups of Senators and with individual members. Finally
I asked Senator McCumber, who, in order to secure the
ratification of the treaty was ready to go further toward
the acceptance of the various provisions of the League
Covenant than any other Republican Senator, to come to
my house and lunch with me alone. At that time we took
up the reservation which had been already brought to a
point where I thought I could secure all the Republican
votes for it if I could get the assent of Senator McCumber.
After much discussion he and I agreed upon the reservation in the form in which it was presented to the Senate
and finally adopted. The reservation was as follows:

"3. The United States assumes no obligation to preserve the territorial integrity or political independence of any other country or to interfere in controversies between nations—whether members of the league or not—under the provisions of Article 10, or to employ the military or naval forces of the United States under any article of the treaty for any purpose, unless in any particular case the Congress, which, under the Constitution, has the sole power to declare war or authorize the employment of the military or naval forces of the United States, shall by act or joint resolution so provide."

In some way the draft of the reservation agreed to by Senator McCumber and by me reached President Wilson who read it at a meeting at Salt Lake City on September 23d, 1919. He then said:

"That is a rejection of the covenant. That is an absolute refusal to carry any part of the same responsibility that the other members of the League carry. This [Article 10] is the heart of the covenant."

Such extreme, almost violent, feeling on the part of the President in regard to Article 10 was due in large part, if not entirely, to the fact that this Article, which was the storm center of the debate and did more than all other provisions put together to defeat the treaty, was President Wilson's own work. In reply to a question at the meeting at the White House on August 19, 1919, on being asked by Senator Brandegee "who was the author of Article 10?", Mr. Wilson replied, "I suppose I was as much as anybody." In his opening statement on the same occasion he said, "Article 10 seems to me to constitute the very backbone of the whole Covenant." In the Bullitt testimony the original American draft of the Covenant appears with Article 10 corrected in the President's own handwriting. In this Article, therefore, in addition to the general determination to insist on the entire Covenant as he brought it to Washington, was the pride of authorship attached to this single clause which made any change in it peculiarly unacceptable to a man of Mr. Wilson's temperament.

Therefore when we came to the final vote on this reservation on the 13th of November the line was sharply drawn, and it was really the test vote on the adoption of what was known as the "Lodge reservations." The reservation was carried by a vote of 46 to 33. Every Republican Senator and five Democrats voted or were paired in favor of the reservation.

Reservation No. 4 was the reservation in regard to mandates, which in the report of the committee was included with Reservation No. 3 covering Article 10. It now appeared as a separate reservation and read as follows:

"No mandate shall be accepted by the United States under Article 22, Part I, or any other provision of the treaty of peace with Germany, except by action of the Congress of the United States."

This reservation was agreed to on November 15th, after the adoption of the clôture rule, without objection or a record vote.

Reservation No. 5, prepared, as I recall, by Senator Kellogg, was as follows:

"The United States reserves to itself exclusively the right to decide what questions are within its domestic jurisdiction and declares that all domestic and political questions relating wholly or in part to its internal affairs, including immigration, labor, coastwise traffic, the tariff, commerce, the suppression of traffic in women and children and in opium and other dangerous drugs, and all other domestic questions, are solely within the jurisdiction of the United States and are not under this treaty to be submitted in any way either to arbitration or to the consideration of the council or of the assembly of the league of nations, or any agency thereof, or to the decision or recommendation of any other power."

This reservation was after some discussion adopted by a vote of 59 to 36, all the Republicans and 10 Democratic Senators being paired or voting in favor of it.

Reservation No. 6 dealt with the Monroe Doctrine and read as follows:

"The United States will not submit to arbitration or to inquiry by the assembly or by the council of the League of Nations, provided for in said treaty of peace, any questions which in the judgment of the United States depend upon or relate to its long-established policy, commonly known as the Monroe Doctrine; said doctrine is to be interpreted by the United States alone and is hereby declared to be wholly outside the jurisdiction of said League of Nations and entirely unaffected by any provision contained in the said treaty of peace with Germany."

Various amendments proposed to this reservation were all defeated, and the reservation was adopted on November 15th by a vote of 55 to 34, nine Democrats voting or being paired in the affirmative.

Reservation No. 7, relating to Shantung, was adopted on November 15th. This reservation provided:

"The United States withholds its assent to Articles 156, 157, and 158, and reserves full liberty of action with respect to any controversy which may arise under said articles between the Republic of China and the Empire of Japan."

This reservation was agreed to by a vote of 53 to 41, five Democrats and all the Republican Senators being paired or voting in favor of it, except Senator McCumber, who voted in the negative.

Reservation No. 8 was agreed to as follows:

"The Congress of the United States will provide by law for the appointment of the representatives of the United States in the assembly and the council of the league of nations, and may in its discretion provide for the participation of the United States in any commission, committee, tribunal, court, council, or conference, or in the selection of any members thereof and for the appointment of members of said commissions, committees, tribunals, courts, councils, or conferences, or any other representatives under the treaty of peace, or in carrying out its provisions, and until such participation and appointment have been so provided for and the powers and duties of such representatives have been defined by law, no person shall represent the United States under either said league of nations or the treaty of peace with Germany or be authorized to perform any act for or on behalf of the United States thereunder, and no citizen of the United States shall be selected or appointed as a member of said commissions, committees, tribunals, courts, councils, or conferences except with the approval of the Senate of the United States."

The vote was taken on November 15th and resulted: Yeas 53, nays 40, five Democrats voting for the reservation.

Reservation No. 9 read as follows:

"The United States understands that the reparation commission will regulate or interfere with exports from the United States to Germany, or from Germany to the United States, only when the United States by Act or Joint Resolution of Congress approves such regulation or interference."

This reservation was adopted on the same day, the yeas being 56 and the nays 39. Seven Democrats voted in favor of it.

Reservation No. 10 regarding contributions to the expenses of the League, provided that:

"The United States shall not be obligated to contribute to any expenses of the League of Nations, or of the Secretariat, or of any commission, or committee, or conference, or other agency, organized under the League of Nations or under the treaty or for the purpose of carrying out the treaty provisions, unless and until an appropriation of funds available for such expenses shall have been made by the Congress of the United States."

On this reservation, adopted November 15th, the vote was 56 yeas, 39 nays, seven Democrats voting or being paired in the affirmative.

Reservation No. 11 dealt with the question of the limitation of armament and read as follows:

"If the United States shall at any time adopt any plan for the limitation of armaments proposed by the council of the league of nations under the provisions of Article 8, it reserves the right to increase such armaments without the consent of the council whenever the United States is threatened with invasion or engaged in war."

It was adopted on November 15th by a vote of 56 to 39, seven Democrats voting or being paired in favor of it.

Reservation No. 12 read as follows:

"The United States reserves the right to permit in its discretion, the nationals of a covenant-breaking State, as defined in Article 16 of the covenant of the league of nations, residing within the United States or in countries other than that violating said Article 16, to continue their commercial, financial, and personal relations with the nationals of the United States."

It was agreed to on the same day, the vote being 53 to 41, and five Democrats voting or being paired in favor of its adoption.

Reservation No. 13 was agreed to as follows:

"Nothing in Articles 296, 297, or in any of the annexes thereto or in any other article, section, or annex of the treaty of peace with Germany shall, as against citizens of the United States, be taken to mean any confirmation, ratification, or approval of any act otherwise illegal or in contravention of the rights of citizens of the United States."

It was adopted on November 15th, the vote resulting in 52 yeas, 41 nays, and four Democrats voting or being paired for it.

Reservation No. 14 was the first reservation proposed by the Committee which failed of adoption by the Senate. That reservation read as follows:

"The United States declines to accept as trustee or in her own right any interest in or any responsibility for the Government or disposition of the overseas possessions of Germany, her rights and titles to which Germany renounces to the Principal Allied and Associated Powers under Articles 119 to 127, inclusive."

Twenty-two Republicans voted or were paired against the adoption of the reservation while three Democrats supported it. The vote was taken on November 17th and resulted: Yeas 29, nays 64.

Reservation No. 15 read as follows:

"The United States reserves to itself exclusively the right to decide what questions affect its honor or its vital interests and declares that such questions are not under this treaty to be submitted in any way either to arbitration or to the consideration of the Council or to the Assembly of the League of Nations, or any agency thereof, or to the decision or recommendation of any other Power."

This was the second committee reservation rejected by the Senate. The vote was taken on November 17th and resulted in 36 yeas, 56 nays; three Democratic Senators voted in the affirmative and fifteen Republicans voted or were paired against its adoption.

These comprised all the reservations reported by the Committee on Foreign Relations, but a large number of other reservations were proposed by individual Senators, which, with two exceptions, were all defeated.

The 14th reservation agreed to by the Senate was one offered by Senator McCumber. It related to the labor organization set up by the treaty and provided that:

"The United States withhold its assent to Part XIII (Articles 387 to 427, inclusive) unless Congress by Act or Joint Resolution shall hereafter make provision for representation in the organization established by said Part XIII, and in such event the participation of the United States will be governed and conditioned by the provisions of such Act or Joint Resolution."

A substitute for this reservation, offered by Senator King, was rejected and the McCumber reservation was then adopted by a vote of 54 to 35. Nine Democrats voted or were paired in favor of the reservation and one Republican, Senator Sherman of Illinois, voted against it.

The 15th reservation adopted by the Senate provided for equality of voting in the Council and Assembly of the League. The first draft was presented by Senator McCumber, to which Senator Johnson, of California, proposed a substitute, which was rejected. A substitute was then offered by Senator Lenroot on November 18th and was agreed to by a vote of 55 to 38. Seven Democrats voted or were paired in favor of the Lenroot substitute, while one Republican, Senator McCumber, voted against it.

On the same day, November 18th, Senator Knox proposed a conditional resolution of ratification, which was rejected by a vote of 30 yeas to 61 nays.

The treaty was then reported to the Senate, action having been completed in the Committee of the Whole. On the next day, November 19th, I presented the resolution of ratification, containing the reservations adopted in Committee of the Whole, and the vote was then taken on the ratification of the treaty with those reservations. The vote resulted in 39 yeas to 55 nays, five Democrats voting with 34 Republicans for ratification and 13 Republicans, the so-called irreconcilables, voting with 42 Democrats against the ratification of the treaty. Senator Fall was absent and a vacancy in the Senate from Delaware accounts for the total membership.

Following this vote on the resolution of ratification, Senator Reed, of Missouri, who had voted in the negative, moved that the Senate reconsider the vote by which they had refused to ratify. The motion was carried by a vote of 63 to 30. Two Senators did not vote. Twelve Repubican Senators, the so-called "mild reservationists," voted with the Democratic majority in support of the motion to reconsider while one Democrat voted against it. The treaty, therefore, was brought again before the Senate, and Senator Pomerene, of Ohio, after a brief speech moved the appointment of a Committee of Conciliation to be appointed by the President of the Senate, among whom should be myself as leader of the majority and Senator Hitchcock, of Nebraska, the leader of the minority, with instructions to prepare and report to the Senate such a resolution of ratification and reservations as in the judgment of the proposed committee should meet with the approval of not less than two-thirds of the Senate. This motion was defeated by a vote of 48 to 42. It received no Republican support and three Democrats voted against it. Senator Hitchcock then moved that the treaty be referred back to the Committee of the Whole with instructions to report it to the Senate with certain mild or interpretative reservations which it is not necessary to print here, and this motion was rejected, 41 Senators voting in the affirmative and 50 in the negative. Three Democrats voted against it and it received no Republican votes.

A second vote was then taken on the resolution of

ratification containing the reservations which had been already adopted by the Senate and which I had previously presented, and again it failed to secure the necessary two-thirds, the result being 41 yeas and 51 nays, two Republicans and one Democrat not voting, 7 Democrats voting with 34 Republicans for ratification and 13 Republicans voting with 38 Democrats against it.

Senator Underwood of Alabama thereupon proposed an unconditional resolution of ratification. This resolution was defeated by a most decisive majority, the result being 38 yeas to 53 nays. Two Republicans and 2 Democrats did not vote; 1 Republican, Senator McCumber, voted with 37 Democrats for unconditional ratification while 7 Democrats and 46 Republicans were recorded in the negative. The vote on the resolution of Senator Underwood had a peculiar importance and is generally forgotten. It demonstrated that the covenant of the League of Nations as proposed by President Wilson could under no circumstances have been accepted by the Senate. Far from receiving two-thirds there was a majority of fifteen against it on a direct vote. This was the final action taken on the first attempt to secure the ratification of the League of Nations and the Treaty of Versailles. It will be noticed that no party line was drawn in the votes which I have given. There were Democratic votes cast with the votes of the Republican majority in every instance, and in some cases Republican votes, especially in the crucial vote on adopting the resolution of advice and consent, cast with that of the majority of the Democrats.

Immediately after the action of the 19th of November, 1919, rejecting the Treaty of Versailles, we adjourned *sine die,* and the first session of the 67th Congress came to an end. We then met on the first Monday in December, under the law. In that brief interval I went to Massachusetts for a few days and while there and after

I reached Washington at the opening of the regular session I found that a situation had developed, both in the Senate and in the country, which was caused by the continued assertion of the friends of the League that the reservations had been added and the defeat of the treaty had been brought about by disputes between the two parties on what were merely verbal differences. The statement was false, but I thought its falsity should be publicly exhibited. It seemed to me very clear, after considering the new conditions thus presented that, in order to make it perfectly plain to the world that the differences between those who supported the treaty and those who opposed it were not verbal but vital and essential, it was most desirable to make an effort, at least, to come to some agreement between the two sides; that is, between the opponents of the reservations and of the treaty and those who favored accepting the League substantially as it was offered. After much discussion among individual Senators I called together what was known as the "Bi-partisan Conference," consisting of representatives of the opposing views upon the reservations. This Bi-partisan Conference consisted of five Republicans and four Democrats and was made up as follows:

Senators Lodge, New, Lenroot, Kellogg, Hitchcock, Simmons, McKellar, Walsh (of Montana), and Owen.

This conference met and sat constantly for two weeks and considered all the reservations. We came to tentative agreements on certain changes in the wording of some of the reservations agreed to in the preceding November; but we could not agree on the reservation relating to the Monroe Doctrine, or the reservation pertaining to the equality of voting in the League, and we failed conspicuously and emphatically to agree on any changes in the reservation relating to Article 10. Those of us who stood for the treaty with reservations could not accept any proposition made by our opponents in regard to these particular reservations because the modifications they asked for were vital and went to the very essence of the reservations involved.

I had made up my mind at the beginning that if the conference was to break up without an agreement it should be on Article 10, which was the crucial point throughout the contest over the covenant of the League of Nations. During the course of the Bi-partisan Conference, reports, more or less inaccurate, as to the proceedings of the Conference, got out and led to all sorts of rumors as to the action of those representing the Republican Party on the Conference. Greatly disturbed by these reports, the Republican "irreconcilables" of the Senate, as they were called, asked me with Senator New to meet them on the afternoon of January 23rd in Senator Johnson's office. Those present, in addition to Senators New and Lodge, were: Senators Borah, Brandegee, Moses, Knox, McCormick, Poindexter and Johnson. They were naturally much disturbed by what they had heard. We had a long discussion of all the phases of the situation. As I made no notes of what was said I cannot give a report of the views expressed by all those present at this gathering, but I assured them, and Senator New joined with me, that there was not the slightest danger of our conceding anything that was essential or that was anything more than a change in wording.

The Bi-partisan Conference went on for some days longer and then we broke on three reservations, as I have said, and especially on that relating to Article 10. On January 31, 1920, I made a statement to the press as to just what had been done in the Conference, the tentative agreements and the points on which we found agreement impossible. Senator Hitchcock made a statement on the subject at the same time and I had them both printed for the information of the Senate. I here print both statements, for they give a contemporary, al-

though condensed, account of what happened in the Bi-
partisan Conference:

"STATEMENT OF SENATOR LODGE
JANUARY 31, 1920.

"For the past two weeks nine Senators—four Democrats and five Republicans—have been meeting to consider the question of changes in the reservations adopted
by the Senate before the adjournment of the last session
of Congress, commonly known as the Lodge reservations. The Senators who thus met did not constitute a
committee. The meetings were entirely informal and it
was understood at the outset that they had no power
or authority whatever to bind anyone. Their only purpose was to see whether there were any changes which
they would be willing to lay before all the other Members of the Senate for their consideration. No final agreement, even to submit any changes to their colleagues in
the Senate, was reached. Some tentative agreements
were obtained. Reservations 3 (4.),* 8 (9.), 12 (13.), and
13 were tentatively accepted by all without change. It
was tentatively agreed to submit the following changes
to all the other Senators for their consideration:

"RESOLVING CLAUSE (1.)

1 *Resolved (two-thirds of the Senators present*
2 *concurring therein),* That the Senate advise and
3 consent to the ratification of the treaty of peace with

* Numbers in parentheses, introduced here for the sake of clearness,
are those of the Senate print of November 6. 1919, wherein the amendment
to the resolving clause appeared as No. 1 of the fifteen paragraphs in
which it and the fourteen reservations were first laid before the Senate
(see *ante,* pp. 180 *et seq.*). In subsequent printings of the Resolution of
Ratification, however, the resolving clause was properly left unnum-
bered; paragraph No. 2 of the original print thus became Reservation
No. 1, and the numbering of the remaining reservations, as first debated
and adopted, was changed to correspond.

4 Germany concluded at Versailles on the 28th day of
5 June, 1919, subject to the following reservations and
6 understandings, which are hereby made a part and
7 condition of this resolution of ratification, which rati-
8 fication is not to take effect or bind the United States
9 until the said reservations and understandings adopted
10 by the Senate have been accepted by an exchange of
11 notes as a part and a condition of this resolution of
12 ratification by at least three of the four Principal
13 Allied and Associated Powers, to wit, Great Britain,
14 France, Italy, and Japan.'

"The Democrats proposed to strike out all after the
word 'ratification' in line 7 to the end of the clause. The
Republicans proposed the following substitute (new language in bold-face type):

1 *Resolved (two-thirds of the Senators present*
2 *concurring therein)*, That the Senate advise and
3 consent to the ratification of the treaty of peace with
4 Germany concluded at Versailles on the 28th of June,
5 1919, subject to the following reservations and
6 understandings, which are hereby made a part and a
7 condition of this resolution of ratification, which
8 ratification is not to take effect or bind the United
9 States until the said reservations and understand-
10 ings adopted by the Senate have been accepted as
11 a part and a condition of this resolution of ratification
12 by **the Allied and Associated Powers and a failure**
13 **on the part of the Allied and Associated Powers to**
14 **make objection to said reservations and understand-**
15 **ings prior to the deposit of ratifications by the**
16 **United States shall be taken as a full acceptance of**
17 **such reservations and understandings by said**
18 **powers.'**

"This proposal was tentatively agreed to.

"RESERVATION NO. 4. (5.)

1 'The United States reserves to itself exclusively the
2 right to decide what questions are within its domestic
3 jurisdiction and declares that all domestic and politi-
4 cal questions relating wholly or in part to its internal
5 affairs, including immigration, labor, coastwise traffic,
6 the tariff, commerce, the suppression of traffic in
7 women and children and in opium and other danger-
8 ous drugs, and all other domestic questions, are solely
9 within the jurisdiction of the United States and are
10 not under this treaty to be submitted in any way
11 either to arbitration or to the consideration of the
12 council or of the assembly of the League of Nations,
13 or any agency thereof, or to the decision or recom-
14 mendation of any other power.'

"Various changes were suggested to this reservation.
It was finally tentatively agreed to insert the word 'internal' before the word 'commerce,' in line 6, and to
strike out, in line 8, the words 'and all other domestic
questions,' which were a superfluous repetition.

"RESERVATION NO. 6. (7.)

1 'The United States withholds its assent to articles
2 156, 157, and 158, and reserves full liberty of action
3 with respect to any controversy which may arise under
4 said articles between the Republic of China and the
5 Empire of Japan.'

"It was tentatively agreed to strike out the words 'between the Republic of China and the Empire of Japan.'

"RESERVATION NO. 7. (8.)

1 'The Congress of the United States will provide by
2 law for the appointment of the representatives of the
3 United States in the assembly and the council of the

4 League of Nations, and may in its discretion provide
5 for the participation of the United States in any com-
6 mission, committee, tribunal, court, council, or con-
7 ference, or in the selection of any members thereof
8 and for the appointment of members of said commis-
9 sions, committees, tribunals, courts, councils, or con-
10 ferences, or any other representatives under the treaty
11 of peace, or in carrying out its provisions, and until
12 such participation and appointment have been so pro-
13 vided for and the powers and duties of such represen-
14 tatives have been defined by law, no person shall rep-
15 resent the United States under either said League of
16 Nations or the treaty of peace with Germany or be
17 authorized to perform any act for or on behalf of said
18 commissions, committees, tribunals, courts, councils,
19 or conferences except with the approval of the Senate
20 of the United States.'

"It was tentatively agreed to substitute for this reservation the following wording, which is precisely the same
in effect except that under the substitute there is no
promise made to pass such a statute, the original form
containing the words 'The Congress of the United States
will provide.'

1 'No person is or shall be authorized to represent the
2 United States, nor shall any citizen of the United
3 States be eligible as a member of any body or agency
4 established or authorized by said treaty of peace with
5 Germany, except pursuant to an act of the Congress
6 of the United States providing for his appointment
7 and defining his powers and duties.

"RESERVATION NO. 10. (11.)

1 'If the United States shall at any time adopt any
2 plan for the limitation of armaments proposed by the

3 council of the League of Nations under the provisions
4 of Article 8, it reserves the right to increase such
5 armaments without the consent of the council when-
6 ever the United States is threatened with invasion or
7 engaged in war.'

"Many suggestions were made for changes in this reservation, and it was finally tentatively agreed to adopt the
following substitute proposed by the Republicans.

1   'No plan for the limitation of armaments proposed
2 by the council of the League of Nations under the pro-
3 visions of Article 8 shall be held as binding the
4 United States until the same shall have been accepted
5 by Congress.'

"RESERVATION NO. 1. (2.)

1   'The United States so understands and construes
2 article 1 that in case of notice of withdrawal from the
3 League of Nations, as provided in said article, the
4 United States shall be the sole judge as to whether all
5 its international obligations and all its obligations
6 under the said covenant have been fulfilled, and notice
7 of withdrawal by the United States may be given by
8 a concurrent resolution of the Congress of the United
9 States.'

"It was proposed by the Democrats to strike out the
word 'concurrent' in line 8, and insert the word 'joint.'
It was suggested by the Republicans to amend this reservation by striking out all after the word 'given' in line 7,
and inserting 'by the President or whenever a majority
of both Houses of Congress may deem it necessary.'
"No decision was reached as to the changes proposed
in this reservation.

"RESERVATION NO. 9. (10.)

1 'The United States shall not be obligated to con-
2 tribute to any expenses of the League of Nations, or
3 of the secretariat, or of any commission, or committee,
4 or conference, or other agency organized under the
5 League of Nations or under the treaty or for the pur-
6 pose of carrying out the treaty provisions, unless and
7 until an appropriation of funds available for such
8 expenses shall have been made by the Congress of the
9 United States.'

"It was proposed to strike out the word 'or' in line 2 and insert 'except the office force and expenses.' No decision was reached upon this change.

"RESERVATION NO. 11. (12.)

1 'The United States reserves the right to permit, in
2 its discretion, the nationals of a covenant-breaking
3 State, as defined in Article 16 of the covenant of the
4 League of Nations, residing within the United States
5 or in countries other than that violating said Article
6 16, to continue their commercial, financial, and per-
7 sonal relations with the nationals of the United
8 States.'

"It was proposed to strike out the words 'or in countries other than that violating said Article 16.' No decision was reached on this proposal.

"RESERVATION NO. 14.

1 'The United States assumes no obligations to be
2 bound by any election, decision, report, or finding of
3 the council or assembly in which any member of the
4 league and its self-governing dominions, colonies, or
5 parts of empire, in the aggregate have cast more than
6 one vote, and assumes no obligation to be bound by

7 any decision, report, or finding of the council or as-
8 sembly arising out of any dispute between the United
9 States and any member of the league if such member,
10 or any self-governing dominion, colony, empire, or
11 part of empire united with it politically has voted.'

"The following was proposed as a substitute for this reservation:

1   'Until part 1, being the covenant of the League of
2 Nations, shall be so amended as to provide that the
3 United States shall be entitled to cast a number of
4 votes equal to that which any member of the league
5 and its self-governing dominions, colonies, or parts
6 of empire, in the aggregate, shall be entitled to cast,
7 the United States assumes no obligation to be bound,
8 except in cases where Congress has previously given
9 its consent by any election, decision, report, or finding
10 of the council or assembly in which any member of
11 the league and its self-governing dominions, colonies,
12 or parts of empire, in the aggregate have cast more
13 than one vote.
14   'The United States assumes no obligation to be
15 bound by any decision, report or finding of the council
16 or assembly arising out of any dispute between the
17 United States and any member of the league if such
18 member or self-governing dominion, colony, empire,
19 or part of empire, united with it politically, has voted.'

"No decision was reached on this change.

"RESERVATION NO. 2. (3.)

1   'The United States assumes no obligation to pre-
2 serve the territorial integrity or political independence
3 of any other country or to interfere in controversies
4 between nations—whether members of the league or
5 not—under the provisions of article 10, or to employ

6 the military or naval forces of the United States under
7 any article of the treaty for any purpose, unless in any
8 particular case the Congress, which, under the Consti-
9 tution, has the sole power to declare war or authorize
10 the employment of the military or naval forces of the
11 United States, shall by act or joint resolution so pro-
12 vide.'

"Various amendments and substitutes were offered to this reservation in regard to article 10 of the treaty. It was found impossible to agree on any change in this reservation to be presented to the other Senators.

"RESERVATION NO. 5. (6.)

1   'The United States will not submit to arbitration or
2 to inquiry by the assembly or by the council of the
3 League of Nations, provided for in said treaty of
4 peace, any questions which in the judgment of the
5 United States depend upon or relate to its long-es-
6 tablished policy, commonly known as the Monroe doc-
7 trine; said doctrine is to be interpreted by the United
8 States alone, and is hereby declared to be wholly
9 outside the jurisdiction of said League of Nations
10 and entirely unaffected by any provision contained
11 in the said treaty of peace with Germany.'

"It was proposed by the Democrats to strike out in lines 7 and 8 the words 'said doctrine is to be interpreted by the United States alone.' To this consent could not be obtained.

"Speaking for myself alone I have only this to say, that I was unable to agree to any change in reservations 2 and 5 dealing with article 10 and the Monroe doctrine. In my opinion reservation No. 2, which provides that we shall assume no obligation of any kind under article 10 except the one mentioned in the treaty, that we should ourselves respect the boundaries of other nations, can not possibly permit of change.

"The change proposed in reservation No. 5 in regard to the Monroe doctrine was an absolutely vital one, because it was asserted as an official interpretation by the representatives of Great Britain that the Monroe doctrine under the treaty was to be interpreted by the league. To this I for one could never assent, and in view of the statement made in Paris by the British delegation, to which I have referred, I regard the line which it was proposed to strike out as absolutely necessary. The United States has always interpreted the Monroe doctrine alone. It is our policy. No one else has ever attempted to interpret it, and it is something in my judgment which ought never to be permitted even by the most remote implication. If we should strike out that phrase now, after it has been accepted by the Senate, it would lead to a direct inference that we left that question open. The right to interpret the Monroe doctrine pertaining to the United States alone must never be open to question.

"H. C. LODGE."

"STATEMENT OF SENATOR HITCHCOCK.
(From the Washington *Post*, Jan. 31, 1920.)

" 'To-morrow I shan't be here, but Senator Walsh, of Montana, will give notice for me that on Tuesday, February 10, I shall ask the Senate to proceed to the consideration of the peace treaty. I shall be back here before that time. It is my intention to return to Washington from my home in Nebraska Thursday next.

" 'At the meeting to-day we presented the last Taft reservation on article 10 as our proposition of a compromise. There was some conversation as to the exact meaning of the reservation. We urged the Republicans to say whether they could accept it or consider it.

" 'Senator Lodge said definitely he could not accept it. We then asked if the Republicans had a counterproposal or would make one. Senator Lodge replied that he could not make any proposition on article 10 other than the one contained in the Lodge program of reservations. He said he could not consent to any modification. ·

" 'We did not take up the Monroe doctrine, but Senator Lodge was equally positive there could be no alteration of that reservation. We had accepted the reservation on the Monroe doctrine with the exception that we proposed an elimination of the right of the United States alone to interpret it.

" 'I suggested that perhaps we could agree on some way of taking the treaty up in the Senate, but Senator Lodge said he did not care to have any meeting on that subject.'

" 'Do you think you have enough votes to get the treaty up in the Senate?' Senator Hitchcock was asked.

" 'We do not know.'

" 'How many Democrats do you count on?' was the next inquiry.

" 'There will be at least 43 Democratic votes,' replied Senator Hitchcock. 'Before the question of the Senate taking up the treaty comes before it for determination conferences will have been held by the Democrats and possibly the Republicans to decide whether the reservations as tentatively agreed upon in the bi-partisan conferences shall be taken up singly or en bloc.'

" 'There was no dramatic climax to the conferences. It was agreed by all that unless some compromise could be worked out on article 10 it would be useless to continue the meetings.'

" 'Was your move to-day discussed with the White House in advance?' Senator Hitchcock was asked.

" 'It was not. We are running entirely independently of the White House in this action.'

"Senator Hitchcock said he was satisfied that Senator Underwood will make no move to get consideration of his resolution for a formal committee of conciliation until after the effort is made to get the treaty before the Senate for open consideration on the floor."

On February 10, 1920, I reported the treaty back to the Senate, together with the reservations adopted by the Senate in the previous November and in which were embodied so far as possible the tentative changes agreed to informally in the Bi-partisan Conference but to which none of the members of the Conference were bound, as was specifically understood by them. I called the treaty up for action on the following Monday, February 16th.

The first amendment, embodying the tentative agreement of the Bi-partisan Conference, was with reference to withdrawal from the League and provided that the United States might withdraw either *by action of the President* or by Congress alone. The original reservation vested the powers of withdrawal solely in Congress. This amendment was defeated on February 21st by a vote of 32 yeas to 33 nays, 7 Democrats voting or being paired for the amendment and 10 Republicans against it. The committee reservation as originally drawn was then adopted on the same day, 45 to 20, all the Republicans and 10 Democrats voting or being paired for it.

Reservation No. 3 (4.), respecting mandates, was adopted on the 26th of February by a vote of 68 to 4. This was the original reservation.

Reservation No. 4 (5.), relating to domestic questions, was adopted without change on March 2nd by a vote of 56 to 25, 14 Democrats voting with the Republicans for the reservation.

The fifth (sixth) reservation, pertaining to the Monroe Doctrine, was adopted on the same day, the vote being 58 yeas to 22 nays, 15 Democrats being paired or voting with the Republicans in favor of it. No change was proposed in this reservation and it was adopted in the same form as agreed to in the previous November.

Reservation No. 6 (7.), regarding Shantung, was amended on March 4th, on my motion, by striking out the words, "between the Republic of China and the Empire of Japan," the vote being 69 yeas to 2 nays. The reservation as amended was then adopted on the same day with a vote of 48 to 21, 10 Democrats voting or being paired with the Republicans in the affirmative.

Reservation No. 7 (8.), dealing with the question of representation of the United States on the commission set up under the treaty, was amended on motion of Senator Walsh of Montana by a vote of 37 to 32. It was then adopted as amended by a vote of 55 to 14, 17 Democrats voting or being paired in the affirmative and all the Republicans supporting it.

Reservation No. 8 (9.), preventing interference by the reparations commission with exports from the United States, was adopted on the 5th of March, the vote resulting in 41 yeas to 22 nays, all the Republicans and 6 Democrats voting or being paired for it.

Reservation No. 9 (10.) related to contributions to the expenses of the League. To this reservation, as originally drawn, an amendment was adopted on motion of Senator Kellogg, by a vote of 55 to 12, 10 Republicans and 2 Democrats opposing it. The amendment added the following words:

"Provided, that the foregoing limitations shall not apply to the United States' proportionate share of the expenses of the office force and the salary of the Secretary General."

This amendment was one of those considered in the Bipartisan Conference. The reservation as amended was then adopted 46 to 25, 8 Democrats and all the Republicans supporting it.

Reservation No. 10 (11.) related to the Limitation of Armaments. A substitute for the original reservation was offered by Senator New and an amendment to the substitute was proposed by Senator McCormick. The changes proposed were not important, and were agreed to. The reservation as amended was then adopted on March 8th by a vote of 49 to 26, 9 Democrats joining with the Republicans in favor of its adoption.

Reservation No. 11 (12.), originally proposed by Senator Wadsworth, permitted the nationals of any State violating the League covenant to continue commercial and personal relations with the nationals of the United States. It was agreed to on March 8th with a slight perfecting amendment, the vote being 44 to 28, all Republicans and 5 Democrats supporting it.

Reservation No. 12 (13.) provided that nothing in the treaty should, as against citizens of the United States, be considered an approval of any acts otherwise illegal or in contravention of the rights of citizens of the United States. It was adopted on March 8th, the vote resulting in 45 yeas, 28 nays; 8 Democrats were paired or voted with the Republicans in support of it.

Reservation No. 13 withheld the assent to part 13 of the treaty establishing the International Labor Office, and was adopted on March 8th, the vote being 44 to 27, 6 Democrats voting or being paired in favor of the reservation.

Reservation No. 14 covered the question of equality of voting in the Council and Assembly of the League. This was one of the reservations on which no agreement was reached by the Bi-partisan Conference, and finally we agreed in the Senate on a draft made by Senator Lenroot of Wisconsin who offered it. I accepted it and it was then agreed to on March 9th by a vote of 57 to 20, 16 Democrats voting or being paired for it.

Reservation No. 2 (3.) was then taken up. This was

the most contested of all the reservations because it related to Article 10, which as I have previously said was, the subject of long and bitter debate in the Senate, and which was described by President Wilson as "the heart of the covenant."

On March 15th this reservation, as originally drawn, was amended on my motion by inserting the words, "including all controversies relating to territorial integrity or political independence" and as amended was then adopted by a vote of 56 to 26, 12 Democrats voting or being paired in favor of it.

On the same day an additional reservation, No. 15, was offered by Senator Gerry of Rhode Island with respect to Ireland. This reservation had not been either considered or approved by the Foreign Relations Committee but it was adopted by the Senate by a vote of 38 to 36. Eighteen Republicans and 20 Democrats voted for the reservation and 20 Republicans and 16 Democrats voted against it.

On March 18th the resolution of ratification was presented to the Senate together with the reservations already adopted in the Committee of the Whole. It was voted upon on March 19th and received 49 votes in the affirmative, 35 votes being cast against it. The total number of Republicans in the Senate was 49, and there were 47 Democrats. Twenty-three Democrats voted or were paired in favor of ratification and 24 Democrats and 14 Republicans voted or were paired against giving the advice and consent of the Senate to the ratification of the treaty, with the reservations. As I thought that the time had now come to make final disposition of the treaty of Versailles, I moved to return it to the President. The vote in favor of this resolution stood 47 to 37; all the Republicans and six Democrats voted or were paired in favor of sending the treaty back to the President. This order was carried out and the Versailles treaty since that day has remained in the hands of the Executive. This vote following the second vote upon the treaty, of March 19, 1920, ended the contest over the covenant of the League of Nations and the treaty of Versailles in the Senate of the United States. I had proposed and offered with a few exceptions all the reservations in behalf of the Committee and had drafted some of them myself. I voted twice for the treaty with reservations and gave to the reservations and to the treaty with the reservations a genuine support; in fact, if I had not given a genuine support I should never have sought for and brought to pass, as I did, the second vote upon the treaty on March 19, 1920. I believed that the reservations approved by the committee and finally adopted by the Senate made the League safe for the United States. Without the reservations nothing would have induced me to vote for the treaty as Mr. Wilson laid it before the Senate. In its original form I considered it full of danger to the people and the Government of the United States and that view I have never changed. I am as convinced of it now as I was in 1919 and 1920. I shall not attempt here to set forth my reasons which compelled or the arguments which led to and supported the conclusions I have just stated. I gave them in outline in a speech during the debate delivered on August 12, 1919, and this speech I print in Appendix V.

The presidential election in November, 1920, followed quickly the action of the Senate upon the treaty of Versailles and Mr. Harding was elected by the greatest popular majority ever received by a candidate for the presidency, something over seven millions. Attempts have been made to show that the people were not voting upon the question of the League of Nations. It must first be remembered and borne in mind that so far as the Senate was concerned the Republican National Convention at Chicago on June 10th, 1920, formally approved the action of the Republican Senators upon the Versailles treaty.* Thus was the issue squarely made. Once made, it was neither neglected nor disregarded. On the contrary, it was pushed to the front and kept there throughout the whole campaign. It was the predominant issue and completely overshadowed all others. I know this of my own knowledge acquired by the widest opportunities. I found that the audiences everywhere were not only crowded but invariably deeply interested and always desired to hear but one subject discussed—the League of Nations. This state of feeling among the voters was made plain in every possible way. If ever a political issue was decided by a popular vote, that decision was rendered upon the League of Nations by the American people in November, 1920. Others who were speaking in the campaign in different parts of the country had precisely the same experience. The League of Nations was the one question above all others which the people wished to hear discussed. Mr. Wilson desired and had demanded an appeal to the people. That appeal was duly made and fully met and the result is history.

I will frankly confess that in the time which has elapsed since the Senate's discussion of the League I have become more and more satisfied, although I voted in the opposite way, that the final decision of the Senate was correct. Every day of the League's existence has convinced me of the wisdom of the United States in holding itself aloof from its useless and at the same time danger-

* The declaration in the Republican platform read as follows:

"The unfortunate insistence of the President upon having his own way, without any change and without any regard to the opinions of a majority of the Senate, which shares with him the treaty-making power, and the President's demand that the Treaty should be ratified without any modification, created a situation in which Senators were required to vote upon their consciences and their oaths according to their judgment against the Treaty as it was presented, or submit to the commands of a dictator in a matter where the authority and the responsibility under the Constitution was theirs, and not his.

"The Senators performed their duty faithfully. We approve their conduct and honor their courage and fidelity."

ous provisions. In practice the League has thus far proved futile for the purpose for which it was ostensibly designed and loudly proclaimed.* It has done nothing to stop wars. The title to the Aland Islands, so much the subject of League boasting, although quite unknown to the world, would never have led to war. The great powers never would have permitted Sweden and Finland to fight, even if they had desired to, over the possession of those islands, the largest of which has a population of only some ten thousand. The boundary of Jugo-Slavia, involving the absorption of Albania by Serbia, and the division of Silesia were both arranged by the great powers, and the League was merely the instrument of governments backed by force. In the nature of things and in its own being the League cannot do anything to stop wars. As a meeting of the representatives of the governments, not of the people, of the different nations, it has engaged in a great deal of debate and conversation; but it has effected nothing of vital consequence to the cause of world peace. Those matters in which it has taken action were in some instances innocent and meritorious and in others trifling or futile. Really to fulfill the advertised intention of its framers, it would have been necessary to put force behind the League, and if there had been an international army and an international commander to carry out the behests of the assembly and the council of the League, the covenant would have become a breeder of wars and not a promoter of peace. As it is, it can at least be said of the League that it is harmless and that occasional international conferences or conversations may be beneficial. The value of the great and, I think I may say, historic debate in the Senate was that every day the American people learned more clearly what

* At this time (October, 1924) an effort is being made at Geneva to make the decisions of the Court and of the Council and Assembly effective by putting force behind them in principle as originally proposed in the Versailles Treaty.

the covenant of the League of Nations which Mr. Wilson presented to them really meant, what dangers it threatened and what perilous purposes it might conceal. It was a very remarkable debate. It rendered an immense service in the instruction of the people. It vindicated the wisdom of the provisions of the American Constitution in regard to the treaty-making power and also the capacity of the Senate as a body to rise to the heights of a very great occasion. The failure of the Senate to give its advice and consent to the ratification of the Treaty of Versailles on the second vote, in March, 1920, however, came much nearer defeat than is generally realized. Those who voted for the acceptance of the Treaty voted in good faith; so did those of the Democrats who voted against it, and all the Republicans. Without a thought of self they were guided by a deep sense of duty to this country. As the final vote drew near, however, I felt convinced that it was quite possible that the treaty with the reservations would be adopted by the Senate because it was obvious to me that on this final and crucial test a majority of the Democrats would be unwilling to vote against ratification. But I also felt convinced that President Wilson would prevent the acceptance of the treaty with reservations if he possibly could. I based this opinion on the knowledge which I had acquired as to Mr. Wilson's temperament, intentions and purposes. I had learned from a careful study of the President's acts and utterances during those trying days—and it was as important for me to understand him as it was for his closest friends—that the key to all he did was that he thought of everything in terms of Wilson. In other words, Mr. Wilson in dealing with every great question thought first of himself. He may have thought of the country next, but there was a long interval, and in the competition the Democratic Party, I will do him the justice to say, was a poor third. Mr. Wilson was devoured by the desire for power. If he had been a soldier and a man of fighting temperament, the Government of the United States would have been in grave danger. He was obstinate and up to a certain point determined, but he was not a fighting man and he never could have led an army or controlled those who would have led it for him, as was done by a very inferior type of man, the 3rd Napoleon. When it came to actual conflict he lacked nerve and daring, although with his temperament I doubt if he lacked the will. He had as great an opportunity as was ever given in human history to one man. He could have settled the affairs of the world from the White House and taken a position both at the time and in the opinion of posterity which it would have been hard to rival. He would have had the world at his feet, but he could think only of himself, and his own idea was and had been for a long time that the part for him to play was that of the great peacemaker. First there was to be no war; we were "too proud to fight." Then when the war came, it was to be "a little war"; then it was to be "a peace without victory." When the great forces let loose by the war got beyond his control and the final settlement came, his one thought appeared to be, as disclosed by his words and acts, to create a system of which he would be the head, and to that everything was made subservient. The people with whom he was associated during his visits to Europe soon discovered this, and by yielding to his demand for the establishment of a League of Nations at just that time, and then by judiciously threatening its defeat, they compelled him to do everything they desired, and many of the evil things that were done and to which Mr. Wilson unwillingly assented, notably the surrender of Shantung to Japan, it is only fair to say were forced upon him because he was ready to sacrifice everything to his own purposes, to the League upon which he had pinned his hopes; in other words, to himself.

The most striking illustration of his absorption in himself to the exclusion of everything else was shown at the time of the last vote in the Senate on the Versailles Treaty. After the vote had been taken and the Treaty defeated, Senator Brandegee, an "irreconcilable," turned to me and said, "We can always depend on Mr. Wilson. He never has failed us. He has used all his powers to defeat the Treaty, because we would not ratify it in just the form which he desired." I replied, "That is quite true. Without his efforts the Treaty would have been accepted by the Senate today." This is shown by the figures. Of the 47 Democratic Senators, we had 23 for the Treaty. Twenty-four Democrats voted against it and, combined with the 15 irreconcilables on the Republican side they were more than enough to deprive the Treaty of the two-thirds vote necessary for ratification. If Mr. Wilson had said a favorable word to his personal supporters, the Treaty with the reservations would have been accepted by the Senate. As it was, he was obliged to exert all his power to prevent its acceptance with the reservations, and two of his Cabinet officers were on the floor of the Senate on that last day using every possible effort to keep enough Democrats in line to assure the defeat of the Treaty.

As I have already said, I do not regret the result now. I think it was a fortunate result. But the Treaty would have been accepted by the Senate on the 19th of March, 1920, if it had not been for Mr. Wilson, and the defeat of the Treaty with the reservations was owing entirely to his determination to have his own way, and to dominate the situation. I do not wish to be unjust to Mr. Wilson in any way, and, therefore, it is only fair for me to say that the final defeat of the Treaty of Versailles and the League of Nations was owing to his efforts and to his unyielding attitude. As proof of this fact, I quote the following letter, addressed to Senator Hitchcock by President Wilson, in November, 1919, just before the first vote on ratification and after the adoption of the reservations by the Senate:

"My dear Senator:
You were good enough to bring me word that the Democratic Senators supporting the treaty expected to hold a conference between the final votes on the Lodge resolution of ratification and that they would be glad to receive a word of counsel from me.

I should hesitate to offer it in any detail but I assume that the Senators only desire it upon the all-important question of the final vote on the resolution containing the many reservations of Senator Lodge. On that I cannot hesitate, for in my opinion the resolution in that form does not provide for ratification, but rather for the nullification of the treaty.

I sincerely hope that the friends and supporters of the treaty will vote against the Lodge resolution of ratification.

I understand that the door will then probably be open for a genuine resolution of ratification.

I trust that all true friends of the treaty will refuse to support the Lodge resolution.

Cordially and sincerely yours,
(Signed) WOODROW WILSON."

Although this letter applied to the first vote upon the treaty on November 18, 1919, it was equally applicable to the second vote of March 19, 1920, and shows perfectly Mr. Wilson's attitude. Rather than yield in any degree or upon any essential point in the treaty which he submitted, he was ready to join with those who were opposed to the covenant of the League of Nations on any terms and defeat the whole treaty of Versailles. He had already in his speech at Salt Lake City declared this position upon Article 10, the article of which he was the author. He would not consult, he would not advise, he

would not consider any change of meaning or consequence. He was determined to have the treaty in every
essential point exactly as he had approved it in Paris,
and nothing else. In other words he was so set upon having his own way that he was ready to destroy the treaty
of Versailles, which was framed to replace a victorious
war with a victorious peace, rather than permit any modification in the terms of the League of Nations which he
had identified with himself. I do not emphasize this
point for the purpose of placing upon Mr. Wilson the responsibility for the defeat in the Senate of the Versailles
treaty. This is a wholly secondary point and there were
plenty of men holding positions of power and with profound convictions, into which no thought of self entered,
who believed that the acceptance of the League of Nations would be a betrayal of this country and who were
quite ready to share with him, although for totally different motives, the responsibility of defeating the treaty.
I have dwelt upon the President's attitude toward the
treaty while pending in the Senate not to criticise or censure him but because his attitude and his action in this
great crisis throw a flood of light upon Mr. Wilson himself, exhibit his temperament and demonstrate the sound-
ness of my estimate of him at the time and the truth of
the proposition that the key to his action always was
to be found in the fact that he thought of everything
and of every question in terms of his own personal interest. The thought of self always overshadowed in the
ultimate decision and effaced every other consideration.
It was shown in his well known dislike to consult with
any one who disagreed with him. It was displayed in
the cold way in which he dropped into the well of for-
getfulness some of those nearest to him, who, whether
rightly or wrongly, had served and followed him with
the utmost loyalty. Take one illustration. Mr. Wilson
desired to defeat, either at the primaries or at the polls,

Senators and some Representatives who had dared to differ from him. It was a natural desire and might be used to show that he was revengeful and vindictive. But that is not at all the point which I wish to make in referring to the well known fact. What is illuminating is the way he expressed his opposition to Senators he had failed to control. One instance covers all. In a letter written in September, 1923, designed to injure and if possible defeat the candidacy of Senator Shields of Tennessee for reelection, Mr. Wilson said: "I regarded him as one of the least trustworthy of my nominal supporters." The offence was Senator Shields' failure to support Mr. Wilson. The same or a similar phrase appears, I think, in all his letters framed to compass the defeat of some Senator who had differed from him. The fact of his opposition to such Senators is not of consequence in reaching an understanding of Mr. Wilson, but the mode of expressing it, and that expression, throws a bright light upon Mr. Wilson's passionate absorption in himself and his own interests and ambitions. It was the same absorption in himself which made him so lonely in all he did because there was no one whom he trusted to protect and advance his interests but himself. His representatives might have done their full duty to the country, but it was impossible for them to care for Mr. Wilson's hopes and purposes as he could himself. Under the Constitution, the President has the entire power of initiation and negotiation in all relations with foreign countries. This power has always been exercised by the President through representatives appointed by him and representing him alone, the Executive, and not the Government of the United States. Setting aside all custom and precedents, even the customs of monarchs, Mr. Wilson went to Paris and negotiated the Treaty of Versailles himself. The four gentlemen who went with him were called delegates, but they were mere surplusage. When the principal exercising all the existing power himself is present and signs the treaty, there is nothing left to delegate, and the signatures of his distinguished companions are as needless and useless as the presence of the conventional fly on the equally conventional wheel of the familiar metaphor.

Following the usual form by which the representation of a nation's sovereignty in relation to other nations is expressed, the Treaty reads: "The President of the United States of America: By: The Honorable Woodrow Wilson, President of the United States, acting in his own name and by his own proper authority."

And so having appointed himself to exercise power which he alone could exercise himself, or in his physical absence, through agents, he so negotiated and so signed the treaty. Of course all was surplusage except the words "President of the United States" with the prefix of the name "Woodrow Wilson." As we look with considerate eyes at this signature as it appears on the treaty our wonder grows, but the explanation is simple; it was the unconscious expression of the devouring passion, the overwhelming thought of self which thrust itself before everything else in this great transaction.

Here in this, as in all other acts of which he was the most conspicuous figure, is to be found the guiding principle of all he did and the secret of his casting away the greatest opportunity ever given to a statesman in modern times and his consequent disastrous failure. A lost opportunity is unforgiving.

> ". . . it is the hour of fate,
> . . . but those who doubt or hesitate,
>
> . . . .
>
> Seek me in vain and uselessly implore,
> I answer not, and I return no more."

This conviction held by me as to the governing quality in Mr. Wilson's mind and character was reached very slowly and only finally arrived at when I found myself confronted with a situation, the gravity of which in its public importance could not be exaggerated, and when a correct analysis of Mr. Wilson's probable attitude was an element of vital moment to me in trying to solve the intricate problem which I and those with whom I acted were compelled to face. These opinions and conclusions in regard to Mr. Wilson were reached by me from close observation and after much reflection.

It is only fair to say that my relations with Mr. Wilson were entirely official. At the beginning of his administration those official relations were perfectly friendly and such as I have already described. My distrust of Mr. Wilson did not grow out of the conditions produced by the great war, still less out of his conduct in regard to the peace and the League of Nations. My distrust of him, which was wholly on public grounds, began with his conduct of our affairs in Mexico. I had ample opportunity to study his character and his qualities as well as his attitude at that time, and I have already described its effect upon me in detail and the reasons for its effect. Of Mr. Wilson prior to his inauguration I had but slight knowledge. I was aware that he had had serious difficulties as president of Princeton that led to his resignation, which, I have reason to believe, was a forced resignation. As I have said, I saw him frequently when he first came in as President, and especially in regard to Mexico, when I first lost confidence in him and his policies. It is only just to say that whenever I met Mr. Wilson he was always most courteous and dignified in his manner and in his conversation when talking with me and the others who were present with me. This continued throughout my relations with him and was true of the meeting of August 19, 1919, when for three hours he discussed the League with the Committee on Foreign Relations.

That he was a man of ability cannot be questioned. He always spoke well, although he was criticised for having an academic manner, which was not to me a disparagement. His style in writing and speaking was clear and forcible. His English was excellent, although he had a fondness for phrasemaking, which, as often happens, proved on several occasions a dangerous gift. He had thought and written much in regard to systems of government, particularly our own, and he was a writer upon and a student of American history. He was entirely capable of thinking for himself and quite independently, as his writings show, containing as they do many statements which attained to a wide subsequent interest when they came into conflict with opinions and views which the events of the time caused him to express after he was President. He was not a scholar in the true sense at all, although the newspapers were fond of applying that term to him, as they are apt to apply it to anyone who has held a position of educational importance. To give one little illustration of what I mean. Universal negatives are always perilous, but I can only say that I have never noticed but once in any of Mr. Wilson's writings or speeches a classical allusion. It occurred in an address made by Mr. Wilson at the rededication of Congress Hall in Philadelphia on October 25, 1913, when he said:

"If you think too much about being re-elected, it is very difficult to be worth re-electing. You are so apt to forget that the comparatively small number of persons, numerous as they seem to be when they swarm, who come to Washington to ask for things, do not constitute an important proportion of the population of the country, that it is constantly necessary to come away from Washington and renew one's contact with the people who do not swarm there, who do not ask for anything, but who do trust you without their personal counsel to do your duty. Unless a man gets these contacts he grows weaker and weaker. *He needs them as Hercules needed the touch of mother earth. If you lift him up too high or he lifts himself too high, he loses the contact and therefore loses the inspiration."* *

The classical allusion is contained in the last lines. I need hardly say that Hercules, who was the son of Jove and Alcmena, gained no strength from touching the earth, but in his wrestling contest with Antæus, who was the son of Neptune and Terra, that is, of the ocean and the earth, he found that Antæus gained strength every time he touched the earth and therefore, according to the story, Hercules held Antæus in the air until the latter weakened for lack of contact with his mother earth so that Hercules was able to crush him to death. The story is as popular as it is old. It is in every classical dictionary and in all the books which boys used to read about the Greek mythology. But as Macaulay says in one of his essays, "I have no desire to detain my reader with this fourth form learning." The point is that it seems incredible that Mr. Wilson should have made a blunder of this sort, which not only would be impossible to a scholar but, one would think, impossible to an educated man.

In this connection I may say that I have also noticed that in Mr. Wilson's speeches, addresses and writings he very rarely made a literary quotation. I do not mean by that a failure to cite authorities for a historical fact or a legal argument, but a quotation simply as an apt expression of a thought. This would seem to indicate that Mr. Wilson, educated as he was in certain directions, politics, history and political economy, was not a widely-read man, for a lover of literature and letters instinctively and almost inevitably thinks of the words of the poet or great prose writer which express better than he can in writing or speaking the idea he is trying to enforce. But in such conversations as I happened to have with him on

* The italics are mine.

different occasions, apart from politics, he always talked well and agreeably and was not without a sense of humor, although his career makes it obvious that he did not possess that master sense in a sufficient degree to save himself, as a large and generous sense of humor would have saved him, from some of his most serious mistakes. He had not a sense of humor sufficient to give him assurance of not mistaking his own relation to the universe. He had, however, a very keen sense of what was for his own political interest—I am not speaking now of the later days when his great opportunity at Paris at the close of the war had to a certain extent unbalanced him, but of the politics of the preceding years. He judged well what was for his own advantage among the people and what would strike happily the popular feeling. Omniscience alone can know with absolute certainty the inmost motives of men and women or read the secrets of the human heart. All that a fellow human being can do is to determine from his study and observation what motives are shown to exist to the exclusion of all others by the acts and words of the man or woman he is endeavoring to understand and to judge justly. This is all I did—all I or anyone could have done; and I did it carefully and with the utmost painstaking, as thoroughly and as fairly as was possible, making ample allowance for the fact that I was opposed to his policies especially as expressed in the Treaty of Versailles. Let me add that although, as I have said, I derived my opinions from firm conviction as to his governing motives, from observation of him as a director of policies to which I was opposed, I think that so far as he was personally concerned I have done him no injustice.

It is not possible, however, to discuss Mr. Wilson, even in the most general way, or to make any attempt to give an impression of his temperament and character without some allusion to what was constantly being said by his unlimited admirers about his idealism—that he was a self-sacrificing idealist; I think the word "martyr'" was not infrequently used. He and a certain group of supporters were especially fond of talking about "vision," and I took occasion to say in my speech of August 12, 1919, which I print in an Appendix, that "vision" and "men of vision" are one thing but that "visionaries" are something entirely different. The same may be said in regard to idealism. Some of the greatest men, not many in number, in our history, as in the history of other nations, have been not only men of vision but men of ideals, and that is very different from idealism in the loose and general way in which it was talked about during the contest over the treaty. The distinction is much the same as that between "sentiment"—attractive almost always, often noble—and "sentimentality," which is usually false and always weak and superficial. Lincoln, to take a very great example, was a man who had ideals, his first and overmastering one being the salvation of the American Union. He tried and succeeded as few men have done in putting his ideals into practice, by knowing the world as it is and under those recognized conditions replacing what is by what ought to be. But the idealism of which we have heard so much in these later years is something entirely different. It is a pleasant, indeed a most attractive thing, to talk about idealism and to regard one's self as an idealist. It has the same engaging qualities that pertain to the comforting occupation of making other people virtuous. People of this sort are apt to forget the second of Browning's well-known lines:

> " 'Tis an awkward thing to play with souls,
>   And matter enough to save one's own."

It is very pleasing to talk about idealism and ideals, and usually without result, inasmuch as the people who like

that sort of talk forget that the men who succeed in con-
verting ideals into realities begin with themselves and
devote their lives to the ideals they cherish, because they
have in addition to a keen sense of existing conditions a
full and abiding comprehension of their own limitations
and shortcomings which breeds both wisdom and toler-
ance. It is also to be noticed, however, that the people
who are continually talking about "idealism" and "lib-
eralism" and "vision" do not realize that other people
have ideals as well as they, although they may not talk
about it, and that all ideals are not necessarily the same.
Those who are so fond, moreover, of discoursing about
ideals and vision and the like, as a kind of stock-in-trade,
are easily satisfied by language. The appeal to ideals and
idealism of any sort has its right place, if accompanied
with practical effort and tolerant wisdom. In a limited
way such appeals are rhetorically legitimate in speech or
writing, but those who, as I have said, make them a stock-
in-trade and use the words without any definite thought
behind them are completely satisfied as a rule if the persons whom they follow use the accepted phrases and the
current dialect in regard to ideals. Mr. Wilson was a
master of the rhetorical use of idealism. He spoke the
language very well and he convinced many people who
were content with words that he was a man of vision and
one ready to sacrifice all to his ideals. He had a selection
of phrases which he used very skilfully. I might say, for
instance, that "breaking the heart of the world" was one
and "making the world safe for democracy" was another,
while "vision," "uplift" and "forward-looking" were sel-
dom absent. These are fair examples of his successful use
of this form of popular appeal. But no one who ever
studied Mr. Wilson's acts, whether as an opponent or as
a supporter, if at all clear-sighted, could fail to perceive that in dealing with political or international questions, whether great or small, Mr. Wilson was extremely

practical and always had in view some material and definite purposes which would result, if successful, possibly in benefit to the world, certainly in benefit to himself. Anyone who attempted to deal with Mr. Wilson, therefore, in opposition or in support, who proceeded on the theory that he was a "visionary" and an "idealist" was certain to meet with disappointment. M. Clemenceau is reported to have said, and the saying had wide currency, that "Mr. Wilson talked like Jesus Christ and acted like Lloyd George." It was a rough gibe but, like many another, it had a strong foundation in truth, and M. Clemenceau knew Mr. Wilson very well and had come into very sharp contact and conflict with him. If President Wilson had been a true idealist, in regard to the covenant of the League of Nations, for example, he would have saved his covenant and secured its adoption by the Senate of the United States by accepting some modification of its terms, since the man who really seeks the establishment of an ideal will never sacrifice it because he cannot secure everything he wants at once, and always estimates the principle as more important than its details and qualifications. If it had been a real ideal with Mr. Wilson and tinged with no thought of self, he would have succeeded in large measure, just as Lincoln did when he put aside for the time the emancipation of the slaves, on which his heart was set, in order to preserve the Union, which to him was the highest ideal and the dominant purpose at the moment.

In support of my opinion I might make a long list of men who suffered extinction, who were simply dropped down the *oubliette,* so far as can be discerned, because their advice had not been agreeable to Mr. Wilson. Their honest opinions had in some degree differed from his and they had ventured to tell him the whole truth as they understood and believed it. I think I may say that if I needed any outside support of my estimate of Mr.

Wilson, who to me was simply an element to be calmly and coolly considered in a great problem of international politics, I could find it in some of those utterances of his close friends to which I have referred. But I am content to leave it where it stands and can only say that the theory which I adopted as to the motives for Mr. Wilson's actions and which therefore would enable me to forecast his coming attitude on any question were never misleading or inaccurate. As the strenuous days which were filled by the contest over the League of Nations passed by, almost every one bringing its difficulty and its crucial question, I made no mistake in my estimate of what President Wilson would do under certain conditions. He, of course, was not only a leading element in my problem, but because he had been thrown into the Presidency by the lottery of presidential nominations he was of necessity a chief figure in the composition of the scene which I have attempted to depict.

There are those still extant who speak of Mr. Wilson as a "very great man." An able man in certain ways, an ambitious man in all ways he certainly was; by no means a commonplace man. But "very great men" are extremely rare. Mr. Wilson was not one of them. He was given the greatest opportunity ever given to any public man in modern times which we may date from the Revival of Learning in Europe. Having this opportunity he tried to use it and failed. The failure necessarily equalled the opportunity in magnitude and the failure was complete and was all his own. No one could have destroyed such a vast opportunity except the man to whom it was given, and in this work of destruction unaided and alone Mr. Wilson was entirely successful. Difficult as such an achievement in the face of such an opportunity was, it does not warrant describing the man who wrought the destruction in any sense as a "very great man."

APPENDIX I

Speech made in the Senate on February 28, 1919.

MR. LODGE. Mr. President, all people, men and women alike, who are capable of connected thought abhor war and desire nothing so much as to make secure the future peace of the world. Everybody hates war. Everyone longs to make it impossible. We ought to lay aside once and for all the unfounded and really evil suggestion that because men may differ as to the best method of securing the world's peace in the future, anyone is against permanent peace, if it can be obtained, among all the nations of mankind. Because one man goes to the Capitol in Washington by one street and another man by a different street it does not follow that they are not both going to the Capitol. We all earnestly desire to advance toward the preservation of the world's peace, and difference in method makes no distinction in purpose. It is almost needless to say that the question now before us is so momentous that it transcends all party lines. Party considerations and party interests disappear in dealing with such a question as this. I will follow any man and vote for any measure which in my honest opinion will make for the maintenance of the world's peace. I will follow no man and vote for no measure which, however well intended, seem in my best judgment to lead to discussions rather than to harmony among the nations or to injury, peril, or injustice to my country. No question has ever confronted the United States Senate which equals in importance that which is involved in the league of nations intended to secure the future peace of the world. There should be no undue haste in considering it. My one desire is that not only the Senate, which is charged with responsibility, but that the press and the people of the country should investigate every proposal with the utmost thoroughness and weigh them all carefully before they make up their minds. If there is any proposition or any plan which will not bear, which will not court the most thorough and most public discussion, that fact makes it an object of suspicion at the very outset. Beware of it; be on your guard against it. Demand that those who oppose the plan now offered present arguments and reasons, based on facts and history, and that those who favor it meet objections with something more relative than rhetoric, personal denunciation, and shrill shrieks that virtue is to be preferred to vice and that peace is better than war. Glittering and enticing generalities will not serve. We must have fact, details, and sharp, clear-cut definitions. The American people cannot give too much thought to this subject, and that they shall look into it with considerate eyes is all that I desire.

In the first place, the terms of the league—the agreements which we make,—must be so plain and so explicit that no man can misunderstand them. We must, so far as it can be done by human ingenuity, have every agreement which we make so stated that it will not give rise to different interpretations and to consequent argument. Misunderstandings as to terms are not a good foundation for a treaty to promote peace. We now have before us the draft of a constitution for a league of nations, prepared by a commission or committee, which is to be submitted to the representatives of the nations. The nations, through their delegates, have not agreed to it. It has not passed beyond the stage of a committee report. It is open to amendment and change in the peace conference. The Senate can take no action upon it, but it lies open before us for criticism and discussion. What is said in the Senate ought to be placed before the peace conference and published in Paris, so that the foreign Governments may be informed as to the various views expressed here.

In this draft prepared for a constitution of a league of nations, which is now before the world, there is hardly a clause about the interpretation of which men do not already differ. As it stands there is serious danger that the very nations which sign the constitution of the league will quarrel about the meaning of the various articles before a twelvemonth has passed. It seems to have been very hastily drafted, and the result is crudeness and looseness of expression, unintentional, I hope. There are certainly many doubtful passages and open questions obvious in the articles which can not be settled by individual inference, but which must be made so clear and so distinct that we may all understand the exact meaning of the instrument to which we are asked to set our hands. The language of these articles does not appear to me to have the precision and unmistakable character which a constitution, a treaty, or a law ought to present. The language only too frequently is not the language of laws or statutes. The article concerning mandatories, for example, contains an argument and a statement of existing conditions. Arguments and historical facts have no place in a statute or a treaty. Statutory and legal language must assert and command, not argue and describe. I press this point because there is nothing so vital to the peace of the world as the sanctity of treaties. The suggestion that we can safely sign because we can always violate or abrogate is fatal not only to any league but to peace itself. You can not found world peace upon the cynical "scrap of paper" doctrine so dear to Germany. To whatever instrument the United States sets its hand it must carry out the provisions of that instrument to the last jot and tittle, and observe it absolutely both in letter and in spirit. If this is not done the instrument will become a source of controversy instead of agreement, of dissension instead of harmony. This is all the more essential because it is evident, although not expressly stated, that this league is intended to be indissoluble, for there is no provision for its termination or for the withdrawal of any signatory. We are left to infer that any nation withdrawing from the league exposes itself to penalties and probably to war. Therefore, before we ratify, the terms and language in which the terms are stated must be as exact and as precise, as free from any possibility of conflicting interpretations, as it is possible to make them.

The explanation or interpretation of any of these doubtful passages is not sufficient if made by one man, whether that man be the President of the United States, or a Senator, or anyone else. These questions and doubts must be answered and removed by the instrument itself.

It is to be remembered that if there is any dispute about the terms of this constitution there is no court provided that I can find to pass upon differences of opinion as to the terms of the constitution itself. There is no court to fulfill the function which our Supreme Court fulfills. There is provision for tribunals to decide questions submitted for arbitration, but there is no authority to decide differing interpretations as to the terms of the instrument itself.

What I have just said indicates the vast importance of the form and the manner in which the agreements which we are to sign shall be stated. I now come to questions of substance, which seem to me to demand the most careful thought of the entire American people, and particularly of those charged with the responsibility of ratification. We abandon entirely by the proposed constitution the policy laid down by Washington in his Farewell Address and the Monroe doctrine. It is worse than idle, it is not honest, to evade or deny this fact, and every fairminded supporter of this draft plan for a league admits it. I know that some of the ardent advocates of the plan submitted to us regard any suggestion of the importance of the Washington policy as foolish and irrelevant. Perhaps it is. Perhaps the time has come when the policies of Washington should be abandoned; but if we are to cast them aside I think that at least it should be done respectfully and with a sense of gratitude to the great man who formulated them. For nearly a century and a quarter the policies laid down in the Farewell Address have been followed and adhered to by the Government of the United States and by the American people. I doubt if any purely political declaration has even been observed by any people for so long a time. The principles of the Farewell Address in regard to our foreign relations have been sustained and acted upon by the American people down to the present moment. Washington declared against permanent alliances. He did not close the door on temporary alliances for particular purposes. Our entry in the great war just closed was entirely in accord with and violated in no respect the policy laid down by Washington. When we went to war

with Germany we made no treaties with the nations engaged in the war against the German Government. The
President was so careful in this direction that he did not
permit himself ever to refer to the nations by whose side
we fought as "allies," but always as "nations associated
with us in the war." The attitude recommended by
Washington was scrupulously maintained even under the
pressure of the great conflict. Now, in the twinkling of
an eye, while passion and emotion reign, the Washington
policy is to be entirely laid aside and we are to enter
upon a permanent and indissoluble alliance. That which
we refuse to do in war we are to do in peace, deliberately,
coolly, and with no war exigency. Let us not overlook
the profound gravity of this step.

Washington was not only a very great man but he was
also a very wise man. He looked far into the future and
he never omitted human nature from his calculations.
He knew well that human nature had not changed fundamentally since mankind had a history. Moreover, he
was destitute of any personal ambitions to a degree never
equaled by any other very great man known to us. In
all the vital questions with which he dealt it was not
merely that he thought of his country first and of himself
second. He thought of his country first and never
thought of himself at all. He was so great a man that
the fact that this country had produced him was enough
of itself to justify the Revolution and our existence as a
Nation. Do not think that I overstate this in the fondness of patriotism and with the partiality of one of his
countrymen. The opinion I have expressed is the opinion
of the world. Fifteen years after Washington's death
Byron wrote the famous and familiar lines:

> "Where may the wearied eye repose
>   When gazing on the Great;
> Where neither guilty glory glows,
>   Nor despicable state?
> Yes—One—the first—the last—the best—
> The Cincinnatus of the West,
>   Whom Envy dared not hate,
> Bequeathed the name of Washington,
> To make man blush there was but one!"

That was the opinion of mankind then, and it is the opinion of mankind to-day, when his statue has been erected in Paris and is about to be erected in London. If we throw aside the political testament of such a man, which has been of living force down to the present instant, because altered circumstances demand it, it is a subject for deep regret and not for rejoicing. When Washington prepared the Farewell Address he consulted Hamilton, perhaps the greatest constructive mind among modern statesmen, who prepared a large part of the draft; Madison, one of the chief framers of the Constitution and President of the United States; John Jay, Chief Justice and one of the great lawyers in our history. Following them came Thomas Jefferson, James Monroe, and John Quincy Adams, bringing the Monroe doctrine to complete and round out the principles of Washington to which they were all alike devoted. If we are to be driven by modern exigencies to dismiss Washington and his counselors and the men who declared the Monroe doctrine from our consideration, we ought, at least, as these stately figures pass off the stage of guiding influence, to pay our homage to them and not relegate them to the shades of the past with jeers and laughter directed against their teachings.

But if we put aside forever the Washington policy in regard to our foreign relations we must always remember that it carries with it the corollary known as the Monroe doctrine. Under the terms of this league draft reported by the committee to the peace conference the Monroe doctrine disappears. It has been our cherished guide and guard for nearly a century. The Monroe doctrine is based on the principle of self-preservation. To say that it is a question of protecting the boundaries, the political integrity, of the American States, is not to state the Monroe doctrine. Boundaries have been changed among American States since the Monroe doctrine was enunciated. That is not the kernel of the doctrine. The real essence of that doctrine is that American questions shall be settled by Americans alone; that the Americas shall be separated from Europe and from the interference of Europe in purely American questions. That is the vital principle of the doctrine.

I have seen it said that the Monroe doctrine is preserved under article 10; that we do not abandon the
Monroe doctrine, we merely extend it to all the world.
How anyone can say this passes my comprehension. The
Monroe doctrine exists solely for the protection of the
American Hemisphere, and to that hemisphere it was
limited. If you extend it to all the world, it ceases to
exist, because it rests on nothing but the differentiation
of the American Hemisphere from the rest of the world.
Under this draft of the constitution of the league of
nations, American questions and European questions and
Asian and African questions are all alike put within
the control and jurisdiction of the league. Europe will
have the right to take part in the settlement of all
American questions, and we, of course, shall have the
right to share in the settlement of all questions in Europe
and Asia and Africa. Europe and Asia are to take part
in policing the American continent and the Panama
Canal, and in return we are to have, by way of compensation, the right to police the Balkans and Asia Minor
when we are asked to do so. Perhaps the time has come
when it is necessary to do this, but it is a very grave
step, and I wish now merely to point out that the American people ought never to abandon the Washington
policy and the Monroe doctrine without being perfectly
certain that they earnestly wish to do so. Standing always firmly by these great policies, we have thriven and
prospered and have done more to preserve the world's
peace than any nation, league, or alliance which ever
existed. For this reason I ask the press and the public
and, of course, the Senate to consider well the gravity of
this proposition before it takes the heavy responsibility
of finally casting aside these policies which we have adhered to for a century and more and under which we have
greatly served the cause of peace both at home and
abroad.

Very complete proof must be offered of the superiority
of any new system before we reject the policies of Washington and Monroe, which have been in our foreign relations the Palladium of the Republic. Within the memory of those to whom I now speak the Monroe doctrine
stopped the incursions of England upon the territory of

Venezuela and settled the boundary question finally by arbitration. Under the Monroe doctrine we arrested the attempt of Germany to take Venezuelan territory on another occasion. In these two instances the doctrine was enforced by a Democratic President and by a Republican President and they were supported in so doing by all the people of the United States without regard to party. I mention these cases merely to show that we are not cutting away dead limbs from the body politic, but that we are abandoning two cardinal principles of American government, which until the presentation of this draft for the constitution of the league of nations, were as vital as on the day when Washington addressed the people of the United States for the last time or when President Monroe announced his policy to the world. What has happened since November 11, 1918, to make them so suddenly valueless, to cause them to be regarded as injurious obstacles to be cast out upon the dust heaps of history? It seems to me that that is a question which at least deserves our consideration before we take action upon it.

Two other general propositions, and I shall proceed to examine these league articles in detail. In article 10 we, in common, of course, with the other signatories and members of the projected league, guarantee the territorial integrity and the political independence of every member of the league. That means that we ultimately guarantee the independence and the boundaries, as now settled or as they may be settled by the treaty with Germany, of every nation on earth. If the United States agrees to guaranties of that sort we must maintain them. The word of the United States, her promise to guarantee the independence and the boundaries of any country, whether she does it alone or in company with other nations, whether she guarantees one country or all the countries of the world, is just as sacred as her honor—far more important than the maintenance of every financial pledge, which the people of this country would never consent to break.

I do not now say the time has not come when, in the interest of future peace, the American people may not decide that we ought to guarantee the territorial integrity of the far-flung British Empire, including her self-governing dominions and colonies, of the Balkan States, of China, or Japan, or of the French, Italian, and Portuguese colonies in Africa; but I do suggest that it is a very grave, a very perilous promise to make, because there is but one way by which such guaranties, if ever invoked, can be maintained, and that way is the way of force—whether military or economic force, it matters not. If we guarantee any country on the earth, no matter how small or how large, in its independence or its boundaries, that guarantee we must maintain at any cost when our word is once given, and we must be in constant possession of fleets and armies capable of enforcing these guarantees at a moment's notice. There is no need of arguing whether there is to be compulsive force behind this league. It is there in article 10 absolutely and entirely by the mere fect of these guaranties. The ranks of the armies and fleets of the navy made necessary by such pledges are to be filled and manned by the sons, husbands, and brothers of the people of America. I wish them carefully to consider, therefore, whether they are willing to have the youth of America ordered to war by other nations without regard to what they or their representatives desire. I would have them determine after much reflection whether they are willing to have the United States forced into war by other nations against her own will. They must bear in mind constantly that we have only one vote in the executive council, only one vote in the body of delegates, and a majority of the votes rules and is decisive.

I am not here to discuss the constitutional question of the sole right of Congress to declare war. That is a detail, as it relates only to the Constitution, which we may decide later. In my own opinion, we shall be obliged to modify the Constitution. I do not think, and I never can admit, that we can change or modify the Constitution by a treaty negotiated by the President and ratified by the Senate. I think that must be done, and can only be done, in the way prescribed by the Constitution itself, and to promise to amend our Constitution is a serious task and a doubtful undertaking.

I hope the American people will take time to consider

this promise before they make it—because when it is once made it can not be broken—and ask themselves whether this is the best way of assuring perfect peace throughout the future years, which is what we are aiming at, for we all are aiming at the same object. A world's peace which requires at the outset preparations for war—for war either economic or military—in order to maintain that peace, presents questions and awakens thoughts which certainly ought to be soberly and discreetly considered.

The second general proposition to which I would call attention is this: We now in this draft bind ourselves to submit every possible international dispute or difference either to the league court or to the control of the executive council of the league. That includes immigration, a very live question, to take a single example. Are we ready to give to other nations the power to say who shall come into the United States and become citizens of the Republic? If we are ready to do this, we are prepared to part with the most precious of sovereign rights, that which guards our existence and our character as a Nation. Are we ready to leave it to other nations to determine whether we shall admit to the United States a flood of Japanese, Chinese, and Hindu labor? If we accept this plan for a league, this is precisely what we promise to do. I know that by following out all the windings of the provision for referring to the council or allowing the council to take charge of what has been called hitherto a conjusticiable question, we shall probably reach a point where it would not be possible to secure unanimous action by the league upon the question of immigration. But, Mr. President, I start with the proposition that there should be no jurisdiction in the league at all over that question; that it should be separated absolutely and entirely from any jurisdiction of the league. Are we prepared to have a league of nations —in which the United States has only one vote, which she could not cast on a dispute to which she was a party —open our doors, if they see fit, to any and all immigration from all parts of the world?

Mr. Taft has announced, in an article which appeared in the National Geographic Magazine, that the question of immigration will go before the international tribunal, and he says now that all organized labor is for the league. If American labor favors putting the restriction of immigration in the control of other nations they must have radically changed their minds and abandoned their most cherished policy. Certainly the gravity of such promises as are involved in the points I have suggested is sufficient to forbid haste. If such promises are to be given they must be given in cold blood with a full realization of what they mean and after the American people and those who represent them here have considered all that is involved with a serious care such as we have never been called upon to exercise before. We are asked to abandon the policies which we have adhered to during all our life as a Nation. We are asked to guarantee the political independence and the territorial integrity of every nation which chooses to join the league—and that means all nations as the President stated in his speech at Manchester. We are asked to leave to the decision of other nations, or to the jurisdiction of other nations, the question of what immigrants shall come to the United States. We are asked also to give up in part our sovereignty and our independence and subject our own will to the will of other nations, if there is a majority against our desires. We are asked, therefore, in a large and important degree to substitute internationalism for nationalism and an international state for pure Americanism. Certainly such things as these deserve reflection, discussion, and earnest thought.

I am not contending now that these things must not be done. I have no intention of opposing a blank negative to propositions which concern the peace of the world, which I am as anxious to see promoted as any living man can be; but I do say, in the strongest terms, that these things I have pointed out are of vast importance not only to us but to the entire world, and a mistake now in making the league of nations might result in more war and trouble than the old system in its worst days. What I ask, and all I ask, is consideration, time, and thought.

The first and most practical question for us to consider and decide is whether the terms of this committee draft of a constitution for the league of nations really make for harmony among the nations or will tend to produce dissension and controversy. We all desire peace, but in our zeal for peace we must be careful not to create new obligations and new and untried conditions, which may lead to fostering war rather than peace. For this reason I am going now to examine the articles in the draft of the constitution for the league of nations one by one.

Upon the preamble we need not pause. It states purposes and objects, with which everybody of course is in sympathy.

Article 1 deals with the officers and the delegates, and they are sufficiently and clearly provided for, and also that there shall be an international secretariat. I think nothing is omitted so far as the creation of offices goes.

Nothing is said about how the delegates shall be chosen. That, of course, is a matter which is left to each nation to determine, but I venture, with all respect, to suggest that delegates representing the United States in what is to be a world state, to which we are to give a portion of our sovereignty and independence, ought to represent the United States; they ought to be selected by the people of the United States or appointed as ambassadors and consuls are appointed. I think these delegates, who are certainly as important as ambassadors or consuls, should be appointed by the usual method of the President and the Senate, and not ever be allowed to be irresponsible personal agents. That, however, is something we can attend to here, I think, when the league of nations is submitted to us in treaty form.

Article 2 refers to the meetings of the body of delegates, and also provides that "each of the high contracting parties shall have one vote but may not have more than three representatives." Therefore the voting in the body of delegates proceeds on the well-settled principle of international law that each national sovereignty is equal to every other national sovereignty, and the United States will have one vote and so will Siam.

In Article 3 we come to the executive council, which is of the greatest possible importance, for it is in the provision stated here—and also I am sure, as practice will show—the controlling force of the entire league:

"The executive council shall consist of representatives of the United States of America, the British Empire, France, Italy, and Japan, together with representatives of four other States, members of the league."

What other States shall be selected has not yet been disclosed to us, but there must be four other States. The executive council now has five members—three from Europe, one from Asia, and one from America. Ultimately it will have nine members. I assume, and I think I have the right to assume, on the best authority, that there is no intention of making Germany one of the four nations to be added to the existing five which will compose the nine members of the executive council. I think it is probable that Germany will have a period of probation before she is even admitted to the league, and that seems to me to be eminently wise.

Then the article provides for the meeting of the council, and then says in the last paragraph:

"Invitations shall be sent to any power to attend a meeting of the council at which matters directly affecting its interests are to be discussed, and no decision taken at any meeting will be binding on such powers unless so invited."

This, of course, looks to having the executive council consider the affairs of every country in the world, whether they are members of the league or not, and all the council has to do in order to make its action binding on such powers is to invite them to be present. It is a paragraph not without importance.

"ARTICLE 4. All matter of procedure at meetings of the body of delegates or the executive council, including the appointment of the committees to investigate particular matters, shall be regulated by the body of delegates or the executive council, and may be decided by a majority of the States represented at the meetings."

It is to be decided by the executive council, where we shall have one vote in five, or, when the council is enlarged, one vote in nine, and in the body of delegates, of course, only one vote.

Then comes article 5, which provides for the secretariat and concerns only offices and provisions for expenses. The words creating offices and providing for salaries leave no room for doubts or questionings.

Article 6 is a matter of course. It simply gives the delegates diplomatic immunities and privileges.

Article 7 covers the admission to the league of States and, when a State is invited to adhere, "requires the assent of not less than two-thirds of the States represented in the body of delegates, and shall be limited to fully self-governing countries, including dominions and colonies."

The inclusion of dominions and colonies, of course, covers the four great self-governing dominions of Great Britain. I have no fault to find with the arrangement. Canada, New Zealand, South Africa, and Australia are far more worthy and more valuable members of a league of nations than some of the nations which I think will find their way into the body. But the fact remains that in the body of delegates England has five votes to one vote of any other country.

The next paragraph says:

"No State shall be admitted to the league unless it is able to give effective guaranties of its sincere intention to observe its international obligations."

I do not wish to seem hypercritical, but I think that in a document of this kind we should know a little better what an "effective guaranty of a sincere intention" is.

How can we have an effective guaranty of a sincere intention?

I merely throw this out as one of the points which it seems to me ought to be made clear. Let us know what it means. How are we to test the sincerity of the intention? How are we to get a guaranty for the sincerity of the intention in advance, I think it would be well to have that more precisely defined.

We now come to article 8, which refers to disarmament, a most important question, one of the most important in the constitution of the league, with the purpose of which everybody must be in the keenest sympathy. The reduction of armaments, if it can be brought about successfully, will be of the greatest value to the world and relieve the people of all countries from a burden of taxation which has become intolerable. But its very importance makes it necessary, in my opinion, to express what is to be done with the utmost clearness. The article says:

"The high contracting parties recognize the principle that the maintenance of peace will require the reduction of national armaments to the lowest point consistent with national safety and the enforcement by common action of international obligations—"

That is, the reduction must be consistent with the "enforcement by common action of international obligation," words to be considered and which the instrument itself must explain.

Here we are dealing solely with military force which we are seeking to reduce, and it is recognized that in disarmament one of the elements to be considered is the "enforcement by common action of international obligations," which, I assume—we have to assume more or less as we pass along through these articles—refers to the obligations of the league. We certainly owe no international obligation to anybody else to-day as to what fleets and armies we shall have. Yet this article contemplates as one of the tests of disarmament the amount of force which will be needed to carry out the purposes of the league. The article continues:

"—having special regard to the geographical situation and circumstances of each State, and the executive council shall formulate plans for effecting such reduction."

I do not know how far the formulation has a binding effect, but the article goes on to say:

"The executive council shall also determine for the consideration and action of the several Governments what military equipment and armament is fair and reasonable in proportion to the scale of forces laid down in the program of disarmament—"

"Laid down." Again I have to interpret. Laid down, I assume, by the executive council itself, because it is they who make the program—

"—and these limits when adopted, shall not be exceeded without the permission of the executive council."

There comes in an absolutely binding provision. It says "when adopted." Adopted by whom? The natural inference is, adopted by the several governments, if you trace it back through the wording of the previous paragraphs. Ought not an instrument of this vital character to be drafted with the ordinary care which a clerk gives in drafting a clause in an appropriation bill for a Senate committee? Ought it not to be stated clearly, "thus adopted by the several governments," and then there can be no question that each government will decide on the program itself and its own share before it is put in a position where it can never exceed that program without the permission of the executive council—I assume the majority of the executive council. That is another thing which apparently it has not been thought worth while to state, but I do not think you can be too clear when you are exacting from nations these great promises and laying upon them these heavy burdens.

"The high contracting parties agree that the manufacture by private enterprise of munitions and implements of war lends itself to grave objections, and direct the executive council to advise how the evil effects attendant upon such manufacture can be prevented."

That, I take it, is mere advice to be laid before the body of delegates, but it is not explained how far the advice goes.

"The high contracting parties—"

The last paragraph says—

"—undertake in no way to conceal from each other the condition of such of their industries as are capable of being adapted to warlike purposes or the scale of their armaments, and agree that there shall be full and frank interchange of information as to their military and naval program."

An admirable proposition! Certainly it can not but add to the prospect of the peace of the world if every nation shall explain to every other nation just what military and naval program it has; but there seems to be no method expressed here by which they can be compelled to give that information, except by saying that if they do not do it, they fail in a moral obligation and will be guilty of what some people might define as "moral obliquity."

Article 9 says:

"A permanent commission shall be constituted to advise the league on the execution of the provisions of article 8 and on military and naval questions generally."

A very useful body, but constituted by whom? There is not one syllable in the article to show by whom it shall be constituted. It may be unnecessary to do it; we may be able to infer it; but when you get into the misty region of inferences by individuals you must have some tribunal established like our Supreme Court, which can declare whether the inference is correct or not.

Article 10 is probably the most important article in the whole constitution—I have already referred to it—because to me it is graver than anything else with perhaps one exception in this entire treaty. It is also perfectly clear.

"The high contracting parties undertake to respect and preserve as against external aggression the territorial integrity and existing political independence of all States members of the league. In case of any such aggression, or in case of any threat or danger of such aggression, the executive council shall advise upon the means by which the obligation shall be fulfilled."

The executive council is to have the power of advice, which I do not suppose is binding at all, but the guaranty remains, and, as I have already said, it cannot be too often repeated, that when one nation guarantees the political independence and the territorial integrity of another, that guaranty must be maintained, and guaranties can only be maintained by the exercise in the last resort of the force of the nation. If we were to guarantee the political independence and territorial integrity of Mexico or Guatemala, or any of those States, we should have to stand behind them with our armies and our fleets when the guaranty was invoked, and there is no escape from that obligation. Those plain words demand it. I am not now arguing whether we should give the guaranty or whether we should not give the guaranty, but I beg my fellow countrymen to consider well before they give this promise to invoke the mighty power of the United States in order to enforce a guaranty which extends to the boundaries of every State on the face of the earth. It is a tremendous promise, and if we give it this country must carry it out. The United States must never be guilty of in any way impairing the sanctity of treaties. But let us think well before we do it. Let us consider it. In the presence of such promises as that, is it unreasonable to ask that the American people should have time to consider, to realize, just what it means before they give the promise? If they decide coolly and deliberately, there is nothing more to be said; we bow to it, and Congress will fulfill it; but that is too weighty a promise to make by simply saying, "I am in favor of a league of nations and of the eternal peace of the world." A mere title does not carry with it any explanation of the responsibility which is undertaken.

"ARTICLE 11. Any war or threat of war, whether immediately affecting any of the high contracting parties or not, is hereby declared a matter of concern to the league, and the high contracting parties reserve the right to take any action that may be deemed wise and effectual to safeguard the peace of nations."

"Any action" covers war—

"It is hereby also declared and agreed to be the friendly right of each of the high contracting parties to draw the attention of the body of delegates—"

Which I suppose means the five who are now assigned and the four who are to join with them, making nine in all—

"—to draw the attention of the body of delegates or of the executive council to any circumstances affecting international intercourse which threaten to disturb international peace or the good understanding between nations upon which peace depends."

Everyone must agree to that, except for the slight uncertainties of statement; but it embodies in practice one of the paragraphs of the Hague convention.

Now we come to the disputes. Those articles relating to the settlement of disputes would require a long time by themselves, if we touched nothing else, to discuss, and also to understand. I merely wish to call attention to a few points which occur on a casual reading. It says in article 12 "disputes." It says in article 13 "any disputes." That means any dispute that may arise among nations, of any kind, whether involving domestic or internal matters or foreign relations. The words "any disputes" cover everything. On that point I wish to reiterate what I have already said. I am not going further into it.

It is no reply to the point that is made about immigration to say that, if you follow it through all the windings of the provisions here for justiciable and nonjusticiable questions you will find it reaches a point where the league could do nothing about immigration into the United States unless it was unanimous, and that it is very unlikely they would ever be unanimous. Granted; it is unlikely that the league will ever be unanimous about anything, but the possibility is there. I deny the jurisdiction. I do not think we should leave to the league any question as to immigration, because immigration lies at the very root of national character and national economy; it ought to be made plain that the league has no jurisdiction whatever over such questions in any way. We do not want a narrow alley of escape from the jurisdiction of the league. We want to prevent any jurisdiction whatever. As we stand to-day no nation or nations can say who shall come into the United States. There is only one rule as to that, and that is the rule of the United States. It should so remain. What I say for the United States I mean for every other nation. No nation should be compelled to admit anyone within its borders whom it does not choose to admit.

Some of these points I think it might be well for those who prepared this draft to consider. Perhaps I do not regard the drafting committee with the veneration which the Senator from Nebraska (Mr. Hitchcock) feels toward them; I know some of them, and, without reflecting upon them in any way, I do not think their intellect or position in the world are so overpowering that we can not suggest amendments to this league. I can not say I know them all; I do not believe anybody here could get up and say who the 14 members of that commission are.

But there is a practical question to which I was about to call attention. This constitution here says until three months there shall be "no resort to war without previously submitting the question and matters involved either to arbitration or to inquiry by the executive council and until three months after award by the arbitrators or a recommendation by the executive council."

That binds the members of the league; but there have been outlaws among the nations before now. As a matter of history, the sudden manner in which Frederick the Great threw aside all his most solemn promises and poured his armies over Silesia, which Prussia has held ever since he tore it from Austria. How was this present war begun? By the sudden precipitation of an enormous war machine on the unprepared lands of Belgium and the nearly unprepared territory of France.

Suppose we had a Mexican raid across our border. It

has happened. Perhaps Mexican nature has changed and it will never happen again, but it may happen. We are members of the league, we will suppose, and mean to carry out, as we must, every provision in absolute good faith. Mexico does not happen, we will say, to be a member of the league, or she is a member and breaks her covenants; she has not yet given "effective guaranties of sincere intention"; she breaks across our border, and under this article we have got to wait three months before we do anything. That, I think, would be a little hard on the people who live on the border.

Article 13 reads:

"The high contracting parties agree that whenever any dispute or difficulty shall arise between them which they recognize to be suitable for submission to arbitration—"

That is, disputes which a majority of the high contracting parties recognize to be suitable for submission to arbitration—

"—and which cannot be satisfactorily settled by diplomacy, they will submit the whole matter to arbitration."

Of course, the only people who can submit a matter to arbitration are the people who are parties to the dispute. Those who have no dispute can not submit anything to arbitration, because they have nothing to submit.

The reason I bring this apparently trivial point up at this time is that it will be well to differentiate these "theys" and show that in one case the reference is to the high contracting parties who agree that any dispute that arises among them suitable for submission shall be submitted, and, in the other that those between whom the dispute arises will submit it. This is clearly the meaning, I think, but it might be expressed a little more luminously.

The executive council "proposes," I suppose, by a majority, although it does not say so; and how binding the proposal is does not appear. I think it ought to be explicitly stated that a majority of the executive council shall have the power to propose and declare whether the proposal is binding or not. The word "propose" does not imply a binding character, I am well aware; but I should like to get rid of one of the implications of which this document is full.

Article 14 provides that "the executive council shall formulate plans for the establishment of a permanent court of international justice."

Then comes article 15, which is very important, and which provides for those disputes "likely to lead to rupture," which are not submitted to arbitration, but which the high contracting parties agree they will refer to the executive council through the secretary general. They are to make their statements of the case there and such recommendations are to be made as the executive council thinks just and proper for the settlement of the dispute, and "if the report is unanimously agreed to by the members of the council other than the parties to the dispute the high contracting parties agree that they will not go to war with any party which complies with the recommendations."

Unless the council is unanimous, I take it, they are at liberty to go to war. And "if any party shall refuse so to comply the council shall propose measures necessary to give effect to the recommendation." There is no explanation of what measures. I presume we must take it to mean all measures. I will not follow the referred dispute through all its tortuous pathway, but it comes eventually to the body of delegates, and in that connection the proposed constitution says:

> "All the provisions of this article and of article 12 relating to the action of the executive council shall apply to the action and powers of the body of delegates."

This means that the body of delegates, as I take it, must unanimously agree, and, if they do not unanimously agree it appears to me to leave the whole matter open. This may be a protection in certain cases, but in other

cases, it seems to me, it does not offer a very strong resistance or create a very serious obstacle to war.

Now we come to article 16, which says that:

"Should any of the high contracting parties break
or disregard its covenants under article 12 it shall
thereby ipso facto be deemed to have committed an
act of war against all the other members of the league,
which hereby undertake immediately to subject it to
the severance of all trade or financial relations, the
prohibition of all intercourse between their nationals
and the nationals of the covenant-breaking State, and
the prevention of all financial, commercial, or personal
intercourse between the nationals of the covenant-
breaking State and the nationals of any other State,
whether a member of the league or not."

There can be no doubt, under the conditions given,
that we shall be called upon to enter on an economic
war with any State on earth, whether a member of the
league or not, if that State breaks or disregards any of
the covenants relating to arbitration. I merely call attention to it because I venture to think that cutting off
our intercourse with another nation and opening our
territory to the passage of troops is a very serious promise to make; and I think it ought to be honored with
more consideration than perhaps it has yet received.

Article 16 contemplates also the duties of the executive
council in such cases "to recommend what effective military or naval forces the members of the league shall
severally contribute to the armed forces to be used to
protect the covenants of the league."

Here it is apparent that there can be no question that
the armed forces of the United States are to be called
upon for work of this kind; and if we are to act in good
faith, it seems to me we are morally bound by this
clause to contribute what the executive council recommends to the armed forces called forth to protect the
covenants of this league. We may say their recommendation does not bind, but it certainly binds us morally if
we agree to it; and I do not think that we can afford to

enter a league of nations for the preservation of the peace of the world with any misunderstanding on a point of this kind. It seems to me that, in any event, this is a direct interference with the power of Congress to raise armies and maintain navies, and we shall be compelled to have a constitutional amendment in order that this provision may be carried out. However, I am not going at this time to enter upon constitutional questions, which are regarded by most advocates of the league as either humorous or academic.

Article 17 refers to the case of disputes between members of the league and other States not members, and makes various provisions raising many of the questions which are raised by the preceding article.

Article 19 is one of the great articles of the proposed constitution. It provides for the States of the league being mandatories and taking charge of other States classified under various descriptions in the article, which I will not read. Oddly enough, it does not say who is to select the mandatories; at least, I can find nothing in the article stating who is to choose the mandatories, whether the body of the delegates or the executive council; nor does it appear whether a mandatory is bound if once selected. I presume not; but it is not stated. I do not think it is hypercriticism to suggest that when a mandatory is to be selected to take charge of the fortunes of another people, or of another State, there should be some provision for the selection of the mandatory, and it should be made clear, at least, whether the nation so selected is bound.

I am not going into the general question of taking up the work of the mandatories and holding States in tutelage. That was so thoroughly covered by the Senator from Iowa (Mr. Cummins) that it is not necessary for me to take the time of the Senate to discuss it further; but I suggest this thought—and I shall keep on suggesting it—that before the United States binds itself in any way it should be made clear to what extent it is bound, for I have no sympathy with the proposition that we can refuse this and refuse that; in other words, that we can violate the principles of the treaty whenever we feel like it. I think that idea ought to be finally dismissed.

What we are bound to in honor we are bound to do, and I think whether we should be prepared to take charge of other countries and of other people is an important question for the American people to decide. I am not speaking now of States which we are to establish as a result of the war. We must help in the establishment of such States. But that belongs to the German peace. The peace with Germany will settle the boundaries of Poland and the Jugo-Slav and the Czecho-Slovak States and the rest. That is part of the German peace which we are bound to see through; but this article 19 is a promise to enter upon the work of trusteeship for all time, and I venture to think it is very serious and deserves much thoughtful consideration.

Of course article 20, for securing or maintaining fair and humane conditions of labor for men, women, and children is an article in which everyone must sympathize.

Now, article 21:

> "The high contracting parties agree that provision shall be made through the instrumentality of the league to secure and maintain freedom of transit and equitable treatment for the commerce of all States members of the league—"

"Freedom of transit." Does that mean transit by land alone, or does it mean transit by land and water? If it means transit by land and water we shall have to repeal our coastwise laws.

"Equitable treatment for the commerce of all States members of the league." Under that phrase every tariff duty which any other nation thought was inequitable, the league of nations could take hold of, and "recommend" or "advise," or "decide," whatever the word may be. If we leave this loose language there, the tariff and all import duties of every nation will come before the league. If we think that there is an unjust discrimination against some American goods by any country, we have a right to take it before the league and see if we can not get equitable treatment. I think this opens up a wide field of dispute. It does not seem to me, moreover, that to throw all questions of tariff or of import duties

into the jurisdiction of the league can do anything to
promote peace. I think, on the contrary, it will be a
breeder of dissension. I do not see how it can be anything else.

That is the first very vital objection to it in my mind;
but I also have a feeling—and, of course, I am aware
it is an old-fashioned one—that the Constitution gives
to the House of Representatives the right to originate all
bills to raise revenue; and this meddling of the league
with tariff rates, of course, would affect revenue very
seriously.

Next come the international bureaus, in article 22, to
which no one would object.

Then comes article 23, which provides that no such
treaty or international engagement, when once made,
shall be binding until it has been registered by the secretary general. Our Constitution says that it shall become
binding after it has been ratified by the Senate and ratifications have been exchanged; and this seems to add a
new condition to the constitutional conditions. I am
told by friends of this treaty that we can hold back
ratification until the registry has taken place, but while
this ingenious scheme undoubtedly slips by the Constitution, it seems to me that it would be just as well to make
it plain and avoid a constitutional objection which would
get into our courts if nowhere else.

Article 24 is not very clear, but it says:

"It shall be the right of the body of delegates from
time to time to advise the reconsideration by State
members of the league of treaties which shall become
inapplicable and of international conditions of which
the continuance may endanger the peace of the world."

I confess I do not clearly understand what is meant
by this. I have no doubt that there are Senators, who
like the league just as it is printed, who perhaps can
explain that thoroughly; but "international conditions
of which the continuance may endanger the peace of
the world" needs some examination.

Article 25 provides that we solemnly engage not to
enter hereafter into any engagements inconsistent with

the terms of the league of nations. Now, that is a distinct limitation upon the treaty-making power of the Constitution. That is a new provision which must be added, in my judgment, by constitutional amendment if this article remains unchanged. The Constitution gives us very well-defined powers as to treaty-making, and here we promise that we will not enter upon any engagement inconsistent with the terms of the league of nations. The object is excellent, of course, but it nevertheless raises a very obvious constitutional difficulty.

The provision for amendments to the constitution of the league makes amendment very difficult, if not practically impossible. That is another reason why I am anxious, perhaps unduly anxious, as to the importance of having these articles clear and precise now, before we are asked to approve them. When our Constitution was formed we had in the convention some 50 of the ablest men in the country, and some of the ablest men, I believe, in the world. They took some three months, as I recall, in their work. They had a committee on style, headed by Gouverneur Morris, and that is the reason the language of the Constitution of the United States is so extremely clear, precise, and excellent; and yet, precise and clear as those articles are, under them, and especially under the grant in regard to commerce between the States, have arisen questions, the decisions of which by the Supreme Court would fill volumes, showing the extreme difficulty and also the need of extreme care in phraseology. I think a committee on style in this league, to redraft the proposed constitution and put it in legal language, would not have been amiss.

Finally, as I come to the end, the Senate will observe that there is no provision for withdrawal. That is very important. We are making an indissoluble treaty. The old fashion of treaties, always beginning by swearing eternal friendship, common certainly as late as the seventeenth century, has been abandoned in modern times entirely. Almost all treaties now contain provisions for terminating the treaty on due notice. Others limit the life of the treaty. An indissoluble treaty, without the right of withdrawal, is very unusual.

It has been pointed out to me—not once but many

times—that we can abrogate, that we can violate, that we can overrule any treaty by the action of Congress. I know that. We can denounce it. I know that. I think, however, that to form a league of this kind and leave it in such a form that no nation can get out of it except by abrogation, by violation, or by denunciation— action which usually in the intercourse of nations means war—is very serious. If the right of withdrawal were preserved, a nation could withdraw—on due notice, of course—without shattering the league or impairing in any way the sanctity of treaties. It seems to me there ought to be some such provision. If you leave a country—I am not speaking merely of the United States—tied hard and fast so that they can not get out of this league without tearing everything to pieces by denouncing it or by abrogating it or violating it, you create a situation which in my mind does not promote the peace of nations, but the very reverse.

I have seen here not so many years ago an occasion when, in a burst of passion, the House of Representatives swept away a treaty with a friendly nation, which contained provisions for notice and withdrawal, without any regard for the terms of the treaty. The resolution was modified here so as to avoid insult and offense; but that was the way it passed the House in a moment of anger and excitement. Passion and emotion are not going to perish or die out of men because we sign an agreement for a league of nations. They will remain. The case to which I have referred, which was with Russia, involved the good relations of the United States with one nation; but such treatment of the provisions of the league would involve a similar feeling on the part of all nations of the earth, practically all members of the league. I think this is a very serious danger, a danger to that peace of the world which we are all seeking to promote. It must be avoided by a simple amendment.

Thus, very imperfectly, I have reviewed these articles. I have stated some of the doubts and questionings which have arisen in my own mind, and I could print in the *Record* letters which I have received showing other points and questions which have occurred to other minds. This demonstrates the uncertainties which cloud this instrument from beginning to end. When the United States enters into an indissoluble permanent alliance there ought to be, as I have said, no uncertainties in the terms of the agreement. I earnestly desire to do everything that can be done to secure the peace of the world, but these articles as they stand in this proposed constitution seem to give a rich promise of being fertile in producing controversies and misunderstandings. They also make some demands which I do not believe any nation would submit to in a time of stress. Therefore this machinery would not promote the peace of the world, but would have a directly opposite effect. It would tend to increase the subjects of misunderstanding and dispute among the nations. Is it not possible to draft a better, more explicit, less dangerous scheme than the one here and now presented? Surely we are not to be shut up to this as the last and only word to take or leave.

To those who object that the criticism of this tentative draft plan of the committee of the peace conference must be not only destructive but constructive it might be said that the burden of proof lies upon those who propose, in order to establish the future peace of the world, that the United States must curtail its independence, part with a portion of its sovereignty, and abandon all the international policies which have been so successful for more than a hundred years. Those who support the present draft of the constitution for the league must demonstrate that it is an improvement before they can expect its general acceptance. But the Senate can not at this time undertake to make plans for a league; because we are in the process of negotiation, and the Senate does not begin to act until the stage of ratification is reached. At the same time there are certain constructive propositions which it would be well, I think, for the peace conference to consider. If it is said that you can preserve the Monroe doctrine by extending it, which appears to me clearly to mean its destruction and to be a contradiction in terms, then let us put three lines into the draft for the league which will preserve the Monroe doctrine beyond any possibility of doubt or question. It is easily done. Let us also have, if we enter the league, a complete exclusion from the league's jurisdiction of such questions as are involved in immigration and the right of each country to say who shall come within its borders and become citizens. This and certain other questions vital to national existence ought to be exempted from any control or jurisdiction by the league or its officials by a very few words, such as can be found in the arbitration treaties of 1907. There should be some definite provision for peaceful withdrawal from the league if any nation desires to withdraw. Lastly, let us have a definite statement in the constitution of the league as to whether the league is to have an international force of its own or is to have the power to summon the armed forces of the different members of the league. Let it be stated in plain language whether the "measures," the "recommendations," or the suggestions of the executive council are to be binding upon the members of the league and are to compel them, technically or morally, to do what the league delegates and the executive council determine to be necessary. On the question of the use of force we should not proceed in the dark. If those who support the league decline to make such simple statements as these—I mean statements in the body of the instrument, not individual statements—it is impossible to avoid the conclusion that they are seeking to do by indirection and the use of nebulous phrases what they are not willing to do directly, and nothing could be more fatal to the preservation of the world's peace than this, for every exercise of power by the executive council which the signatories to the league might fairly consider to be doubtful would lead to very perilous controversies and to menacing quarrels.

Unless some better constitution for a league than this can be drawn, it seems to me, after such examination as I have been able to give, that the world's peace would be much better, much more surely promoted, by allowing the United States to go on under the Monroe doctrine, responsible for the peace of this hemisphere, without any danger of collision with Europe as to questions among the various American States, and if a league is desired it might be made up by the European nations whose interests are chiefly concerned, and with which the United States could coöperate fully and at any time, whenever coöperation was needed. I suppose I shall make myself the subject of derision for quoting from the Farewell Address, but it states a momentous truth so admirably that I can not refrain from giving it, for I think it ought to be borne in mind. Washington says:

"Europe has a set of primary interests which to us have none or a very remote relation. Hence she must be engaged in frequent controversies the causes of which are essentially foreign to our concerns. Hence, therefore, it must be unwise in us to implicate ourselves by artificial ties in the ordinary vicissitudes of her politics or the ordinary combinations and collisions of her friendships or enmities."

It must be remembered that if the United States enters any league of nations it does so for the benefit of the world at large, and not for its own benefit. The people of the United States are a peace-loving people. We have no boundaries to rectify, no schemes, and no desires for the acquisition or conquest of territory. We have in the main kept the peace in the American hemisphere. The States of South America have grown constantly more stable, and revolutions have well-nigh disappeared in the States south of those bordering on the Caribbean. No one questions that the United States is able to prevent any conflicts in the American hemisphere which would involve the world in any way or be more than passing difficulties, which in most cases could be settled by arbitration. If we join a league, therefore, it must be with a view to maintaining peace in Europe, where all the greatest wars have originated, and where there is always danger of war, and in Asia, where serious conflicts may arise at any moment. If we join a league, of course, we have in mind the danger of European conflicts springing up in such a way as to involve us in the defense of civilization, as has just happened in the war with Germany. But such wars as that are, fortunately, rare; so rare that one has never before occurred, and when the time came we took our part; but in the main our share in any league must be almost wholly for the benefit of others. We have the right, therefore, to demand that there shall be nothing in any agreement for the maintenance of the world's peace which is likely to produce new causes of difference and dissension, or which is calculated to injure the United States, or compel from us undue sacrifice, or put us in a position where we may be forced to serve the ambitions of others. There is no gain for peace in the Americas to be found by annexing the Americas to the European system. Whatever we do there we do from almost purely altruistic motives, and therefore we are entitled to consider every proposition with the utmost care in order to make sure that it does not do us injustice or render future conditions worse instead of better than they are at present.

To me the whole subject is one of enormous difficulties. We are all striving for a like result; but to make any real advances toward the future preservation of the world's peace will take time, care, and long consideration. We can not reach our objects by a world constitution hastily constructed in a few weeks in Paris in the midst of the excitement of a war not yet ended. The one thing to do, as I said in the Senate some time ago, and that which I now wish above all others, is to make the peace with Germany—to make a peace which by its terms will prevent her from breaking out again upon the world; to exclude Turkey from Europe, strengthen Greece, and give freedom and independence to the Armenians and to the Jewish and Christian populations of Asia Minor; to erect the barrier States for the Poles, Czecho-Slovaks, and Jugo-Slavs; to take possession of the Kiel Canal; to establish the Baltic States and free them from Russia and restore Danish Schleswig to Denmark. Provision must be made for indemnities or reparation, or by whatever name we choose to call the damages to be exacted from Germany. We ought, in my judgment, to receive indemnities which would enable us to provide for the *Lusitania* claims and for the destruction of our ships by submarines—to go no further. But the enormous losses of England and Italy in shipping should be made good, either in money or in kind. Belgium must be restored and fully compensated for her terrible injuries.

Finally there is France, and the indemnities to France ought to be ample and complete. The machinery taken from her factories should be restored. The cattle driven from her fields should be brought back. The debt of the free and civilized world to France is inestimable. Our own debt to her is very large. France has been our outpost and our bulwark. She has bared her breast to the storm and stood between us and the advancing hordes of Germany in the darkest days. It was France, aided by the small but gallant army of England, which checked the onrush of the Germans at the first battle of the Marne. It is her land which has been desolated and her villages and cities which have been destroyed. She should have compensation to the utmost limit in every way. Eternal justice demands it. But it is also to our immediate and selfish interest as a Nation that France should be made as strong as possible. Alsace and Lorraine she must have without question and without reduction, and other barriers if necessary to make her impregnable to German assault, for on the strength of France more than anything else, because she is the neighbor of Germany, rests the future peace of the world. We ought then to make this peace with Germany and make it at once. Much time has been wasted. The delays have bred restlessness and confusion everywhere. Germany is lifting her head again. The whining after defeat is changing to threats. She is seeking to annex nine millions of Germans in German Austria. She is reaching out in Russia and reviving her financial and commercial penetration everywhere. Her fields have not been desolated nor her factories destroyed. Germany is again threatening, and the only source of a great war is to be found in the future as in the past in Germany. She should be chained and fettered now and this menace to the world's peace should be removed at once. Whatever else we fought for certainly our first and paramount purpose was to defeat Germany. The victory over Germany is not yet complete. Let it be made so without delay.

That which I desire above everything else, that which is nearest to my heart, is to bring our soldiers home. The making of a league of nations will not do that. We can only bring our soldiers home, entirely and completely, when the peace with Germany is made and proclaimed. Let that peace be made and I can assure the world that when the treaty of peace with Germany comes in this

Chamber there will be no delay in the Senate of the United States. We must bring our men back from France —the men who fought the war, the men who made the personal sacrifice. Let us get them back at once, and to that end let us have the peace made with Germany, made now, and not delay it until the complicated questions of the league of nations can be settled with the care and consideration which they demand. What is it that delays the peace with Germany? Discussions over the league of nations; nothing else. Let us have peace now, in this year of grace 1919. That is the first step to the future peace of the world. The next step will be to make sure if we can that the world shall have peace in the year 1950 or 2000. Let us have the peace with Germany and bring our boys home.

This is the immediate thing to do toward the establishment of the world's peace, but there is an issue involved in the league constitution presented to us which far overshadows all others. We are asked to depart now for the first time from the foreign policies of Washington. We are invited to move away from George Washington toward the other end of the line at which stands the sinister figure of Trotsky, the champion of internationalism.

We have in this country, a Government of the people, for the people, and by the people, the freest and best Government in the world, and we are the great rampart to-day against the anarchy and disorder which have taken possession of Russia and are trying to invade every peaceful country in the world. For Lincoln's Government of the people, for the people, and by the people we are asked to substitute in the United States on many vital points government of, for, and by other people. Pause and consider well before you take this fateful step. I do not say that agreements may not be made among the nations which stand for ordered freedom and civilization, which will do much to secure and preserve the peace of the world; but no such agreement has yet been presented to us. We must beware of the dangers which beset our path. We must not lose by an improvident attempt to reach eternal peace all that we have won by war and sacrifice. We must build no bridges across the chasm which now separates American freedom and order from Russian anarchy and destruction. We must see to it that the democracy of the United States, which has prospered so mightily in the past, is not drawn by any hasty error or by any glittering delusions, through specious devices of supernational government, within the toils of international socialism and anarchy. I wish nothing but good to all the· races of men. I hope and pray that peace, unbroken peace, may reign everywhere on earth. But America and the American people are first in my heart now and always. I can never assent to any scheme, no matter how fair its outward seeming, which is not for the welfare and for the highest and best interest of my own beloved people of whom I am one—the American people —the people of the United States.

APPENDIX II

GENTLEMEN OF THE SENATE: On the eighteenth of
December last I addressed an identic note to the governments of the nations now at war requesting them to state,
more definitely than they had yet been stated by either
group of belligerents, the terms upon which they would
deem it possible to make peace. I spoke on behalf of
humanity and of the rights of all neutral nations like our
own, many of whose most vital interests the war puts in
constant jeopardy. The Central Powers united in a reply
which stated merely that they were ready to meet their
antagonists in conference to discuss terms of peace. The
Entente Powers have replied much more definitely and
have stated, in general terms, indeed, but with sufficient
definiteness to imply details, the arrangements, guarantees, and acts of preparation which they deem to be
the indispensable conditions of a satisfactory settlement.
We are that much nearer a definite discussion of the
peace which shall end the present war. We are that
much nearer the discussion of the international concert
which must thereafter hold the world at peace. In every
discussion of the peace that must end this war it is taken
for granted that that peace must be followed by some
definite concert of power which will make it virtually
impossible that any such catastrophe should ever over-
whelm us again. Every lover of mankind, every sane and
thoughtful man must take that for granted.

I have sought this opportunity to address you because
I thought that I owed it to you, as the council associated
with me in the final determination of our international
obligations, to disclose to you without reserve the thought
and purpose that have been taking form in my mind in
regard to the duty of our Government in the days to

come when it will be necessary to lay afresh and upon a new plan the foundations of peace among the nations.

It is inconceivable that the people of the United States should play no part in that great enterprise. To take part in such a service will be the opportunity for which they have sought to prepare themselves by the very principles and purposes of their polity and the approved practices of their Government ever since the days when they set up a new nation in the high and honourable hope that it might in all that it was and did show mankind the way to liberty. They cannot in honour withhold the service to which they are now about to be challenged. They do not wish to withhold it. But they owe it to themselves and to the other nations of the world to state the conditions under which they will feel free to render it.

That service is nothing less than this, to add their authority and their power to the authority and force of other nations to guarantee peace and justice throughout the world. Such a settlement cannot now be long postponed. It is right that before it comes this Government should frankly formulate the conditions upon which it would feel justified in asking our people to approve its formal and solemn adherence to a League for Peace. I am here to attempt to state those conditions.

The present war must first be ended; but we owe it to candour and to a just regard for the opinion of mankind to say that, so far as our participation in guarantees of future peace is concerned, it makes a great deal of difference in what way and upon what terms it is ended. The treaties and agreements which bring it to an end must embody terms which will create a peace that is worth guaranteeing and preserving, a peace that will win the approval of mankind, not merely a peace that will serve the several interests and immediate aims of the nations engaged. We shall have no voice in determining what those terms shall be, but we shall, I feel sure, have a voice in determining whether they shall be made lasting or not by the guarantees of a universal covenant; and our judgment upon what is fundamental and essential as a condition precedent to permanency should be spoken now, not afterwards when it may be too late.

No covenant of cooperative peace that does not include the peoples of the New World can suffice to keep the future safe against war; and yet there is only one sort of peace that the peoples of America could join in guaranteeing. The elements of that peace must be elements that engage the confidence and satisfy the principles of the American governments, elements consistent with their political faith and with the practical convictions which the peoples of America have once for all embraced and undertaken to defend.

I do not mean to say that any American government would throw any obstacle in the way of any terms of peace the governments now at war might agree upon, or seek to upset them when made, whatever they might be. I only take it for granted that mere terms of peace between the belligerents will not satisfy even the belligerents themselves. Mere agreements may not make peace secure. It will be absolutely necessary that a force be created as a guarantor of the permanency of the settlement so much greater than the force of any nation now engaged or any alliance hitherto framed or projected that no nation, no probable combination of nations could face or withstand it. If the peace presently to be made is to endure, it must be a peace made secure by the organized major force of mankind.

The terms of the immediate peace agreed upon will determine whether it is a peace for which such a guarantee can be secured. The question upon which the whole future peace and policy of the world depends is this: Is the present war a struggle for a just and secure peace, or only for a new balance of power? If it be only a struggle for a new balance of power, who will guarantee, who can guarantee, the stable equilibrium of the new arrangement? Only a tranquil Europe can be a stable Europe. There must be, not a balance of power, but a community of power; not organized rivalries, but an organized common peace.

Fortunately we have received very explicit assurances on this point. The statesmen of both of the groups of nations now arrayed against one another have said, in terms that could not be misinterpreted, that it was no part of the purpose they had in mind to crush their an-

tagonists. But the implications of these assurances may
not be equally clear to all,—may not be the same on
both sides of the water. I think it will be serviceable if
I attempt to set forth what we understand them to be.

They imply, first of all, that it must be a peace without
victory. It is not pleasant to say this. I beg that I
may be permitted to put my own interpretation upon it
and that it may be understood that no other interpretation was in my thought. I am seeking only to face realities and to face them without soft concealments. Victory
would mean peace forced upon the loser, a victor's terms
imposed upon the vanquished. It would be accepted in
humiliation, under duress, at an intolerable sacrifice, and
would leave a sting, a resentment, a bitter memory upon
which terms of peace would rest, not permanently, but
only as upon quicksand. Only a peace between equals
can last. Only a peace the very principle of which is
equality and a common participation in a common benefit. The right state of mind, the right feeling between
nations, is as necessary for a lasting peace as is the just
settlement of vexed questions of territory or of racial
and national allegiance.

The equality of nations upon which peace must be
founded if it is to last must be an equality of rights; the
guarantees exchanged must neither recognize nor imply
a difference between big nations and small, between those
that are powerful and those that are weak. Right must
be based upon the common strength, not upon the individual strength, of the nations upon whose concert peace
will depend. Equality of territory or of resources there
of course cannot be; nor any other sort of equality not
gained in the ordinary peaceful and legitimate development of the people themselves. But no one asks or expects anything more than an equality of rights. Mankind is looking now for freedom of life, not for equipoises
of power.

And there is a deeper thing involved than even equality
of right among organized nations. No peace can last,
or ought to last, which does not recognize and accept the
principle that governments derive all their just powers
from the consent of the governed, and that no right anywhere exists to hand peoples about from sovereignty to

sovereignty as if they were property. I take it for granted, for instance, if I may venture upon a single example, that statesmen everywhere are agreed that there should be a united, independent, and autonomous Poland, and that henceforth inviolable security of life, of worship, and of industrial and social development should be guaranteed to all peoples who have lived hitherto under the power of governments devoted to a faith and purpose hostile to their own.

I speak of this, not because of any desire to exalt an abstract political principle which has always been held very dear by those who have sought to build up liberty in America, but for the same reason that I have spoken of the other conditions of peace which seem to me clearly indispensable,—because I wish frankly to uncover realities. Any peace which does not recognize and accept this principle will inevitably be upset. It will not rest upon the affections or the convictions of mankind. The ferment of spirit of whole populations will fight subtly and constantly against it, and all the world will sympathize. The world can be at peace only if its life is stable, and there can be no stability where the will is in rebellion, where there is not tranquillity of spirit and a sense of justice, of freedom, and of right.

So far as practicable, moreover, every great people now struggling towards a full development of its resources and of its powers should be assured a direct outlet to the great highways of the sea. Where this cannot be done by the cession of territory, it can no doubt be done by the neutralization of direct rights of way under the general guarantee which will assure the peace itself. With a right comity of arrangement no nation need be shut away from free access to the open paths of the world's commerce.

And the paths of the sea must alike in law and in fact be free. The freedom of the seas is the *sine qua non* of peace, equality, and cooperation. No doubt a somewhat radical reconsideration of many of the rules of international practice hitherto thought to be established may be necessary in order to make the seas indeed free and common in practically all circumstances for the use of mankind, but the motive for such changes is convincing and compelling. There can be no trust or intimacy between the peoples of the world without them. The free, constant, unthreatened intercourse of nations is an essential part of the process of peace and of development. It need not be difficult either to define or to secure the freedom of the seas if the governments of the world sincerely desire to come to an agreement concerning it.

It is a problem closely connected with the limitation of naval armaments and the cooperation of the navies of the world in keeping the seas at once free and safe. And the question of limiting naval armaments opens the wider and perhaps more difficult question of the limitation of armies and of all programmes of military preparation. Difficult and delicate as these questions are, they must be faced with the utmost candour and decided in a spirit of real accommodation if peace is to come with healing in its wings, and come to stay. Peace cannot be had without concession and sacrifice. There can be no sense of safety and equality among the nations if great preponderating armaments are henceforth to continue here and there to be built up and maintained. The statesmen of the world must plan for peace and nations must adjust and accommodate their policy to it as they have planned for war and made ready for pitiless contest and rivalry. The question of armaments, whether on land or sea, is the most immediately and intensely practical question connected with the future fortunes of nations and of mankind.

I have spoken upon these great matters without reserve and with the utmost explicitness because it has seemed to me to be necessary if the world's yearning desire for peace was anywhere to find free voice and utterance. Perhaps I am the only person in high authority amongst all the peoples of the world who is at liberty to speak and hold nothing back. I am speaking as an individual, and yet I am speaking also, of course, as the responsible head of a great government, and I feel confident that I have said what the people of the United States would wish me to say. May I not add that I hope and believe that I am in effect speaking for liberals and friends of humanity in every nation and of every programme of liberty? I would fain believe that I am speaking for the silent mass of mankind everywhere who have as yet had no place or opportunity to speak their real hearts out concerning the death and ruin they see to have come already upon the persons and the homes they hold most dear.

And in holding out the expectation that the people and Government of the United States will join the other civilized nations of the world in guaranteeing the permanence of peace upon such terms as I have named I speak with the greater boldness and confidence because it is clear to every man who can think that there is in this promise no breach in either our traditions or our policy as a nation, but a fulfilment, rather, of all that we have professed or striven for.

I am proposing, as it were, that the nations should with one accord adopt the doctrine of President Monroe as the doctrine of the world; that no nation should seek to extend its policy over any other nation or people, but that every people should be left free to determine its own polity, its own way of development, unhindered, unthreatened, unafraid, the little along with the great and powerful.

I am proposing that all nations henceforth avoid entangling alliances which would draw them into competitions of power, catch them in a net of intrigue and selfish rivalry, and disturb their own affairs with influences intruded from without. There is no entangling alliance in a concert of power. When all unite to act in the same sense and with the same purpose all act in the common interest and are free to live their own lives under a common protection.

I am proposing government by the consent of the governed; that freedom of the seas which in international conference after conference representatives of the United States have urged with the eloquence of those who are the convinced disciples of liberty; and that moderation of armaments which makes of armies and navies a power for order merely, not an instrument of aggression or of selfish violence.

These are American principles, American policies. We could stand for no others. And they are also the principles and policies of forward looking men and women everywhere, of every modern nation, of every enlightened community. They are the principles of mankind and must prevail.

APPENDIX III

Speech of February 28, 1917, in reply to the President's Address of January 22, 1917.

MR. LODGE. Let me say, first, Mr. President, that I shall make no allusion whatever to the note from Germany which has startled the country this morning. That note is in the hands of the President, in the hands of the Chief Executive. It places upon him a great responsibility, and no word shall fall from my lips which by any possibility could embarrass him in dealing with that note. I shall confine myself absolutely to the propositions of the recent address by the President to the Senate.

Mr. President, I have cherished an earnest hope that we might conclude the necessary business of Congress before the 4th of March and spare to ourselves and to the country the misfortune of another summer session. It is therefore with extreme reluctance that I venture to take any time in discussing a subject not immediately connected with the measures now demanding action if we are to avoid an extra session. I can find justification for doing so only in the extreme seriousness of the questions forced upon the attention of Congress by the President's address delivered in the Senate Chamber on Monday, the 22d of January. Moreover, the President was kind enough to say that he sought this opportunity to address us because he thought that he owed it to us, as the council associated with him in the final determination of our international obligations, to disclose to us without reserve the thought and purpose that had been taking form in his mind in regard to the duty of our Government in the days to come when it will be necessary to lay afresh and upon a new plan the foundations of peace among the nations.

The President has thus recognized the duties imposed upon the Senate by the Constitution in regard to our foreign relations and has invited an expression of our opinions. We have abundant evidence of the gravity of the questions thus presented. The newspaper press and others, employing generous if inaccurate language, have decorated the speech with the adjective "epochal," which calls at once to mind the movement of glaciers and vast tracts of geologic time. I shall content myself with a simpler word and say that the President's utterances in this Chamber, especially as he declared that he said what the people of the United States would wish him to say, and that he was setting forth the principles of mankind, are in a high degree important. I do not think that the failure on the part of the Senate to discuss the President's statements would imply either approval or disapproval or would by implication bind either the Senate or the country to any given course of action. But none the less it seems to me most desirable that as we were chosen in this instance to be the medium of communication with foreign nations and with the people of the United States we should at least give our own understanding of what the President proposed.

It is not necessary, of course, to say anything as to the many general and just observations made by the President in regard to the horrors and miseries of war, or the dangers and complications with which the present conflict threatens the United States, or as to his or our duty as servants of humanity. Of course, we all agree most heartily with the proposition that peace—just and righteous peace—is infinitely better than war; that virtue is better than vice; that, in Browning's words:

"It's wiser being good than bad;
It's safer being meek than fierce:
It's fitter being sane than mad."

In all these declarations we must be cordially and thoroughly of one mind. All that I desire to do is to speak briefly of the substantive propositions contained in the President's address and, by analysis, discover, if I can, to precisely what policies and course of action he is undertaking to commit the country. We have a right—indeed, it is our duty—to learn, if possible, just what the President means and whither he is trying to lead us. To attain this object we must, in his own language, "uncover the realities."

As I understand it, the President is aiming at two objects, both in the highest degree admirable—to bring to an end the war now raging in Europe, and to make provision for the future and permanent peace of the world. It is to the promotion of the second purpose that he proposes action on the part of the United States, saying that we should frankly formulate the conditions upon which this Government would feel justified in asking our people to approve its firm and solemn adherence to a league for peace. He then proceeds to state the two purposes in this way:

"The present war must first be ended; but we owe it to candor and to a just regard for the opinion of mankind to say that, so far as our participation in guarantees of future peace is concerned, it makes a great deal of difference in what way and upon what terms it is ended. The treaties and agreements which bring it to an end must embody terms which will create a peace that is worth guaranteeing and preserving, a peace that will win the approval of mankind, not merely a peace that will serve the several interests and immediate aims of the nations engaged. We shall have no voice in determining what those terms shall be, but we shall, I feel sure, have a voice in determining whether they shall be made lasting or not by the guarantees of a universal covenant; and our judgment upon what is fundamental and essential as a condition precedent to permanency should be spoken now, not afterwards, when it may be too late."

It will be observed that in this paragraph of his address the President says explicitly that the first condition precedent to any action for a league for peace must be the ending of the present war. He then declares that the treaties and agreements which bring the war to an end must create a peace which is worth guaranteeing and preserving. He says further that we shall have no voice in determining what those terms shall be, but that they can never be lasting or permanent unless they meet with our approval. It seems to me that this is equivalent to saying that we are to have no voice in what the terms of the peace which ends the present war shall be, but that at the same time the terms must be what we approve or we shall not be able to enter into any future league to preserve the peace of the world. In other words, our action is to be conditioned upon the terms of a peace which we have no voice in determining. If the belligerents when they come to make peace do not make all the terms satisfactory to us, they cannot look to us to aid in making that peace lasting and permanent. The President then goes on to lay down the general principles upon which the terms of the peace, in which we are to have no voice, shall be based if the peace thus obtained is to be a peace worth having.

In the first place, it must be "a peace without victory." It is not quite clear just what this means, unless it is intended to be a declaration in the interest of one group of belligerents who, having abandoned the original hope of complete victory, wish to make peace in the most advantageous way now open to them. This interpretation must be at once dismissed, for it is not to be supposed for a moment that this can be the President's object, because we all know how devoted he is to neutrality—how it has been his belief from the beginning that it was the duty of the American people to be neutral even in their thoughts—and he is, of course, well aware that it is as easy to be unneutral in forcing a peace favorable to one side as it is to help one side against the other while war is raging. Peace without victory can only mean therefore that neither side is to gain anything by the terms of peace through victory in the field, because if there are no victories on either side there can be neither gains nor losses in the final settlement except through the voluntary self-sacrifice and generosity of the combatants; in other words, all the lives have been given in this war and all the money spent in vain and Europe is to emerge from the conflict in exactly the same situation as when she entered it. It seems to me incredible that people who have made such awful sacrifices as have been made by the belligerents should be content to forego the prospect of victory, in the hope of bringing the war to an end, with everything left just as it was. In such a result they might well think that all their efforts and losses, all their miseries and sorrows and sacrifices were a criminal and hideous futility. Both sides have been inspired by the hope of victory; both sides are still so inspired. Some of the belligerents, at least, believe that the one object of the war is to win a victory which will assure a permanent peace, and would regard a reproduction of the old conditions, with all their menacing possibilities, as something far worse than war. They are determined that the dark peril which has overshadowed their own lives and threatened the independence and very existence of their own countries shall not be permitted to darken the future and be a curse to their children and their children's children. For this they are fighting and suffering and dying. Perhaps they ought not to think in this way; perhaps they ought to feel as the President does. But we must deal with things as they are; we must uncover realities, and there is no doubt of the reality of the desire among many of the great nations of Europe to close this war with a victory which will give them a peace worth having, and not a mere breathing space filled with the upbuilding of crushing armaments and then another and a worse war. Such, I think, is their point of view; but as a practical question for us, dealing with a condition on which we are to build a future league for peace to which we are to be a party, how are we going to provide that it shall be a peace without victory? How are we to arrange that there shall be no victories?

The President says that a peace won by victory would leave a bitter memory upon which peace terms could not rest permanently but only as upon quicksand. There has been pretty constant fighting in this unhappy world ever since the time when history begins its records, and in speaking of lasting peace in terms of history we can only speak comparatively. I think, however, that I am not mistaken in saying that since the fall of the Roman Empire the longest period of general peace which Europe and the Western World have enjoyed was during the forty years following the Battle of Waterloo. During that time there were, of course, a few small and unimportant wars, but there was no great general conflict among great nations anywhere, and yet the peace of 1815 was a peace imposed upon France by the victorious allies if ever such a thing happened in the history of mankind. There was an attempt to settle that Napoleonic war by a treaty "without victory" and between equals. The treaty was signed at Amiens on March 27, 1802. This "peace without victory" lasted exactly thirteen months and nineteen days, and then war came again and continued for twelve years, and was ended by a peace through victory of the most absolute kind, and that peace has lasted between England and France for a hundred years and has never been broken. Our war with Spain ended with a peace based on the complete victory of the United States by land and sea. There is no reason to suppose that because it was a peace obtained by victory it is not a lasting peace. I might cite other examples, but one affirmative instance is enough to shatter a universal negative. As the Frenchman said, "No generalization is ever completely true, not even this one." It is a little hasty, therefore, to say that no peace can endure which is the fruit of victory. The peace which lasts is the peace which rests on justice and righteousness, and if it is a just and righteous peace it makes no difference whether it is based on the compromises and concessions of treaties or upon victories in the field. But I return to and repeat the main question before I leave this point. If peace without victory is to be a condition precedent of lasting peace to be maintained by the covenant in which we are to take part, how are we practically to compel or secure the existence of such a condition?

The next condition precedent stated by the President without which we can have no peace that "can last or ought to last" is the universal acceptance of the idea that governments derive all their just powers from the consent of the governed and that any peace which does not recognize and accept this principle will inevitably be upset. Must the fact that any given government rests on the consent of the governed be determined by a popular vote or by the general acceptance by the people of the existing form of government? Who is to decide whether the principle is recognized under the different governments of the world with whom we are to form the League for Peace "supported by the organized major force of mankind"? If the recognition of this principle is to be essential to the lasting peace which we are to support—and every American, of course, believes in and admires the principle—what is to be done about Korea, or Hindustan, or Alsace-Lorraine, or the Trentino, or the Slav Provinces of Austria, or the Danish Duchies? Does the government of Armenia by Turkey, with its organized massacres, rest on the consent of the governed, and if it does not are we to take steps to remedy it, or is Turkey to be excluded from the league, or is the league to coerce Turkey to an observance of our principles? As a preliminary of the peace which we are to help enforce must we insist that it cannot exist if there are any people under any government who have been handed from sovereignty to sovereignty as if they were property? I am not contesting the justice of the principle—far from it— but we may well ask how we are going to compel the adoption of that principle by other governments, and this is no idle question but a real and practical one which cannot be evaded. If we enter upon this most desirable reform of other nations, there may be people sufficiently malevolent to ask whether we secured Louisiana by a vote of the people of that Territory, or California and other acquisitions from Mexico, or the Philippines, or Porto Rico, or even Alaska, where there were Russian inhabitants who were handed over for a price, very much like property or as serfs *adscripti glebæ*.

The next condition precedent where I should like to "uncover the reality" is that to obtain a firm and lasting peace we must have "freedom of the seas." The President does not say whether it is the high seas or all seas. Let us assume that it is the high seas. The demand must apply either to time of war or time of peace, or both; but for many, many years there has been no interference with the freedom of the seas in time of peace. I think we may therefore assume again that the President's "freedom of the seas" must mean the freedom of the seas in time of war. Is the plan, then, to compel all nations to abandon the rights of belligerents to blockade a hostile port in time of war or to seize contraband going to their enemy? To attain this end we should have to begin by sweeping away all existing doctrines as to the rights of belligerents at sea in time of war—doctrines which were so widely extended in regard to contraband and blockade by the decisions of our own Supreme Court during our Civil War. These doctrines were established by us in the face of very general opposition and have been since accepted and acted upon by belligerents in other wars as the sound construction of international rights. We should therefore have to begin at once by tearing down the fabric of law on this point which we ourselves created and built up.

In the *Congressional Record* of January 26, on page 2376, there is a printed code prepared by a committee of the American Institute of International Law, which has been accepted by the institute and is to be presented to the twenty-one American Republics. This code deals with the freedom of commerce, the rights and duties of belligerents, and the rights and duties of neutrals in time of war. The committee was appointed to deal with this subject on the suggestion of Mr. Lansing, and this code is the result. I have no right to infer that this code represents what the President meant by the freedom of the seas in his recent address, but it embodies in concrete form some of the supposed cases which I have just suggested to the Senate. To state the propositions of the code fully—still more to discuss its details—would occupy hours, and I have only minutes to spare; but what Mr. Temple said when he presented it covers, in a general way, the general purposes of the code. Mr. Temple said:

"The seas are already free in time of peace. The new code provides for the freedom of the seas in time of war. It abolishes blockade entirely, forbids interference with the mails, declares that merchant ships of the enemy, as well as those of neutrals, shall be free from capture, and abolishes the right of visit and search. Even vessels carrying contraband may in no case be confiscated or sunk under any pretext whatever, though the contraband itself may be confiscated or destroyed by the captor."

These are the radical changes which I have just been imagining as possible, and this code, if adopted, would sweep away practically all the most important belligerent rights at sea which have hitherto existed, as well as the doctrines which we extended and laid down during our Civil War and the decisions of our Supreme Court. I do not suppose that there is any idea of overthrowing and sweeping away international law, the work of centuries, in regard to belligerent rights at sea during the present war, which began with the old system fully recognized by the world and which could not now be altered, except by an entire breach of neutrality if attempted by neutrals. I assume that this new code is to take effect after the war.

There are only two comments which I desire to make upon it. One is that if it embodies the freedom of the seas spoken of by the President in general terms it would require for its enforcement the navies of all nations who were parties to the league for peace, for, if belligerents engaged in war rested their rights on existing law and long-established usage they could only be brought into obedience to the new code by force, and, as I have already said, we should then, as a party to the league, be obliged by force of arms to take our share in preventing the exercise of these long-established rights. The conference of neutrals provided for in the code would be looked to for its maintenance and the occurrences of the present war do not give us much hope that such a conference would be very effective in future wars.

My other comment is this: There has been no violation of the rights of neutrals so glaring as the planting of contact mines on the high seas. That is a method of destruction without warrant of international law or the customs and usages of nations. A contact mine is no respecter of persons. It is just as likely to destroy a perfectly innocent ship, without contraband and on a perfectly innocent voyage, as it is to destroy the warship of a belligerent. No worse attack upon the rights of neutrals could have been made than by this planting of contact mines on the high seas. So far as I am aware no neutral has protested against it—certainly no neutral has protested effectively—and I observe with some surprise that in all this long code for the protection of neutral rights upon the seas in time of war there is not one word said to prevent the planting of contact mines upon the high seas. If this code represents the President's conception of the freedom of the high seas it is in this respect, at least, very imperfect. It will also be observed that in this code it is provided that—

"In important cases the conference may authorize severe measures against the belligerent or against the neutrals refusing to respect the rights and duties of neutrality.

"Such measures may be public blame, pecuniary indemnity, commercial boycott, and even the use of international force, to be determined by the conference."

So that whether or not a league for peace is created, under the conference of neutrals proposed by this code we should be obliged to take very strong measures for the enforcement of neutral rights as agreed to by the conference, and at the bidding of the majority of the conference we should be forced into war in order to compel the belligerents to obey our rules. Therefore this proposal does not differ in essence from the league for peace supported by the major force of mankind. Whether the cases which I have supposed or the new code suggested by the Institute represent the freedom of the seas, it would seem as if the enforcement of this new doctrine would surely involve us, and those nations which sign the covenant with us, in every war which might occur between maritime nations.

Closely allied with this proposition for the freedom of the seas, the President tells us, is the limitation of armaments and the cooperation of the navies of the world in keeping the seas free and safe. This, as I have just pointed out, would involve the use of our Navy in any war where the belligerents saw fit to exercise their long-established rights. The limitation of armaments, although not made by the President a condition precedent for lasting peace, is treated by him as of great importance and opens up some very difficult questions. If all naval armaments are to be limited, or, still more, if they are to be abolished, the result would be to leave the nation having the largest mercantile marine in complete control of the seas if war occurred, because, if there were no naval ships, the nation which could arm and put afloat the greatest number of merchant vessels for naval purposes would, of course, be supreme in the absence of ships of war. Before entering upon the freedom of the seas, allied with the limitation of armaments, it would be well to consider whether the world would thereby be left under a system which, in time of war, would confer absolute power upon the nation possessing the largest mercantile marine.

It will also be necessary for the firm and lasting peace, which the league proposed by the President is to bring about, that every great people now struggling toward a full development of its resources and its powers be assured a direct outlet to the sea. The President confines this important right to the "great peoples," which does not seem to harmonize entirely with his earlier proposition that there must be no difference, recognized or implied, between big nations and small, "between those which are powerful and those which are weak," or with the declaration that the equality of nations, upon which peace must be founded, must be an .equality of rights. If the right of access to the sea is to be confined, as the President says, to "every great people," small nations are excluded. We have ample access to two great oceans, so that this proposed reform of the President has the enormous advantage of being wholly altruistic. It is entirely for the benefit of others.

Coming down to the practical question, in order that we may obtain lasting peace are we to see to it that a direct right of way to Constantinople shall be secured to Russia that she may reach the Mediterranean, and to Germany that she may have a direct route to Bagdad and the Persian Gulf? Must we see to it that if Italy regains the Trentino, Trieste shall be kept open so that Germany and Austria may have access to the Mediterranean, and are Serbia and Switzerland to be deprived of the right of way giving them access to the sea because they are small? Are we to bring the doctrine into the American Hemisphere and provide that Bolivia and Paraguay shall have direct access to the sea? Are we to carry the doctrine to Asia and make sure that Afghanistan has a right of way to the sea, or is Afghanistan excluded as a small power? It seems to me that this plan for securing free access to the sea to all the great nations of Europe, and still more to the nations, both great and small, would involve us in some very difficult questions wholly outside our proper sphere of influence; and yet the President states this as one of the essentials for the lasting peace which we are to covenant to bring about and to enforce.

The President says that he proposes, as it were, that the nations with one accord should adopt the doctrine of President Monroe as the doctrine of the world. In the effort which I am making to uncover the realities which lie behind the President's propositions and to avoid "the soft concealments" to which he justly objects, I do not find it easy to determine precisely what is meant by making the doctrine of President Monroe the doctrine of the world. Let me begin by quoting the doctrine as stated by President Monroe. The Monroe doctrine appears, as everyone knows, in the President's annual message of December 2, 1823. It is found in two separate passages. The first is connected with the statement made by the President as to the proposition of the Russian Government to arrange by negotiation the respective rights of the two nations upon the northwest coast of this continent. President Monroe then says:

"In the discussions to which this interest has given rise and to the arrangements by which they may terminate the occasion has been judged proper for asserting, as a principle in which the rights and interests of the United States are involved, that the American continents, by the free and independent condition which they have assumed and maintain, are henceforth not to be considered as subjects for future colonization by any European powers."

The second declaration of the doctrine occurs in connection with that portion of the message devoted to South

America and to the purposes of the Holy Alliance, and is as follows:

"We owe it, therefore, to candor and to the amicable relations existing between the United States and those powers to declare that we should consider any attempt on their part to extend their system to any portion of this hemisphere as dangerous to our peace and safety. With the existing colonies or dependencies of any European power we have not interfered, and shall not interfere. But with the Governments who have declared their independence, and maintained it, and whose independence we have, on great consideration and on just principles, acknowledged, we could not view any interposition for the purpose of oppressing them or controlling in any other manner their destiny by any European power in any other light than as the manifestation of an unfavorable disposition toward the United States."

John Quincy Adams, who formulated, and President Monroe, who proclaimed the doctrine which rightly bears the latter's name, were eminent men of very large experience, both in public affairs at home and in diplomacy. They knew well the values of words. Mr. Adams was a scholar with a remarkable power of expression. No doubt they could both, if they had seen fit, have said something which meant nothing, for that is an art as old as language itself. But it may be doubted if either was able or would have consented to say something which might mean anything. They were upright, straightforward men, and Mr. Monroe stated his famous doctrine in plain, unmistakable terms which he who ran might read. When we examine the message of 1823 it will be observed that the Monroe doctrine is strictly local in its application; that is, it applies only to the American Hemisphere and is based on the theory that there are two spheres in the world which are entirely separate in their political interests. How are we to reframe the first portion of the Monroe doctrine so as to give it a world-wide application? It asserts that the American Continents are not to be considered as subjects for future colonization by

any European power. How is this proposition to be
turned into a world doctrine? If all the European powers
accepted that doctrine and agreed with us that they would
attempt no colonization here we should have the recognition of the doctrine by European powers, but the doctrine would apply to the same territory as before. How
are we to make it a world doctrine in any other way?
How are we to turn into a world doctrine President Monroe's second statement that he should regard it as an
unfriendly act if any European power interfered with
the independence of any American Government? Is the
transformation to be effected by having Europe and Asia
and Africa adopt a doctrine that there shall be no colonies established by any power on any of those great
continents and that if, for example, any European power
should establish a new colony somewhere in Africa we
should regard it as an unfriendly act? It has been suggested that the Monroe doctrine would cover the protection of small nations. The Monroe doctrine has nothing
to do with the rights of small or great powers as such.
Its declared purpose was simply to protect the independence of all American States, great and small, from the
interference of Europe and to prohibit European colonization. How can it be said that it concerns the rights of
small States when Argentine and Brazil have taken control of Paraguay, when Chile has by force of arms annexed part of Peru, and when we took by conquest the
larger part of Mexico, and no one either at home or
abroad, ever suggested that these acts constituted in any
way an infraction of the Monroe doctrine? The Monroe
doctrine defined our position and defined nobody else's
position, and if we are to extend that doctrine to the
other nations the only sanction it would carry would be
that we should regard European colonization in all continents as an unfriendly act. Or does the President's
proposition mean that the Monroe doctrine is to be extended to all the world and thereby be abandoned under
the law laid down by John Fiske in regard to myths—
that when we find a story of something which has happened everywhere we may be quite sure that it never
happened anywhere—so that if we have a Monroe doctrine everywhere we may be perfectly certain that it will

not exist anywhere? If we are to abandon the Monroe doctrine, this is one way of doing it.

I have tried very briefly to set forth the conditions precedent which the President says are essential to a lasting peace. I have endeavored in a very general and imperfect way to "uncover the realities" and to get rid of all "soft concealments." Now, having clearly in our minds these conditions precedent, vital to the establishment of a lasting peace which we are to help bring about, I desire to consider the part which we are to take in maintaining it. Let me say at the outset by way of preface that it seems to me unwise to entangle the question of what shall be done to make peace permanent after the conclusion of the present war with the peace which is to terminate this war. It confuses two wholly distinct questions, and is certainly injurious to the prospect of the success of any attempt to make the peace which comes at the end of this war permanent. It tends also to create ill feeling toward the United States on one side or the other, and perhaps on both, and the influence of the United States in behalf of the future peace of the world will not be increased but will, I fear, be sadly diminished if we endeavor, directly or indirectly, to meddle with the terms of the peace which shall conclude the present war, because in so doing we should inevitably take sides with one group of belligerents or with another.

Let us now consider what has already been done in behalf of world peace and what it is proposed we shall do in the future, because that question has been forced upon us. All international associations or agreements for the promotion of the world's peace have hitherto been voluntary; that is, there has been no sanction behind the decisions of the international tribunals or behind the international agreements. If any signatory of the agreements or treaties, or any party to an arbitration, declined to be bound by a decision of the tribunal which had been created or by the provisions of an international convention, there was no means of compelling such signatory to abide by them, a fact which has been most dismally demonstrated since this war began.

The chief practical result of international associations for the promotion of peace has taken the form of arrangements for the arbitration of disputed questions. The subjects of these arbitrations have been limited and the submission of the nations to the international tribunals and their decisions has been purely voluntary. Much good has been obtained by voluntary arbitration. Many minor questions which a hundred years ago led to reprisals, and sometimes to war, have been removed from the region of armed hostilities and brought within the range of peaceable settlement. Voluntary arbitrations, which have gone on in steadily increasing number and in the promotion of which the United States has played a large, creditable, and influential part, have now reached, as they were certain to do, their natural limits; that is, they have been made to include in practice all the questions which can at present be covered by voluntary arbitration. The efforts which have been made to carry voluntary arbitration beyond its proper sphere—like our recent treaties involving a year's delay and attempting to deal with the vital interests of nations—are useless but by no means harmless. They are indeed distinctly mischievous, because in time of stress and peril no nation would regard them, and a treaty which cannot be or will not be scrupulously fulfilled is infinitely worse than no treaty at all. No greater harm can be done to the cause of peace between the nations than to make treaties which will not be under all conditions scrupulously observed. The disregard of treaties is a most prolific cause of war. Nothing has done more to envenom feeling in the present war or to prolong it than the disregard of the treaty guaranteeing the neutrality of Belgium and the further disregard of The Hague conventions, for this has implanted in the minds of men the belief that treaties bring no settlement and are not worth the paper upon which they are written; that the only security of peace is to be found in the destruction of the enemy and in placing an opponent in a physical condition where he is unable to renew war, because there is no assurance of safety in a duly ratified treaty.

If, then, voluntary arbitration and voluntary agreements, by convention or otherwise, without any sanction, have reached their limits, what is the next step? There is only one possible advance, and that is to put a sanction behind the decision of an international tribunal or behind an agreement of the nations; in other words, to create a power to enforce the decree of the international courts or the provisions of the international agreements. There is no other solution. I have given a great deal of thought to this question and I admit that at first it seemed to me that it might be possible to put force behind the world's peace. The peace and order of towns and cities, of states and nations, are all maintained by force. The force may not be displayed—usually there is no necessity for doing so—but order exists in our towns, in our cities, in our States, and in our Nation, and the decrees of our courts are enforced solely because of the existence of overwhelming force behind them. It is known that behind the decrees of the courts of the United States there is an irresistible force. If the peace of the world is to be maintained as the peace of a city or the internal peace of a nation is maintained, it must be maintained in the same way—by force. To make an agreement among the nations for the maintenance of peace and leave it to each nation to decide whether its force should be used in a given case to prevent war between two or more other nations of the world, does not advance us at all; we are still under the voluntary system. There is no escape from the conclusion that if we are to go beyond purely voluntary arbitration and purely voluntary agreements, actual international force must be placed behind the decisions of the agreements. There is no halfway house to stop at. The system must be either voluntary or there must be force behind the agreement or the decision. It makes no difference whether that force is expressed by armies and navies, or by economic coercion, as suggested by Sir Frederick Pollock, it is always force, and it is of little consequence whether the recalcitrant nation is brought to obedience by armed men and all the circumstance of war, or by commercial ruin, popular suffering and perhaps starvation, inflicted by the major force of mankind under the direction of the League for Peace. It is ever and always force.

Everyone must feel, as I do, the enormous importance of securing in some way the peace of the world and relieving the future of humanity from such awful struggles

as that which is now going on in Europe, but if the only
advance is to be made through the creation of an international force we are brought face to face with the difficulties of that system. The President sees this clearly.
He proposes that we should adhere to a league for peace
and then says:

"It will be absolutely necessary that a force be created as a guarantor of the permanency of the settlement so much greater than the force of any nation now
engaged or any alliance hitherto formed or projected
that no nation, no probable combination of nations
could face or withstand it. If the peace presently to
be made is to endure, it must be a peace made secure
by the organized major force of mankind."

Nothing could be plainer or more direct than that
statement, and if we are to advance from the voluntary
stage it must be, as the President says, by a league for
peace behind which is the organized major force of mankind. I fully agree with the President that if we are to
have a league such as he describes and are to enforce
peace it must be done in just the way he has stated. As
a general proposition nothing could be more attractive
for those who desire the peace of the world. I confess
that when I first began to consider it some two years ago
it presented great attraction to me; but the more I have
thought about it the more serious the difficulties in the
way of its accomplishment seem to be. This is a matter
which cannot be determined by verbal adherence to a
general principle. Everything here depends upon the
details. In the first place, a league to enforce the peace
of the world and create a major force of mankind to
carry out the purposes of the league, must be made by
treaty or convention among the nations agreeing. The
agreement must be of the most solemn and binding kind.
When disputes arise among nations, whether such nations
are members of the league or not, those disputes must
either be determined by an international tribunal created by the treaties agreed to by the members of the
league, or they must be settled by representatives of the
league after due consideration. So far all is simple. It

is no new thing to create international tribunals or to make agreements as to methods to be employed in war, the rights of neutrals, and the many other subjects now covered by the voluntary Hague conventions. The first difficulty comes when the league is confronted by the refusal of a nation involved in dispute with another nation to abide by the decision of the league when that decision has been rendered by an international tribunal, or in any other way. Submission to such a decision can only be compelled as submission to a decision of the court is compelled—by force—in this case the organized major force of mankind. If, therefore, a decision has been made in a dispute between nations by the tribunal and authority of the league, all the members of the league are bound by their treaties to contribute their share toward the enforcement of the decision, and if a recalcitrant nation resists, it means war and the vindication of the power of the league which has the control of the major force of organized mankind. The authorities of the league would, of necessity, have the power to call on every member of the league to send out its quota to the forces of the league, and the nations forming the league would find themselves, of necessity, involved in war.

The first question that would occur to any one of us is what the number of the league force will be. I will not venture a guess myself, but I will quote the opinion of Prof. Albert Bushnell Hart, the distinguished historian, a close student and high authority on all American policies and a most friendly critic of the President's address. In a very interesting article in the New York *Times* of January 28, 1917, Professor Hart says:

"He [the President] does incline toward the general plan which is pushed by the League to Enforce Peace. For he says: 'It will be absolutely necessary that a force be created as a guarantor of the permanency of the settlement so much greater than the force of any nation now engaged, or any alliance hitherto formed or projected that no nation, no probable combination of nations could face or withstand it.'

"If that means anything definite, it means an international police force of not less than 5,000,000 men, in which the share of the United States would be at least 500,000."

There is the estimate of a dispassionate and competent observer. Will it not be worth while to pause a moment before we commit ourselves to an army of 500,000 men, to be held ready for war at the pleasure of other nations in whose councils we shall have but one vote if we are true to the President's policy of the equality of nations?

Arrangements would have to be made for the command of the forces of the league, and the commander would have to be taken from some one of the signatory nations. The quota or units of the international army and navy would have to be inspected at least annually. The inspectors would be of necessity officers of the league's army and navy. Are we ready to have our Army and Navy inspected and reported upon at regular intervals by the officers of foreign services? It may be said by those who wish to have the world's peace assured by force, without using force to do it, why conjure up these phantoms of unpleasant possibilities? My reply is that they are not phantoms but simply the realities which it is our duty to uncover and upon which the whole scheme is founded. You cannot make effective a league for peace, "supported by the organized major force of mankind," by language or high-sounding phrases, which fall so agreeably upon the ear, when there is no thought behind it. The forces of the league must consist of an army and navy. They must have rifles and machine guns and cannon, battleships and battle cruisers, submarines and aeroplanes, and all the terrific machinery of modern war. They cannot set that machinery in motion by "calling spirits from the vasty deep" like Glendower. They must have men of flesh and blood to man their ships and fight their guns, and these men must be officered and commanded. Then when they order these forces to move they can enforce peace, and they will do it by war, if necessary, in which each member of the league must bear its part. Representatives of the league would thus be vested with the authority to make war and to put the league forces under the control of some commander whom they should select.

If we are to adhere to the principle of the equality of

nations laid down by the President, each nation, great and small, having equality of rights, would have an equal voice in the decision of the league, and a majority would set the forces of the league in motion. It might happen that the majority would be composed of the smaller and weaker nations, who, if they are to have equality of rights, would thus be enabled to precipitate the greater nations into war, into a war perhaps with one of the greatest nations of the league. In the present state of human nature and public opinion is it probable that any nation will bind itself to go to war at the command of other nations and furnish its army and navy to be disposed of as the majority of other nations may see fit? It seems to me that it is hardly possible, and yet in what other way can we come to the practical side of this question? In what other way are you to enforce the decisions of the league? If you undertake to limit the questions of disputes between nations which the league shall decide, you will not be able to go beyond the limits already imposed in voluntary arbitration and there will be no need of force. If a real advance is to be made, you must go beyond those limitations, you must agree to submit to the decision of the league questions which no nations will now admit to be arbitrable. You would be compelled, if a decree of the league were resisted, to go to war without any action on the part of Congress and wholly on the command of other nations. We are all anxious to promote peace in every possible way, but if we are to maintain the peace of the world by force it can only be maintained in the way I have described, and no amount of shouting about the blessings of peace will relieve us from the obligations or the necessities imposed by putting force behind the peace of the world as we put it behind the peace of a city.

Let us now consider this plan from our own point of view alone and with reference solely to the United States. The policy of the United States hitherto has been the policy laid down by Washington, and its corollary expressed in the message of President Monroe. Washington declared that we had a set of interests separate from those of Europe and that European political questions did not concern us. Monroe declared that we had a set of questions which did not concern Europe, and that, as we did not meddle with Europe, Europe must not meddle with us.   These doctrines were approved and stated with great force and explicitness by Jefferson.   From the time of their enunciation these policies have been followed and adhered to by the United States.   I have the greatest possible reverence for the precepts of Washington; no wiser, no more far-seeing man ever lived.   I only wish that we had followed all his precepts as closely as we have that which he laid down as to our relations with Europe.   But I have no superstition in regard to Washington's policy, nor do I think he had.   He set forth his policy under conditions not unlike those which now exist, and he stated very explicitly that we should not involve ourselves in any way in the ordinary vicissitudes of European politics.   I think he meant that we should hold ourselves aloof and that this should be our guiding rule.   I am far from thinking that the man who won the Revolution largely through the alliance with France would have suggested that there could be no possible situation in which it might not be well for us to form an alliance with some other nation or nations.   But that situation certainly has hitherto never arisen.   The wisdom of Washington's policy, supplemented by that of Monroe, has been demonstrated by the experience of more than a century, and this at least must be said, that we should not depart from it without most powerful reasons and without knowing exactly where that departure would lead. We are now invited to depart from it by giving our adherence to a league for peace when the present war closes, without knowing how far it is proposed to go or what is to be demanded of us.   If an effective league for peace among the nations is to be made it must be one backed by the force which the President has described. Are we prepared to commit ourselves to a purely general proposition without knowing where we are going or what is to be demanded of us, except that we shall be compelled to furnish our quota of military and naval forces to the service of a league in which we shall have but one voice?   We are asked to place ourselves in a position where our military forces could be used for war by the decree of other nations.   This would be a very momentous step.   Surely we ought to pause and consider very carefully and know every detail before we commit our-selves to any vague, general propositions involving such serious results and responsibilities.

The first service which the United States can render to the cause of peace is to preserve its own. I do not mean within its own borders, but to preserve its peace with the other nations of the earth. This can be done in only one way—by the most absolute and scrupulous ob-servance of every treaty or agreement that we enter into; by the termination of all treaties for arbitration, which we know well we should not under certain conditions and in time of stress regard, for no such war-breeding treaties ought to cumber the ground; and, lastly, by the estab-lishment of such national defenses, both by land and sea, as to insure our country, so far as it can be done, from wanton attack. When we have taken steps to insure our own peace and have national defenses sufficient for that purpose, the next step, if we are to become members of this league for peace would be to put our national forces, or a portion of them, at the disposition of the league under conditions established by the terms of the treaty which creates the league. If we are not prepared to take these obligations; if we are not ready to submit questions which we consider of vital interest to the decision of the league; if we are not fully prepared to carry out all our obliga-tions which a league for peace would necessarily require, we had better restrict ourselves to the voluntary arbi-tration, which we know can be carried out, until the people of the United States are ready to go further. A league for peace has a most encouraging sound, but this is altogether too grave a question to be satisfied with words. We must realize that a league for peace means putting force behind peace and making war on any na-tion which does not obey the decisions of the league. It may be that the world's peace can be secured in this man-ner, but we should not attempt it without a full appre-ciation of just what it involves. Effective leagues for peace can not be sustained by language alone nor by moral suasion as their only weapons. I reiterate with all possible emphasis that when they pass beyond the pres-ent voluntary stage they must be sustained by men and arms, and if we are ready to assume that responsibility then we may proceed to take the necessary steps, but not otherwise.

Let me take two examples of questions which we must be prepared to face as members of a league for peace "supported by the major force of mankind." If, as I have already said, such a league is formed, it must deal with questions of vital interest and go beyond the limitations of voluntary agreements, for if it does not there will be no advance on the present conditions. Assume that such a league has been formed, with the powers which I have outlined. China and Japan, we will say, acting on the principles of the brotherhood of man which this league is to embody, come before the representatives of the league and demand for their people the right of free emigration to Canada, Australia, and New Zealand, which now practically exclude them. Suppose the league decides that the people of China and Japan ought not to be deprived of the right to migrate anywhere, and that Canada, Australia, and New Zealand, backed by England, decline to accept this decision. The league will then proceed to enforce its decision, and we shall find ourselves obliged to furnish our quota to a force which will compel the admission of Asiatic labor to Canada. Are we prepared to make war upon Canada in such a cause as this, our quota of the forces of the league perhaps being under the orders of a Japanese commander in chief? Let us turn the question the other way. Suppose the Asiatic powers demand the free admission of their labor to the United States, and we resist, and the decision of the league goes against us, are we going to accept it? Is it possible that anyone who wishes to preserve our standards of life and labor can be drawn into a scheme, veiled by glittering and glancing generalities, which would take from us our sovereign right to decide alone and for ourselves the vital question of the exclusion of Mongolian and Asiatic labor? These are not fanciful cases drawn from the region of the imagination. They are actual, living questions of the utmost vitality and peril to-day. In them is involved that deepest of human instincts which seeks not only to prevent an impossible competition in labor but to maintain the purity of the race. Are we prepared to make any agreement which would put us in such a position as that? Before we give our adhesion to a league for peace let us consider all these contingencies. The time will not be wasted which we give to such consideration.

I hear already the clamor of those who have been shrieking for peace at any price and denouncing all armaments, rising around us with the passionate demand that we shall immediately join a league for peace, about the details of which they neither know nor care, but which will compel the establishment of large naval and military forces and which may plunge us into war in any quarter of the globe at any moment at the bidding of other nations. Such is the magic of a word to those who are content with vocal sounds and ask only that the word they love be shouted with sufficient loudness. But they, too, if they persist, will meet the day when words are vain, when there is no help or shelter in language, and when they must face relentless, unforgiving realities. I know well the question which can be put to me, and probably will be put to me here and elsewhere: "Are you, then, unwilling to use the power and influence of the United States for the promotion of the permanent peace of the world?" Not at all. There is nothing that I have so much at heart. But I do not, in my eagerness to promote the permanent peace of the world, desire to involve this country in a scheme which may create a situation worse than that which now exists. Sometimes it is better to "bear the ills we have than fly to others that we know not of." There are measures which will promote peace and which are wholly practicable. The first and most important is the protection of our own peace against foreign attack. That can only be done by national defense, and we have no adequate national defense now. We have no means of repelling the invasion of a great power as it must be repelled, and such weakness, combined with great wealth, constitutes an invitation and a temptation to war. Against that danger we should insure ourselves by adequate national defenses, and by reducing the danger of war being forced upon us we to that extent promote the peace of mankind and we likewise put ourselves in a position where our influence and power in the world for the maintenance of general peace would be enormously increased. The next thing to which we ought to address ourselves on the conclusion of this war should be the rehabilitation and reestablishment of international law. International law represents a great mass of customs and usages which have become law and which have been observed, cited, and referred to by the nations. International law has had an ever-increasing power in guiding and controlling the conduct of nations toward each other. The fact that it has been violated and disregarded in many instances during the present conflict is no reason for adopting the counsel of despair and saying that it is of no value and must be abandoned. It is of enormous value and should be restored and up-built on the conclusion of this war with all the energy and influence which we can bring to bear. We should try also, within the necessary and natural limits, to ex-tend the use of voluntary arbitration, so far as possible, and create, as we can well do, a powerful public opinion behind the system and behind the maintenance of peace. We can also do much in urging a general reduction of armaments by all nations.

It may be said that these are but slight improvements and but moderate advances. This may all be true, but what I propose has at least this merit—it is not visionary, and I suggest nothing which is not practical and reason-able and which will not, within its limitations, do sub-stantial good. If there is any way in which we can go further without creating a worse condition nobody will be more rejoiced than I; but I do not wish to plunge blindly forward, misled by phrases and generalities, into undertakings which threaten worse results than the im-perfect conditions now existing. We are as a people al-together too prone to be satisfied with words; to believe that we advance the cause of peace or any good cause merely by shouting for it. When we approach such ques-tions as are involved in our relations with the other na-tions of the earth and such a mighty issue as the main-tenance of the world's peace, to be misled by words and to take words for deeds would be a fatal error. What-ever we decide to do, let us know precisely what we are doing and what we may reasonably expect.

As an example of what I mean, let me call your

attention to the resolution offered by the Senator from Idaho. It meets with my full approval at the present time, for I now see in this tortured and distracted world nothing but peril in abandoning our long and well established policies, which have behind them not only the authority of Washington and Jefferson and Adams and Monroe but a long acceptance by the American people. Let it not be forgotten that if we pass that resolution we close the door for the time being, so far as the Senate is concerned, upon a proposition that we should join a league for peace backed by the organized major force of mankind. This resolution commits us without reserve to the policy in regard to foreign nations, of Washington, Monroe, and Jefferson, whose statements are as clear as the unclouded sun at noonday, and are not reflections of double meaning words under which men can hide and say they mean anything or nothing. Let there be no mistake about what we are doing in this direction. I would not have our action misunderstood there any more than I should wish to see a mistake made if resolutions were adopted in a sense to which I was opposed. There is no lurking place for a league for peace "supported by the organized major force of mankind" in the sentences of George Washington and Thomas Jefferson set forth in the preamble to which the resolution of the Senator from Idaho declares our allegiance.

This war will end; the passions of mankind will die down; individual ambitions will vanish with the evanescent beings who cherish them; but the Republic and the American people will remain. Let us beware how we take any steps which may precipitate this country and the people who are to come after us, and whose inheritance it is, into dangers which no man can foresee. We can not secure our own safety or build up the lasting peace of the world upon peace at any price. The peace of the world, to be enduring, must be based on righteousness at any cost.

APPENDIX IV

CONFERENCE AT THE WHITE HOUSE

August 19, 1919

The committee met at the White House at 10 o'clock A.M., pursuant to the invitation of the President, and proceeded to the East Room, where the conference was held.

Present: Hon. Woodrow Wilson, President of the United States, and the following members of the committee: Senators Lodge (chairman), McCumber, Borah, Brandegee, Fall, Knox, Harding, Johnson, of California, New, Moses, Hitchcock, Williams, Swanson, Pomerene, Smith, and Pittman.

STATEMENT OF THE PRESIDENT

The PRESIDENT. Mr. Chairman, I have taken the liberty of writing out a little statement in the hope that it might facilitate discussion by speaking directly on some points that I know have been points of controversy and upon which I thought an expression of opinion would not be unwelcome. I am absolutely glad that the committee should have responded in this way to my intimation that I would like to be of service to it. I welcome the opportunity for a frank and full interchange of views.

I hope, too, that this conference will serve to expedite your consideration of the treaty of peace. I beg that you will pardon and indulge me if I again urge that practically the whole task of bringing the country back to normal conditions of life and industry waits upon the decision of the Senate with regard to the terms of the peace.

297

I venture thus again to urge my advice that the action of the Senate with regard to the treaty be taken at the earliest practicable moment because the problems with which we are face to face in the readjustment of our national life are of the most pressing and critical character, will require for their proper solution the most intimate and disinterested cooperation of all parties and all interests, and can not be postponed without manifest peril to our people and to all the national advantages we hold most dear. May I mention a few of the matters which can not be handled with intelligence until the country knows the character of the peace it is to have? I do so only by a very few samples.

The copper mines of Montana, Arizona, and Alaska, for example, are being kept open and in operation only at a great cost and loss, in part upon borrowed money; the zinc mines of Missouri, Tennessee and Wisconsin are being operated at about one-half their capacity; the lead of Idaho, Illinois, and Missouri reaches only a portion of its former market; there is an immediate need for cotton belting, and also for lubricating oil, which can not be met—all because the channels of trade are barred by war when there is no war. The same is true of raw cotton, of which the Central Empires alone formerly purchased nearly 4,000,000 bales. And these are only examples. There is hardly a single raw material, a single important foodstuff, a single class of manufactured goods which is not in the same case. Our full, normal profitable production waits on peace.

Our military plans of course wait upon it. We can not intelligently or wisely decide how large a naval or military force we shall maintain or what our policy with regard to military training is to be until we have peace not only, but also until we know how peace is to be sustained, whether by the arms of single nations or by the concert of all the great peoples. And there is more than that difficulty involved. The vast surplus properties of the Army include not food and clothing merely, whose sale will affect normal production, but great manufacturing establishments also which should be restored to their former uses, great stores of machine tools, and all sorts of merchandise which must be idle until peace and military policy are definitely determined. By the same token there can be no properly studied national budget until then.

The nations that ratify the treaty, such as Great Britain, Belgium, and France, will be in a position to lay their plans for controlling the markets of central Europe without competition from us if we do not presently act. We have no consular agents, no trade representatives there to look after our interests.

There are large areas of Europe whose future will be uncertain and questionable until their people know the final settlements of peace and the forces which are to administer and sustain it. Without determinate markets our production can not proceed with intelligence or confidence. There can be no stabilization of wages because there can be no settled conditions of employment. There can be no easy or normal industrial credits because there can be no confident or permanent revival of business.

But I will not weary you with obvious examples. I will only venture to repeat that every element of normal life amongst us depends upon and awaits the ratification of the treaty of peace; and also that we can not afford to lose a single summer's day by not doing all that we can to mitigate the winter's suffering, which, unless we find means to prevent it, may prove disastrous to a large portion of the world, and may, at its worst, bring upon Europe conditions even more terrible than those wrought by the war itself.

Nothing, I am led to believe, stands in the way of the ratification of the treaty except certain doubts with regard to the meaning and implication of certain articles of the covenant of the league of nations; and I must frankly say that I am unable to understand why such doubts should be entertained. You will recall that when I had the pleasure of a conference with your committee and with the Committee of the House of Representatives on Foreign Affairs at the White House in March last the questions now most frequently asked about the league of nations were all canvassed with a view to their immediate clarification. The covenant of the league was then in its first draft and subject to revision. It was pointed out that no express recognition was given to the Monroe

doctrine; that it was not expressly provided that the
league should have no authority to act or to express a
judgment on matters of domestic policy; that the right
to withdraw from the league was not expressly recognized; and that the constitutional right of the Congress
to determine all questions of peace and war was not
sufficiently safeguarded. On my return to Paris all these
matters were taken up again by the commission on the
league of nations and every suggestion of the United
States was accepted.

The views of the United States with regard to the
questions I have mentioned had, in fact, already been
accepted by the commission and there was supposed to
be nothing inconsistent with them in the draft of the
covenant first adopted—the draft which was the subject
of our discussion in March—but no objection was made
to saying explicitly in the text what all had supposed to
be implicit in it. There was absolutely no doubt as to
the meaning of any one of the resulting provisions of the
covenant in the minds of those who participated in
drafting them, and I respectfully submit that there is
nothing vague or doubtful in their wording.

The Monroe doctrine is expressly mentioned as an
understanding which is in no way to be impaired or interfered with by anything contained in the covenant and
the expression "regional understandings like the Monroe
doctrine" was used, not because anyone of the conferees
thought there was any comparable agreement anywhere
else in existence or in contemplation, but only because it
was thought best to avoid the appearance of dealing in
such a document with the policy of a single nation. Absolutely nothing is concealed in the phrase.

With regard to domestic questions article 16 of the
covenant expressly provides that, if in case of any dispute
arising between members of the league the matter involved is claimed by one of the parties "and is found by
the council to arise out of a matter which by international
law is solely within the domestic jurisdiction of that
party, the council shall so report, and shall make no
recommendation as to its settlement." The United States
was by no means the only Government interested in the
explicit adoption of this provision, and there is no doubt

in the mind of any authoritative student of international law that such matters as immigration, tariffs, and naturalization are incontestably domestic questions with which no international body could deal without express authority to do so. No enumeration of domestic questions was undertaken because to undertake it, even by sample, would have involved the danger of seeming to exclude those not mentioned.

The right of any sovereign State to withdraw had been taken for granted, but no objection was made to making it explicit. Indeed, so soon as the views expressed at the White House conference were laid before the commission it was at once conceded that it was best not to leave the answer to so important a question to inference. No proposal was made to set up any tribunal to pass judgment upon the question whether a withdrawing nation had in fact fulfilled "all its international obligations and all its obligations under the covenant." It was recognized that that question must be left to be resolved by the conscience of the nation proposing to withdraw; and I must say that it did not seem to me worth while to propose that the article be made more explicit, because I knew that the United States would never itself propose to withdraw from the league if its conscience was not entirely clear as to the fulfillment of all its international obligations. It has never failed to fulfill them and never will.

Article 10 is in no respect of doubtful meaning, when read in the light of the covenant as a whole. The council of nations can only "advise upon" the means by which the obligations of that great article are to be given effect to. Unless the United States is a party to the policy or action in question, her own affirmative vote in the council is necessary before any advice can be given, for a unanimous vote of the council is required. If she is a party, the trouble is hers anyhow. And the unanimous vote of the council is only advice in any case. Each Government is free to reject it if it pleases. Nothing could have been made more clear to the conference than the right of our Congress under our Constitution to exercise its independent judgment in all matters of peace and war. No attempt was made to question or limit that right. The United States will, indeed, undertake under article 10 to "respect and preserve as against external aggression the territorial integrity and existing political independence of all members of the league," and that engagement constitutes a very grave and solemn moral obligation. But it is a moral, not a legal, obligation, and leaves our Congress absolutely free to put its own interpretation upon it in all cases that call for action. It is binding in conscience only, not in law.

Article 10 seems to me to constitute the very backbone of the whole covenant. Without it the league would be hardly more than an influential debating society.

It has several times been suggested, in public debate and in private conference, that interpretations of the sense in which the United States accepts the engagements of the covenant should be embodied in the instrument of ratification. There can be no reasonable objection to such interpretations accompanying the act of ratification provided they do not form a part of the formal ratification itself. Most of the interpretations which have been suggested to me embody what seems to me the plain meaning of the instrument itself. But if such interpretations should constitute a part of the formal resolution of ratification, long delays would be the inevitable consequence, inasmuch as all the many governments concerned would have to accept, in effect, the language of the Senate as the language of the treaty before ratification would be complete. The assent of the German Assembly at Weimar would have to be obtained, among the rest, and I must frankly say that I could only with the greatest reluctance approach that assembly for permission to read the treaty as we understand it and as those who framed it quite certainly understood it. If the United States were to qualify the document in any way, moreover, I am confident from what I know of the many conferences and debates which accompanied the formulation of the treaty that our example would immediately be followed in many quarters, in some instances with very serious reservations, and that the meaning and operative force of the treaty would presently be clouded from one end of its clauses to the other.

Pardon me, Mr. Chairman, if I have been entirely un-reserved and plain-spoken in speaking of the great matters we all have so much at heart. If excuse is needed, I trust that the critical situation of affairs may serve as my justification. The issues that manifestly hang upon the conclusions of the Senate with regard to peace and upon the time of its action are so grave and so clearly insusceptible of being thrust on one side or postponed that I have felt it necessary in the public interest to make this urgent plea, and to make it as simply and as unreservedly as possible.

I thought that the simplest way, Mr. Chairman, to cover the points that I knew to be points of interest.

The CHAIRMAN. Mr. President, so far as I am per-sonally concerned—and I think I represent perhaps the majority of the committee in that respect—we have no thought of entering upon argument as to interpretations or points of that character, but the committee is very desirous of getting information on certain points which seem not clear and on which they thought information would be of value to them in the consideration of the treaty which they, I think I may say for myself and others, desire to hasten in every possible way.

Your reference to the necessity of action leads me to ask one question. If we have to restore peace to the world it is necessary, I assume, that there should be treaties with Austria, Hungary, Turkey, and Bulgaria. Those treaties are all more or less connected with the treaty with Germany. The question I should like to ask is, what the prospect is of our receiving those treaties for action?

The PRESIDENT. I think it is very good, sir, and, so far as I can judge from the contents of the dispatches from my colleagues on the other side of the water, the chief delay is due to the uncertainty as to what is going to happen to this treaty. This treaty is the model for the others. I saw enough of the others before I left Paris to know that they are being framed upon the same set of principles and that the treaty with Germany is the model. I think that is the chief element of delay, sir.

The CHAIRMAN. They are not regarded as essential to the consideration of this treaty?

The PRESIDENT. They are not regarded as such; no, sir; they follow this treaty.

The CHAIRMAN. I do not know about the other treaties, but the treaty with Poland, for example, has been completed?

The PRESIDENT. Yes, and signed; but it is dependent on this treaty. My thought was to submit it upon the action on this treaty.

The CHAIRMAN. I should like, if I may, to ask a question in regard to the plans submitted to the commission on the league of nations, if that is the right phrase.

The PRESIDENT. Yes, sir.

The CHAIRMAN. You were kind enough to send us the draft of the American plan. When we were here in February, if I understood you rightly—I may be incorrect but I understood you to say that there were other drafts or plans submitted by Great Britain, by France, and by Italy. Would it be possible for us to see those other tentative plans?

The PRESIDENT. I would have sent them to the committee with pleasure, Senator, if I had found that I had them. I took it for granted that I had them, but the papers that remain in my hands remain there in a haphazard way. I can tell you the character of the other drafts. The British draft was the only one, as I remember, that was in the form of a definite constitution of a league. The French and Italian drafts were in the form of a series of propositions laying down general rules and assuming that the commission, or whatever body made the final formulation, would build upon those principles if they were adopted. They were principles quite consistent with the final action.

I remember saying to the committee when I was here in March—I have forgotten the expression I used—something to the effect that the British draft had constituted the basis. I thought afterwards that that was misleading, and I am very glad to tell the committee just what I meant.

Some months before the conference assembled, a plan for the league of nations had been drawn up by a British committee, at the head of which was Mr. Phillimore—I

believe the Mr. Phillimore who was known as an authority on international law. A copy of that document was
sent to me, and I built upon that a redraft. I will not
now say whether I thought it was better or not an improvement; but I built on that a draft which was quite
different, inasmuch as it put definiteness where there had
been what seemed indefiniteness in the Phillimore suggestion. Then, between that time and the time of the
formation of the commission on the league of nations, I
had the advantage of seeing a paper by Gen. Smuts, of
South Africa, who seemed to me to have done some very
clear thinking, particularly with regard to what was to
be done with the pieces of the dismembered empires.
After I got to Paris, therefore, I rewrote the document
to which I have alluded, and you may have noticed that
it consists of a series of articles and then supplementary
agreements. It was in the supplementary agreements
that I embodied the additional ideas that had come to me
not only from Gen. Smuts's paper but from other discussions. That is the full story of how the plan which
I sent to the committee was built up.

The CHAIRMAN. Of course, it is obvious that the Gen.
Smuts plan has been used. That appears on the face of
the document.

The PRESIDENT. Yes.

The CHAIRMAN. Then there was a previous draft in
addition to the one you have sent to us? You spoke of
a redraft. The original draft was not submitted to the
committee?

The PRESIDENT. No; that was privately, my own.

The CHAIRMAN. Was it before our commission?

The PRESIDENT. No; it was not before our commission.

The CHAIRMAN. The one that was sent to us was a
redraft of that?

The PRESIDENT. Yes. I was reading some of the discussion before the committee, and some one, I think
Senator Borah, if I remember correctly, quoted an early
version of article 10.

Senator BORAH. That was Senator Johnson.

Senator JOHNSON of California. I took it from the
Independent.

The PRESIDENT. I do not know how it was obtained, but that was part of the draft which preceded the draft which I sent to you.

Senator JOHNSON of California. It was first published by Mr. Hamilton Holt in the *Independent;* it was again subsequently published in the *New Republic,* and from one of those publications I read it when examining, I think, the Secretary of State.

The PRESIDENT. I read it with the greatest interest, because I had forgotten it, to tell the truth, but I recognized it as soon as I read it.

Senator JOHNSON of California. It was the original plan?

The PRESIDENT. It was the original form of article 10; yes.

The CHAIRMAN. I was about to ask in regard to article 10 as the essence of it appears in article 2 of the draft which you sent, whether that was the British plan —the Smuts plan—or the other plan?

Of course if there are no drafts of these other plans, we can not get them.

The PRESIDENT. I am very sorry, Senator. I thought I had them, but I have not.

The CHAIRMAN. Mr. Lansing, the Secretary of State, testified before us the other day that he had prepared a set of resolutions covering the points in the league, which was submitted to the American commission. You saw that draft?

The PRESIDENT. Yes.

The CHAIRMAN. No specific action was taken upon it?

The PRESIDENT. Not in a formal way.

The CHAIRMAN. Mr. President, I have no prepared set of questions, but there are one or two that I wish to ask, and will go to an entirely different subject in my next question. I desire to ask purely for information. Is it intended that the United States shall receive any part of the reparation fund which is in the hands of the reparation commission?

The PRESIDENT. I left that question open, Senator, because I did not feel that I had any final right to decide it. Upon the basis that was set up in the reparation clauses the portion that the United States would receive would be very small at best, and my own judgment was frequently expressed, not as a decision but as a judgment, that we should claim nothing under those general clauses. I did that because I coveted the moral advantage that that would give us in the counsels of the world.

Senator McCumber. Did that mean we could claim nothing for the sinking of the *Lusitania?*

The President. Oh, no. That did not cover questions of that sort at all.

The Chairman. I understood that pre-war claims were not covered by that reparation clause.

The President. That is correct.

The Chairman. I asked that question because I desired to know whether under the reparation commission there was anything expected to come to us.

The President. As I say, that remains to be decided.

The Chairman. By the commission?

The President. By the commission.

The Chairman. Going on now to another question, as I understand the treaty the overseas possessions of Germany are all made over to the five principal allied and associated powers, who apparently, as far as the treaty goes, have power to make disposition of them, I suppose by way of mandate or otherwise. Among those overseas possessions are the Ladrone Islands, except Guam, the Carolines, and, I think, the Marshall Islands. Has there been any recommendation made by our naval authorities in regard to the importance of our having one island there, not for territorial purposes, but for naval purposes?

The President. There was a paper on that subject, Senator, which has been published. I only partially remember it. It was a paper laying out the general necessities of our naval policy in the Pacific, and the necessity of having some base for communication upon those islands was mentioned, just in what form I do not remember. But let me say this, there is a little island which I must admit I had not heard of before.

Senator Williams. The island of Yap?

The President. Yap. It is one of the bases and centers of cable and radio communication on the Pacific, and I made the point that the disposition, or rather the control, of that island should be reserved for the general conference which is to be held in regard to the ownership and operation of the cables. That subject is mentioned and disposed of in this treaty and that general cable conference is to be held.

The CHAIRMAN. I had understood, or I had heard the report, that our General Board of the Navy Department and our Chief of Operations, had recommended that we should have a footing there, primarily in order to secure cable communications.

The PRESIDENT. I think you are right, sir.

The CHAIRMAN. That we were likely to be cut off from cable communication—that is, that the cables were likely to pass entirely into other hands—unless we had some station there, and it seemed to me a matter of such importance that I asked the question.

I wish to ask this further question: There was a secret treaty between England and Japan in regard to Shantung; and in the correspondence with the British ambassador at Tokyo, when announcing the acquiescence of Great Britain in Japan's having the German rights in Shantung, the British ambassador added:

"It is, of course, understood that we are to have the islands south of the Equator and Japan to have the islands north of the Equator."

If it should seem necessary for the safety of communication for this country that we should have a cable station there, would that secret treaty interfere with it?

The PRESIDENT. I think not, sir, in view of the stipulation that I made with regard to the question of construction by this cable convention. That note of the British ambassador was a part of the diplomatic correspondence covering that subject.

The CHAIRMAN. That was what I understood.

Senator MOSES. Was the stipulation that that should be reserved for the consideration of the cable conference a formally signed protocol?

The PRESIDENT. No; it was not a formally signed protocol, but we had a prolonged and interesting discussion on the subject, and nobody has any doubt as to what was agreed upon.

The CHAIRMAN. I asked the question because it seemed to me a matter of great importance.

The PRESIDENT. Yes; it is.

The CHAIRMAN. As a matter of self-protection, it seemed on the face of it that the treaty would give the five principal allied and associated powers the authority to make such disposition as they saw fit of those islands, but I did not know whether the secret treaty would thwart that purpose. I have no further questions to ask, Mr. President.

Senator BORAH. Mr. President, if no one else desires to ask a question, I want, so far as I am individually concerned, to get a little clearer information with reference to the withdrawal clause in the league covenant. Who passes upon the question of the fulfillment of our international obligations, upon the question whether a nation has fulfilled its international obligations?

The PRESIDENT. Nobody.

Senator BORAH. Does the council have anything to say about it?

The PRESIDENT. Nothing whatever.

Senator BORAH. Then if a country should give notice of withdrawal it would be the sole judge of whether or not it had fulfilled its international obligations—its covenants—to the league?

The PRESIDENT. That is as I understand it. The only restraining influence would be the public opinion of the world.

Senator BORAH. Precisely; but if the United States should conceive that it had fulfilled its obligations that question could not be referred to the council in any way, or the council could not be called into action.

The PRESIDENT. No.

Senator BORAH. Then, as I understand, when the notice is given, the right to withdraw is unconditional?

The PRESIDENT. Well, when the notice is given it is conditional on the faith of the conscience of the withdrawing nation at the close of the two-year period.

Senator BORAH. Precisely; but it is unconditional so far as the legal right or the moral right is concerned.

The PRESIDENT. That is my interpretation.

Senator BORAH. There is no moral obligation on the

part of the United States to observe any suggestion made by the council?

The PRESIDENT. Oh, no.

Senator BORAH. With reference to withdrawing?

The PRESIDENT. There might be a moral obligation if that suggestion had weight, Senator, but there is no other obligation.

Senator BORAH. Any moral obligation which the United States would feel, would be one arising from its own sense of obligation?

The PRESIDENT. Oh, certainly.

Senator BORAH. And not by reason of any suggestion by the council?

The PRESIDENT. Certainly.

Senator BORAH. Then the idea which has prevailed in some quarters that the council would pass upon such obligation is an erroneous one, from your standpoint?

The PRESIDENT. Yes, entirely.

Senator BORAH. And as I understand, of course, you are expressing the view which was entertained by the commission which drew the league?

The PRESIDENT. I am confident that that was the view. That view was not formulated, you understand, but I am confident that that was the view.

Senator McCUMBER. May I ask a question right here? Would there be any objection, then, to a reservation declaring that to be the understanding of the force of this section?

The PRESIDENT. Senator, as I indicated at the opening of our conference, this is my judgment about that: Only we can interpret a moral obligation. The legal obligation can be enforced by such machinery as there is to enforce it. We are therefore at liberty to interpret the sense in which we undertake a moral obligation. What I feel very earnestly is that it would be a mistake to embody that interpretation in the resolution of ratification, because then it would be necessary for other governments to act upon it.

Senator McCUMBER. If they all recognized at the time that this was the understanding and the construction that should be given to that portion of the treaty, would it be necessary for them to act on it again?

The PRESIDENT. I think it would, Senator.

Senator McCUMBER. Could they not accept it merely by acquiescence?

THE PRESIDENT. My experience as a lawyer was not very long, but that experience would teach me that the language of a contract is always part of the debatable matter, and I can testify that in our discussions in the commission on the league of nations we did not discuss ideas half as much as we discussed phraseologies.

Senator McCUMBER. But suppose, Mr. President, we should make a declaration of that kind, which would be in entire accord with your view of the understanding of all of the nations, and without further comment or action the nations should proceed to appoint their commissions, and to act under this treaty, would not that be a clear acquiescence in our construction?

The PRESIDENT. Oh, it might be, Senator, but we would not know for a good many months whether they were going to act in that sense or not. There would have to be either explicit acquiescence, or the elapsing of a long enough time for us to know whether they were implicitly acquiescing or not.

Senator McCUMBER. I should suppose that when the treaty was signed, under present world conditions, all nations would proceed to act immediately under it.

The PRESIDENT. In some matters; yes.

Senator HARDING. Mr. President, assuming that your construction of the withdrawal clause is the understanding of the formulating commission, why is the language making the proviso for the fulfillment of covenants put into the article?

The PRESIDENT. Merely as an argument to the conscience of the nations. In other words, it is a notice served on them that their colleagues will expect that at the time they withdraw they will have fulfilled their obligations.

Senator HARDING. The language hardly seems to make that implication, because it expressly says, "Provided it has fulfilled its obligations."

The PRESIDENT. Yes.

Senator HARDING. If it were a matter for the nation

itself to judge, that is rather a far-fetched provision, is it not?

The PRESIDENT. Well, you are illustrating my recent remark, Senator, that the phraseology is your difficulty, not the idea. The idea is undoubtedly what I have expressed.

Senator PITTMAN. Mr. President, Senator McCumber has drawn out that it is your impression that the allied and associated powers have the same opinion of the construction of these so-called indefinite articles that you have. Is that construction also known and held by Germany?

The PRESIDENT. I have no means of knowing.

Senator PITTMAN. Germany, then, has not expressed herself to the commission with regard to these mooted questions?

The PRESIDENT. No; we have no expression from Germany about the league, except the expression of her very strong desire to be admitted to it.

Senator PITTMAN. And is it your opinion that if the language of the treaty were changed in the resolution of ratification, the consent of Germany to the change would also be essential?

The PRESIDENT. Oh, undoubtedly.

The CHAIRMAN. Mr. President, in that connection—I did not mean to ask another question—I take it there is no question whatever, under international law and practice, that an amendment to the text of a treaty must be submitted to every signatory, and must receive either their assent or their dissent. I had supposed it had been the general diplomatic practice with regard to reservations—which apply only to the reserving power, and not to all the signatories, of course—that with regard to reservations it had been the general practice that silence was regarded as acceptance and acquiescence; that there was that distinction between a textual amendment, which changed the treaty for every signatory, and a reservation, which changed it only for the reserving power. In that I may be mistaken, however.

The PRESIDENT. There is some difference of opinion among the authorities, I am informed. I have not had time to look them up myself about that; but it is clear to me that in a treaty which involves so many signatories, a series of reservations—which would ensue, undoubtedly —would very much obscure our confident opinion as to how the treaty was going to work.

Senator WILLIAMS. Mr. President, suppose for example that we adopted a reservation, as the Senator from Massachusetts calls it, and that Germany did nothing about it at all, and afterwards contended that so far as that was concerned it was new matter, to which she was never a party. Could her position be justifiably disputed?

The PRESIDENT. No.

Senator BORAH. Mr. President, with reference to article 10—you will observe that I am more interested in the league than any other feature of this discussion— in listening to the reading of your statement I got the impression that your view was that the first obligation of article 10, to wit—

"The members of the league undertake to respect and preserve as against external aggression the territorial integrity and existing political independence of all members of the league—"

was simply a moral obligation.

The PRESIDENT. Yes, sir; inasmuch as there is no sanction in the treaty.

Senator BORAH. But that would be a legal obligation so far as the United States was concerned if it should enter into it, would it not?

The PRESIDENT. I would not interpret it in that way, Senator, because there is involved the element of judgment as to whether the territorial integrity or existing political independence is invaded or impaired. In other words, it is an attitude of comradeship and protection among the members of the league, which in its very nature is moral and not legal.

Senator BORAH. If, however, the actual fact of invasion were beyond dispute, then the legal obligation, it seems to me, would immediately arise. I am simply throwing this out in order to get a full expression of views. The legal obligation would immediately arise if the fact of actual invasion were undisputed?

The PRESIDENT. The legal obligation to apply the automatic punishments of the covenant, undoubtedly; but not the legal obligation to go to arms and actually to make war. Not the legal obligation. There might be a very strong moral obligation.

Senator McCUMBER. Just so that I may understand definitely what your view is on that subject, Mr. President, do I understand you to mean that while we have two different remedies, and possibly others, we would be the sole judge of the remedy we would apply, but the obligation would still rest upon us to apply some remedy to bring about the result?

The PRESIDENT. Yes. I can not quite accept the full wording that you used, sir. We would have complete freedom of choice as to the application of force.

Senator McCUMBER. Would we not have the same freedom of choice as to whether we would apply a commercial boycott? Are they not both under the same language, so that we would be bound by them in the same way?

The PRESIDENT. Only in regard to certain articles. The breach of certain articles of the covenant does bring on what I have designated as an automatic boycott, and in that we would have no choice.

Senator KNOX. Mr. President, allow me to ask this question: Suppose that it is perfectly obvious and accepted that there is an external aggression against some power, and suppose it is perfectly obvious and accepted that it can not be repelled except by force of arms, would we be under any legal obligation to participate?

The PRESIDENT. No, sir; but we would be under an absolutely compelling moral obligation.

Senator KNOX. But no legal obligation?

The PRESIDENT. Not as I contemplate it.

Senator WILLIAMS. Mr. President, each nation, if I understand it, is, of course, left to judge the applicability of the principles stated to the facts in the case, whether there is or is not external aggression?

The PRESIDENT. Yes.

Senator WILLIAMS. And if any country should conclude that there was not external aggression, but that

France or some other country had started the trouble indirectly, we would have the same right, if I understand it, that Italy had to declare that her alliance with Germany and Austria was purely defensive, and that she did not see anything defensive in it; so when you come to judgment of the facts, outside of the international law involved, each nation must determine, if I understand, whether or not there has been external aggression?

The PRESIDENT. I think you are right, sir. Senator (addressing Senator Knox), you were about to ask something?

Senator KNOX. I only wanted to tell you that I asked that question because I was a little confused by the language of your message transmitting the proposed Franco-American treaty to the Senate, in which you said, in substance, and, I think, practically in these terms, that this is only binding us to do immediately what we otherwise would have been bound to do under the league of nations?

The PRESIDENT. Yes.

Senator KNOX. Perhaps I am mistaken with respect to its having been in that message. I am sure I am mistaken; it was not in that message; it was in the message that Mr. Tumulty gave out—

The CHAIRMAN. May 10.

Senator KNOX. Yes.

The PRESIDENT. Yes.

Senator KNOX. That it was merely binding us to do immediately, without waiting for any other power, that which we would otherwise have been bound to do under the terms of the league of nations.

The PRESIDENT. I did not use the word "bound," but "morally bound." Let me say that you are repeating what I said to the other representatives. I said, "Of course, it is understood we would have to be convinced that it was an unprovoked movement of aggression," and they at once acquiesced in that.

Senator MCCUMBER. Mr. President, there are a number of Senators who sincerely believe that under the construction of article 10, taken in connection with other clauses and other articles in the treaty, the council can suggest what we should do, and of course, while they admit the council can only advise and suggest, that it is nevertheless our moral duty to immediately obey the council, without exercising our own judgment as to whether we shall go to war or otherwise. Now, the public, the American people, a great proportion of them, have that same conviction, which is contrary to your view. Do you not think, therefore, that it would be well to have a reservation inserted in our resolution that shall so construe that section as to make it clear, not only to the American people but to the world, that Congress may use its own judgment as to what it will do, and that its failure to follow the judgment of the council will not be considered a breach of the agreement?

The PRESIDENT. We differ, Senator, only as to the form of action. I think it would be a very serious practical mistake to put it in the resolution of ratification; but I do hope that we are at liberty, contemporaneously with our acceptance of the treaty, to interpret our moral obligation under that article.

Senator PITTMAN. Mr. President, I understand that, under the former method, in your opinion, it would have to go back to Germany and the other countries; while under the latter method it would not be required to go back for ratification.

The PRESIDENT. Yes, sir; that is my judgment.

Senator KNOX. Mr. President, is it not true that such matters are ordinarily covered by a mere exchange of notes between powers, stating that they understand in this or that sense, or do not so understand?

The PRESIDENT. Yes, sir; ordinarily.

Senator KNOX. That would be a matter that would require very little time to consummate it, if these constructions have already been placed upon it in their conversations with you.

The PRESIDENT. But an exchange of notes is quite a different matter from having it embodied in the resolution of ratification.

Senator KNOX. If we embody in our resolution of ratification a statement that we understand section 10 or section 16 or section something else in a particular sense, and this Government, through its foreign department, transmits the proposed form of ratification to the chancellors of the other nations that are concerned in this treaty, and if those interpretations are the same as you have agreed upon with them in your conversations, I do not see how we would need anything more than a mere reply to that effect.

The PRESIDENT. It would need confirmation.

Senator KNOX. Yes; it would need confirmation in that sense.

The PRESIDENT. My judgment is that the embodying of that in the terms of the resolution of ratification would be acquiescence not only in the interpretation but in the very phraseology of the interpretation, because it would form a part of the contract.

Senator KNOX. It might with us, because we have so much machinery for dealing with treaties but in other countries where it is much more simple I should think it would not be.

The PRESIDENT. It is simple legally, Senator; but, for example, this treaty has been submitted to legislatures to which the Government was not, by law, obliged to submit it, and it is everywhere being treated as a legislative matter—I mean, so far as the ratification is concerned.

Senator KNOX. You mean in countries where, under their constitutions, there are provisions that treaties ordinarily are not submitted to the legislative branch of the Government, this treaty is being so submitted?

The PRESIDENT. So I understand.

Senator KNOX. Where there are two branches of the legislative department, an upper and a lower branch, do you know whether it is being submitted to both?

The PRESIDENT. I think not, sir. I am not certain about that, but my memory is it is not.

Senator FALL. Mr. President, the idea has struck me and I have entertained the view, since reading the treaty and the league, that Germany having signed the treaty but not being a member of the league, any reservations which we might make here would be met by Germany either joining the league or refusing to join the league. It would not be submitted to her at all now; because she is not a member of the league? You catch the point?

The PRESIDENT. Yes. I differ with you there, Senator.

One of the reasons for putting the league in the treaty was that Germany was not going to be admitted to the league immediately, and we felt that it was very necessary that we should get her acknowledgment—acceptance —of the league as an international authority, partly because we were excluding her, so that she would thereafter have no ground for questioning such authority as the league might exercise under its covenant.

Senator FALL. Precisely.

The PRESIDENT. Therefore, I think it would be necessary for her to acquiesce in a league the powers of which were differently construed.

Senator FALL. Precisely; but her acquiescence would be by her accepting the invitation, when extended, either to join the league or not to join the league. In other words, upon ratification by three of the powers, a status of peace is established, and as to those three powers and Germany all the rules and regulations contained in the treaty of peace become operative. As to the other nations which have not ratified, the status of peace exists; that is, war has terminated. Now, that being the case, and Germany being out of the league—not having been invited to join the league—if in ratifying the treaty we ratify it with certain explanations or reservations, even in the ratifying resolution, when the time comes and Germany is invited to become a member of the league, or when she applies, under the admission clause of the league, for membership therein, if she enters she of course accepts our reservations. If she makes a qualified application, then it is for the league itself to consider whether she will be admitted?

The PRESIDENT. I do not follow your reasoning in the matter, Senator, because this is not merely a question of either membership or nonmembership. The covenant is a part of the treaty, it is a part of the treaty which she has signed, and we are not at liberty to change any part of that treaty without the acquiescence of the other contracting party.

Senator FALL. Well, Mr. President, of course it is not my purpose to enter into an argument, but we are here for information. There are provisions for the amendment of the articles. Germany is out of the league. Any amendment proposed by the other members of the league prior to her coming into the league would not be submitted to her, would it, she not being a member?

The PRESIDENT. I will admit that that point had not occurred to me. No, she would not.

Senator FALL. Then so far as we are concerned we could make a recommendation in the nature of an amendment.

Senator PITTMAN. She has already agreed by this treaty that she has signed that the members may amend it.

The PRESIDENT. Yes.

Senator FALL. Precisely, and we could come in with an amendment.

Senator HITCHCOCK. Did I understand your first reply to Senator Fall to be that Germany under this treaty already had a relationship to the league by reason of its international character, and its participation in a number of questions that Germany was interested in?

The PRESIDENT. Yes.

Senator HITCHCOCK. So that it has a relationship to the league of nations even before the time that it may apply for membership.

The PRESIDENT. Yes.

Senator McCUMBER. Mr. President, you answered one question that I think possibly may need a little elucidation. If I remember rightly, in reference to reparation your statement was that the commission would have to decide whether the United States should claim her proportion of the reparation.

The PRESIDENT. That the commission would have to do it? No; we decide whether we claim it or not.

Senator McCUMBER. That is what I want to make clear. I think the question was asked if the commission was to decide that, and I thought your answer said yes. That is the reason I asked the question.

The PRESIDENT. The claim would have to come from us, of course.

Senator McCUMBER. It would have to be through an act of Congress, would it not?

The PRESIDENT. I would have to be instructed about that, Senator. I do not know.

Senator McCumber. Whatever right the United States would receive under the treaty for reparation or indemnity is one that runs to the United States, and therefore to divest ourselves of that right would require an act of Congress.

The President. To divest ourselves of it? I suppose so.

Senator Knox. In the question of the Japanese indemnity, that was done by a joint resolution.

Senator McCumber. I thought the President said it would have to be decided by the constituted authority.

Senator Knox. I did not understand that he said that.

Senator Swanson. I understand that the reparation is to be decided upon a representation made by the associated powers. It would seem that the President under that agreement with France, Great Britain, and other nations would have to submit it to the Senate for ratification, and the agreement would have to be reported.

Senator McCumber. In each case it would have the force of law.

Senator Swanson. If the Senate wanted to ratify it, it would take an act of Congress.

Senator Williams. This question of reparation does not in any way affect our rights to prewar indemnities?

The President. That is expressly stated.

Senator Williams. That is expressly stated. Now, then, one other question. Germany has signed this treaty with the covenant of the league in it, and she is subject to be dealt with as a nonmember under the treaty, and has very much fewer privileges than a member?

The President. Yes.

Senator New. Mr. President, may I ask a question there? What effort was made by the delegates there to prevent the proceedings of the reparations committee being required to be secret?

The President. I beg your pardon, Senator.

Senator New. What effort, if any, was made by the American delegates to prevent the proceedings of the reparation commission from being required to be secret, and did the American delegates protest that America be omitted from this commission on account of that thing?

The PRESIDENT. Nothing was said about it, that I remember.

Senator BORAH. Mr. President, coming back for a moment to the subject from which we were diverted a moment ago, and coupling with article 10 article 11, in order that we may have the construction of the committee which framed the league as to both of those articles, as I understand it from your statement, the committee's view was that the obligations under articles 10 and 11 whatever they are, are moral obligations.

The PRESIDENT. Remind me of the eleventh. I do not remember that by number.

Senator BORAH (reading):

"Any war or threat of war, whether immediately affecting any of the members of the league or not, is hereby declared a matter of concern to the whole league, and the league shall take any action that may be deemed wise and effectual to safeguard the peace of nations."

What I am particularly anxious to know is whether or not the construction which was placed upon these two articles by the committee which framed the league was that it was a binding obligation from a legal standpoint, or merely a moral obligation.

The PRESIDENT. Senator, I tried to answer with regard to article 10.

Senator BORAH. Yes; exactly.

The PRESIDENT. I would apply it equally with regard to article 11, though I ought to hasten to say that we did not formulate these interpretations. I can only speak from my confident impression from the debates that accompanied the formulation of the covenant.

Senator BORAH. Yes; I understand; and your construction of article 11 is the same as that of article 10?

The PRESIDENT. Yes.

Senator BORAH. As to the question of legal obligation. That is all I desire to ask at present.

Senator HARDING. Right there, Mr. President, if there is nothing more than a moral obligation on the part of any member of the league, what avail articles 10 and 11?

The PRESIDENT. Why, Senator, it is surprising that that question should be asked. If we undertake an obligation we are bound in the most solemn way to carry it out.

Senator HARDING. If you believe there is nothing more to this than a moral obligation, any nation will assume a moral obligation on its own account. Is it a moral obligation? The point I am trying to get at is, Suppose something arises affecting the peace of the world, and the council takes steps as provided here to conserve or preserve, and announces its decision, and every nation in the league takes advantage of the construction that you place upon these articles and says, "Well, this is only a moral obligation, and we assume that the nation involved does not deserve our participation or protection," and the whole thing amounts to nothing but an expression of the league council.

The PRESIDENT. There is a national good conscience in such a matter. I should think that was one of the most serious things that could possibly happen. When I speak of a legal obligation I mean one that specifically binds you to do a particular thing under certain sanctions. That is a legal obligation. Now a moral obligation is of course superior to a legal obligation, and, if I may say so, has a greater binding force; only there always remains in the moral obligation the right to exercise one's judgment as to whether it is indeed incumbent upon one in those circumstances to do that thing. In every moral obligation there is an element of judgment. In a legal obligation there is no element of judgment.

Senator JOHNSON of California. But, Mr. President, when a moral obligation is undoubted it will impel action more readily than a legal obligation.

The PRESIDENT. If it is undoubted, yes; but that involves the circumstances of the particular case, Senator.

Senator JOHNSON of California. Yes; necessarily.

Senator HARDING. In answering Senator Knox a moment ago you spoke of a compelling moral obligation. Would you think that any less binding than a specific legal obligation?

The PRESIDENT. Not less binding, but operative in a different way because of the element of judgment.

Senator HARDING. But not less likely to involve us in armed participation?

The PRESIDENT. In trifling matters, very much less likely.

Senator HARDING. To clear my slow mind, let me take a specific case. Suppose the allotted territory which comes under the control of Italy should in some way be assailed from the Balkan States and the council of the league should immediately look upon that as a threat of war involving other nations and should say that the nations of the league should immediately contribute an armed force to stop that war or to bring the attacking nation to terms, would we be a perfidious people, if I may use that term, or would we violate our obligations, if we failed to participate in the defense of Italy?

The PRESIDENT. We would be our own judges as to whether we were obliged in those circumstances to act in that way or not.

Senator HITCHCOCK. In such a case the council would only act unanimously, and our representative on the council of course would have to concur in any advice given.

The PRESIDENT. Certainly; we would always in such case advise ourselves.

Senator WILLIAMS. But if in such case, Mr. President, we concluded that the case provided for and prescribed had arisen and that the extraneous attack existed and that it fell within the terms of the treaty, then we would be untrue if we did not keep our word?

The PRESIDENT. Certainly.

Senator BORAH. In other words, then, that transfers the power to decide whether we should act from the Congress of the United States to one individual who sits on the council.

Senator WILLIAMS. No, it does not; it merely provides that when the council acts in accordance with the prescribed terms and we see that it has acted, then Congress will, as a matter of faith keeping, act itself; and, if Congress does not, Congress will do a dishonorable thing.

Senator BORAH. Precisely so; so that the matter gets

back to the point where one individual has bound Con-gress.

Senator HITCHCOCK. I hope my question to the President will not be interpreted in that way. My question to the President was whether the matter would even come before this country as the advice of the council until the American representative had concurred with the other eight members of the council. After he had concurred it would then be up to Congress to decide.

The PRESIDENT. You are quite right, Senator. And let me suggest that I find nothing was more clearly in the consciousness of the men who were discussing these very important matters than that most of the nations concerned had popular governments. They were all the time aware of the fact that it would depend upon the approving or disapproving state of opinion of their countries how their representatives in the council would vote in matters of this sort; and it is inconceivable to me that, unless the opinion of the United States, the moral and practical judgment of the people of the United States, approved, the representative of the United States on the council should vote any such advice as would lead us into war.

Senator BORAH. Mr. President, does the special alliance treaty with France which has been submitted to us rest upon any other basis as to legal and moral obligation than that of Article 10 and Article 11 which you have just described?

The PRESIDENT. No, sir.

Senator BORAH. That is also, as you understand it, simply our moral obligations which we enter into with France?

The PRESIDENT. Yes.

Senator WILLIAMS. All international obligations are moral ones.

Senator PITTMAN. There is one thing I do not understand about Senator Borah's question. He has stated that he gathers from what you said that it all rests with our representative on the council. Even if our representative on the council advises as a member of the council, and the council is unanimous, is it not then still up to Congress either to accept or reject that advice?

The PRESIDENT. Oh, yes; but I understood the Senator to mean that it would be dependent on our representative.

Senator JOHNSON of California. May I take the example that was just suggested concerning the Balkan States and a possible attack upon the new territories of Italy. Assuming that that is a case of external aggression by the Balkan States concerning the new territory that Italy has acquired by the peace treaty, upon us rests a compelling moral obligation to do our part in preventing that, does there not?

The PRESIDENT. Yes.

Senator JOHNSON of California. And that compelling moral obligation would require us to use such means as would seem appropriate, either economic or force? Is not that correct?

The PRESIDENT. Deemed appropriate by whom? That is really the point.

Senator JOHNSON of California. Of course, deemed appropriate for the purpose of preventing and frustrating the aggression.

The PRESIDENT. Deemed by us appropriate?

Senator JOHNSON of California. I assume of necessity it would have to be deemed by us to bind us as a compelling moral obligation to prevent the aggression in the case named.

The PRESIDENT. Yes.

Senator McCUMBER. Mr. President, I think, due to my own fault, I do not fully comprehend your distinction between a moral and a legal obligation in a treaty. If we enter into a treaty with France to defend her against aggression from Germany for any length of time, that is a legal obligation, is it not?

The PRESIDENT. Legal in the sense that a treaty is of binding force; yes.

Senator McCUMBER. Yes; that is what I meant. It is as legal as any treaty could be made legal, and there is also a moral obligation to keep that treaty, is there not?

The PRESIDENT. Yes, sir. I happened to hear Senator Knox say what I am glad to adopt. It is a legal obligation with a moral sanction.

Senator BORAH. That is true generally, is it not?

The PRESIDENT. Yes, Senator; but I have already defined in what special sense I use the word "legal."

Senator McCUMBER. To my mind those two articles are legal obligations to be carried out by the moral conscience of the American people if the conditions justify it.

The PRESIDENT. You see we are speaking of two different fields, and therefore the language does not fit. In international law the word "legal" does not mean the same as in national law, and the word hardly applies.

Senator BORAH. I wish to ask some questions in regard to the secret treaties. I do not feel as free about those matters as I do about the league, because there are certain things that I recognize may not be entirely open for public consideration, but, nevertheless, in so far as we can, I should like to know when the first knowledge came to this Government with reference to the secret treaties between Japan, Great Britain, Italy, and France concerning the German possessions in Shantung.

The PRESIDENT. I thought that Secretary Lansing had looked that up and told you. I can only reply from my own knowledge, and my own knowledge came after I reached Paris.

Senator BORAH. We did get a reply from Mr. Lansing to the same effect so far as he was concerned. When did the secret treaties between Great Britain, France, and the other nations of Europe with reference to certain adjustments in Europe first come to your knowledge? Was that after you had reached Paris also?

The PRESIDENT. Yes; the whole series of understandings were disclosed to me for the first time then.

Senator BORAH. Then we had no knowledge of these secret treaties so far as our Government was concerned, until you reached Paris?

The PRESIDENT. Not unless there was information at the State Department of which I knew nothing.

Senator BORAH. Do you know when the secret treaties between Japan, Great Britain, and other countries were first made known to China?

The PRESIDENT. No, sir; I do not. I remember a meeting of what was popularly called the council of ten, after our reaching Paris, in which it was first suggested that all these understandings should be laid upon the table of the conference. That was some time after we reached there, and I do not know whether that was China's first knowledge of these matters or not.

Senator BORAH. Would it be proper for me to ask if Great Britain and France insisted upon maintaining these secret treaties at the peace conference as they were made?

The PRESIDENT. I think it is proper for me to answer that question, sir. I will put it in this way. They felt that they could not recede from them, that is to say, that they were bound by them, but when they involved general interests such as they realized were involved, they were quite willing, and indeed I think desirous, that they should be reconsidered with the consent of the other parties. I mean with the consent, so far as they were concerned, of the other parties.

Senator MOSES. Were all those treaties then produced, Mr. President?

The PRESIDENT. Oh, yes.

Senator MOSES. Did that include the secret arrangement with reference to Avlona?

The PRESIDENT. I do not recall that agreement, Senator. You mean with regard to Italy having Avlona?

Senator MOSES. Yes.

The PRESIDENT. If it did, I did not see it. I heard of it, but I cannot say confidently that the terms were laid before us.

Senator MOSES. I recall in some statements you made in connection with Fiume that you referred to Italy receiving Avlona under some agreement previously arrived at, and in that statement you held that to be part compensation at least for any loss she might sustain in not having Fiume.

The PRESIDENT. I was referring to what I understood to be the agreement. I am simply now answering your question that I did not see that agreement in written terms.

Senator MOSES. Then, they were not produced in textual form?

The PRESIDENT. I do not know; they may have been and I may not have picked them up in the great mass of papers before me.

Senator MOSES. The purpose of my inquiry was to ascertain whether there was laid before the council of ten any textual agreements which transferred parts of the territory of one independent nation to another.

The PRESIDENT. Only those that have been spoken of.

Senator MOSES. That is to say, Shantung and Avlona?

The PRESIDENT. I say only those that we have had under general discussion. I cannot enumerate them, but there are none that have not been produced so far as I know. That answers the question.

Senator McCUMBER. The secret treaties to which you refer are those treaties which were made from time to time as the exigencies of the war required during the period of the war?

The PRESIDENT. Yes.

Senator McCUMBER. And not treaties that were made prior to the war?

The PRESIDENT. Yes.

Senator WILLIAMS. Mr. President, I wish to ask you a question in order to see if the facts are clear in my own mind. As I understand the situation—and I should like to have you correct me if I am wrong—France and Great Britain both have stated that they were bound by certain treaties with Japan and they were perfectly willing, with Japan's consent, to reconsider those treaties, but that they were themselves bound if the other party to the treaty did not consent to reconsider. Is that about it?

The PRESIDENT. Yes.

Senator WILLIAMS. That is what I thought. Bound in honor is the only way a nation is bound in international affairs.

Senator SWANSON. Can you tell us, or would it be proper to do so, of your understanding with Japan as to the return of Shantung? That is a question which has been very much discussed.

The PRESIDENT. I have published the wording of the understanding, Senator. I cannot be confident that I quote it literally, but I know that I quote it in substance. It was that Japan should return to China in full sovereignty the old Province of Shantung so far as Germany had had any claims upon it, preserving to herself the right to establish a residential district at Tsingtao, which is the town of Kiaochow Bay; that with regard to the railways and mines she should retain only the rights of an economic concession there, with the right, however, to maintain a special body of police on the railway, the personnel of which should be Chinese under Japanese instructors nominated by the managers of the company and appointed by the Chinese Government. I think that is the whole of it.

Senator POMERENE. That is, that the instructors should be confirmed by the Chinese Government?

The PRESIDENT. No; not exactly that. The language, as I remember it, was that they should be nominated by the managers of the railway company, and appointed by the Chinese Government.

Senator BORAH. Was that understanding oral?

Senator WILLIAMS. This rather curious question presents itself to my mind: As I understand, Japan has retained sovereignty for the 99 years of the lease only at Kiaochow, and 5 kilometers, or some such distance, back from the bay.

The PRESIDENT. She has not retained sovereignty over anything.

Senator WILLIAMS. She has not?

The PRESIDENT. I mean, she has promised not to.

Senator WILLIAMS. During the period of the lease?

The PRESIDENT. No; she has promised not to retain sovereignty at all. Senator Borah asked whether this understanding was oral or otherwise. I do not like to describe the operation exactly if it is not perfectly discreet, but as a matter of fact this was technically oral, but literally written and formulated, and the formulation agreed upon.

Senator JOHNSON of California. When, Mr. President, is the return to be made?

The PRESIDENT. That was left undecided, Senator, but we were assured at the time that it would be as soon as possible.

Senator JOHNSON of California. Did not the Japanese decline to fix the date?

The PRESIDENT. They did at that time, yes; but I think it is fair to them to say not in the spirit of those who wished it be within their choice, but simply that they could not at that time say when it would be.

Senator JOHNSON of California. The economic privileges that they would retain would give them a fair mastery over the province, would they not, or at least the Chinese think so? Let me put it in that fashion, please.

The PRESIDENT. I believe they do, Senator. I do not feel qualified to judge. I should say that that was an exaggerated view.

Senator JOHNSON of California. But the Chinese feel that way about it, and have so expressed themselves?

The PRESIDENT. They have so expressed themselves.

Senator KNOX. Mr. President, the economic privileges that they originally acquired in Korea, and subsequently in inner and outer Mongolia, and in northern and southern Manchuria, have almost developed into a complete sovereignty over those countries, have they not?

The PRESIDENT. Yes, Senator; in the absence of a league of nations they have.

Senator KNOX. You think the league of nations would have prevented that, do you?

The PRESIDENT. I am confident it would.

Senator NEW. Mr. President, does not this indefinite promise of Japan's suggest the somewhat analogous case of England's occupation of Malta? She has occupied Malta for something like a century, I believe, under a very similar promise.

The PRESIDENT. Well, Senator, I hope you will pardon me if I do not answer that question.

Senator FALL. Mr. President, speaking of the duty of defense in reference to sovereignty, and of aggression with reference to sovereignty, in construing these different articles of the league, I have been curious to know who will defend the mandate territories or colonies if there should be external aggression.

The PRESIDENT. Primarily, the mandatory power.

Senator FALL. The mandatory power would have that character of sovereignty over the possession which would compel it as a duty to defend the mandate province?

The PRESIDENT. Yes.

Senator FALL. Then a qualified sovereignty would in that instance, at any rate, compel the mandatory of the league first to defend the colony?

The PRESIDENT. I should put it this way. Senator:

We have in mind throughout the whole discussion of the mandate idea the analogy of trustees. The States taking those under mandates would be in the nature of trustees, and of course it is part of the trustee's duty to preserve intact the trust estate.

Senator FALL. But out of the funds of the trust estate?

The PRESIDENT. Oh, yes.

Senator FALL. Mr. President, I will not pursue that line at this time. I will say very frankly that I have prepared some questions which I wanted, for my own purposes, to put down in writing, and I had expected to ask them in sequence of you after the other Senators had concluded. It will, however, evidently take quite a long while if we pursue the line which we are now pursuing, and particularly if the Senators themselves argue their own interpretations of the different clauses in the treaty.

Senator McCUMBER. Mr. President, I should like to get as definite an understanding as I can, at least, of how these promises of Japan to return Shantung are evidenced to-day. In what form do they appear?

The PRESIDENT. They are evidenced in a *procès verbal* of the so-called council of four—the name that we ourselves used was very much more pretentious; we called ourselves the council of the principal allied and associated powers—but the four who used to confer, or rather the five, because Japan was there of course at that time.

Senator McCUMBER. The principal points were taken down in writing and read over and compared and preserved, were they?

The PRESIDENT. Not read over and compared, but preserved. The process each day was this, Senator: The matters discussed were summarized, and the conclusions reached were recorded in a *procès verbal,* copies of which were distributed within 24 hours; and of course it was open to any one of the conferees to correct anything they might contain. Only in that sense were they corrected.

Senator McCUMBER. Where are those records kept now?

The PRESIDENT. They are in Paris, sir.

Senator McCUMBER. Is there any objection to their being produced for the committee?

The PRESIDENT. I think there is a very serious objection, Senator. The reason we constituted that very small conference was so that we could speak with the utmost absence of restraint, and I think it would be a mistake to make use of those discussions outside. I do not remember any blazing indiscretion of my own, but there may be some.

Senator McCUMBER. In those conversations it was fully understood that Japan was to return Shantung as soon as possible?

The PRESIDENT. Yes, sir.

Senator McCUMBER. Was there anything stated as to what was meant by "as soon as possible"—that is, to place it within any definite period at all?

The PRESIDENT. No, sir; no. We relied on Japan's good faith in fulfilling that promise.

Senator McCUMBER. Was there anything outside? If I go too far in my questions you can signify it, Mr. President.

The PRESIDENT. How do you mean outside, Senator?

Senator McCUMBER. Was there anything said by Japan as to anything that she would want to do before she turned the territory over to China?

The PRESIDENT. No; nothing was mentioned.

Senator McCUMBER. Then "as soon as possible" would naturally mean, would it not, as soon as the treaty has been signed under which she accepts the transfer from Germany?

The PRESIDENT. Well, I should say that it would mean that the process should begin then. Of course there would be many practical considerations of which I know nothing that might prolong the process.

Senator McCUMBER. And all that Japan reserves is the same that other great nations have reserved—certain concessions?

The PRESIDENT. A residential concession and economic concession; yes, sir.

Senator McCUMBER. The same as Great Britain and France and other countries have retained there?

The PRESIDENT. Yes; and I ought to say that the representatives of Japan showed every evidence of wishing to put the matter upon just the same basis that the dealings of other nations with China have rested upon for some time.

Senator McCumber. The whole purpose of my question, Mr. President, is to satisfy my mind, if I can, that Japan will in good faith carry out her agreement.

The President. I have every confidence that she will, sir.

Senator Pomerene. Mr. President, if I may, I should like to ask a question or two along that same line. If this treaty should fail of ratification, then would not the opportunity be open to Japan to treat the Shantung question just as she has treated the Manchurian situation?

The President. I think so; yes.

Senator Pomerene. So that if the treaty should fail of ratification, China, so far as Shantung is concerned, would be practically at the mercy of Japan; whereas if the treaty is ratified, then at least she will have the benefit of the moral assistance of all the other signatory powers to the treaty to aid in the protection of Chinese rights?

The President. Senator, I conceive one of the chief benefits of the whole arrangement that centers in the league of nations to be just what you have indicated—that it brings to bear the opinion of the world and the controlling action of the world on all relationships of that hazardous sort, particularly those relationships which involve the rights of the weaker nations. After all, the wars that are likely to come are most likely to come by aggression against the weaker nations. Without the league of nations they have no buttress or protection. With it, they have the united protection of the world; and inasmuch as it is the universal opinion that the great tragedy through which we have just passed never would have occurred if the Central Powers had dreamed that a number of nations would be combined against them, so I have the utmost confidence that the notice beforehand that the strong nations of the world will in every case be united will make war extremely unlikely.

Senator Moses. Mr. President, are these *procès verbaux* to be deposited anywhere as a matter of public record?

The President. That had not been decided, Senator. Of course, if they were deposited as a matter of public record, there would be certain very great disadvantages.

Senator MOSES. Are they to be deposited with the secretariat of the league of nations?

The PRESIDENT. No, sir.

Senator MOSES. Without some such depository, how otherwise would this engagement of Japan, as embodied in the *procès verbal,* be brought forward for enforcement?

The PRESIDENT. There would be as many copies of the *procès verbal* as there were members of the conference in existence much longer than the time within which we shall learn whether Japan will fulfill her obligations or not.

Senator MOSES. You mean in the private papers of the personnel of the council of four?

The PRESIDENT. I would not call them private papers. I have a copy, Senator. I regard them as a public trust, not private papers, and I can assure you that they will not be destroyed.

Senator MOSES. Suppose that each member of the council of four had passed out of office, out of any position of power, at a time when it became evident that Japan was not keeping the engagement as it was embodied in the *procès verbal* on the day when this record was made, in what manner would you expect that engagement to be brought forward for enforcement?

The PRESIDENT. I should deem it my duty—I cannot speak for the others—to leave those papers where they could be made accessible.

Senator POMERENE. Mr. President, I have another question or two on the Shantung proposition that I should like to ask, if I may.

Assuming for the sake of the argument that there were to be some undue delay on the part of Japan in turning back to China her rights in Shantung, and that China were to make complaint to the council provided for in the league of nations, have you any doubt but that it would be taken up promptly by all the members of that council for their consideration and determination?

The PRESIDENT. No, sir; I have not any doubt of it.

Senator POMERENE. Another question. On yesterday Dr. Millard was before the committee, and he made the statement that there were twenty regional understandings similar to the Monroe doctrine. I desire to say, however, that in answer to a question—

The PRESIDENT. Did he name any of them?

Senator POMERENE. I asked him some questions afterwards, and in explanation he qualified that statement by saying that these were written agreements somewhat akin to the Lansing-Ishii agreement, so-called, and as to these with relation to China a part of them were as between Japan and China, and a part as between Great Britain and China, and he instanced the secret agreement with Japan respecting Shantung. What I desired to ask was this: Did any information come to the commission indicating that there were any regional understandings similar to the Monroe doctrine?

The PRESIDENT. None, whatever. The only agreements that I can imagine he was referring to are contained in the exchange of notes which occurred between the Japanese and Chinese Governments in 1915 and 1918 with regard to the method and conditions of the return of Shantung Province to China.

Senator HITCHCOCK. Mr. President, I think it should be said also that later on in his testimony, either in answer to a question by Senator Pomerene, or perhaps in response to a question by Senator Swanson, while the witness, Dr. Millard, stated that he deemed them regional understandings—those that he had in mind—he said very emphatically that they were totally unlike the Monroe doctrine, and would not come under that category.

The PRESIDENT. And in his sense every treaty that concerns territory anywhere affects a region, and is a regional understanding; but that is a very broad and vague meaning to attach to the word.

Senator JOHNSON of California. Mr. President, I am quite hesitant about asking certain questions which I wish to ask. I apologize in advance for asking them, and I trust you will stop me at once if they are questions which you deem inappropriate, or that ought not to be asked.

The PRESIDENT. Thank you.

Senator JOHNSON of California. First, we have pending now treaties of peace with Austria, with Hungary, with Bulgaria, and with the Ottoman Empire, all of which involve tremendous new territorial adjustments; and under those new territorial adjustments we will have our obligations, moral or otherwise, under the league of nations, of course. The new territorial adjustments about to be determined upon in these various treaties are really greater in extent, or quite as important, at least, as those that are provided for by the German treaty; are they not?

The PRESIDENT. I should say so; yes.

Senator JOHNSON of California. They will deal not only with the creation of the boundaries of new nations, but possibly with the subject of mandatories, too?

The PRESIDENT. Well, the treaties will not themselves deal with the mandatories. That is a matter that will be decided by the league.

Senator JOHNSON of California. Oh, yes.

The PRESIDENT. But the treaties will no doubt create certain territories which fall under the trusteeship which will lead to mandatories.

Senator JOHNSON of California. So that there is a very important—in fact, the most important—part of the territorial world settlement yet to be made?

The PRESIDENT. Well, in extent, yes, Senator; so far as the amount of territory covered is concerned, yes.

Senator JOHNSON of California. Not only in extent, but in their character, and in the numbers of peoples involved, too, Mr. President. Is not that accurate?

The PRESIDENT. Well, you may be right, Senator; I do not know.

Senator JOHNSON of California. I think you answered to Senator Borah the question I am about to ask, so pardon me if it is repetitive. It is this: Was the United States Government officially informed, at any time between the rupture of diplomatic relations with Germany and the signing of the armistice, of agreements made by the allied Governments in regard to the settlement of the war?

The PRESIDENT. No; not so far as I know.

Senator JOHNSON of California. So far as you are aware, was it unofficially informed during that period?

The PRESIDENT. I would be more clear in my answer, Senator, if I knew just what you were referring to.

Senator JOHNSON of California. I am referring to the

so-called secret treaties which disposed of territory among the belligerents.

The PRESIDENT. You mean like the treaty of London?

Senator JOHNSON of California. Yes; like the London pact.

The PRESIDENT. No; no, sir.

Senator JOHNSON of California. Could you state whether or not any official investigation was made by our Government to ascertain whether or not there were any such treaties of territorial disposition?

The PRESIDENT. There was no such investigation.

Senator JOHNSON of California. These specific treaties, then—the treaty of London, on the basis of which Italy entered the war; the agreement with Roumania, in August, 1916; the various agreements in respect to Asia Minor, and the agreements consummated in the winter of 1917 between France and Russia relative to the frontiers of Germany, and particularly in relation to the Saar Valley and the left bank of the Rhine—none of these did we (and when I say "we" I mean you, Mr. President) have any knowledge of prior to the conference at Paris?

The PRESIDENT. No, sir. I can confidently answer that "No," in regard to myself.

Senator McCUMBER. Senator Johnson, may I ask the President right here whether or not after we entered into the war any treaties were made between any of our cobelligerents that were not given to us?

The PRESIDENT. No, sir; I do not know of any.

Senator McCUMBER. Then the secret treaties that you have reference to were made prior to the time we entered into the war?

The PRESIDENT. Yes, sir.

Senator McCUMBER. After that, our cobelligerents withheld nothing from us; did they?

The PRESIDENT. They entered into no agreements.

Senator BORAH. Well, you asked, Senator, if they withheld anything from us. They withheld all that they had had previously?

The PRESIDENT. No, no; but he means, Did they withhold any agreement that they made after we entered the war?

Senator McCUMBER. That is just what I meant.

Senator JOHNSON of California. We do not know of any engagements which have been made subsequent to our entering into the war?

The PRESIDENT. No, sir.

Senator JOHNSON of California. Those that I have referred to—and I say this, Senator, so that you will have no error in respect to it—I referred wholly, I think, to the treaties that were prior to our entry into the war.

The PRESIDENT. Yes.

Senator JOHNSON of California. Were you familiar, Mr. President, please, with any agreements that were made by the allied Governments with the Czecho-Slovak National Council, the Polish National Council, and the Jugo-Slav National Committee?

The PRESIDENT. I was aware of arrangements similar to those that we had ourselves made recognizing those national committees as provisional representatives of the people.

Senator JOHNSON of California. But merely as recognizing governments, and that these committees represented the peoples of the various countries?

The PRESIDENT. Yes; and the recognition was purely informal. It was not an international recognition, but an agreement to deal with them as representatives.

Senator JOHNSON of California. When our Government through you, Mr. President, in January, 1918, made the 14 points as the basis for peace, were those points made with the knowledge of the existence of the secret agreements?

The PRESIDENT. No; oh, no.

Senator JOHNSON of California. It was not intended, then, by the expression of these 14 points, to supplant the aims contained in the secret treaties?

The PRESIDENT. Since I knew nothing of them, necessarily not.

Senator JOHNSON of California. Yes; quite so. Do you know, Mr. President, or is it permissible for us to be told, whether France has special military agreements with Poland and Czecho-Slovakia?

The PRESIDENT. I know of none, sir.

Senator JOHNSON of California. Did China enter the war upon our advice—the advice of the United States?

The PRESIDENT. I cannot tell, sir. We advised her to enter, and she soon after did. She had sought our advice. Whether that was the persuasive advice or not, I do not know.

Senator JOHNSON of California. Do you recall, Mr. President, that preceding that advice we had asked China, as one of the neutral nations, to sever diplomatic relations with Germany?

The PRESIDENT. Whether we had asked her?

Senator JOHNSON of California. Yes, sir.

The PRESIDENT. I do not recall, Senator. I am sure Mr. Lansing can tell, though, from the records of the department.

Senator JOHNSON of California. Do you know, Mr. President, whether or not our Government stated to China that if China would enter the war we would protect her interests at the peace conference?

The PRESIDENT. We made no promises.

Senator JOHNSON of California. No representations of that sort?

The PRESIDENT. No. She knew that we would as well as we could. She had every reason to know that.

Senator JOHNSON of California. Pardon me a further question: You did make the attempt to do it, too; did you not?

The PRESIDENT. Oh, indeed, I did; very seriously.

Senator JOHNSON of California. And the decision ultimately reached at the peace conference was a disappointment to you?

The PRESIDENT. Yes, sir; I may frankly say that it was.

Senator JOHNSON of California. You would have preferred, as I think most of us would, that there had been a different conclusion of the Shantung provision, or the Shantung difficulty or controversy, at the Paris peace conference?

The PRESIDENT. Yes; I frankly intimated that.

Senator JOHNSON of California. Did it require the unanimous consent of the members of the peace conference to reach a decision like the Shantung decision?

The PRESIDENT. Every decision; yes, sir.

Senator JOHNSON of California. Do you recall, Mr.

President, prior to the decision on the territorial question of Shantung, or of German rights in Shantung, the racial equality question coming before the peace conference?

The PRESIDENT. I remember that at one of the sessions called plenary sessions a resolution regarding that matter was introduced by the Japanese representatives, but rather as an expression of opinion or hope, and it was not pressed for action.

Senator JOHNSON of California. Mr. President, the press at that time stated that it had gone to a vote—and I trust some one will correct me if I am in error—and that the vote was 11 to 6 upon the proposition. The dispatches at that time were to that effect.

The PRESIDENT. I was misled, Senator. You are referring to the commission on a league of nations?

Senator JOHNSON of California. Yes.

The PRESIDENT. There was a vote there. There never was a vote on any subject in the peace conference.

Senator JOHNSON of California. I confounded the two.

The PRESIDENT. Yes.

Senator JOHNSON of California. May I ask, if permissible, how the representatives of the United States voted upon that particular proposition?

The PRESIDENT. Senator, I think it is very natural you should ask that. I am not sure that I am at liberty to answer, because that touches the intimacy of a great many controversies that occurred in that conference, and I think it is best, in the interest of international good understanding, that I should not answer.

Senator JOHNSON of California. Do you know, Mr. President, whether or not the American Commission at Paris urged that a definite sum of reparation be fixed in the treaty?

The PRESIDENT. It did.

Senator JOHNSON of California. Will you state, if appropriate, why that view did not prevail?

The PRESIDENT. No, Senator, I cannot; and yet I dislike to decline, because it may create a misapprehension on your part. Let me see if I can explain it, without indiscretion; I would be very glad, gentlemen, to tell you all about it, if you will leave it out of the notes. May

I do that?—because I do not wish to leave any wrong impression on your minds. The explanation is perfectly simple.

Senator BRANDEGEE. What is the question, please?

The PRESIDENT. The question is, Why was the policy urged by the United States, that we fix a definite sum of reparation in the treaty, not adopted?

Senator BORAH. I would be content to have it left out of the notes upon your request; but I am afraid it would still get to the public, and that would put us in an embarrassing position.

The PRESIDENT. It is not an explanation discreditable to anybody, but it is an international secret. I am quite at liberty to say that the United States' financial representatives—who, by the way, made an admirable impression upon everybody over there—did advocate the fixing of a definite sum for reparation.

Senator FALL. Mr. President, may I ask, to clear up a difficulty in my own mind, whether you regard the answering of these questions as an indiscretion because of the fact that there are other negotiations pending which might be affected?

The PRESIDENT. Oh, no, sir; simply because they affect the internal political affairs of other countries.

Senator FALL. Then, in your judgment, these matters should never be given publicity?

The PRESIDENT. Matters of this sort.

Senator FALL. I say, matters of this sort that have been referred to, should, in your judgment, never be given publicity; and it is not because of pending or other negotiation?

The PRESIDENT. Oh, no; I think they should not be given publicity.

Senator JOHNSON of California. I thank you very much, Mr. President. That is all I desire to ask.

The PRESIDENT. You have been very considerate in putting your questions.

Senator FALL. Mr. President, as I suggested, I have prepared several written questions, for the purpose of concentrating my own ideas, and several of them, I may say, are somewhat in sequence, and I feel that if we are going to hold hearings all day—that is, if we are all going to have the time and do not get into arguments among ourselves—possibly it might be just to you to submit these questions, as I have prepared them, to you first, and allow you to look them over before I pursue the line of inquiry. However, that is, of course, entirely with you. They do not all refer directly to provisions of the treaty nor to the construction of the treaty, but to other matters relating to the treaty.

Senator JOHNSON of California. Before you do that, Senator, with the President's permission may I ask one or two more questions concerning Shantung which I omitted or forgot?

The PRESIDENT. Certainly, Senator.

Senator JOHNSON of California. First, did Japan decline to sign the award as made or provided in the peace treaty?

The PRESIDENT. Her representatives informed us, Senator, that they were instructed not to sign in that event.

Senator JOHNSON of California. Was the determination finally reached a balancing of the difficulties or the disadvantages that might arise because of the balancing of those advantages or disadvantages?

The PRESIDENT. I do not know that I could answer that either "yes' or "no," Senator. It was a matter of many conversations and of many arguments and persuasions.

Senator JOHNSON of California. Was the decision reached—if you will pardon the perfectly blunt question—because Japan declined to sign unless that decision was reached in that way?

The PRESIDENT. No; I do not think it would be true to say "yes" to that question. It was reached because we thought it was the best that could be got, in view of the definite engagements of Great Britain and France, and the necessity of a unanimous decision, which we held to be necessary in every case we have decided.

Senator JOHNSON of California. Great Britain and France adhered to their original engagements, did they not?

The PRESIDENT. They said that they did not feel at liberty to disregard them.

Senator JOHNSON of California. And you, Mr. Presi-

Senator HITCHCOCK. We have an engagement to-morrow morning for the committee.

The CHAIRMAN. I think we must have some consideration for the President's time.

Senator HARDING. I just want to reserve one question.

Senator BRANDEGEE. Do you not want to ask it now?

The CHAIRMAN. We have until 1 o'clock.

Senator BRANDEGEE. I have here the President's statement which he read to us when we met here this morning, and in it he states:

"Nothing, I am led to believe, stands in the way of the ratification of the treaty except certain doubts with regard to the meaning and implication of certain articles of this covenant of the league of nations, and I must frankly say that I am unable to understand why such doubts should be entertained."

Now, I do not believe the President is correctly informed as to the situation if he believes that. There are things in the treaty itself which militate against the ratification, in my opinion, of the treaty without amendment. Did you have in mind, Mr. President, when you read that to us, the Shantung provision of the treaty?

The PRESIDENT. I certainly had that in mind, Senator, but I did not understand that that stood in the way of ratification. I am, of course, acting only upon such information as I have received.

Senator BRANDEGEE. I understand—and that is the reason of taking the liberty of suggesting to you that you may not be well informed in this respect. Of course there is opposition by a great many Senators to the entire covenant of the league of nations, which I have no doubt you know, that is, article 1 of the treaty of Versailles. Then there is opposition to the various parts of the covenants of the league and not to the whole league, by other Senators. Then there is a great opposition, fundamental and sincere, to the Shantung provision, which is in the body of the treaty itself, and which can only be cured by an amendment. As I understand it, no reservation that we could make in the resolution of ratification would be effective to strike out the

Shantung provision. It must be cured, if it is cured, by a straight out-and-out amendment, striking that from the treaty. That, of course, would necessitate the resubmission of the treaty to the signatories who have already signed it.

Now, you state later on that every suggestion of the United States was accepted, that is after you went back, after you had your conference with us last March, and having obtained our views as to the necessity for certain changes in the first draft of the covenant, you state [reading]:

"The view of the United States with regard to the questions I have mentioned had, in fact, already been accepted by the commission and there was supposed to be nothing inconsistent with them in the draft of the covenant first adopted."

And omitting a few lines which do not apply to that you say [reading]:

"There was absolutely no doubt as to the meaning of any one of the resulting provisions of the covenant in the minds of those who participated in drafting them, and I respectfully submit that there is nothing vague or doubtful in their wording."

Of course that is your opinion, if I may say so.

The PRESIDENT. Yes, sir.

Senator BRANDEGEE. But you are familiar with the statements, I have no doubt, that ex-Senator Root, Justice Hughes, Mr. Taft, and other able lawyers of the country have made with respect to the necessity for reservations if we are to ratify the treaty, are you not?

The PRESIDENT. Yes, sir.

Senator BRANDEGEE. That is, you admit that there are grave doubts among the ablest lawyers of the country as to the necessity for reservations or the alternative between reservations and ratifying the whole treaty, as it is expressed in the vernacular, without the dotting of an "i" or the crossing of a "t."

The PRESIDENT. I admit that there are those difficulties in a great many minds.

Senator BRANDEGEE. Now, of course, it is true, is it

not, that if difficulties arise as to the construction of any provision of the treaty after we have passed from the scene, what we thought the provisions of the treaty or of the covenant meant, will not be very powerful in the construction that may be placed upon it by those who then have to determine what it means, will it?

The PRESIDENT. The vote of the United States will be essential.

Senator BRANDEGEE. I do not mean that. The fact that you think now that everything in the treaty is plain and that there is no doubt about the meaning of any provisions, and the fact that I think there is grave doubt about many of the provisions, will not seriously affect the opinion of the council or of the arbitrator that finally passes upon the true meaning of the treaty when dispute arises.

The PRESIDENT. No, Senator; but the plain wording of the treaty will have a great deal to do, and the meaning of the wording is plain.

Senator BRANDEGEE. That is simply another way of stating, is it not, that you are clear in your opinion that the provisions of the treaty are plain? But I am suggesting that there will be a dispute between nations as to what the treaty means after we have passed from the scene.

The PRESIDENT. No, sir; it is a question of being confident of what language means, not confident of an opinion.

Senator BRANDEGEE. I mean, we derive our opinions as to the meanings of the treaty from the language of the treaty, do we not?

The PRESIDENT. Yes.

Senator BRANDEGEE. Now they would derive their construction of what the treaty means from the language of it, we not being there?

The PRESIDENT. Yes.

Senator BRANDEGEE. So that what we think about it now will not be determinative in an international court or before an arbitrator 20 years hence in case of a dispute between two nations as to the meaning of the treaty?

The PRESIDENT. Certainly not, but the language will.

Senator BRANDEGEE. Of course they will have the language before them, but the language which determines it is now in dispute between you and certain lawyers of the country and certain Senators as to its meaning. Now what provision is there in the treaty for the determination of a dispute as to the interpretation of a clause of the treaty if such dispute arises?

The PRESIDENT. The covenant states that there are certain questions which are acknowledged as being especially suitable for submission to arbitration. One of those is the meaning of the treaty.

Senator BRANDEGEE. What does the treaty provide about that?

The PRESIDENT. You have it there, sir.

Senator BRANDEGEE. Yes, sir; I wondered if you remembered it.

The PRESIDENT. I think I do so, but you have the language.

Senator BRANDEGEE. Yes. Article 12 of the league provides (reading):

"The members of the league agree that if there should arise between them any dispute likely to lead to a rupture, they will submit the matter either to arbitration or to inquiry by the council, and they agree in no case to resort to war until three months after the award by the arbitrators or the report by the council."

That is, if there is a dispute, as I construe this, between members of the league as to the meaning of the covenant or any article thereof, it shall be referred to the arbitrators.

The PRESIDENT. Only if the parties agree.

Senator BRANDEGEE. Or to the council?

The PRESIDENT. Or to the council; yes.

Senator BRANDEGEE. That is, the council is to determine the meaning of the covenant?

The PRESIDENT. No, Senator; I beg your pardon. There are two processes. If the parties agree to submit to arbitration, of course, it is submitted to arbitration, and the decision is final. If they think it is a question that they are not willing to submit to arbitration, then they must submit it to the council for an expression of opinion and a recommendation, but that opinion and recommendation do not bind.

Senator BRANDEGEE. Is there any possible way authoritatively of determining without war what the treaty means?

The PRESIDENT. That is true of every treaty, Senator. If you re-express it in the language of the Senators to whom you refer and there is a dispute about the meaning of that, the same would apply. You cannot use any language, I assume, which could not possibly give rise to some sort of dispute.

Senator BRANDEGEE. I assume that if it provided that if there should arise between the members of the league any dispute in relation to the construction of any article of the covenant of the league of nations, such dispute should be referred to an arbitrator, and the members would agree to be bound by its decision; that would be an agreement for an authoritative determination of what the treaty meant.

The PRESIDENT. Yes.

Senator BRANDEGEE. Now, as it is they will submit the matter either to arbitration or to inquiry by the council, and so forth. Now you say that the opinion of the council to which the dispute has been submitted is only advisory?

The PRESIDENT. Yes, sir.

Senator BRANDEGEE. Then suppose one party to the dispute against whom the council decides declines to abide by it?

The PRESIDENT. Then there is war, but not within three months of the opinion of the council.

Senator BRANDEGEE. Under Article 10 the members of the league undertake to respect and preserve as against external aggression the territorial integrity and existing political independence of all members of the league. That is a contract between the signatories. We say: "We undertake to preserve the territorial integrity of the members against external aggression," which means that we contract to do it, does it not?

The PRESIDENT. We engage to do it.

Senator BRANDEGEE. It means an international contract, does it not, a compact, an agreement?

The PRESIDENT. Yes.

Senator BRANDEGEE. Whether that is a moral or legal obligation, it is an obligation?

The PRESIDENT. Yes.

Senator BRANDEGEE. Of course, it is a moral duty to keep a promise, and this is an international promise; so that the distinction between a moral obligation and a legal one seems to me to be not of great importance, because we are obligated in any event.

The PRESIDENT. Pardon me; I think it is of the greatest importance because the element of judgment enters into it as it does not in the other.

Senator BRANDEGEE. You mean the judgment as to whether or not it is a moral obligation?

The PRESIDENT. No. For example, a question is submitted to arbitration and it is agreed that the decision shall be final. The judgment of one of the parties to the controversy may be that the decision is a very bad one, but it has to accept it; the element of judgment is excluded altogether, but, with regard to the method of fulfilling the obligations of a covenant like that under consideration there is freedom of judgment on the part of the individual members of the league. It seems to me that makes a very considerable difference.

Senator HARDING. Will the Senator permit me to interrupt right there?

Senator BRANDEGEE. I will.

Senator HARDING. I dislike to interrupt the Senator.

Senator BRANDEGEE. I yield to the Senator.

Senator HARDING. The President expressed a while ago surprise that I raised a question as to the value of this compact because of the moral obligation feature. Let me premise by the statement that I look upon a moral obligation as that which the conscience of the contracting party impels. The conscience of any nation in Europe, for example, may be warped by its prejudices, racial, geographical, and otherwise. If that be true and any nation may put aside or exercise its judgment as to the moral obligation in accepting any recommendation of the league, really what do we get out of this international compact in the enforcement of any decree?

The PRESIDENT. We get the centering upon it generally of the definite opinion of the world, expressed through the authoritative organs of the responsible governments.

Senator HARDING. Another question. That is surrendering the suggestion of a moral obligation for this Republic to the prejudices or necessities of the nations of the Old World, is it not?

The PRESIDENT. I do not understand that we make such a surrender.

Senator HARDING. Would you not understand a decree by the council to be a suggestion of this moral obligation?

The PRESIDENT. Certainly I would, but we would have to concur in that before it had any force of any kind.

Senator HARDING. Would it not be quite as moral for this Republic itself to determine its moral obligations?

The PRESIDENT. Undoubtedly, Senator; but in the meantime the world would not have the knowledge before it that there will be concerted action by all the responsible governments of the world in the protection of the peace of the world. The minute you do away with that assurance to the world you have reached the situation which produced the German war.

Senator HARDING. What becomes of our standing among nations if the council fixes a moral obligation upon us and we reject the judgment of the council as to the moral obligation?

The PRESIDENT. Pardon me if I remind you that we always have to concur in that.

Senator HARDING. Precisely; but the council states what constitutes the moral obligation, if we agree; but if we do not agree, then in the eyes of the world we have rejected its judgment as to a moral obligation.

The PRESIDENT. Certainly; and I hold that we are at liberty to do that, if our moral judgment honestly differs from the moral judgment of the world.

Senator HARDING. Then, let us go back to the original inquiry. What permanent value is there, then, to this compact?

The PRESIDENT. The greatest permanent value, Senator, is the point that I have raised. We are assuming that the United States will not concur in the general

moral judgment of the world. In my opinion, she generally will. If it had been known that this war was coming on, her moral judgment would have concurred with
that of the other Governments of the world, with that of
the other people of the world; and if Germany had known
that there was a possibility of that sort of concurrence,
she never would have dared to do what she did. Without
such notice served on the powers that may wish to repeat the folly that Germany commenced, there is no assurance to the world that there will be peace even for a
generation, whereas if they know beforehand that there
will be that concert of judgment there is the most tremendous guaranty.

Senator HARDING. But, Mr. President, nobody expressed for us our moral obligation to enter into this war.
That was our own expression, was it not?

The PRESIDENT. Certainly; it was our concurrence in
the judgment of the world.

Senator HARDING. One of the points I am getting at, if
I can make it clear, is the necessity of a written compact
for this Republic to fulfill its moral obligations to civilization.

The PRESIDENT. Senator, this Republic, if I interpret
it rightly, does not need a suggestion from any quarter to
fulfill its moral obligations.

Senator HARDING. I quite agree with that.

The PRESIDENT. But it steadies the whole world by its
promise beforehand that it will stand with other nations
of similar judgment to maintain right in the world.

Senator FALL. Mr. President, then if the commissioner
of the United States on the council were to join with the
other members of the council in fixing a moral obligation
upon the United States, and the Congress and the President, acting as part of the legislative branch of the Government, were to reject that judgment, would it not have
a very disastrous effect upon the league, throw the world
into chaos, and undo all that has been done?

The PRESIDENT. It might; but you are assuming a
case——

Senator FALL. Certainly; we have to assume cases.

The PRESIDENT. Where we would have to assume that
responsibility, because, being part of the Government, we

would in every case really express the judgment of the American people, and if the unhappy time should ever come when that judgment is against the judgment of the rest of the world we would have to express it.

Senator FALL. Certainly. Mr. President, I am possibly looking, as Bacon said, at a distance.

Senator McCUMBER. Would our moral conviction of the unrighteousness of the German war have brought us into this war if Germany had not committed any acts against us, without the league of nations, as, of course, we had no league of nations at that time?

The PRESIDENT. I hope it would eventually, Senator, as things developed.

Senator McCUMBER. Do you think if Germany had committed no act of war or no act of injustice against our citizens that we would have gotten into this war?

The PRESIDENT. I do think so.

Senator McCUMBER. You think we would have gotten in anyway?

The PRESIDENT. I do.

Senator BRANDEGEE. If I may be allowed to resume, for I kept still all morning——

Senator FALL. If the Senator will pardon me a moment, I am going to ask the President to excuse me, as I have an engagement.

The PRESIDENT. I am sorry, Senator, that you are obliged to leave.

Senator FALL. I regret, sir, that I have an engagement with my wife, who is not in very good health.

Senator BRANDEGEE. Now, if I may proceed without interruption, which breaks the continuity of my thought and uses a great deal of time, I will be through in a very few minutes. As I understand the President, his construction of article 10 is that if the council considers the question of external aggression upon a member of the league, we, having signed this treaty with article 10 in it, in which we undertake to preserve against external aggression the territorial integrity of all members of the league, can then say, it is a moral question into which the element of judgment enters and we, considering our judgment binding at the time, do not care to agree to the recommendation of the council. If every member of the league is at liberty to take that view of its moral and legal obligations under article 10, and declines to do what the council recommends, and if it is known in advance that that is the construction placed upon article 10 by those who framed it, it does not seem to me—and this is merely my opinion—that the terror to wrongdoers by what is hoped to be the united concerted action of the members of the league in the concentration of its powers to suppress the wrongdoer will have the effect that the President thinks it will. In other words, I do not think that Germany would have refrained from war if she had known that article 10 was in existence.

Article 10 says:

> "In case of any such aggression, or in case of any threat or danger of such aggression, the council shall advise upon the means by which the obligation shall be fulfilled."

There is no doubt that that is an obligation in a contract, and I know of but one way to perform an obligation that you have contracted to perform, and that is to perform it. I do not think that it admits of any qualifications after you sign the treaty. I want to call attention also to the fact that the external aggression which we undertake, if we sign this treaty, to repel or guarantee against is not stated in the treaty at all to be an unwarranted aggression. I wish to ask the President, if the league were in existence and Hungary and Roumania were members of it, and Roumania were in the position she now is, having raided the territorial integrity of Hungary and marched through its capital and occupied it, and the council, as its duty would be under the covenant, considered what was best to be done and advised us to send immediately to co-operate with them 100,000 men, whether we would be at liberty to discuss whether we were morally bound by article 10 of the covenant and decline to send the men, and, if we were, could we do it without risking being called an "international slacker" by the other members of the league?

The PRESIDENT. Senator, since you have made the case a concrete one I am afraid I ought not to answer it, because it involves a judgment as between Roumania and Hungary.

Senator BRANDEGEE. I withdraw the names of the two countries, and assume the circumstances.

The PRESIDENT. Let me say that I take it for granted that in practically every case the United States would respond; but that does not seem to be the question. I quite agree with you that a moral obligation is to be fulfilled, and I am confident that our Nation will fulfill it, but that does not remove from each individual case the element of judgment which we are free to exercise in two stages: We are, first, free to exercise it in the vote of our representative on the council, who will of course act under instructions from the home Government; and, in the second place, we are to exercise it when the President, acting upon the action of the council, makes his recommendation to Congress. Then, Congress is to exercise its judgment as to whether or not the instructions of the Executive to our member of the council were well founded, and whether the case is one of distinct moral obligation.

Senator BRANDEGEE. Suppose that each member of the council, as you say, acting under instructions from its home Government, including our representative on the council, should think, for instance, that Roumania was entirely right in some invasion of Hungary, and public sentiment was that way, but that our Government instructed our representative to vote with the foreign members of the council to support Hungary—suppose the public sentiment of the other members and of the people of this country were in favor of Roumania, what sort of a position would we be in to fulfill our guaranty?

The PRESIDENT. In order to answer that question I must go a little bit afield. In the first place, I understand that article to mean that no nation is at liberty to invade the territorial integrity of another. That does not mean to invade for purposes of warfare, but to impair the territorial integrity of another nation. Its territorial integrity is not destroyed by armed intervention; it is destroyed by the retention of territory, by taking territory away from it; that impairs its territorial integrity. I understand the covenant to mean that that is in no case permissible by the action of a single nation against another; that there is only one permissible method and that is, if territorial arrangements are unsatisfactory, that they should be brought to the attention of the world through the league and that then the league should exercise such rights as it may be able to exercise for a readjustment of boundaries.

I believe that territorial aggression, in the sense of territorial capture, is, by the wording of the act, made illegitimate.

Senator BRANDEGEE. The words are not "territorial aggression," but "external aggression."

The PRESIDENT. But it says the preservation of its territorial integrity against external aggression.

Senator BRANDEGEE. Suppose the external aggressor, having gotten within the territory of the aggressee, stays there?

The PRESIDENT. Then that impairs the territorial integrity.

Senator BRANDEGEE. Certainly; and then on a call by the council for us to perform our international contract under article 10, if Congress does not favor performing it, you think we would not be subject to criticism by the other members of the league?

The PRESIDENT. Oh, we might be subject to criticism; but I think Congress would be at liberty to form its own judgment as to the circumstances.

Senator BRANDEGEE. I agree with you entirely, and under our Constitution Congress would have to do so.

The PRESIDENT. Yes; that is understood by all.

Senator BRANDEGEE. Of course; but I am assuming if the council should advise us to do a certain thing, and Congress refused to do it—and if every nation's representative assembly can do the same thing, it seems to me like a rope of sand and not an effective tribunal which would result in promoting peace.

The PRESIDENT. The reason I do not agree with you, Senator, is that I do not think such a refusal would likely often occur. I believe it would be only upon the gravest grounds—and in case Congress is right, I am indifferent to foreign criticism.

Senator BRANDEGEE. Of course, we would always think we were right, I assume. Now, I wish to call your attention to article 15. I do this simply because you think all these provisions are clear, and I want to say in that connection that we had Mr. Miller, who described himself as the technical expert or adviser to the American Peace Commission, especially, I think, on questions of international law.

The PRESIDENT. The league of nations.

Senator BRANDEGEE. We had him before our committee, and he answered this question, that I am about to ask, in three different ways, and we could not, of course, get much information from him; and he promised to take it under advisement and to give us his considered opinion, but he has not done so. Now, article 15, in the last two paragraphs provides:

"The council may in any case under this article refer the dispute to the assembly. The dispute shall be so referred at the request of either party to the dispute, provided that such request be made within 14 days after the submission of the dispute to the council.

"In any case referred to the assembly, all the provisions of this article and of article 12 relating to the action and powers of the council shall apply to the action and powers of the assembly, provided that a report made by the assembly, if concurred in by the representatives of those members of the league represented on the council and of a majority of the other members of the league, exclusive in each case of the representatives of the parties to the dispute, shall have the same force as a report by the council concurred in by all the members thereof other than the representatives of one or more of the parties to the dispute."

Now, in the first place, it says "represented on the council and of a majority of the other members of the league." Does that mean that the various members of the league have got to act upon that as separate Governments, or does it mean the representatives of the other members of the league?

The PRESIDENT. I do not quite understand that question.

Senator BRANDEGEE. It says:

"A report made by the assembly, if concurred in by the representatives of those members of the league represented on the council and of a majority of the other members of the league."

Does that mean there "and a majority of the other representatives of members of the league in the assembly"?

The PRESIDENT. Yes; I assume so.

Senator BRANDEGEE. But it does not say so. It leaves it as though the members of the league could act independently of their representatives and the assembly.

The PRESIDENT. Oh, no.

Senator BRANDEGEE. I assume it means what you say.

The PRESIDENT. Yes; I assume that.

Senator BRANDEGEE. Very well. Now, the question; Supposing there were a dispute between the United States and that portion of the British Empire known as the United Kingdom—England, Ireland, Scotland and Wales —as to some right of one of our ships to enter an English port, for instance, and that dispute should come before the council, and, upon the request of Great Britain, it should be removed to the assembly. The article I have just read provides for a report concurred in "exclusive in each case of the representatives of the parties to the dispute."

The PRESIDENT. Yes.

Senator BRANDEGEE. Now, all the self-governing colonies of England, or at least five of them, have a vote in the assembly, and the British Empire also has a vote. I assume in the case of the dispute which I have supposed, of course, the United States would be excluded from voting, as being a party to the dispute; and I assume the British Empire would be excluded, but I am not sure.

The PRESIDENT. Yes, sir; that is what I assume.

Senator BRANDEGEE. Do you assume also that Australia, New Zealand, Canada, and India would be excluded?

The PRESIDENT. They are parts of the British Empire.

Senator BRANDEGEE. They are parts of the British Empire, but are they parties to the dispute which I have supposed to have arisen between us and England?

The PRESIDENT. I admit, Senator, that that is a complicated question; but my judgment about it is quite clear. I think I can give one instead of three answers.

Senator BRANDEGEE. Yes.

The PRESIDENT. Disputes can arise only through the Governments which have international representation. In other words, diplomatically speaking there is only one "British Empire." The parts of it are but pieces of the whole. The dispute, therefore, in the case you have supposed, would be between the United States as a diplomatic unit and the British Empire as a diplomatic unit. That is the only ground upon which the two nations could deal with one another, whether by way of dispute or agreement. Therefore, I have assumed, and confidently assumed, that the representatives of all parts of the British Empire would be excluded.

Senator BRANDEGEE. I should think that would be only fair, and I would assume that; but Mr. Miller answered that question by saying, first, that he was in doubt; secondly, that the self-governing colonies of Great Britain or of the British Empire would not be excluded, because they were not parties to the dispute; and then, third, that they would be excluded because they were parts of the British Empire; and if the legal adviser of the commission was that much confused, I feel that I need not apologize for being confused myself.

The PRESIDENT. No; but the commission was not confused.

Senator KNOX. May I say this; I was not present at the meeting when Mr. Miller testified. The fact is that while it is technically true, as the President says, that the British self-governing colonies deal diplomatically through the British foreign office, it is only true in a most technical sense. They are absolutely autonomous, even in their diplomatic dealings, as to matters that affect them. For instance, I remember when the Canadian reciprocity agreement was negotiated in 1911 the delegates sent to negotiate the agreement were from Canada. Great Britain did not appear at the hearings or conferences at all, and in every sense Canada was just as autonomous in conducting her international negotiations as she would have been if she had been an absolutely independent Government.

The PRESIDENT. Yes; but this, you see, Senator, is a combination of definite Governments that have definite international relations with each other.

Senator KNOX. But the fact that you give representation to Canada and Australia and New Zealand and other autonomous self-governing British colonies rather contradicts the idea, does it not, that they are one Government?

The PRESIDENT. I think not, sir; because in making up the constitution of the council it was provided, to speak with technical accuracy, that the five principal allied or associated Governments should each have one representative in the league; and in the opening paragraph of the treaty itself those powers are enumerated, and among others is the British Empire. "The Empire of Great Britain," I think, is the technical term. Therefore their unity is established by their representation in the council.

Senator BRANDEGEE. Mr. President, I read from the treaty——

The CHAIRMAN. I was going to ask, if I may, what function do these five Dominions of the British Empire have in the assembly?

The PRESIDENT. None, except the general powers of the assembly itself.

The CHAIRMAN. They have votes in the assembly?

The PRESIDENT. They have votes, but in a matter involving the British Empire, they would have but one vote among them.

The CHAIRMAN. But on all other matters, they would each have one vote?

The PRESIDENT. Yes.

Senator BRANDEGEE. I want to call the President's attention to the first page of the treaty with Germany, which says, after the preamble setting forth the desirability of the condition existing being replaced by a just and durable peace, "For this purpose, the high contracting parties represented as follows," and then it names them, and in the list is "His Majesty, the King of the United Kingdom of Great Britain and Ireland, and of the British Dominions beyond the seas, Emperor of India, by his duly accredited officials, and the Dominion of Canada,

the Commonwealth of Australia, the Dominion of South
Africa, the Dominion of New Zealand," etc. Now, they
are "high contracting parties"?

The PRESIDENT. Yes.

Senator BRANDEGEE. And if one of those high contracting parties has a dispute with another of the high
contracting parties, by what inference are other high contracting parties made parties to the dispute?

The PRESIDENT. I think by the inference that I
thought I established, sir——

Senator BRANDEGEE. But, if you will allow me to say
so, it does not say that these parties, the self-governing
British colonies, shall be excluded from participating in
the deliberations because they may have some interest in
the controversy.

The PRESIDENT. No.

Senator BRANDEGEE. They must be parties to the dispute. Now, if we have a dispute with England about the
right of an American ship to enter an English port, how
can it be said that New Zealand or Australia is a party to
that dispute?

The PRESIDENT. Because, Senator, in case of the worst
coming to the worst, and war ensuing, we would be at war
with all of them.

Senator BRANDEGEE. It may be that a blunder has
been made in creating such a situation. It would not be
determinative, in my opinion.

Now, on page 7 of the print that I have, which is Senate
Document No. 49, Sixty-sixth Congress, first session, the
last thing in the treaty is this statement:

"From the coming into force of the present treaty
the state of war will terminate. From that moment
and subject to the provisions of this treaty, official relations with Germany, and with any of the German
States, will be resumed by the allied and associated
powers."

The treaty itself provides that when Germany and
three of the allied and associated powers have ratified the
treaty it has come into force.

The PRESIDENT. As between those parties.

Senator BRANDEGEE. It does not say so.

The PRESIDENT. I beg your pardon, I think it does.

Senator BRANDEGEE. Here it is, Mr. President. [Handing pamphlet to the President.] I have read it, and there is no such language in it that I can discover.

The PRESIDENT. No; not the part that you read; I did not mean that; but in the part where the provision is referred to about ratification by Germany and three of the principal allied and associated powers.

Senator BRANDEGEE. I have read that with some care, and I have not seen it.

Senator KNOX. The language to which the President refers is the concluding paragraph of the treaty, and it provides that when the process of ratification shall have been completed by Germany and any three powers, the treaty shall come into force.

The PRESIDENT. As between them.

Senator KNOX. No; I beg your pardon, Mr. President. In a subsequent clause dealing with what I think is an entirely different matter—that is, the adjustments as between the nations, not adjustments as between the allied and associated powers and Germany—it comes into force whenever the ratifications are made; but if you will take the body of the treaty you will find that everything that Germany is to do is to be done within a certain number of days after the ratification has been made; and a certain number of months afterwards she is to demobilize, give up her ships, and do all things that will make her practically a noncombatant, within a number of days after ratification by three of the powers; so she is either at peace with the world, or she is only partially at peace with the world, and as the requirements of the treaty are specific that she is to go out of the war business altogether, there is a conclusive inference in my mind that she is at peace with the world when those three ratifications have been made.

The PRESIDENT. I can not agree with you there. You see, the theory is this: That when three of the principal allied and associated powers ratify this treaty, Germany having ratified it, then the treaty is in force; that is to say, she has then engaged to do the things provided in the treaty, and her engagement is with those three powers, among the rest, and she must then proceed to do what she has promised; but it does not establish peace between her and other countries.

Senator KNOX. I think that language shows that it establishes peace and provides for a resumption of diplomatic and all other relations with Germany. I intend, within a short time, to try to make my views upon that clear.

The PRESIDENT. Yes.

Senator BRANDEGEE. I went into that question rather thoroughly—"from the coming into force of the present treaty the state of war will terminate." Then it says, "From that moment, and subject to the provisions of this treaty, official relations with Germany and with any of the German States will be resumed by the allied and associated powers," which I assume means all of them.

Now, to revert to another point, Mr. President, have you any knowledge—and I ask all these questions, of course, subject to your determination as to whether it is proper for you to answer them, or to make any statement about them——

The PRESIDENT. Yes.

Senator BRANDEGEE. Are the Austrian, Bulgarian, and Turkish treaties, which I assume are in process of being made——

The PRESIDENT. Yes.

Senator BRANDEGEE [continuing]. Intertwined with the covenant of the league of nations as is the treaty with Germany?

The PRESIDENT. The covenant of the league constitutes a part of each of those treaties.

Senator BRANDEGEE. Would you feel at liberty to state what percentage of progress they have made up to the present time, or how nearly completed they are?

The PRESIDENT. I think they are all practically completed, Senator, with the exception of some debatable questions of territorial boundaries.

Senator BRANDEGEE. Inasmuch as our Constitution provides that treaties shall be made by the President by and with the advice and consent of two-thirds of the Senators present, do you think that it is constitutional for us to approve the Franco-American treaty which provides that before it goes into operation—or substantially, I would say, before it goes into operation—it must secure the approval of the council of the league of nations?

The PRESIDENT. Why, yes; we can consent. We have the sovereign right to consent to any process that we choose, surely.

Senator BRANDEGEE. We have the right to consent, but of course the Senate has the constitutional right to ratify the treaty, negotiated and presented by the Executive; but my point is, have we a right to provide that in addition to the constitutional requirements for the making of a valid treaty there shall also be required the consent of the council of the league of nations, which the Constitution was not aware of?

The PRESIDENT. If that is a part of the treaty; yes, I think we have.

Senator BRANDEGEE. But you do not think that the treaty can in any way amend the Constitution or the constitutional requirements for executing a treaty.

The PRESIDENT. No.

Senator BRANDEGEE. Then by what process of ratiocination do you assume that the treaty can compel the consent of the council before this covenant is approved?

The PRESIDENT. Suppose you would determine that when any group of nations adopted a treaty then we could adopt the treaty that contained certain provisions that we wished to put in, and to make the operation of the treaty contingent upon its acceptance by the other nations in the group. It seems to me that that is an entirely analogous case. In other words I am assuming that we adopt the treaty with Germany. In that case we will be members of the league. We are in effect saying that we have become members of the league. If the council of the league accepts this we agree to put it in force. It is a means of being consistent with the thing that we have already done in becoming a member of the league.

Senator BRANDEGEE. I get your viewpoint about that. Now, do you think it is wise for us to adopt the Franco-American treaty which in substance provides that we can not denounce it until the council of the league of nations gives us permission to do so or agrees to denounce it?

The PRESIDENT. I do, Senator. I have a very strong

feeling with regard to our historical relations with France, and also a very keen appreciation of her own sense of danger, and I think it would be one of the handsomest acts of history to enter into that.

Senator BRANDEGEE.   I feel just as cordially toward her heroic conduct as anybody can.   But that was not the question.   The question was whether it was wise to so tie ourselves to any foreign nation as that we never could repudiate—I will not use the word "repudiate"—can never cancel our treaties without due notice, without the consent of a body not yet created.

The PRESIDENT.   Of course I am assuming that body will be created before we adopt the Franco-American treaty, and in that case that provision that you are alluding to is only a completion of the plea of the treaty, namely, as I have been quoted as saying, this is an agreement on our part to anticipate the advice of the council of the league, as we shall take such and such measures to defend France.   Inasmuch as we are anticipating that, we are assuming the action of the league, and therefore it is with the league and its action that the whole matter is bound up, and I think that the provision you allude to, therefore, is consistent and almost logically necessary.

Senator BRANDEGEE.   Well, now, inasmuch as you have stated in your message—and I have of course agreed to it and have no doubt that it is true—that the Franco-American treaty is only designed for temporary purposes, the defense of France until the league says that it is competent to do it, or words to that effect——

The PRESIDENT.   Yes.

Senator BRANDEGEE.   Would it not be the part of prudence for us to include in the Franco-American treaty, if it should be ratified, a provision that it shall have some time limit put upon it, that it shall exist for not more than 10 years, say.   I assume if the league is ever going to be effective to preserve the territorial integrity and political independence of its various members, it will be in the course of 10 years, and there is no objection to having some time limit on the treaty.

The PRESIDENT.   Only a psychological objection, the sentiment between the two countries.

Senator BRANDEGEE.   The other alternative is to guarantee it forever or until the council of the league loosens us from it, is it not?

The PRESIDENT. Yes; when the council of the league will exist, among other uses should be that the whole international influence that could be brought to bear for the management of all these things will be present there to bring about this rearrangement.

Senator BRANDEGEE. Yes; I understand that. But the fact that we have a vote to loose ourselves does not help us, as unanimous action is required by nine gentlemen, any one of whom can prevent us.

The PRESIDENT. No, Senator; but the diplomatic relations of the different countries in that council will be such, if I may judge, that those things may be accomplished.

Senator BRANDEGEE. That is an optimistic view to take, if you will pardon my opinion about it.

The PRESIDENT. Perhaps it is.

Senator BRANDEGEE. I want to call your attention to the fact that this era of good feeling which exists between the allied and associated powers after their common experience and suffering in this great war may not always exist, in view of future commercial contests and separate interests of different nationalities which may occur in the future, and what some of us feel is that we ought to be careful in making these definite international engagements which we are wisely determined to carry out in good faith if we should make them, and we feel that now is the time to understand exactly the obligations we are to be held to before we affix our signature, and I have no doubt that you agree to that.

The PRESIDENT. Yes.

Senator BRANDEGEE. I want to ask you a word or two about this so-called American draft. The American draft of the league which was sent to us in response to Senate resolution was the draft which was submitted by the American commission to the conference abroad?

The PRESIDENT. No.

Senator BRANDEGEE. It was the draft which was submitted by you as the head of the American commission to the American commission. Is that correct?

The PRESIDENT. Why, Senator, it was done as all

other things of this sort were done over there. We circulated the draft among the representatives of the 14 States who were represented in the general league of nations, and they had 10 days or more to examine it. I also submitted it to my colleagues, not for any formal discussion but in order to have their opinion if they chose to express it. Then when the commission got down to its real work they appointed a committee.

Senator BRANDEGEE. Of the commission?

The PRESIDENT. No; of two officers of the commission. Well, they did form a committee, but that committee employed the services of two technical advisers. Mr. Miller was one of them and Mr. Hurst—not the Mr. Hurst that Mr. Miller mentioned.

Senator BRANDEGEE. He gave his initials as C. J. B.

The PRESIDENT. I have forgotten the initials.

Senator BRANDEGEE. He said he was an employee of the British State Department.

The PRESIDENT. Yes; he is a very able man. He was on the general drafting committee of the treaty, and Mr. Miller took the various documents that we have been reading and discussing and made a combined draft and it was that combined draft which was the subject of formal discussion and amendment and addition by the committee.

Senator BRANDEGEE. And that was the combined draft, the one that you sent to us the other day?

The PRESIDENT. No; Secretary Lansing was asked for it.

The CHAIRMAN. It was a composite draft. It came in yesterday.

Senator BRANDEGEE. I beg your pardon. I did not know about it. Was there any draft, no matter how incomplete, any skeleton draft or enumeration or substance for a draft for the so-called American plan for the covenant of the league of nations which you took with you from this country or was prepared over there by you?

The PRESIDENT. Only the one that I referred to earlier in the conference, Senator, when I had taken the Phillimore report as more or less of a basis of my work.

Senator BRANDEGEE. That was the only thing that you

had in the nature of a skeleton draft when you left the country?

The PRESIDENT.   Yes.

Senator BRANDEGEE.   Did the Phillimore draft or report, whatever the proper term may be, contain anything like what is now article 10 of the covenant of the league?

The PRESIDENT.   I do not remember.

Senator BRANDEGEE.   You do not remember whether there was anything like that in that?

The PRESIDENT.   Let me say this in regard to article 10. I believe this to be a part of the history of it. It is so far as I am concerned. Early in my administration, as I think many of the members know, I tried to get the American States, the States of Central and South America, to join with us in an arrangement in which a phrase like this constituted the kernel, that we guaranteed to each other territorial integrity and political independence. "Under a republican form of government" was added in that case. But that is another matter. As I represented to them at that time, it was a desire on my part at any rate to show the way to them of keeping things steady and preventing the kind of aggression they have had.

The CHAIRMAN.   That was the subject of the Niagara conference?

Senator BRANDEGEE.   The A. B. C. powers.

The PRESIDENT.   I do not think it was discussed there, Senator. We discussed it diplomatically.

The CHAIRMAN.   It was taken up at that time?

The PRESIDENT.   It was taken up at that time.

Senator BRANDEGEE.   Who was the author of article 10?

The PRESIDENT.   I suppose I was as much as anybody.

Senator BRANDEGEE.   And you recommended it to your fellow American commissioners?

The PRESIDENT.   Yes.

Senator BRANDEGEE.   How many Americans were on the commission which framed the covenant for the league of nations?

The PRESIDENT.   Two—Col. House and myself.

Senator BRANDEGEE.   The total membership was what? Fifteen, was it not?

The PRESIDENT.   Fourteen nations, and five principal

nations had two members, which would make 19, would it not? Yes, 19 members.

Senator Brandegee. Did they have the unit rule, so to to speak, casting one vote for each member?

The President. In only one or two instances did we vote at all. I presided and the final form was this, "If there are no objections we will regard that as accepted."

Senator Brandegee. As we say in the Senate, "without objection it is agreed to."

The President. Yes; and that is the way the whole thing was agreed to.

Senator Brandegee. Did these commissions to which the plenary conference delegated certain subjects to prepare reports upon have any co-ordination with each other? Did each commission know what the other commissions were doing?

The President. No; the subjects were too unlike.

Senator Brandegee. Was there any debate on the completed draft of the covenant of the league of nations when it was submitted to the plenary council just before you came over in March?

The President. Yes; there were speeches.

Senator Brandegee. I do not call those debates. I read that there were no debates as to what each particular government demanded.

The President. No; because there were so many of those represented, and they had all been canvassed in the process of formulation.

Senator Brandegee. You replied to a resolution of the Senate requesting a copy of a letter of Gen. Tasker H. Bliss, which was also signed by Secretary Lansing——

The President. And Mr. White.

Senator Brandegee. And Mr. White—you stated, if I recollect, in substance, that you would be glad to furnish us with a copy of it but for the fact that Gen. Bliss had mentioned the names of certain Governments and you thought it was a matter of delicacy not to make it public. Would it not be possible to furnish us with the general drift of the arguments, leaving out the names of the Governments, etc.?

The President. There was not any argument. He said flatly that it was unjust. It was not a reason.

Senator Brandegee. It was an opinion.

The President. It was an opinion.

Senator Brandegee. A conclusion.

Senator Johnson of California. With that, you agreed, Mr. President, did you not?

The President. Senator, I do not think I ought to say any more than I have said.

Senator Brandegee. I do not think I care to ask anything more.

Senator Hitchcock. Will you permit me to read into the record these two paragraphs from the conclusion of the treaty and ask whether they are what you refer to when you express the opinion that the treaty would go into effect when Germany and three of the contracting parties had signed it, and only as to them?

The Chairman. That is explicitly stated.

Senator Hitchcock. I thought it was left in some doubt. I would like to read them into the record [reading]:

"A first *procès verbal* of the deposit of ratifications will be drawn up as soon as the treaty has been ratified by Germany on the one hand, and by three of the principal allied and associated powers on the other hand.

"From the date of the first *procès verbal* the treaty will come into force between the high contracting parties who have ratified it. For the determination of all periods of time provided for in the present treaty this date will be the date of the coming into force of the treaty."

I just wanted to make it clear that the treaty is not in effect except as to those that have ratified it.

The President. I could not put my hand on it, but I was sure.

Senator McCumber. Mr. President, just one question on this French treaty. If we should adopt this present treaty with the league of nations and with section 10 in it, which brings all of the great nations of the league to the protection of France, if war should be made against her by Germany, what necessity is there for any other special treaty with France?

The PRESIDENT. To meet the possibility of delay in action on the part of the council of the league.

Senator McCUMBER. But the agreement of section 10 comes into effect, does it not, the moment we adopt the treaty?

The PRESIDENT. Yes; but the council has to act and formulate its advice, and then the several Governments have to act and form their judgment upon that advice.

Senator McCUMBER. Do you not think under the present situation that that could be done as quickly as Germany could get ready for a second war on France?

The PRESIDENT. Oh, as quickly as she could get ready, yes; but not as quickly as she could act after she got ready.

Senator BRANDEGEE. Mr. President, the situation is this: If Germany has surrendered her navy, demobilized her army, and been shorn of large portions of her territory; if we have no demand for reparation or indemnity against her; if, as you stated in your addresses to the Congress, the war is over; if there is no fighting going on; if Germany has signed the peace treaty, and you have signed the peace treaty; if, in fact, there is a condition of peace, and only the joint resolution of Congress that a state of war existed a year ago—if that is all so, is there no way by which the condition of peace which actually exists can be made legally effective except by the adoption of the proposed treaty?

The PRESIDENT. Senator, I would say that there is no way which we ought to be willing to adopt which separates us, in dealing with Germany, from those with whom we were associated during the war.

Senator BRANDEGEE. Why?

The PRESIDENT. Because I think that is a moral union which we are not at liberty to break.

Senator BRANDEGEE. If we have rescued our fellow belligerents from the German peril voluntarily and without any charge, and if we prefer not to have any entanglements or connections with European powers, but to pursue our course as we did before the war, where is the moral obligation to merge ourselves with Europe forever?

The PRESIDENT. I do not construe it as merging ourselves, but I do think we are under the plainest moral obligation to join with our associates in imposing certain conditions of peace on Germany.

Senator BRANDEGEE. Even if we ratify the German so-called peace treaty, with or without the Shantung provision in it, and strike out article 1 of the peace treaty, the covenant of the league of nations, we still join with those with whom we have co-operated in establishing peace with Germany, do we not, and are at liberty to trade with her?

The PRESIDENT. An unworkable peace, because the league is necessary to the working of it.

Senator BRANDEGEE. Well, suppose they have a league, and we ratify the treaty with the reservation that we are not bound by article 1, which is the covenant of the League—then they have a league of nations covenant.

The PRESIDENT. Yes, and we are tied into every other part of the treaty by reason of the fact that we are supposed to be members of the league of nations.

Senator BRANDEGEE. Supposing we also adopt the 21 amendments that Senator Fall has pending before the Committee on Foreign Relations, striking us out of these commissions to which we are tied, and just cutting the Gordian knot which ties us to the covenant: We establish peace with Germany just the same, I fancy. The other powers could accept our amendments to the treaty or not, as they chose. In either case Germany would be at peace, and they would be in the league, and we would be out of it. We could have peace and resume all our business in relation to copper mines and zinc mines, etc., and we could export to Germany, and re-establish the consular service; could we not?

The PRESIDENT. We could, sir; but I hope the people of the United States will never consent to do it.

Senator BRANDEGEE. There is no way by which the people can vote on it.

The CHAIRMAN. Are we not trading with Germany now, as a matter of fact?

The PRESIDENT. Not so far as I know, sir.

The CHAIRMAN. Licenses certainly have been issued. It is advertised in all the New York papers.

The PRESIDENT. We removed the restrictions that were formerly placed upon shipments to neutral countries which we thought were going through to Germany.

The CHAIRMAN. Yes; I see them advertised broadly in the New York papers.

Senator JOHNSON of California. Mr. President, does the moral obligation to which you have alluded compel us to maintain American troops in Europe?

The PRESIDENT. Which moral obligation, Senator?

Senator JOHNSON of California. You referred to the moral obligation resting upon us to carry out the peace terms and the like in conjunction with our associates, and felt that it would be, as I understood you, a breaking, a denial of the moral obligation to make a separate peace or to act by ourselves.

The PRESIDENT. Yes.

Senator JOHNSON of California. Does that obligation go to the extent of compelling us to maintain American troops in Europe?

The PRESIDENT. Such small bodies as are necessary to the carrying out of the treaty, I think; yes.

Senator JOHNSON of California. And will those troops have to be maintained under the various treaties of peace until the ultimate consummation of the terms of those treaties?

The PRESIDENT. Yes, Senator; but that is not long. In no case, as I remember, does that exceed 18 months.

Senator JOHNSON of California. I was rather under the impression that the occupation of Germany was to be for 15 years.

The PRESIDENT. Oh, I beg your pardon.

The CHAIRMAN. Along the Rhine.

The PRESIDENT. Along the Rhine; yes. I was thinking of Upper Silesia, and the other places where plebiscites are created, or to be carried out. It is the understanding with the other Governments that we are to retain only enough troops there to keep our flag there.

Senator JOHNSON of California. The idea in my mind was this: Will we be maintaining American troops upon the Rhine for the next 15 years?

The PRESIDENT. That is entirely within our choice, Senator; but I suppose we will.

Senator JOHNSON of California. Do you know, Mr.

President, whether or not we have American troops in Budapest at present?

The PRESIDENT. We have not. There are some American officers there, Senator, sent with a military commission, but no American troops.

Senator JOHNSON of California. Returning, if you do not mind, Mr. President, to one last question about Shantung, do you recall the American experts reporting that the Japanese promise, the verbal promise, which has been referred to, to return Shantung, meant in reality the returning of the shell but retaining the kernel of the nut?

The PRESIDENT. I remember their saying that; yes, sir.

Senator JOHNSON of California. That is all.

The PRESIDENT. But I do not agree with them.

Senator NEW. Mr. President, if no one else has any questions to ask, I have a few.

The PRESIDENT. Proceed, Senator, if you will.

Senator NEW. These questions, Mr. President, are more or less general and haphazard, referring to no particular feature of the treaty, but to all of them.

First, was it the policy of the American delegates to avoid participation by the United States in strictly European questions and their settlement; and, if so, what were the matters in which America refused to participate, or endeavored to avoid participation?

The PRESIDENT. I could not give you a list in answer to the last part of your question, sir; but it certainly was our endeavor to keep free from European affairs.

Senator NEW. What did the American delegates say or do to secure nonparticipation by the United States in the cessions of Danzig, Memel, and in the various boundary commissions, reparations commissions, and other agencies set up in the treaty for the disposition of questions in which America has no national interest?

The PRESIDENT. I did not get that, Senator, it is so long.

Senator NEW. I will divide it. What did the American delegates say or do to secure nonparticipation by the United States in the cessions of Danzig and Memel?

The PRESIDENT. Why, Senator, the process of the whole peace was this: Each nation had associated with it certain expert advisers, college professors and bankers and men who were familiar with ethnical and geographical and financial and business questions. Each question was referred to a joint commission consisting of the specialists in that field representing the principal allied and associated powers. They made a report to this smaller council, and in every instance the American representatives were under instructions to keep out of actual participation in these processes so far as it was honorably possible to do so.

Senator New. The second half of the question is this; What did the American delegates do to secure nonparticipation by the United States in the reparations commission?

The President. Why, we were disinclined to join in that, but yielded to the urgent request of the other nations that we should because they wanted our advice and counsel.

Senator New. What agreement, written or verbal, has been entered into by the American delegates touching the assignment to various States of mandatories under the provisions of article 22?

The President. None whatever.

Senator New. If it be understood that Great Britain or her dominions will act as mandatories of the territory in Africa lately held by Germany, what advantage of a practical nature is expected to accrue, and whom will it benefit, from subjecting the British or dominion administration to the mandatories of such nations as Liberia, Italy, or any others?

The President. Mandatories of Liberia?

Senator New. Yes.

The President. I do not understand, Senator. The whole system of mandates is intended for the development and protection of the territories to which they apply—that is to say, to protect their inhabitants, to assist their development under the operation of the opinion of the world, and to lead to their ultimate independent existence.

Senator New. Mr. President, it seems that there is more than a suspicion; there is a general conviction in the world, I think, that Germany is promoting the dissemination of Bolshevist propaganda in the countries of the Allies, including the United States. That being the case, I am prompted to ask what provision in the treaty obligates Germany to prohibit Bolshevik propaganda from German sources in the United States and allied countries?

The PRESIDENT. None.

Senator NEW. No provision? Was any proposal considered by the peace conference directed toward securing the names of German propaganda agents in the United States and the allied countries, or to obtain the records of the disbursements made in support of Bolshevik or other propaganda intended to weaken or disrupt the United States?

The PRESIDENT. We made every effort to trace everything that we got rumor of, Senator; and traced everything that we could; but no provisions were feasible in the treaty itself touching that.

Senator NEW. Did not France yield under pressure at least partly exerted by the American delegates to abandon certain guaranties of the security of her German frontiers which she had been advised by Marshal Foch were indispensable; and is not the present frontier, in French military opinion, less secure than the one which France was induced to abandon?

The PRESIDENT. Senator, do you think I ought to redebate here the fundamental questions that we debated at Paris? I think that would be a mistake, sir.

Senator JOHNSON of California. Mr. President, it is on that very theory that I refrained from asking many of those things, the thoughts of which crowd one's mind, and which one would like to ask.

The PRESIDENT. Of course. You see, you are going into the method by which the treaty was negotiated. Now, with all respect, sir, I think that is a territory that we ought not to enter.

Senator NEW. Of course, if there is any reason why it should not be answered, I will withdraw it. Is there objection to answering this, Mr. President: What was France's solution proposed for administration of the Saar Basin?

The PRESIDENT. I do not think I ought to answer those questions, Senator, because of course they affect the policy and urgency of other Governments. I am not at liberty to go into that.

Senator NEW. Mr. President, would our position in the War of 1812 and the Spanish-American War have been secure under the league covenant?

The PRESIDENT. Oh, Senator, you can judge of that as well as I could. I have tried to be a historical student, but I could not quife get the league back into those days clearly enough in my mind to form a judgment.

Senator NEW. What would have been the procedure under the covenant in those two cases, in your opinion?

The PRESIDENT. Why, Senator, I could figure that out if you gave me half a day, because I would have to refresh my mind as to the circumstances that brought on the wars; but that has not been regarded as a profitable historical exercise—hypothetically to reconstruct history.

Senator NEW. Well, I do not want to press for answers, then.

Senator MOSES. Mr. President, under the terms of the treaty, Germany cedes to the principal allied and associated powers all of her overseas possessions?

The PRESIDENT. Yes.

Senator MOSES. We thereby, as I view it, become possessed in fee of an undivided fifth part of those possessions.

The PRESIDENT. Only as one of five trustees, Senator. There is no thought in any mind of sovereignty.

Senator MOSES. Such possession as we acquire by means of that cession would have to be disposed of by congressional action.

The PRESIDENT. I have not thought about that at all.

Senator MOSES. You have no plan to suggest or recommendation to make to Congress?

The PRESIDENT. Not yet, sir; I am waiting until the treaty is disposed of.

The CHAIRMAN. Mr. President, I do not wish to interfere in any way, but the conference has now lasted about three hours and a half, and it is half an hour after the lunch hour.

The PRESIDENT. Will not you gentlemen take luncheon with me? It will be very delightful.

(Thereupon, at 1 o'clock and 35 minutes p.m the conference adjourned.)

APPENDIX V

Speech of Henry Cabot Lodge in the Senate of the
United States, August 12, 1919.

TREATY OF PEACE WITH GERMANY

Mr. LODGE. Mr. President, in the Essays of Elia, one
of the most delightful is that entitled "Popular Fallacies." There is one very popular fallacy, however,
which Lamb did not include in his list, and that is the
common saying that history repeats itself. Universal
negatives are always dangerous, but if there is anything
which is fairly certain, it is that history never exactly
repeats itself. Popular fallacies, nevertheless, generally
have some basis, and this saying springs from the undoubted truth that mankind from generation to generation is constantly repeating itself. We have an excellent
illustration of this fact in the proposed experiment now
before us, of making arrangements to secure the permanent peace of the world. To assure the peace of the
world by a combination of the nations is no new idea.
Leaving out the leagues of antiquity and of mediæval
times and going back no further than the treaty of
Utrecht, at the beginning of the eighteenth century, we
find that at that period a project of a treaty to establish
perpetual peace was brought forward in 1713 by the
Abbé de Saint-Pierre. The treaty of Utrecht was to be
the basis of an international system. A European league
or Christian republic was to be set up, under which the
members were to renounce the right of making war
against each other and submit their disputes for arbitration to a central tribunal of the allies, the decisions of
which were to be enforced by a common armament. I
need not point out the resemblance between this theory
and that which underlies the present league of nations.
It was widely discussed during the eighteenth century, re-

ceiving much support in public opinion; and Voltaire said that the nations of Europe, united by ties of religion, institutions, and culture, were really but a single family. The idea remained in an academic condition until 1791, when under the pressure of the French Revolution Count Kaunitz sent out a circular letter in the name of Leopold, of Austria, urging that it was the duty of all the powers to make common cause for the purpose of "preserving, public peace, tranquillity of States, the inviolability of possession, and the faith of treaties," which has a very familiar sound. Napoleon had a scheme of his own for consolidating the Great European peoples and establishing a central assembly, but the Napoleonic idea differed from that of the eighteenth century, as one would expect. A single great personality dominated and hovered over all. In 1804 the Emperor Alexander took up the question and urged a general treaty for the formation of a European confederation. "Why could one not submit to it," the Emperor asked, "the positive rights of nations, assure the privilege of neutrality, insert the obligation of never beginning war until all the resources which the mediation of a third party could offer have been exhausted, until the grievances have by this means been brought to light, and an effort to remove them has been made? On principles such as these one could proceed to a general pacification, and give birth to a league of which the stipulations would form, so to speak, a new code of the law of nations, while those who should try to infringe it would risk bringing upon themselves the forces of the new union."

The Emperor, moved by more immediately alluring visions, put aside this scheme at the treaty of Tilsit and then decided that peace could best be restored to the world by having two all-powerful emperors, one of the east and one of the west. After the Moscow campaign, however, he returned to his early dream. Under the influence of the Baroness von Krudener he became a devotee of a certain mystic pietism which for some time guided his public acts, and I think it may be fairly said that his liberal and popular ideas of that period, however vague and uncertain, were sufficiently genuine. Based upon the treaties of alliance against France, those of

Chaumont and of Vienna, was the final treaty of Paris, of November 20, 1815. In the preamble the signatories, who were Great Britain, Austria, Russia, and Prussia, stated that it is the purpose of the ensuing treaty and their desire "to employ all their means to prevent the general tranquillity—the object of the wishes of mankind and the constant end of their efforts—from being again disturbed; desirous, moreover, to draw closer the ties which unite them for the common interests of their people, have resolved to give to the principles solemnly laid down in the treaties of Chaumont of March 1, 1814, and of Vienna of March 25, 1815, the application the most analogous to the present state of affairs, and to fix beforehand by a solemn treaty the principles which they propose to follow, in order to guarantee Europe from dangers by which she may still be menaced."

Then follow five articles which are devoted to an agreement to hold France in control and checks, based largely on other more detailed agreements. But in article 6 it is said:

"To facilitate and to secure the execution of the present treaty, and to consolidate the connections which at the present moment so closely unite the four sovereigns for the happiness of the world, the high contracting parties have agreed to renew their meeting at fixed periods, either under the immediate auspices of the sovereigns themselves, or by their respective ministers, for the purpose of consulting upon their common interests, and for the consideration of the measures which at each of those periods shall be considered the most salutary for the repose and prosperity of nations and for the maintenance of the peace of Europe."

Certainly nothing could be more ingenuous or more praiseworthy than the purposes of the alliance then formed, and yet it was this very combination of powers which was destined to grow into what has been known, and we might add cursed, throughout history as the Holy Alliance.

As early as 1818 it had become apparent that upon this innocent statement might be built an alliance which was to be used to suppress the rights of nationalities and every attempt of any oppressed people to secure their freedom. Lord Castlereagh was a Tory of the Tories, but at that time, only three years after the treaty of Paris, when the representatives of the alliance met at Aix-la-Chapelle, he began to suspect that this new European system was wholly inconsistent with the liberties to which Englishmen of all types were devoted. At the succeeding meetings, at Troppau and Laibach, his suspicion was confirmed, and England began to draw away from her partners. He had indeed determined to break with the alliance before the Congress of Verona, but his death threw the question into the hands of George Canning, who stands forth as the man who separated Great Britain from the combination of the continental powers. The attitude of England, which was defined in a memorandum where it was said that nothing could be more injurious to the idea of government generally than the belief that their force was collectively to be prostituted to the support of an established power without any consideration of the extent to which it was to be abused, led to a compromise in 1818 in which it was declared that it was the intention of the five powers, France being invited to adhere, "to maintain the intimate union, strengthened by the ties of Christian brotherhood, contracted by the sovereigns; to pronounce the object of this union to be the preservation of peace on the basis of respect for treaties." Admirable and gentle words these, setting forth purposes which all men must approve.

In 1820 the British Government stated that they were prepared to fulfill all treaty obligations, but that if it was desired "to extend the alliance, so as to include all objects, present and future, foreseen and unforeseen, it would change its character to such an extent and carry us so far that we should see in it an additional motive for adhering to our course at the risk of seeing the alliance move away from us, without our having quitted it." The Czar Alexander abandoned his Liberal theories and threw himself into the arms of Metternich, as mean a tyrant as history can show, whose sinister designs probably caused as much misery and oppression in the years which followed as have ever been evolved by one man of second-rate abilities. The three powers, Russia, Austria, and Prussia, then put out a famous protocol in which it was said that the "States which have undergone a change of government due to revolution, the results of which threaten other States, *ipso facto* cease to be members of the European alliance and remain excluded from it until their situation gives guaranties for legal order and stability. If, owing to such alterations, immediate danger threatens other States, the powers bind themselves, by peaceful means, or, if need be, by arms, to bring back the guilty State into the bosom of the great alliance." To this point had the innocent and laudable declaration of the treaty of Paris already developed. In 1822 England broke away, and Canning made no secret of his pleasure at the breach. In a letter to the British minister at St. Petersburg he said:

"So things are getting back to a wholesome state again. Every nation for itself, and God for us all. The time for Areopagus, and the like of that, is gone by."

He also said, in the same year, 1823:

"What is the influence we have had in the counsels of the alliance, and which Prince Metternich exhorts us to be so careful not to throw away? We protested at Laibach; we remonstrated at Verona. Our protest was treated as waste paper; our remonstrances mingled with the air. Our influence, if it is to be maintained abroad, must be secured in the source of strength at home; and the sources of that strength are in sympathy between the people and the Government; in the union of the public sentiment with the public counsels; in the reciprocal confidence and cooperation of the House of Commons and the Crown."

These words of Canning are as applicable and as weighty now as when they were uttered and as worthy of consideration.

The Holy Alliance, thus developed by the three continental powers and accepted by France under the Bourbons, proceeded to restore the inquisition in Spain, to establish the Neapolitan Bourbons, who for 40 years were to subject the people of southern Italy to one of the most detestable tyrannies ever known, and proposed further to interfere against the colonies in South America which had revolted from Spain and to have their case submitted to a congress of the powers. It was then that Canning made his famous statement, "We have called a new world into existence to redress the balance of the old." It was at this point also that the United States intervened. The famous message of Monroe, sent to Congress on December 2, 1823, put an end to any danger of European influence in the American Continents. A distinguished English historian, Mr. William Alison Phillips, says:

"The attitude of the United States effectually prevented the attempt to extend the dictatorship of the alliance beyond the bounds of Europe, in itself a great service to mankind."

In 1825 Great Britain recognized the South American Republics. So far as the New World was concerned the Holy Alliance had failed. It was deprived of the support of France by the revolution of 1830, but it continued to exist under the guidance of Metternich and its last exploit was in 1839, when the Emperor Nicholas sent a Russian army into Hungary to crush out the struggle of Kossuth for freedom and independence.

I have taken the trouble to trace in the merest outline the development of the Holy Alliance, so hostile and dangerous to human freedom, because I think it carries with it a lesson for us at the present moment, showing as it does what may come from general propositions and declarations of purposes in which all the world agrees. Turn to the preamble of the covenant of the league of nations now before us, which states the object of the league. It is formed "in order to promote international cooperation and to achieve international peace and security by the acceptance of obligations not to resort to war, by the prescription of open, just, and honorable relations between nations, by the firm establishment of the understandings of international laws as the actual rule of conduct among governments and by the maintenance of justice and a scrupulous respect for all treaty obligations in the dealings of organized peoples with one another."

No one would contest the loftiness or the benevolence of these purposes. Brave words, indeed! They do not differ essentially from the preamble of the treaty of Paris, from which sprang the Holy Alliance. But the covenant of this league contains a provision which I do not find in the treaty of Paris, and which is as follows:

"The assembly may deal at its meetings with any matter within the sphere of action of the league or affecting the peace of the world."

There is no such sweeping or far-reaching provision as that in the treaty of Paris, and yet able men developed from that treaty the Holy Alliance, which England, and later France were forced to abandon and which, for 35 years, was an unmitigated curse to the world. England broke from the Holy Alliance and the breach began three years after it was formed, because English statesmen saw that it was intended to turn the alliance—and this league is an alliance—into a means of repressing internal revolutions or insurrections. There was nothing in the treaty of Paris which warranted such action, but in this covenant of the league of nations the authority is clearly given in the third paragraph of article 3, where it is said:

"The assembly may deal at its meetings with any matter within the sphere of action of the league or affecting the peace of the world."

No revolutionary movement, no internal conflict of any magnitude can fail to affect the peace of the world. The French Revolution, which was wholly internal at the beginning, affected the peace of the world to such an extent that it brought on a world war which lasted some 25 years. Can anyone say that our Civil War did not affect the peace of the world? At this very moment, who would deny that the condition of Russia, with internal conflicts raging in all parts of that great Empire, does not affect the peace of the world and therefore come properly within the jurisdiction of the league. "Any matter affecting the peace of the world" is a very broad statement which could be made to justify almost any interference on the part of the league with the internal affairs of other countries. That this fair and obvious interpretation is the one given to it abroad is made perfectly apparent in the direct and vigorous statement of M. Clemenceau in his letter to Mr. Paderewski, in which he takes the ground in behalf of the Jews and other nationalities in Poland that they should be protected, and where he says that the associated powers would feel themselves bound to secure guaranties in Poland "of certain essential rights which will afford to the inhabitants the necessary protection, whatever changes may take place in the internal constitution of the Polish Republic." He contemplates and defends interference with the internal affairs of Poland—among other things—in behalf of a complete religious freedom, a purpose with which we all deeply sympathize. These promises of the French prime minister are embodied in effective clauses in the treaties with Germany and with Poland and deal with the internal affairs of nations, and their execution is intrusted to the "principal allied and associated powers"; that is, to the United States, Great Britain, France, Italy, and Japan. This is a practical demonstration of what can be done under article 3 and under article 11 of the league covenant, and the authority which permits interference in behalf of religious freedom, an admirable object, is easily extended to the repression of internal disturbances which may well prove a less admirable purpose. If Europe desires such an alliance or league with a power of this kind, so be it. I have no objection, provided they do not interfere with the American Continents or force us against our will but bound by a moral obligation into all the quarrels of Europe. If England, abandoning the policy of Canning, desires to be a member of a league which has such powers as this, I have not a word to say. But I object in the strongest possible way to having the United States agree, directly or indirectly, to be controlled by a league which may at any time, and perfectly lawfully and in accordance with the terms of the covenant, be drawn in to deal with internal conflicts in other countries, no matter what those conflicts may be. We should never permit the United States to be involved in any internal conflict in another country, except by the will of her people expressed through the Congress which represents them.

With regard to wars of external aggression on a member of the league the case is perfectly clear. There can be no genuine dispute whatever about the meaning of the first clause of article 10. In the first place, it differs from every other obligation in being individual and placed upon each nation without the intervention of the league. Each nation for itself promises to respect and preserve as against external aggression the boundaries and the political independence of every member of the league. Of the right of the United States to give such a guaranty I have never had the slightest doubt, and the elaborate arguments which have been made here and the learning which has been displayed about our treaty with Granada, now Colombia, and with Panama, were not necessary for me, because, I repeat, there can be no doubt of our right to give a guaranty to another nation that we will protect its boundaries and independence. The point I wish to make is that the pledge is an individual pledge. We have, for example, given guaranties to Panama and for obvious and sufficient reasons. The application of that guaranty would not be in the slightest degree affected by 10 or 20 other nations giving the same pledge if Panama, when in danger, appealed to us to fulfill our obligation. We should be bound to do so without the slightest reference to the other guarantors. In article 10 the United States is bound on the appeal of any member of the league not only to respect but to preserve its independence and its boundaries, and that pledge if we give it, must be fulfilled.

There is to me no distinction whatever in a treaty between what some persons are pleased to call legal and moral obligations. A treaty rests and must rest, except where it is imposed under duress and securities and hostages are taken for its fulfillment, upon moral obligations. No doubt a great power impossible of coercion can cast aside a moral obligation if it sees fit and escape from the performance of the duty which it promises. The pathway of dishonor is always open. I, for one, however, cannot conceive of voting for a clause of which I disapprove because I know it can be escaped in that way. Whatever the United States agrees to, by that agreement she must abide. Nothing could so surely destroy all prospects of the world's peace as to have any powerful nation refuse to carry out an obligation, direct or indirect, because it rests only on moral grounds. Whatever we promise we must carry out to the full, "without mental reservation or purpose of evasion." To me any other attitude is inconceivable. Without the most absolute and minute good faith in carrying out a treaty to which we have agreed, without ever resorting to doubtful interpretations or to the plea that it is only a moral obligation, treaties are worthless. The greatest foundation of peace is the scrupulous observance of every promise, express or implied, of every pledge, whether it can be described as legal or moral. No vote should be given to any clause in any treaty or to any treaty except in this spirit and with this understanding.

I return, then, to the first clause of article 10. It is, I repeat, an individual obligation. It requires no action on the part of the league, except that in the second sentence the authorities of the league are to have the power to advise as to the means to be employed in order to fulfill the purpose of the first sentence. But that is a detail of execution, and I consider that we are morally and in honor bound to accept and act upon that advice. The broad fact remains that if any member of the league suffering from external aggression should appeal directly to the United States for support the United States would be bound to give that support in its own capacity and without reference to the action of other powers because the United States itself is bound, and I hope the day will never come when the United States will not carry out its promises. If that day should come, and the United States or any other great country should refuse, no matter how specious the reasons, to fulfill both in letter and spirit every obligation in this covenant, the United States would be dishonored and the league would crumble into dust, leaving behind it a legacy of wars. If China should rise up and attack Japan in an effort to undo the great wrong of the cession of the control of Shantung to that power, we should be bound under the terms of article 10 to sustain Japan against China, and a guaranty of that sort is never involved except when the question has passed beyond the stage of negotiation and has become a question for the application of force. I do not like the prospect. It shall not come into existence by any vote of mine.

Article 11 carries this danger still further, for it says:

"Any war or threat of war, whether immediately affecting any of the members of the league or not, is hereby declared a matter of concern to the whole league, and the league shall take any action that shall be deemed wise and effectual to safeguard the peace of nations."

"Any war or threat of war"—that means both external aggression and internal disturbance, as I have already pointed out in dealing with article 3. "Any action" covers military action, because it covers action of any sort or kind. Let me take an example, not an imaginary case, but one which may have been overlooked because most people have not the slightest idea where or what a King of the Hedjaz is. The following dispatch appeared recently in the newspapers:

"HEDJAZ AGAINST BEDOUINS.

"The forces of Emir Abdullah recently suffered a grave defeat, the Wahabis· attacking and capturing Kurma, east of Mecca. Ibn Savond is believed to be working in harmony with the Wahabis. A squadron of the royal air force was ordered recently to go to the assistance of King Hussein."

Hussein I take to be the Sultan of Hedjaz. He is being attacked by the Bedouins, as they are known to us, although I fancy the general knowledge about the Wahabis and Ibn Savond and Emir Abdullah is slight and the names mean but little to the American people. Nevertheless, here is a case of a member of the league—for the King of Hedjaz is such a member in good and regular standing and signed the treaty by his representatives, Mr. Rustem Haidar and Mr. Abdul Havi Aouni.

Under article 10, if King Hussein appealed to us for aid and protection against external aggression affecting his independence and the boundaries of his Kingdom, we should be bound to give that aid and protection and to send American soldiers to Arabia. It is not relevant to say that this is unlikely to occur; that Great Britain is quite able to take care of King Hussein, who is her fair creation, reminding one a little of the Mosquito King, a monarch once developed by Great Britain on the Mosquito Coast of Central America. The fact that we should not be called upon does not alter the right which the King of Hedjaz possesses to demand the sending of American troops to Arabia in order to preserve his independence against the assaults of the Wahabis or Bedouins. I am unwilling to give that right to King Hussein, and this illustrates the point which is to me the most objectionable in the league as it stands; the right of other powers to call out American troops and American ships to go to any part of the world, an obligation we are bound to fulfill under the terms of this treaty. I know the answer well—that of course they could not be sent without action by Congress. Congress would have no choice if acting in good faith, and if under article 10 any member of the league summoned us, or if under article 11 the league itself summoned us, we should be bound in honor and morally to obey. There would be no escape except by a breach of faith, and legislation by Congress under those circumstances would be a mockery of independent action. Is it too much to ask that provision should be made that American troops and American ships should never be sent anywhere or ordered to take part in any conflict except after the deliberate action of the American people, expressed according to the Constitution through their chosen representatives in Congress?

Let me now briefly point out the insuperable difficulty which I find in article 15. It begins: "If there should arise between members of the league any dispute likely to lead to a rupture." "Any dispute" covers every possible dispute. It therefore covers a dispute over tariff duties and over immigration. Suppose we have a dispute with Japan or with some European country as to immigration. I put aside tariff duties as less important than immigration. This is not an imaginary case. Of late years there has probably been more international discussion and negotiation about questions growing out of immigration laws than any other one subject. It comes within the definition of "any dispute" at the beginning of article 15. In the eighth paragraph of that article it is said that "if the dispute between the parties is claimed by one of them, and is found by the council to arise out of a matter which, by international law, is solely within the domestic jurisdiction of that party, the council shall so report and shall make no recommendation as to its settlement." That is one of the statements, of which there are several in this treaty, where words are used which it is difficult to believe their authors could have written down in seriousness. They seem to have been put in for the same purpose as what is known in natural history as protective coloring. Protective coloring is intended so to merge the animal, the bird, or the insect in its background that it will be indistinguishable from its surroundings and difficult, if not impossible, to find the elusive and hidden bird, animal, or insect. Protective coloring here is used in the form of words to give an impression that we are perfectly safe upon immigration and tariffs, for example, because questions which international law holds to be solely within domestic jurisdiction are not to have any recommendation from the council, but the dangers are there just the same, like the cunningly colored insect on the tree or the young bird crouching motionless upon the sand. The words and the coloring are alike intended to deceive. I wish somebody would point out to me those provisions of international law which make a list of questions which are hard and fast within the domestic jurisdiction. No such distinction can be applied to tariff duties or immigration, nor indeed finally and conclusively to any subject. Have we not seen the school laws of California, most domestic of subjects, rise to the dignity of a grave international dispute? No doubt both import duties and immigration are primarily domestic questions, but they both constantly involve and will continue to involve international effects. Like the protective coloration, this paragraph is

wholly worthless unless it is successful in screening from
the observer the existence of the animal, insect, or bird
which it is desired to conceal. It fails to do so and the
real object is detected. But even if this bit of decep-
tion was omitted—and so far as the question of immigration or tariff questions are concerned it might as well be
—the ninth paragraph brings the important point clearly
to the front. Immigration, which is the example I took,
cannot escape the action of the league by any claim of
domestic jurisdiction; it has too many international as-
pects.

Article 9 says:

"The council may, in any case under this article,
refer the dispute to the assembly."

We have our dispute as to immigration with Japan
or with one of the Balkan States, let us say. The council has the power to refer the dispute to the assembly.
Moreover the dispute shall be so referred at the request
of either party to the dispute, provided that such request
be made within 14 days after the submission of the dispute to the council. So that Japan or the Balkan States,
for example, with which we may easily have the dispute,
ask that it be referred to the assembly and the immigration question between the United States and Jugoslavia
or Japan as the case may be, goes to the assembly. The
United States and Japan or Jugoslavia are excluded from
voting and the provision of article 12, relating to the
action and powers of the council apply to the action and
powers of the assembly provided, as set forth in article 15,
that a report made by the assembly "if concurred in by
the representatives of those members of the league represented on the council and of a majority of the other
members of the league, exclusive in each case of the representatives of the parties to the dispute, shall have the
same force as a report by the council concurred in by all
the members thereof other than the representatives of
one or more of the parties to the dispute." This course
of procedure having been pursued, we find the question
of immigration between the United States and Japan is
before the assembly for decision. The representatives of
the council, except the delegates of the United States and

of Japan or Jugoslavia, must all vote unanimously upon
it as I understand it, but a majority of the entire assembly, where the council will have only seven votes,
will decide. Can anyone say beforehand what the decision of that assembly will be, in which the United States
and Jugoslavia or Japan will have no vote? The question in one case may affect immigration from every
country in Europe, although the dispute exists only for
one, and in the other the whole matter of Asiatic immigration is involved. Is it too fanciful to think that it
might be decided against us? For my purpose it matters
not whether it is decided for or against us. An immigration dispute or a dispute over tariff duties, met by the
procedure set forth in ·article 15, comes before the assembly of delegates for a decision by what is practically
a majority vote of the entire assembly. That is something to which I do not find myself able to give my assent. So far as immigration is concerned, and also so
far as tariff duties, although less important, are concerned, I deny the jurisdiction. There should be no possibility of other nations deciding who shall come into
the United States, or under what conditions they shall
enter. The right to say who shall come into a country is
one of the very highest attributes of sovereignty. If a
nation cannot say without appeal who shall come within
its gates and become a part of its citizenship it has ceased
to be a sovereign nation. It has become a tributary and
a subject nation, and it makes no difference whether it is
subject to a league or to a conqueror.

If other nations are willing to subject themselves to
such a domination, the United States, to which many immigrants have come and many more will come, ought
never to submit to it for a moment. They tell us that
so far as Asiatic emigration is concerned there is not the
slightest danger that that will ever be forced upon us by
the league, because Australia and Canada and New Zealand are equally opposed to it. I think it highly improbable that it would be forced upon us under those
conditions, but it is by no means impossible. It is true
the United States has one vote and that England, if
you count the King of the Hedjaz, has seven—in all
eight—votes; yet it might not be impossible for Japan

and China and Siam to rally enough other votes to defeat us; but whether we are protected in that way or not does not matter. The very offering of that explanation accepts the jurisdiction of the league, and personally, I cannot consent to putting the protection of my country and of her workingmen against undesirable immigration, out of our own hands. We and we alone must say who shall come into the United States and become citizens of this Republic, and no one else should have any power to utter one word in regard to it.

Article 21 says:

"Nothing in this covenant shall be deemed to affect the validity of international engagements, such as treaties of arbitration or regional understandings like the Monroe doctrine for securing the maintenance of peace."

The provision did not appear in the first draft of the covenant, and when the President explained the second draft of the convention in the peace conference he said:

"Article 21 is new."

And that was all he said. No one can question the truth of the remark, but I trust I shall not be considered disrespectful if I say that it was not an illuminating statement. The article was new, but the fact of its novelty, which the President declared, was known to everyone who had taken the trouble to read the two documents. We were not left, however, without a fitting explanation. The British delegation took it upon themselves to explain article 21 at some length, and this is what they said:

"Article 21 makes it clear that the covenant is not intended to abrogate or weaken any other agreements, so long as they are consistent with its own terms, into which members of the league may have entered or may hereafter enter for the assurance of peace. Such agreements would include special treaties for compulsory arbitration and military conventions that are genuinely defensive.

"The Monroe doctrine and similar understandings are put in the same category. They have shown themselves in history to be not instruments of national ambition, but guarantees of peace. The origin of the Monroe doctrine is well known. It was proclaimed in 1823 to prevent America from becoming a theater for intrigues of European absolutism. At first a principle of American foreign policy, it has become an international understanding, and it is not illegitimate for the people of the United States to say that the covenant should recognize that fact.

"In its essence it is consistent with the spirit of the covenant, and, indeed, the principles of the league, as expressed in article 10, represent the extension to the whole world of the principles of the doctrine, while, should any dispute as to the meaning of the latter ever arise between the American and European powers, the league is there to settle it."

The explanation of Great Britain received the assent of France.

"It seems to me monumentally paradoxical and a trifle infantile—"

Says M. Lausanne, editor of the *Matin* and a chief spokesman for M. Clemenceau—

"to pretend the contrary.

"When the executive council of the league of nations fixes the 'reasonable limits of the armament of Peru'; when it shall demand information concerning the naval program of Brazil (art. 7 of the covenant); when it shall tell Argentina what shall be the measure of the 'contribution to the armed forces to protect the signature of the social covenant' (art. 16); when it shall demand the immediate registration of the treaty between the United States and Canada at the seat of the league, it will control, whether it wills or not, the destinies of America.

"And when the American States shall be obliged to take a hand in every war or menace of war in Europe (art. 11) they will necessarily fall afoul of the fundamental principle laid down by Monroe.

"* * * If the league takes in the world, then Europe must mix in the affairs of America; if only Europe is included, then America will violate of necessity her own doctrine by intermixing in the affairs of Europe."

It has seemed to me that the British delegation traveled a little out of the precincts of the peace conference when they undertook to explain the Monroe doctrine and tell the United States what it was and what it was not proposed to do with it under the new article. That, however, is merely a matter of taste and judgment. Their statement that the Monroe doctrine under this article, if any question arose in regard to it, would be passed upon and interpreted by the league of nations is absolutely correct. There is no doubt that this is what the article means. Great Britain so stated it, and no American authority, whether friendly or unfriendly to the league, has dared to question it. I have wondered a little why it was left to the British delegation to explain that article, which so nearly concerns the United States, but that was merely a fugitive thought upon which I will not dwell. The statement of M. Lausanne is equally explicit and truthful, but he makes one mistake. He says, in substance, that if we are to meddle in Europe, Europe cannot be excluded from the Americas. He overlooks the fact that the Monroe doctrine also says:

"Our policy in regard to Europe, which was adopted at an early stage of the wars which have so long agitated that quarter of the globe, nevertheless remains the same, which is not to interfere in the internal concerns of any of the powers."

The Monroe doctrine was the corollary of Washington's neutrality policy and of his injunction against permanent alliances. It reiterates and reaffirms the principle. We do not seek to meddle in the affairs of Europe and keep Europe out of the Americas. It is as important to keep the United States out of European affairs as to keep Europe out of the American Continents. Let us maintain the Monroe doctrine, then, in its entirety, and not only preserve our own safety, but in this way best promote the real peace of the world. Whenever the preservation of freedom and civilization and the overthrow of a menacing world conqueror summon us we shall respond fully and nobly, as we did in 1917. He who doubts that we could do so has little faith in America. But let it be our own act and not done reluctantly by the coercion of other nations, at the bidding or by the permission of other countries.

Let me now deal with the article itself. We have here some protective coloration again. The Monroe doctrine is described as a "regional understanding" whatever that may mean. The boundaries between the States of the Union, I suppose, are "regional understandings," if anyone chooses to apply to them that somewhat swollen phraseology. But the Monroe doctrine is no more a regional understanding than it is an "international engagement." The Monroe doctrine was a policy declared by President Monroe. Its immediate purpose was to shut out Europe from interfering with the South American Republics, which the Holy Alliance designed to do. It was stated broadly, however, as we all know, and went much further than that. It was, as I have just said, the corollary of Washington's declaration against our interfering in European questions. It was so regarded by Jefferson at the time and by John Quincy Adams, who formulated it, and by President Monroe, who declared it. It rested firmly on the great law of self-preservation, which is the basic principle of every independent State.

It is not necessary to trace its history or to point out the extensions which it has received or its universal acceptance by all American statesmen without regard to party. All Americans have always been for it. They may not have known its details or read all the many discussions in regard to it, but they knew that it was an American doctrine and that, broadly stated, it meant the exclusion of Europe from interference with American affairs and from any attempt to colonize or set up new States within the boundaries of the American Continent. I repeat it was purely an American doctrine, a purely American policy, designed and wisely designed for our defense. It has never been an "international engagement." No nation has ever formally recognized it. It has been the subject of reservation at international conventions by American delegates. It has never been a "regional understanding" or an understanding of any kind with anybody. It was the declaration of the United States of America, in their own behalf, supported by their own power. They brought it into being, and its life was predicated on the force which the United States could place behind it. Unless the United States could sustain it it would die. The United States has supported it. It has lived—strong, efficient, respected. It is now proposed to kill it by a provision in a treaty for a league of nations.

The instant that the United States, who declared, interpreted, and sustained the doctrine, ceases to be the sole judge of what it means, that instant the Monroe doctrine ceases and disappears from history and from the face of the earth. I think it is just as undesirable to have Europe interfere in American affairs now as Mr. Monroe thought it was in 1823, and equally undesirable that we should be compelled to involve ourselves in all the wars and brawls of Europe. The Monroe doctrine has made for peace. Without the Monroe doctrine we should have had many a struggle with European powers to save ourselves from possible assault and certainly from the necessity of becoming a great military power, always under arms and always ready to resist invasion from States in our near neighborhood. In the interests of the peace of the world it is now proposed to wipe away this American policy, which has been a bulwark and a barrier for peace. With one exception it has always been successful, and then success was only delayed. When we were torn by civil war France saw fit to enter Mexico and endeavored to establish an empire there. When our hands were once free the empire perished, and with it the unhappy tool of the third Napoleon. If the United States had not been rent by civil war no such attempt would have been made, and nothing better illustrates the value to the cause of peace of the Monroe doctrine. Why, in the name of peace, should we extinguish it? Why, in the name of peace, should we be called upon to leave the interpretation of the Monroe doctrine to other nations? It is an American policy. It is our own. It has guarded us well, and I, for one, can never find consent in my heart to destroy it by a clause in a treaty and hand over its body for dissection to the nations of Europe. If we need authority to demonstrate what the Monroe doctrine has meant to the United States we cannot do better than quote the words of Grover Cleveland, who directed Mr. Olney to notify the world that "to-day the United States is practically sovereign on this continent, and its fiat is law to which it confines its interposition." Theodore Roosevelt, in the last article written before his death, warned us, his countrymen, that we are "in honor bound to keep ourselves so prepared that the Monroe doctrine shall be accepted as immutable international law." Grover Cleveland was a Democrat and Theodore Roosevelt was a Republican, but they were both Americans, and it is the American spirit which has carried this country always to victory and which should govern us to-day, and not the international spirit which would in the name of peace hand the United States over bound hand and foot to obey the fiat of other powers.

Another point in this covenant where change must be made in order to protect the safety of the United States in the future is in article 1, where withdrawal is provided for. This provision was an attempt to meet the very general objection to the first draft of the league, that there was no means of getting out of it without denouncing the treaty; that is, there was no arrangement for the withdrawal of any nation. As it now stands it reads that—

"Any member of the league may, after two years' notice of its intention to do so, withdraw from the league, provided that all its international obligations, and all its obligations under this covenant shall have been fulfilled at the time of its withdrawal."

The right of withdrawal is given by this clause, although the time for notice, two years, is altogether too long. Six months or a year would be found, I think, in most treaties to be the normal period fixed for notice of withdrawal. But whatever virtue there may be in the right thus conferred is completely nullified by the proviso. The right of withdrawal cannot be exercised until all the international obligations and all the obligations of the withdrawing nations have been fulfilled. The league alone can decide whether "all international obligations and all obligations under this covenant" have been fulfilled, and this would require, under the provisions of the league, a unanimous vote so that any nation desiring to withdraw could not do so, even on the two years' notice, if one nation voted that the obligations had not been fulfilled. Remember that this gives the league not only power to review all our obligations under the covenant but all our treaties with all nations for every one of those is an "international obligation."

Are we deliberately to put ourselves in fetters and be examined by the league of nations as to whether we have kept faith with Cuba or Panama before we can be permitted to leave the league? This seems to me humiliating to say the least. The right of withdrawal, if it is to be of any value whatever, must be absolute, because otherwise a nation desiring to withdraw could be held in the league by objections from other nations until the very act which induces the nation to withdraw had been completed; until the withdrawing nation had been forced to send troops to take part in a war with which it had no concern and upon which it did not desire to enter. It seems to me vital to the safety of the United States not only that this provision should be eliminated and the right to withdraw made absolute but that the period of withdrawal should be much reduced. As it stands it is practically no better in this respect than the first league draft which contained no provision for withdrawal at all, because the proviso here inserted so incumbers it that every nation to all intents and purposes must remain a member of the league indefinitely unless all the other members are willing that it should retire. Such a provision as this, ostensibly framed to meet the objection, has the defect which other similar gestures to give an impression of meeting objections have, that it apparently keeps the promise to the ear but most certainly breaks it to the hope.

I have dwelt only upon those points which seem to me most dangerous. There are, of course, many others, but these points, in the interest not only of the safety of the United States but of the maintenance of the treaty and the peace of the world, should be dealt with here before it is too late. Once in the league the chance of amendment is so slight that it is not worth considering. Any analysis of the provisions of this league covenant, however, brings out in startling relief one great fact. Whatever may be said, it is not a league of peace; it is an alliance, dominated at the present moment by five great powers, really by three, and it has all the marks of an alliance. The development of international law is neglected. The court which is to decide disputes brought before it fills but a small place. The conditions for which this league really provides with the utmost care are political conditions, not judicial questions, to be reached by the executive council and the assembly, purely political bodies without any trace of a judicial character about them. Such being its machinery, the control being in the hands of political appointees whose votes will be controlled by interest and expedience, it exhibits that most marked characteristic of an alliance—that its decisions are to be carried out by force. Those articles upon which the whole structure rests are articles which provide for the use of force; that is, for war. This league to enforce peace does a great deal for enforcement and very little for peace. It makes more essential provisions looking to war than to peace, for the settlement of disputes.

Article 10 I have already discussed. There is no question that the preservation of a State against external aggression can contemplate nothing but war. In article 11, again, the league is authorized to take any action which may be necessary to safeguard the peace of the world. "Any action" includes war. We also have specific provisions for a boycott, which is a form of economic warfare. The use of troops might be avoided but the enforcement of a boycott would require blockades in all probability, and certainly a boycott in its essence is simply an effort to starve a people into submission, to ruin their trade, and, in the case of nations which are not self-supporting, to cut off their food supply. The misery and suffering caused by such a measure as this may easily rival that caused by actual war. Article 16 embodies the boycott and also, in the last paragraph, provides explicitly for war. We are told that the word "recommends" has no binding force; it constitutes a moral obligation, that is all. But it means that if we, for example, should refuse to accept the recommendation, we should nullify the operation of article 16 and, to that extent, of the league. It seems to me that to attempt to relieve us of clearly imposed duties by saying that the word "recommend" is not binding is an escape of which no nation regarding the sanctity of treaties and its own honor would care to avail itself. The provisions of article 16 are extended to States outside the league who refuse to obey its command to come in and submit themselves to its jurisdiction; another provision for war.

Taken altogether, these provisions for war present what to my mind is the gravest objection to this league in its present form. We are told that of course nothing will be done in the way of warlike acts without the assent of Congress. If that is true, let us say so in the covenant. But as it stands there is no doubt whatever in my mind that American troops and American ships may be ordered to any part of the world by nations other than the United States, and that is a proposition to which I for one can never assent. It must be made perfectly clear that no American soldiers, not even a corporal's guard, that no American sailors, not even the crew of a submarine, can ever be engaged in war or ordered anywhere except by the constitutional authorities of the United States. To Congress is granted by the Constitution the right to declare war, and nothing that would take the troops out of the country at the bidding or demand of other nations should ever be permitted except through congressional action. The lives of Americans must never be sacrificed except by the will of the American people expressed through their chosen Representatives in Congress. This is a point upon which no doubt can be permitted. American soldiers and American sailors have never failed the country when the country called upon them. They went in their hundreds of thousands into the war just closed. They went to die for the great cause of freedom and of civilization. They went at their country's bidding and because their country summoned them to service. We were late in entering the war. We made no preparation as we ought to have done, for the ordeal which was clearly coming upon us; but we went and we turned the wavering scale. It was done by the American soldier, the American sailor, and the spirit and energy of the American people. They overrode all obstacles and all shortcomings on the part of the administration or of Congress, and gave to their country a great place in the great victory. It was the first time we had been called upon to rescue the civilized world. Did we fail? On the contrary, we succeeded, we succeeded largely and nobly, and we did it without any command from any league of nations. When the emergency came we met it and we were able to meet it because we had built up on this continent the greatest and most powerful nation in the world, built it up under our own policies, in our own way, and one great element of our strength was the fact that we had held aloof and had not thrust ourselves into European quarrels; that we had no selfish interest to serve. We made great sacrifices. We have done splendid work. I believe that we do not require to be told by foreign nations when we shall do work which freedom and civilization require. I think we can move to victory much better under our own command than under the command of others. Let us unite with the world to promote the peaceable settlement of all international disputes. Let us try to develop international law. Let us associate ourselves with the other nations for these purposes. But let us retain in our own hands and in our own control the lives of the youth of the land. Let no American be sent into battle except by the constituted authorities of his own country and by the will of the people of the United States.

Those of us, Mr. President, who are either wholly opposed to the league or who are trying to preserve the independence and the safety of the United States by changing the terms of the league and who are endeavoring to make the league, if we are to be a member of it, less certain to promote war instead of peace, have been reproached with selfishness in our outlook and with a desire to keep our country in a state of isolation. So far as the question of isolation goes, it is impossible to isolate the United States. I well remember the time, 20 years ago, when eminent Senators and other distinguished gentlemen who were opposing the Philippines and shrieking about imperialism, sneered at the statement made by some of us, that the United States had become a world power. I think no one now would question that the Spanish War marked the entrance of the United States into world affairs to a degree which had never obtained before. It was both an inevitable and an irrevocable step, and our entrance into the war with Germany certainly showed once and for all that the United States was not unmindful of its world responsibilities. We may set aside all this empty talk about isolation. Nobody expects to isolate the United States or to make it a hermit Nation, which is a sheer absurdity. But there is a wide difference between taking a suitable part and bearing a due responsibility in world affairs and plunging the United States into every controversy and conflict on the face of the globe. By meddling in all the differences which may arise among any portion or fragment of humankind we simply fritter away our influence and injure ourselves to no good purpose. We shall be of far more value to the world and its peace by occupying, so far as possible, the situation which we have occupied for the last 20 years and by adhering to the policy of Washington and Hamilton, of Jefferson and Monroe, under which we have risen to our present greatness and prosperity. The fact that we have been separated by our geographical situation and by our consistent policy from the broils of Europe has made us more than any one thing capable of performing the great work which we performed in the war against Germany, and our disinterestedness is of far more value to the world than our eternal meddling in every possible dispute could ever be.

Now, as to our selfishness. I have no desire to boast that we are better than our neighbors, but the fact remains that this Nation in making peace with Germany had not a single selfish or individual interest to serve. All we asked was that Germany should be rendered incapable of again breaking forth, with all the horrors incident to German warfare, upon an unoffending world, and that demand was shared by every free nation and indeed by humanity itself. For ourselves we asked absolutely nothing. We have not asked any government or governments to guarantee our boundaries or our political independence. We have no fear in regard to either. We have sought no territory, no privileges, no advantages, for ourselves. That is the fact. It is apparent on the face of the treaty. I do not mean to reflect upon a single one of the powers with which we have been associated

alone. We forced our way upward from the days of the Revolution, through a world often hostile and always indifferent. We owe no debt to anyone except to France in that Revolution, and those policies and those rights on which our power has been founded should never be lessened or weakened. It will be no service to the world to do so and it will be of intolerable injury to the United States. We will do our share. We are ready and anxious to help in all ways to preserve the world's peace. But we can do it best by not crippling ourselves.

I am as anxious as any human being can be to have the United States render every possible service to the civilization and the peace of mankind, but I am certain we can do it best by not putting ourselves in leading strings or subjecting our policies and our sovereignty to other nations. The independence of the United States is not only more precious to ourselves but to the world than any single possession. Look at the United States to-day. We have made mistakes in the past. We have had shortcomings. We shall make mistakes in the future and fall short of our own best hopes. But none the less is there any country to-day on the face of the earth which can compare with this in ordered liberty, in peace, and in the largest freedom? I feel that I can say this without being accused of undue boastfulness, for it is the simple fact, and in making this treaty and taking on these obligations all that we do is in a spirit of unselfishness and in a desire for the good of mankind. But it is well to remember that we are dealing with nations every one of which has a direct individual interest to serve and there is grave danger in an unshared idealism. Contrast the United States with any country on the face of the earth to-day and ask yourself whether the situation of the United States is not the best to be found. I will go as far as anyone in world service, but the first step to world service is the maintenance of the United States. You may call me selfish if you will, conservative or reactionary, or use any other harsh adjective you see fit to apply, but an American I was born, an American I have remained all my life. I can never be anything else but an American, and I must think of the United States first, and when I think of the United States first in

an arrangement like this I am thinking of what is best
for the world, for if the United States fails the best hopes
of mankind fail with it.   I have never had but one allegiance—I cannot divide it now.   I have loved but one
flag and I cannot share that devotion and give affection
to the mongrel banner invented for a league.   Internationalism, illustrated by the Bolshevik and by the men to
whom all countries are alike provided they can make
money out of them, is to me repulsive.   National I must
remain, and in that way I, like all other Americans, can
render the amplest service to the world.   The United
States is the world's best hope, but if you fetter her in
the interests and quarrels of other nations, if you tangle
her in the intrigues of Europe, you will destroy her
power for good and endanger her very existence.   Leave
her to march freely through the centuries to come as in
the years that have gone.   Strong, generous, and confident, she has nobly served mankind.   Beware how you
trifle with your marvelous inheritance, this great land of
ordered liberty, for if we stumble and fall, freedom and
civilization everywhere will go down in ruin.

We are told that we shall "break the heart of the
world" if we do not take this league just as it stands.
I fear that the hearts of the vast majority of mankind
would beat on strongly and steadily and without any
quickening if the league were to perish altogether.   If it
should be effectively and beneficently changed the people
who would lie awake in sorrow for a single night could
be easily gathered in one not very large room, but those
who would draw a long breath of relief would reach to
millions.

We hear much of visions and I trust we shall continue
to have visions and dream dreams of a fairer future for
the race.   But visions are one thing and visionaries are
another, and the mechanical appliances of the rhetori-
cian designed to give a picture of a present which does
not exist and of a future which no man can predict are
as unreal and shortlived as the steam or canvas clouds,
the angels suspended on wires, and the artificial lights
of the stage.   They pass with the moment of effect and
are shabby and tawdry in the daylight.   Let us at least
be real.   Washington's entire honesty of mind and his

fearless look into the face of all facts are qualities which can never go out of fashion and which we should all do well to imitate.

Ideals have been thrust upon us as an argument for the league until the healthy mind, which rejects cant, revolts from them. Are ideals confined to this deformed experiment upon a noble purpose, tainted as it is with bargains, and tied to a peace treaty which might have been disposed of long ago to the great benefit of the world if it had not been compelled to carry this rider on its back? *"Post equitem sedet atra cura,"* Horace tells us, but no blacker care ever sat behind any rider than we shall find in this covenant of doubtful and disputed interpretation as it now perches upon the treaty of peace.

No doubt many excellent and patriotic people see a coming fulfillment of noble ideals in the words "league for peace." We all respect and share these aspirations and desires, but some of us see no hope, but rather defeat, for them in this murky covenant. For we, too, have our ideals, even if we differ from those who have tried to establish a monopoly of idealism. Our first ideal is our country, and we see her in the future, as in the past, giving service to all her people and to the world. Our ideal of the future is that she should continue to render that service of her own free will. She has great problems of her own to solve, very grim and perilous problems, and a right solution, if we can attain to it, would largely benefit mankind. We would have our country strong to resist a peril from the West, as she has flung back the German menace from the East. We would not have our politics distracted and embittered by the dissensions of other lands. We would not have our country's vigor exhausted or her moral force abated by everlasting meddling and muddling in every quarrel, great and small, which afflicts the world. Our ideal is to make her ever stronger and better and finer, because in that way alone, as we believe, can she be of the greatest service to the world's peace and to the welfare of mankind. [Prolonged applause in the galleries.]

INDEX

"A. B. C. Powers," the, 370; mediation of, in Mexican dispute, 18-20

Adams, John Quincy, 144, 232, 296, 398; Monroe doctrine formulated by, 282

Adriatic, the, territorial settlements on eastern shores of, 57

Addresses: of Senator Lodge, on armed intervention in Mexico, 16; of Senator Lodge, on the *Lusitania* notes, 35 ff., 40-43, 44; of President Wilson, to Congress, January, 1918, 84-92; of Senator Lodge, opposing a league of nations, 96-98; of Senator Lodge, before League to Enforce Peace, 131-133; of Senator Lodge, on inconsistency, 136-145; of President Wilson, at Congress Hall, Philadelphia, 220; of Senator Lodge, February, 1919, on League of Nations, 227-261; of President Wilson, on a league to enforce peace, 262-269; of Senator Lodge, February, 1917, in reply to President Wilson's address, 270-296; of Senator Lodge, on Treaty of Peace with Germany, 380-410

Aland Islands, the, 211

Alexander, Emperor, 381, 383

Allies, the, Wilson's statement that there were no understandings with, 81, 82

Alsace-Lorraine, 89

Amendments, proposed, to Versailles Treaty, 161-163, 170-172; rejection of, by Senate, 178 ff.; distinction between reservations and, 312; were not to be submitted to Germany, 316-319

American Association of Commerce and Trade, dinner given Ambassador Gerard by, 75

American Institute of International Law, code prepared by, 277

Americanization of people of the United States, 406, 407

Americans, protection to, in foreign countries or on high seas, 67-69; Treaty reservation concerning rights of, adopted, 207

Amiens, treaty of, 275

Ancona, S.S., 69

Anderson, Chandler, 124

Annin, Robert Edwards, his "Woodrow Wilson, a Character Study" quoted, 56-61

Arabic, S.S., 69

Arbitration, clause on, in League Covenant, 246-248; voluntary, 285 ff.

Argentine Republic, the, 18-20

Armaments, on merchantmen, 70-72; reduction of, 88, 93; reservation regarding limitation of, 188, 198, 199; adoption of reservation, 207; Senator Lodge's address on, 241-243, 279, 280; President Wilson on, 267, 268

Armistice, the, acceptance of, by Germany, 96

Arnold, Matthew, quoted, 132

Arredondo, note of, 21, n.

Article 10 of League Covenant, authorship of, 184, 370; "the heart of the Covenant," 184, 208, 302; the reservations to, 173, 182 ff., 193, 201-204; the crucial point in contest over Covenant, 94; adoption of reservation concerning, 208; and the Monroe doctrine, 233; Senator Lodge's address on, 234-237, 243, 244, 388-390; Wilson's explanation of, 301, 302, 313-317, 321; the original form of, 305, 306; discussed with Wilson, 351, 355-358; Wilson's account of the history of, 370

Asia Minor, 337; policing of, 233

Associated Press, the, 57, 58

Austria, the treaty with, 303, 335, 365; and the Holy Alliance, 382 ff.